Approaches to Teaching
the Middle English *Pearl*

Approaches to Teaching the Middle English *Pearl*

Edited by

Jane Beal

and

Mark Bradshaw Busbee

The Modern Language Association of America
New York   2018

MLA and the MODERN LANGUAGE ASSOCIATION are trademarks
owned by the Modern Language Association of America.
For information about obtaining permission to reprint material from
MLA book publications, send your request by mail (see address below)
or e-mail (permissions@mla.org).

Library of Congress Cataloging-in-Publication Data

Names: Beal, Jane, editor. | Busbee, Mark Bradshaw, editor.
Title: Approaches to teaching the Middle English Pearl / edited
by Jane Beal and Mark Bradshaw Busbee.
Description: New York : The Modern Language Association of America, 2018. |
Series: Approaches to Teaching World Literature series ; 143 |
Includes bibliographical references and index.
Identifiers: LCCN 2017021511 (print) | LCCN 2017021650 (e-book) |
ISBN 9781603292931 (EPUB) | ISBN 9781603292948 (Kindle) | ISBN 9781603292917
(cloth : alk. paper) | ISBN 9781603292924 (pbk. : alk. paper)
Subjects: LCSH: Pearl (Middle English poem)—Study and teaching. |
Christian poetry, English (Middle)—History and criticism.
Classification: LCC PR2111 (e-book) | LCC PR2111 .A77 2017 (print) | DDC 821/.1—dc23
LC record available at https://lccn.loc.gov/2017021511

Cover illustration of the paperback and electronic editions:
The Dreamer Resting by a Mound.
© The British Library Board. Cotton Nero A.x.art.3, folio 41r.

Published by The Modern Language Association of America
85 Broad Street, suite 500, New York, New York 10004-2434
www.mla.org

CONTENTS

ACKNOWLEDGMENTS

Many people helped shape this Approaches to Teaching volume, and we are thankful to the respondents to our initial MLA survey, to the authors who contributed essays to this book, and to the internal and external reviewers of the MLA for their constructive feedback on our book manuscript at every stage. We are particularly thankful to James Hatch, the MLA's senior acquisitions editor, for his support, guidance, and encouragement. We are thankful for the detail-oriented attention of our copyeditors, too. We owe a debt of gratitude to our colleague, co-contributor, and friend, Ann Meyer, for her initial help in proposing this volume to the MLA for publication.

We wish to express our gratitude to the Howard College of Arts and Sciences at Samford University, particularly Dean David Chapman, for generous financial support in procuring copyrights for the images included here; faculty members in the Department of English, who tolerated their chair's time commitment to this volume, and especially the department administrative assistant, Gretchen Sexton, who assisted with a number of issues related to the creation of this book; and department research assistants Caitlyn Branum and Adam Quinn.

We would be remiss if we did not thank the professors who first taught this beautiful poem to us: Helen Dunn of Sonoma State University; Anne Middleton of the University of California, Berkeley; Caron Cioffi of the University of California, Davis; and John Fyler of Tufts University. To each of them, for their insights, we are thankful. We are thankful to the members of the Pearl-Poet Society, who meet annually at the International Congress on Medieval Studies, in Kalamazoo, Michigan, for the many informative panels on *Pearl* that we have had the opportunity to attend and participate in over the years; to our colleagues in the field of *Pearl* studies who have edited, translated, and interpreted the poem so well; to the readers who have helped refine our understanding of *Pearl*, and to the editors who have published our work on *Pearl* in the past, especially Edward Donald Kennedy, James H. Forse, and Nicola Masciandaro. Librarians at the Shields Library of UC Davis, the Fowler Library of Colorado Christian University, the Buswell Library of Wheaton College, and the Harwell Goodwin Davis Library at Samford University have supported our research, and we are thankful to all of them, especially Roberto Delgadillo at UC Davis.

We are both thankful for the positive, collaborative experience we have had as coauthors and coeditors, bringing this volume together. We are thankful to all the diligent teacher-scholars who contributed their time, thought, effort, and energy to writing essays for this volume and to our students, who inspired us. We wish to express our thankfulness to the many students to whom we have taught *Pearl* over the years, especially those at Colorado Christian University, Florida Gulf Coast University, Samford University, UC Davis, and Wheaton College. Their curiosity and questions kept us on our toes! They inspired us to find new ways to teach the poem and explain its complexities. This book exists because of them and for the many teachers and students who will read *Pearl* in the future.

PREFACE

The poetic masterpiece known as *Pearl* appears in one late-fourteenth-century manuscript known as Cotton Nero A.x, which is now preserved in the British Library. The first of four alliterative poems in that manuscript, *Pearl* is followed by *Cleanness, Patience*, and *Sir Gawain and the Green Knight*. All the poems seem to have been composed by a single anonymous poet writing in the Middle English dialect of the North-West Midlands region of England. All demonstrate their author's wide reading, thorough immersion in the teachings of medieval Catholicism, and deep insights into the human condition. Single authorship might also signal that the poems share a united purpose. But while *Cleanness* and *Patience* are so overtly didactic in their Christian message that they might be classed as literary homilies and while *Sir Gawain* fits in plot and theme the description of a medieval romance, *Pearl* is a dream vision, a genre that has religious and secular antecedents. Its 101-stanza, 1,212-line first-person narrative concentrates on a dreamer's interiority—how his anguished mental and spiritual states change as a result of a revelatory and comforting vision of his lost beloved Pearl and of a hopeful, redemptive Paradise. Thus, *Pearl* embodies some of the elements of its companion poems in the manuscript, particularly the didacticism of *Cleanness* and *Patience* and the journey format of *Sir Gawain*. Along with its artful narrative, poignant message, and intricate design, *Pearl*'s overlapping techniques—ranging from sophisticated symbolism (images to numbers) to intertextual networks of meaning—compel reflection on universal aspects of the human condition, such as love, loss, grief, and, finally, hope.

The editors of *Approaches to Teaching the Middle English* Pearl believe that the powerful beauty of this medieval masterpiece is reason enough for a book devoted to its teaching. We believe students should be given the opportunity to study it with instructors who are confident in their approaches. We also realize that a poem of *Pearl*'s intricacy and complexity poses special challenges to twenty-first-century students and teachers. In our MLA survey of college and university professors, we learned that along with general unfamiliarity with *Pearl*, the poem's very foreignness—of historical origin and culture, of genre and form, of Christian doctrine and ideology, of allegory and symbolism, of topic and theme—seems to influence professors to choose other better-known medieval texts when creating course syllabi. For generations of university students it was a regular part of university literary study, yet *Pearl* is today often passed over for the works of poets like Geoffrey Chaucer, William Langland, or John Gower. Even the romance *Sir Gawain and the Green Knight* retains a secure place in literature curricula, so much so that the poet of both poems is more often called the *Gawain* poet than the *Pearl* poet, as he was frequently called in the past.

In order to refamiliarize teachers with the poem and to assist them and their students as they grapple with its rich meanings, the essays in this volume seek to offer clear explanations of what *Pearl* is as a poem, historical document, and religious experience. The essays offer tools, strategies, and practical suggestions for teaching *Pearl* so that the pedagogical task is less daunting and, in the end, more rewarding. The ultimate goal of this volume is to return *Pearl* to its former prominence so that it once again appears in literature syllabi and in the minds of students long after they finish their formal studies.

Unfortunately, teachers are often overwhelmed by the amount of information (and misinformation) available to them about how best to teach *Pearl*, especially if they depend on the Internet, and they often feel frustrated when they have to rely solely on scholarly texts in their effort to form teaching strategies. We believe that an important first step before teaching the poem is to identify authoritative editions and translations and to gain a clear perspective of its scholarly reception, especially how the poem has been interpreted through the years and which interpretations have gained consensus. In part 1, "Materials," we discuss the various tools (editions, translations, critical works, Web sites, dictionaries, and grammars) that a teacher might need, and we present what scholars have had to say about these tools. This section should be of special interest to teachers and scholars. We discovered when writing "Materials" that no similarly thorough reception history previously existed.

How to fit the poem into a course is one of many issues we address in part 2, "Approaches." One of *Pearl*'s virtues as a course text is that it is an ideal length for a class meeting, a weeklong unit, or an entire section of the course. But to approach it effectively, teachers need to anticipate the time needed to address the cognitive estrangement their students will experience when reading the poem. It is indeed a foreign poem to most students, especially those unaccustomed to highly allusive, theologically informed literature. The essays in part 2, "Approaches," address this problem directly by turning the complex historical, cultural, theological, and literary aspects into opportunities for enquiry. Students are often surprised to learn that while the idea of authorship is a fixation of modern readers, it was less important to people in the Middle Ages. They often struggle to think of the poem as a unique production, part of a work of physical art in the form of a manuscript, and undergraduates often make assumptions about its language without noticing that they are encountering the poem through a filter of translation. Most pressing are the demands of a basic knowledge of the Bible and medieval Catholic doctrine, symbolism, and iconography—knowledge that twenty-first-century students often do not possess. Therefore the essays here frame approaches around the contextual problems that we know students have. For example, one essay offers a way to guide students to analyze how biblical subtexts inform interpretations of the poem, and another focuses on how medieval Christian readers might themselves have employed the same strategies for reading *Pearl* that they used for interpreting the Bible.

However, the essays in this volume do not focus solely on the challenges or opportunities that *Pearl* presents; they also work to situate the poem in the interconnected literary culture of late-fourteenth-century Europe. Students naturally want to connect *Pearl* to the poetry of Chaucer and Langland, to the European tradition represented by Dante and Boccaccio, and even to the classical traditions they are familiar with. This desire fits perfectly with the tendencies of survey courses, and the essays here offer connection points, not only between *Pearl* and other poetry traditions but also within the Cotton Nero A.x manuscript.

The nineteen essays in part 2 address specific contexts and strategies for teaching *Pearl*. These essays work in conjunction with the overview of materials for teaching in part 1 and with a robust list of textual and Internet resources. It is our hope that this volume will aid future students of English literature in their reading of this poetic masterpiece of Middle English literature.

Introduction to the Volume

Jane Beal and Mark Bradshaw Busbee

Since the nineteenth century, *Pearl*'s story about universally shared human experiences of love, loss, longing, and consolation has been well known to students of English literature. *Pearl* has been read alongside other fourteenth-century Middle English alliterative poems, such as *Sir Gawain and the Green Knight*, with which *Pearl* is bound in a unique manuscript called Cotton Nero A.x housed at the British Library, in London. Not long after its first modern printing in 1864, *Pearl* came to be studied as part of anglophone university language and literature curricula, which included interdisciplinary study of medieval aesthetics, culture, religion, and social practice.

Edited and translated numerous times, widely circulated and widely read, the poem has entered the bloodline of Western culture. It has come to be understood as singularly English in language and expression and broadly European in form and content. The poem relies upon biblical and classical allusion and, occasionally, direct reference to make meaning, while its dream-vision plot follows in the tradition of European masterpieces such as Dante's *Divine Comedy*, Guillaume de Lorris and Jean de Meun's *Romance of the Rose*, and Boethius's *Consolation of Philosophy*. The influence of *Pearl* has extended beyond the university into popular culture so far that writers like J. R. R. Tolkien have drawn upon it for inspiration in their creative work.

Despite its canonical status, *Pearl* remains a challenging poem to understand and teach. Intended to assist faculty in meeting the challenge of teaching *Pearl* in the twenty-first century, this volume presents a summary analysis of the poem in this introduction, an overview of teaching materials in "Materials for Teaching *Pearl*: Classroom Texts and Instructor's Library," and a number of essays that articulate specific pedagogical approaches to the poem.

The Plot of Pearl

Pearl tells the story of a man grieving in a garden over the loss of a beloved pearl. He falls asleep and, in a dream, travels to a marvelous land where, as he reaches the banks of a stream, he sees a beautiful maiden. He recognizes her as a young woman he once knew, though now she is transformed into a heavenly queen, a Pearl-Maiden. He expresses his grief at losing her and, after she consoles him, he rejoices at their reunion. Still separated by the stream, they engage in a long, emotional dialogue in which he learns about the nature of innocence, the grace of God, and the virtues of meekness and purity as well as the Pearl-Maiden's spiritual marriage to Christ in heaven. He asks many questions, but he remains confused and longs to cross the water to be reunited with her. The

Pearl-Maiden tells him that is forbidden; he cannot now enter heaven. However, she tells him that she has requested that a sight be shown to him. The Dreamer then has a vision of the New Jerusalem, a procession of 144,000 virgins, including the Pearl-Maiden herself, and the Lamb of God. But the Dreamer's longing for his beloved compels him to attempt to cross the stream as though he were attempting to die. His vision breaks, and he awakes in awe, resolved to live virtuously and to submit to the will of God. For he recognizes that God is his friend and we are all precious pearls to the Prince of heaven.

The Date and Manuscript of Pearl

Pearl probably dates to the reign of Richard II (1377–1400) and could have been composed as early as 1348 and, according to paleographic evidence, as late as 1400, the approximate date of the copying of the Cotton Nero A.x manuscript. The illustrations included in the manuscript are dated to the early fifteenth century. By making connections between the poem and its historical and cultural contexts, John Bowers dates the poem more specifically to 1395, while Susanna Fein dates the poem closer to 1380, by analyzing the use of the twelve-line ballade stanza by the *Pearl* poet and other contemporary English poets.

The Ricardian era was one of national and international tension as well as tremendous literary creativity in England. Richard II had come to the throne shortly after England returned to war with France, just as an unsteady parliament in 1376–77 reversed course, and a few years before an uprising of the English peasant classes took place in 1381. These national events at home were overshadowed and possibly intensified by international tensions in the Christian Church caused by the Great Schism of the papacy (when rival popes sat at Rome and Avignon from 1378 to 1417), and ongoing fear in Europe of the return of the plague. The reign of Richard II also encompassed the literary works of Geoffrey Chaucer, William Langland, and John Gower, a point that led J. A. Burrow to categorize *Pearl* as "Ricardian Poetry," because the poem seems to draw from a shared set of historical and literary contexts.

However, because *Pearl* appears in only one known manuscript, identified as British Library, Cotton Nero A.x, article 3, it is much more mysterious than its fellow Ricardian poems. In contrast, Chaucer's *Canterbury Tales* exists in eighty-three known manuscripts, Langland's *Piers Plowman* in fifty, and Gower's *Confessio Amantis* in forty-nine. The designation "British Library Cotton Nero A.x, article 3" arises from its current location in the British Library (since 1753) and its previous location in the private library of the Renaissance collector of rare books Sir Robert Bruce Cotton (1571–1631), who kept it in a bookcase adorned with the bust of the Roman Emperor Nero, on the top shelf (A), in the tenth position (x).

The designation "article 3" indicates that *Pearl* (together with *Cleanness, Patience*, and *Sir Gawain and the Green Knight*) was the third item in the original Cotton manuscript: it was preceded by article 1, *Justus de Justis De dignitate procerum antiquissimorum Britonicum* (5r–38r), and article 2, *Letter from Justis to John Chedworth* (38v–40r); it was followed by articles 4–6, which are theological tracts. The 1–6 numbering system came from the 1696 Cotton Catalogue in which, it is worth noting, the four Middle English poems are identified as one poem called the *Poema in lingua veteri Anglicana*. In 1964 the composite manuscript was disassembled and rebound in two volumes, one containing items 1 and 3 (or articles 1, 2, 4, 5, and 6) and the other containing the four Middle English poems: *Pearl, Patience, Cleanness*, and *Sir Gawain and the Green Knight* (item 2 or article 3). (For additional information, see the British Library catalog description available online.) The "article 3" designation explains why *Pearl*, as the first poem in the rebound manuscript, is not numbered as the first page, but begins at folio 37, recto, and continues to folio 59, verso. (A folio is a manuscript leaf; its facing page to the right is termed "recto" and to the left "verso." It should be noted that some scholars prefer to use the designations "a" or "r" for recto and "b" or "v" for verso.)

Pearl and the three other related poems appearing together in the manuscript share a set of intellectual and moral beliefs related to orthodox medieval Christianity and a chivalric social morality of the late fourteenth century. The individual poems were originally untitled, but today we generally know them as *Pearl, Cleanness* (or *Purity*), *Patience*, and *Sir Gawain and the Green Knight*, after the titles given to them by the scholars Sir Frederick Madden in 1839 and Richard Morris in 1864. *Cleanness* and *Patience* are literary homilies. Each presents a Christian precept and then illustrates it in practice with material drawn from scripture. To teach the values of purity and innocence, *Cleanness* uses three main exempla: the story of the Great Flood and the destruction of Sodom and Gomorrah, both found in Genesis, and the story of Belshazzar's Feast from the book of Daniel. *Patience* places the biblical story of Jonah at its center to illustrate the best attitude man should assume in his relationship with God. The final poem, *Sir Gawain and the Green Knight*, represents a different form of didacticism from the dream vision of *Pearl* and the homilies of *Cleanness* and *Patience*: it is an Arthurian romance. (For more on that fine poem, we recommend *Approaches to Teaching* Sir Gawain and the Green Knight.)

All four poems in the manuscript are accompanied by color illustrations that relate closely to the passages they are meant to illustrate: four before the opening of *Pearl* (folios 41 recto to 42 verso), two before *Cleanness*, two before *Patience*, as well as one before and three following *Sir Gawain and the Green Knight*. We have included black-and white-reproductions of the illustrations to *Pearl* at the end of this volume (app. 2). The images are also available in full

color online at the Web sites *The Cotton Nero A.x Project* (gawain.ucalgary
.ca) and *Medieval Pearl* (medievalpearl.wordpress.com) as well as through *Wiki
Commons*.

The Dialect of Pearl

Pearl was written in the local dialect of the North-West Midlands in the area
of modern-day Cheshire, some 190 miles from London. This distance suggests
that the poem may have originated apart from the cultural influence of the court
of Richard II. (However, it should be noted that both *Pearl* and *Sir Gawain
and the Green Knight* reveal sophisticated, detailed knowledge of courtly life,
and Richard II had strong ties to the Cheshire region.) The later dominance of
Chaucer's Middle English does not suggest that contemporary speakers of the
North-West Midlands dialect saw their language as provincial or less literary.
The number of extant poems from the region suggests that writers took great
pride in the dialect of their region.

Pearl may have been read aloud or performed, in keeping with common practices in medieval literary culture, as opposed to the ubiquitous silent reading in
our modern culture. Perhaps partially on account of this, the scribe of the manuscript does not use capitalization consistently, and he does not punctuate at all.
Medieval oral readers would supply the pauses and stops that are now indicated
by commas and periods in our texts. Instructors should therefore be aware of the
fact that modern editions of *Pearl* supply these indicators of meaning to create
a version of the poem that meets the expectations and needs of modern readers.

Students and teachers familiar with the language of Chaucer's "Prologue" to
The Canterbury Tales sometimes expect *Pearl* to fit preconceived ideas about
Middle English. As a result they regard the dialect of *Pearl* as quaint. This is
all the more the case when students are used to *The Riverside Chaucer*, which
modernizes Chaucer's letters (and thus, to an extent, his spelling), and then
they come to an edition of *Pearl*, like Malcolm Andrew and Ronald Waldron's
(2008), which preserves medieval orthography, including the unique letters
thorn and *yogh*. So, at first glance, the spelling in *Pearl* may appear unusual,
though teachers and scholars with training in Middle English grammar can explain its patterns. Then *Pearl*'s system of inflexions, or grammatical endings
of words, varies greatly when compared with the Middle English associated
with London and its environs. Word order, though less complicated in the actual
reading of lines in *Pearl*, is problematic because readers cannot know for sure
if an expression is a spoken idiom of the day or an intentionally poetic turn of
phrase. Sometimes phrases are relevant to the content, and sometimes they appear to be metric fillers, added to complete an alliterative line.

Most immediately noticeable to students with prior experience with Chaucer's English is the vocabulary of *Pearl*, which incorporates a high percentage

of words from Old Norse and archaisms from Old English. We believe that with a well-chosen edition or translation, as well as useful knowledge of how to approach the language, teachers will find that the special dialect of *Pearl* presents more opportunities than barriers to enjoyment of the poem.

Authorship of Pearl

One of the most mysterious and compelling aspects of *Pearl*, distinguishing it from the work of Chaucer, Gower, and Langland, is, ironically, its unknown author. In this volume we refer to the poet as the *Pearl* poet. He is also commonly known as the *Gawain* poet.

Many scholars read the poem as autobiographical at some level, and they depend on ideas about the author's identity for clues to meaning. This approach is complicated by a number of unanswered questions. Did the same poet who wrote *Pearl* also write the other three poems in Cotton Nero A.x? Did he also write *Saint Erkenwald*, a poem that does not appear in Cotton Nero A.x, but, like *Pearl*, is written in the North-West Midlands dialect and explores similar themes? Can the *Pearl* poet be co-identified with the narrator of the poem, the Dreamer?

In the introduction to his edition and translation of the five poems attributed to the *Pearl* poet, Casey Finch reviews the names of many men who have been proposed as the poet: Ralph Strode, Huchoun of the Awle Ryale, Enguerrand de Coucy, John Prat, John Donne (a valet of the king's kitchen), John of Erghome, Hugh Massey, and John de Massey (2). Clifford Peterson has made a special case for John de Massey's authorship of all five poems. Today many scholars accept that the poet who wrote *Pearl* also wrote the other three poems contained in the same manuscript, and some also include *Sir Erkenwald* in the poet's corpus, even though it appears separately in Harley 2250. (In point of fact, many manuscripts of medieval English literature are miscellanies, containing a variety of pieces by a number of different authors, so that one poet's work could certainly be contained in different manuscripts without in any way making it less likely that the work was his.) Increasingly, scholars have edited and published all five poems together, and teachers may include all five poems as a group in seminars or sections of survey courses devoted to the *Pearl* poet. Despite this, of the possible authors, who have been named, none has been widely accepted. The *Pearl* poet is generally regarded as an anonymous author.

A more complicated question is whether the poet can be identified with the narrator of the poem. The Chaucerian narrator has long been regarded as an invention created to advance the aims of Chaucer's satire, and other first-person accounts in literary works of the later Middle Ages have been similarly regarded. However, probably because of the highly personal nature of the story, readers of *Pearl* may equate the author with the narrator of the poem. The degree to which students and scholars view the narrator's voice as the author's own largely depends on how they interpret the basic plot of the poem, its contemplative context, and the rules of its genre, the dream vision, as well as how they see that it functions in relation to its sources and analogues.

Sources and Analogues of Pearl

Many readers can see clearly the connection between the symbol of the pearl in the poem and in the Bible. The *Pearl* poet relishes the biblical paraphrase, especially that of the parables of Jesus, the Song of Songs, and the book of Revelation; he alludes to specific episodes from the Gospels like the Transfiguration (J. Allan Mitchell) and Mary Magdalene's surprising, post-resurrection encounter with Christ in the garden where he had been entombed (Johnson, *The Voice of the Gawain-Poet*). Yet in the case of classical and medieval literature, it has been easier for scholars to make a case for analogues than for sources. This stems from nagging uncertainty about the identity of the *Pearl* poet; if we knew more about his life, we might be able to determine what exactly he read that might have influenced his poetry.

Pearl itself seems to allude to the *Consolation of Philosophy*, the *Romance of the Rose*, and Dante's *Divine Comedy*. The poet mentions Aristotle directly in the poem, and Ovid's *Metamorphoses* is the likely source of allusions to Pygmalion in *Pearl*. Ovid's influence may also explain the presence of themes and plot points related to the legend of Orpheus and Eurydice. However, we cannot know for sure the extent of the poet's direct knowledge of these authors and their works. How would he have gotten hold of manuscripts containing these literary works, with or without patronage? How well could he read Latin or French or Italian, irrespective of whether he was a cleric or a courtier or a man in some other role?

Some readers even speculate about whether the *Pearl* poet knew the work of his English contemporaries Chaucer, Gower, and Langland, or the mystical writers Richard Rolle and Julian of Norwich, with whom he shares an interest in divine things. Evidence for making any of these connections is quite slender, though he may have known his London contemporaries through active involvement in the political and social scene of the late fourteenth century. Despite evincing little concrete evidence of the poet's possible relationship to other late medieval writers, *Pearl* does show definitively that the poet was influenced by his cultural milieu.

Pearl *and Medieval Christian Contemplative Devotion*

The literary genre of dream vision flourished in Middle English writings of the late fourteenth century, and at the same time, so did late medieval Christian accounts of visionary experiences. The books of Bridget of Sweden, Julian of Norwich, and Margery Kempe are contemporary examples. Like those auto-biographical, visionary writings, *Pearl* is firmly grounded in the tradition of Christian contemplative devotion or what has sometimes been called, less specifically, mysticism.

In the contemplative tradition, the journey to intimacy with God was sometimes imagined as Jacob's ladder and the rungs of the ladder as steps in the journey. (For the story of the appearance of the ladder in Jacob's dream, see Genesis 28.10–17.) The first step was always humility. In times of sustained prayer, the Christian contemplative seeking God would then experience a season (sometimes very long) of purgation or purification, during which sinful thoughts and actions were burned away. Next would come illumination: the beginning of visionary experience that included glimpses of heavenly things. Inward illumination was fostered and encouraged by outward meditation on icons and images. For a few rare souls, illumination might be followed by unification to Christ, for contemplatives considered themselves individually (as well as corporately) the *sponsa Christi*: the Bride of Christ.

To experience a vision of spiritual marriage to Christ while still living was uncommon, but it was nevertheless acknowledged as an orthodox possibility for the devoted lover of God. This can be seen in several medieval mystical accounts, including those of Christina of Markyate and Margery Kempe as well as later in the Renaissance, in the writings of the English laywoman Aemilia Lanyer and the Spanish nun Teresa of Avila. However, most Christians expected to experience the wedding feast of the Lamb of God only after their death.

The narrative and imagery of *Pearl* clearly reflect the progression (from humility to illumination to purification to unification) that is possible in the ideal Christian spiritual life. The Pearl-Maiden has already experienced it. She tells the Dreamer of her spiritual marriage to Christ multiple times (lines 412–14 and 418, 757–59, and 781–87), but he either does not understand it or does not want to accept it. Despite his hesitancy, the Dreamer is being invited to go on a parallel journey.

The Dreamer is symbolically represented as experiencing humility when he falls asleep on the ground in the garden. (The Latin word for ground is *humus*, from which we get our English word *humility*.) He begins to ascend the ladder of contemplation in his illuminating dream and purgative journey through the dreamscape. The Dreamer's journey might be described as a kind of spiritual pilgrimage. When he meets the Maiden at the stream, and they begin conversing, his illumination and purification continue. He stares at the Maiden during their conversation, and in so doing, he looks upon an individual Bride of Christ: an image of innocence, holiness, and faithfulness. His vision of the New Jerusalem is a vision of the corporate Bride of Christ, led by the Lamb of God: an invitation and promise to him of the fuller joy that can be his after his death.

Although he does not enter into the procession of saints (or brides) following Christ, he witnesses the procession, so he is symbolically very close to unification with Christ, which is the highest stage in the contemplative journey into God.

When the Dreamer awakens once more to earthly existence, he shows that he has been changed by his contemplative ascent from the garden to the dreamscape to the vision of the New Jerusalem because he is no longer resisting the will of God but rather regarding God as his lord and, significantly, his friend (1204). He is also aware that he might have experienced more of Christ's joys had he not attempted to enter the stream. The stream seems parallel to the one that flows from the throne of God (Rev. 22.1); to cross it would mean, in a literal sense, to die on earth in order to enter heaven. However, it is not yet time for the Dreamer to die. His return to the natural world from his vision of the spiritual one gives him the same opportunity as that given to every other medieval Christian: to contemplate what he has been shown, to grow closer to Christ through continued pursuit of righteousness, and to bear witness to others of his own unique experience of God in the context of church teaching and shared communal experience throughout the liturgical year.

Indeed, the imagery of *Pearl* makes clear that the poem is a Paschal one, appropriate to the Easter liturgical season, written in keeping with affective piety: the broadly popular, late medieval movement among Christians to devote themselves, emotionally, to the suffering of Christ on the Cross and to identify with him in his sufferings. This devotion was grounded in meditation on the Passion, which was in turn rooted in *lectio divina*, or divine reading of scripture. The Gospels all contain passion narratives, and the contemplative reader (or hearer) listening to the Passion could imagine, vividly, the experiences of Christ's suffering, death, and resurrection.

The Maiden is represented as performing exactly such an emotional, co-identifying meditation on the Passion of Christ. Her rehearsal of elements from the Gospels, for the listening Dreamer's benefit, encodes the experience in the poem and expands it to embrace the readers and listeners of *Pearl*. Thus *Pearl* represents the practices of medieval Christian contemplative devotion and simultaneously invites readers to experience them.

The Genres of Pearl

Pearl is a dream vision. To be a dream vision, according to J. Stephen Russell in *English Dream Vision: Anatomy of a Form*, a poem must have certain motifs and result from a poet's specific intention to follow the tradition or imitate a generic model (2). At the simplest level, the dream-vision poem depicts someone who falls asleep, beholds a vision in a dream, and awakens, usually with a new insight or understanding.

Like many other earlier, contemporary, and later dream visions, *Pearl* begins with a prologue that introduces the narrator (the soon-to-be dreamer) and portrays him in a state of distress. The causes of the distress are not yet revealed to the readers, a circumstance that generates their sense of curiosity or suspense. In a restless state, the narrator falls asleep and enters his dream.

The prologue is followed by the dream report. The narrator is always a character in his own dream, and he is often represented as talking not to one interlocutor (as in *The Consolation of Philosophy* and *Pearl*) but several (as in *The Romance of the Rose*, *The Divine Comedy*, or *The Vision of Piers Plowman*). These other speakers may be real or allegorical, and one or more may be a figure of authority (e.g., Lady Philosophy, the Pearl-Maiden, or Vergil). The narrative that unfolds may follow several patterns, in diverse settings, examining various themes (such as love, grief, or spiritual pilgrimage). The telling of the dream takes up the majority of the poem.

The dream report is followed by an epilogue, which depicts the awakening of the Dreamer. Together with the prologue, it forms the frame narrative, which contains the dream. In the epilogue the narrator may offer interpretive comments on his recent experience of dreaming. Occasionally he may affirm his intention to record his dream in poetry or prose or to otherwise remember and meditate on his vision. The epilogue provides narrative closure to the poem (even if the dream itself was cut off without total resolution). As Russell suggests, the epilogue challenges the reader to perceive the dream vision's artistic, aesthetic, and architectural completion (6).

The dream-vision genre exists at the intersection of literal and literary dreams. Perhaps precisely because of this, early scholars studying *Pearl* debated whether it is an elegy (a literal recollection of a man's lived experience of love and loss) or an allegory (a spiritual, symbolic narrative meant to point the reader to well-known Christian truth). Naturally, these two genres are not necessarily in binary opposition to one another; Dante's *Divine Comedy* was inspired, in part, by the real loss of Beatrice, a woman who nevertheless came to signify a wide range of elevated meanings in his poem. That being acknowledged, elegiac interpretations generally predominated among scholars of *Pearl* until new readers proposed alternative genres to help understand *Pearl*, notably the consolation.

In classical tradition the consolation was a rhetorical speech, letter, essay, or poem intended to comfort mourners after the death of a loved one. In the medieval period, Christian themes entered the genre. Christian consolations often included theological explanations for suffering and death that stemmed from the story of the Fall in the Garden of Eden; they also offered the hope of resurrection and heavenly reunion. Clearly, based on these criteria, *Pearl* can be considered not only an elegy and an allegory, but a consolation as well.

There are, in fact, many genres that appear to be at play in *Pearl*. It has been considered a contra-*consolatio*, a courtly romance, a dialogue, a debate, a hagiographic account, a spiritual quest, and a revelation. Within its verses, *Pearl* contains smaller units that can be considered, generically, as parables, biblical paraphrases (or vernacular translations), sermons, prayers, lyrics (sacred or secular), and even journeys to the otherworld. As Cynthia Kraman has observed insightfully:

> For critics who do not notice the highly literary and personal quality of *Pearl*, the genre discussion of *Pearl* is rather overwrought, heightened by expectations that it will conform to a single type of literature, unaware that a new and original literature is being created before their eyes.   (360–61)

Yet, all genres considered, *Pearl* is certainly a dream vision, and it is a preeminent one among other late medieval examples. Contemporary dream visions written in Middle English include Langland's *The Vision of Piers Plowman*, Gower's *Confessio Amantis*, and Chaucer's dream visions, *The Book of the Duchess, The House of Fame, The Parliament of Fowls, The Legend of Good Women*, and Chauntecleer's dream from the Nun's Priest's Tale and Troilus's dream from *Troilus and Criseyde*. These had their earliest origins in biblical and classical dream visions, and, as has been noted, they appear to have been influenced by Boethius's *Consolation of Philosophy*, the *Romance of the Rose*, and Dante's *Divine Comedy* as well. When reading *Pearl* it is important to remember that the medieval literary form emerged in the context of Catholic piety, in a culture of belief wherein Christians widely believed that dream visions were not only literary, but literal.

The Settings and Structures of Pearl

In keeping with its medieval contemplative devotional context and its dream-vision genre, the plot of *Pearl* ascends through three settings: a garden on earth, a bejeweled paradise in the dream, and the heavenly city in the vision of the New Jerusalem. These three settings provide contexts for the Dreamer's experience and perceptions in the narrative structure of the poem. The intricate, ornate structure of the poem as a whole has been compared to a cathedral (Meyer; Marti), a reliquary (Chaganti, *Medieval Poetics*), and a royal crown (Bishop; Bowers, *Politics of* Pearl; Gatta). These comparisons intimate the sense that readers of *Pearl* so often have: namely, that the poem enshrines, memorializes, and honors someone infinitely precious. Borrowing metaphors from medieval art, scholars have compared it to a diptych (Harwood) and a triptych (Everett; Bishop; Blenker) as well.

In *Body, Heart, and Text in the Pearl-Poet*, Kevin Marti has made architectural and corporeal comparisons to explain *Pearl*, arguing that the poem has multiple centers, moving outward in concentric circles that are patterned after the rose window and the cathedral, and, simultaneously, the human body with a heart at the center: it is a microcosm (83). Marti observes, "The corporeal symmetry of the poem, together with its corollary relation of each of its parts to the macrocosmic whole, constitutes an essential architectonic frame for any thematic interpretation" (85). The textual heart of *Pearl* is the Parable of the Workers in the Vineyard, which is at the center of the poem (86) and corresponds to the Incarnation of Christ at the center of salvation history (102). Marti adds that "Just as the Virgin's womb contained that which, paradoxically, contained both her and the whole universe, so the pearl is at once smaller and greater than all of its enclosures" (104).

Like Marti, Edward Condren sees a close relation between the microcosm of *Pearl* and the macrocosm of the manuscript (on the one hand) and the universe (on the other). In *The Numerical Universe of the Gawain-Pearl Poet: Beyond Phi* (2002), Condren explores how the *Pearl* poet uses what modern mathematicians call phi and what Renaissance scholars called "the golden section" to structure *Pearl* and the other three poems of the manuscript corporately and individually. He shows that when the lines from all four poems are added together (*Pearl*'s 1,212 lines, *Cleanness*'s 1,812 lines, *Patience*'s 531 lines, and *Sir Gawain and the Green Knight*'s 2,531 lines), they equal 6,086 lines. So the ratio of the whole (6,086) to the sum of the lines in the first and last poems (3,743) is almost the same as the ratio of the sum of the lines of the first and last poems (3,743) to the sum of the lines of the middle two (2,343): 1.62596 and 1.59752, respectively— which is remarkably close to phi: 1.61803. (Readers may well remember at this point that the four poems were treated as one in the 1696 Cotton Catalogue title and called simply, *Poema in lingua veteri Anglicana*, and that there are, in fact, no separating titles in the manuscript.) The poet Vergil used the phi device to structure his *Georgics*, and Horace his *Ars poetica*, and, Condren argues, so too did the *Pearl* poet use it to structure together not only all four Middle English poems of Cotton Nero A.x, but each separately. In the case of *Pearl*, beyond phi, there are geometric implications to the poet's number symbolism. As Michael Edwards aptly summarizes in his review of Condren's study:

> The dodecahedron is also the solid most closely associated with the perfect sphere, the shape of the world-soul in Plato's *Timaeus*. Condren argues that these two shapes, the dodecahedron and the sphere, are combined in *Pearl*: the perfect roundness of the pearl is set in sections of five twelve-line stanzas echoing the twelve pentagonal faces measuring twelve units on a side of Condren's ideal dodecahedron, reflected in turn in the twelve-times-twelve thousand virgins and the Holy City depicted at the end of the poem as well as the total number of lines contained in the poem, which is 1212.   (479)

Respected scholars, such as Chauncey Wood (who reviewed Condren's book for *Speculum*) and Julian Wasserman (who reviewed it for *Arthuriana*), have been convinced by Condren's argument. Subsequent scholars, like Claude Willan, have been influenced by it.

So while the mathematics of Condren's analysis may be difficult for non-mathematicians to grasp, Condren's point is not: "From the perspective of the ancients, division into mean and extreme ratio was a coherent system of relationships that could demonstrate a connection to infinity, the power to replicate itself and expand indefinitely" (*Numerical Universe* 36). In other words, the divine order of things is revealed in proportion; it intimates the existence, intentionality, and profound involvement of an infinitely complex Creator. The microcosm of *Pearl*, understood in relation to and in isolation from the other three poems, corresponds to the macrocosm of the universe. Like the universe, it expands toward the infinite—ultimately, toward the divine.

Pearl is indeed a carefully crafted poem that contains many smaller, supporting structures within its architectural whole. It consists of 101 stanzas, divided into twenty sections of five stanzas each (with the exception of section 15, which has six), and each stanza consists of twelve lines. The numeric significance of these divisions and their possible symbolism has been a subject of much interest.

John Fleming has seen meaning in the 101 stanzas of the poem. He argues in "The Centuple Structure of the *Pearl*" that the promise of a hundredfold return in the gospel Parable of the Sower (Matt. 13.1–23) was often glossed as an *increase* upon an original gift, thus, one plus one hundred. He also shows that many medieval works use 101 as a structural principle, and that these works share the theme of penitential consolation. Thus, the 101 stanzas, instead of being otiose, actually participate in the numeric symbolism of *Pearl*.

Like the 101 stanzas, the grouping of the stanzas into twenty sections has attracted scholarly attention. These sections are marked in the manuscript by an illustrated capital letter and in the poem itself by a repeated concatenation word shared by groups of five stanzas (or, in the case of section 15, shared by a group of six stanzas). Harwood, who sees the poem's structure as chiastic and compares it to a diptych, divides these sections in half (10-10) for analysis. Michael Olmert shares this view, which undergirds his interpretation of the poem's structure as similar to that of a medieval board game ("Game-Playing"). Others, who see the poem as a triptych, have considered the first four and last four sections as the two side panels and the middle twelve sections as the central panel (4-12-4). Sandy Cohen considered the first twelve sections to be the "Song of Earth" and the last eight sections to be the "Song of Heaven."

The twelve lines of the ballade stanzas have also been seen as meaningful. In the Middle Ages, the number twelve was associated with its frequent biblical occurrences: the twelve tribes of Israel, the twelve Prophets, the twelve Apostles, and the twelve gates of the New Jerusalem. It was related to church teaching, especially the twelve articles of the Apostle's Creed. It was further connected to time and eternity: the twelve months of the year, the twelve signs of the zodiac, and the greater cosmic order. Just as it was associated with the macrocosm of the universe, it was associated with the microcosm of man, who was believed to consist of twelve parts. Because heaven could be represented symbolically by the number three, and earth with the number four, twelve (3×4) could represent the intersection of heaven and earth. Susanna Fein has observed that the "twelveness" of the stanza form

> is obviously part of such meaning in a poem—numbering exactly 1,212 lines —that conveys a vision of the Holy Jerusalem teeming with twelves and twelves-squared (a kind of climax of the stanza number). By whatever inspiration, the *Pearl*-poet adopted a metrical style that fits perfectly the poetic content of lament, revelatory vision, and divine order.
>
> ("Twelve-Line Stanza Forms" 372)

Clearly, the *Pearl* poet was aware of the numeric symbolism in his culture and used the number twelve in significant ways in his poem.

Pearl is often described as a poem of 1,212 lines, but in fact, one line is missing entirely in the manuscript. So the poem is actually only 1,211 lines, though most scholars agree this is the fault of the copyist, not the intention of the poet. The significance of 1,212 lines, in a poem preoccupied by the numeric significance of twelve, is apparent. Yet there is more to the linear structure of *Pearl*, for each line contains within it both alliteration and an end-word that rhymes with a subsequent line in the pattern *ababababab bcbc*, a pattern that divides each stanza into an octet and quatrain. The last *c* rhyme, at the end of stanza grouping, introduces a new concatenation word.

A concatenation word is a link word repeated between two or more stanzas. In the case of *Pearl*, the concatenation word is repeated at the beginning and end of each stanza until the new concatenation word is introduced at the end of one section and the beginning of another. The twenty concatenation words (or phrases) of *Pearl* are as follows:

Section	Stanzas	Word or Phrase
1	1–5	*wythouten spot* "without spot"
2	6–10	*adubbement* "adornment"
3	11–15	*more and more*
4	16–20	*pyȝt* "set, fixed, adorned (with gems)"
5	21–25	*juelere* "jeweler"
6	26–30	*deme* "(to) judge, deem"
7	31–35	*grounde of alle my blysse* "ground of all my bliss"
8	36–40	*Quen of cortaysye* "queen of courtesy"
9	41–45	*dere þe date* "precious/noble/costly the date/season/beginning/end"

10	46–50	*more* "more"
11	51–55	*þe grace of god is gret inoghe* "the grace of God is great enough'"
12	56–60	*ryȝt* "right/justification" and *innosent* "innocent"
13	61–65	*perle ma(s)kelles* "spotless/matchless pearl"
14	66–70	*Jerusalem*
15	71–76	*neuer þe less* "nevertheless"
16	77–81	*mote* "city" and "spot"
17	82–86	*apostel John* "Apostle John"
18	87–91	*sunne and mone/mone* "sun and moon"
19	92–96	*gret delyt* "great delight"
20	97–101	*princes paye* "prince's pleasure"

As the modern English translations of these Middle English words suggest, the link words in the poem often have more than one meaning. In many cases they have not only different denotations but also different connotations each time they are used; they may also vary in form or possess a double sense. Sylvia Tomasch has analyzed the *Pearl* poet's punning and wordplay, observing that he uses the techniques of medieval rhetoric:

> According to medieval rhetorical analysis, there are three main varieties of punning wordplay: *traductio*, in which one word is used with more than one connotation (repetition of homonyms); *adnominatio*, in which the form of a word is varied by the use of suffixes, prefixes, or transportation of letters or sounds; and *significatio* in which a word may be taken in more than one sense (double entendre). (2)

The deliberate, highly wrought nature of nearly every word in *Pearl* may well put readers in a state of awe.

The concatenation words are linked not only to one another but to the poet's themes and the poem's overall structure. As Tomasch has also observed: "Throughout the poem, punning wordplay thus carries theme and builds structure . . . The poet's method here, as well as the audience's understanding of it, is predicated upon a recognition of form as having meaning of its own" (20). Significantly, the concatenation words vividly reinforce the interlinked and circular nature of the poem itself. They serve to unify each of the twenty stanzaic sections and to connect the end of the poem to its beginning. Even as they re-initiate the beginning of the poem, they complete its endlessly round structure.

Characters and Points of View in Pearl

The three main characters in *Pearl* are the Dreamer, the Pearl-Maiden, and the Lamb. The poem as a whole is narrated from the first-person point of view of the Dreamer. Andrew and Waldron have written in the introduction to their edition:

The use of the Dreamer as first-person narrator creates a close relationship with the audience, who are thus tacitly encouraged to relate his experience directly to their own lives. This narrative technique also identifies the Dreamer-narrator with the poet himself, and presents the loss and the vision of elements from his actual experience. The effect of this identification (whether fictional or not) on the tone and feeling of the poem as a whole is crucial.   (36)

Without a doubt, first-person narration in *Pearl* increases the sense of immediacy of the Dreamer's feelings, especially the poignancy of his loss, and it deliberately seeks to provoke similar feelings (or the memory of such feelings) in readers.

Yet, there are times in the long discourses of the Pearl-Maiden, naturally expressed in the first person, when readers may see things from the Pearl-Maiden's point of view as well. The dialogue between the Dreamer and the Maiden invites readers to imagine a performance, and because this question-and-answer dialogue sometimes has a debate-like quality to it, readers may find themselves shifting between two perspectives.

Readers do not ever truly see things from the Lamb's point of view. Instead, they receive reports of the Dreamer's feelings and attitudes toward Christ as a result of the loss of his pearl. These feelings of grief and anger, expressed early in the poem, later stand in vivid contrast to the feelings of the Pearl-Maiden. The Pearl-Maiden's feelings about the Lamb are rapturous: they are blissful and joyful, as a new bride's feelings; the Pearl-Maiden not only expresses her love for the Lamb, but she vividly recalls how he expressed his love for her, using the language of the Song of Songs.

Through such recollections, readers become aware of the Lamb's love for the Pearl-Maiden, just as the Dreamer does. The readers may or may not sympathize with the Dreamer's inability to accept the Pearl-Maiden's spiritual marriage to the Lamb, but without their grasping the larger context of medieval Christian contemplative devotion, their ability to interpret may be challenged by the sudden appearance of the Lamb bleeding from his wounded side in the vision of the New Jerusalem. Yet this iconic moment is key to understanding the expression of affective piety in the poem. It represents the Passion and Crucifixion of Christ, which is what makes unification to Christ—including the spiritual marriage of the Pearl-Maiden—possible for God's lovers.

While the triangular tensions between the Dreamer, the Maiden, and the Lamb become apparent in the course of the narrative, the actual nature of the relationship between the Dreamer and the Pearl-Maiden is not made entirely clear. When scholars view *Pearl* as an elegy, they have tended to see the Dreamer as father and the Pearl-Maiden as daughter, perhaps one named Margaret or Margery (as these names mean "pearl," deriving from the Latin *margarita*). But as John Bowers has noted in *The Politics of* Pearl, "The evidence for this identification is remarkably slight, however, and it comes remarkably late in the text" (153). Bowers believes that she may be a figure for one or both of the young queens of Richard II, but as Ian Bishop noted in Pearl *in Its Setting*, the Pearl-Maiden "may have been a godchild, a grandchild or even a younger sister" (8). Still others have seen her as the Dreamer's beloved, lost in life and longed for in death (Carson; Beal, "Pearl-Maiden's").

When the poem is viewed as an allegory, the question shifts slightly from "Who is the Pearl-Maiden?" to "What does she represent?" In this case, allegorical interpreters have seen her as the Dreamer's own soul, a symbol of salvation, or an interlocutor in the tradition of Boethius's Lady Philosophy or Dante's Beatrice, whose role it is to evoke the Dreamer's interior desolation or, in keeping with monastic tradition, "spiritual dryness" (comparable to "the dark night of the soul," which is considered in Mary Madeleva's Pearl: *A Study in Spiritual Dryness*). In Pearl: *Image of the Ineffable* (1983), Theodore Bogdanos sees the relationship as one representing the Dreamer's desire for union with perfection. In "The Signifying Power of *Pearl*," Beal argues that the Pearl-Maiden could stand for the Dreamer's "alleluia," his joy in salvation, which he "lost" (*sic* buried) in a Lenten season but anticipates recovering during the joyful resurrection season of Easter. (For additional allegorical interpretations, see in this volume Beal, "The Relationship between the the Pearl-Maiden and Dreamer.")

The mystery of the nature of the relationship between the Dreamer and the Pearl-Maiden is obviously one deliberately cultivated by the poet. The poem provokes questions about the relationship, but the answer to those questions is certainly not the poet's main point. For *Pearl* suggests that the Dreamer has elevated the importance of his relationship to the Pearl-Maiden above the importance of his relationship to the Lamb. The Pearl-Maiden, however, enjoys such tender intimacy with Christ that she seeks to restore the Dreamer's love for God. Therefore, she requests that the Dreamer be allowed a vision of the New Jerusalem and the Lamb himself. The Dreamer does seek to cross the stream in order to be with the Pearl-Maiden, and not necessarily the Lamb, but when the Dreamer awakens, his anger at Christ over the loss of the pearl has cooled and his sorrow, to some extent, has been comforted. This is clear when he expresses that he now regards God not only as his lord but as his friend. His restoration has begun.

The Symbolism of Pearl

The central symbol of the poem is the pearl. The source of the symbol is in the New Testament Parable of the Pearl of Great Price (Matt. 13.45–46), in which the pearl stands for salvation, which makes possible an entrance into the kingdom of heaven. Certainly this is one of its meanings in *Pearl*. Yet as A. C. Spearing has pointed out, "The pearl symbol is not static but dynamic: it develops in meaning as the poem extends itself in time, and this development in meaning is coordinated with the developing human drama of the relationship between the Dreamer and the Maiden" (*Gawain-Poet* 101). In the preface to their edition of the poems, Cawley and Anderson state that the pearl stands for

> the dead child, as the poet remembers her and all of her loveliness, for the beatified maiden, for the grace of God conferred on her because of her innocence, and for the kingdom of heaven in which she enjoys the reward of eternal felicity. The poet's lost pearl is also a symbol of his own lost innocence, which he sees his way to recovering through meditation on the Pearl-Maiden's death and salvation . . . He recovers his pearl when the conviction grows on him that her soul is safe and that she is the recipient of God's grace through the Christ-given sacrament of baptism. He becomes convinced that he too may receive God's grace through sacramental penance.   (xi)

Clearly, the pearl is not the vehicle of simple metaphor with a one-to-one correspondence to a single tenor, but rather a symbol with many aspects. Indeed, Marie Borroff states, in the preface to her translation of the poem, that the pearl stands for that which is "most precious" to the Dreamer, and that in its roundness the pearl stands for "eternity, the existence of God in a timeless present from the perspective of which human history is a completed, static pattern" (*Gawain Poet* 116).

Other scholars have seen the pearl as connected to the Eucharist (e.g., Garrett; Gatta), which is referred to near the conclusion of the poem, and still others have noted how the narrator states in the final two lines: "He gef vus to be His homly hyne / Ande precious perlez vnto His pay" ("He grants us to be his humble servants / and precious pearls unto his pleasure"). These lines point to the poet's belief that we—his readers and all people made by God—are precious pearls. This is an all-embracing idea and a suitable culmination to the multiple transformations of the symbolism of the pearl.

The symbolism of the poem is not limited to the pearl only. *Pearl* is a highly symbolic poem, incorporating many images that undergo transformation and expansion as they appear or reappear in the three different settings of the poem: the garden, the dreamscape, and the vision of the New Jerusalem. Among these symbols are many elements from the natural world that gain greater significance in the spiritual world of the dream and the vision: flowers, plants, and trees; stones and jewels; birds and beasts; colors of many kinds as well as the contrast between light and dark; the sun and moon; and so on. Some of these symbols are at first described literally but later are used metaphorically. The complex symbolism of *Pearl* is yet another reason that the poem repays multiple rereadings with such rich dividends.

The Themes, Theology, and Conclusion of Pearl

Pearl presents the occasion of the Dreamer's loss as an opportunity to explore the emotions of grief, the frustrations that humans experience when their will is different from God's will, and the possibility of going on a healing journey that restores and transforms the soul. It juxtaposes time and eternity, earth and heaven, in order to put the experiences of this life in a timeless perspective. The central revelation of *Pearl* is the revelation of the Lamb, who, though bleeding from his wounded side, nevertheless has a joyful countenance.

In Christian theology, the blood of the innocent Lamb makes the salvation of humanity possible. The Fall, which took place when Adam and Eve disobeyed God in the Garden of Eden, introduced sin into the world and separated humanity from God. Ancient Israel practiced the blood sacrifice of animals, of unblemished lambs and sheep, to atone for sin. Christians believed that God sent his Son, Jesus ("the Word became flesh and dwelt among us"; John 1.14), to die as a sinless Lamb on a Roman Cross to atone for sin and to reconcile God and humanity for eternity. They believed, as the Apostle Paul wrote, that "if you confess with your mouth that Jesus is Lord and believe in your heart that God raised him from the dead, you will be saved" (Rom. 10.9). That is partly why medieval Catholics made a regular practice of reciting the Apostle's Creed, which, along with the Lord's Prayer, they were expected to memorize (a reality the *Pearl* poet alludes to in the poem at line 485).

Because of this theology, the Crucifixion of Jesus was of central importance to medieval Christians. The *Pearl* poet particularly emphasizes it through the Pearl-Maiden's extensive meditations on the Passion in the poem and through the Dreamer's vision of the bleeding Lamb. Like the Dreamer, the Lamb of God suffered the loss of the one he loved, his Bride—all of humanity. But unlike the Dreamer, he rejoiced to suffer because he had an eternal perspective (see Hebrews 12.2). His suffering was temporary, but his reunion with the Bride will be eternal.

When the Dreamer awakens at the end of the poem, once again in the lovely garden ("erber wlonk") where he fell asleep, he has a better understanding, which was achieved through a sudden, emotional vision of the iconic bleeding Lamb. He has been restored to the right relationship with his Prince in part because he has glimpsed eternity and gained perspective on suffering. To some extent, he is comforted. The ending of the poem does convey a sense, which many readers have perceived, that complete consolation is not possible in this life. Comfort remains partial on earth. Though it can be reexperienced in the community of the church, especially through the taking of the Eucharist, only in heaven will every tear be wiped away.

The poem *Pearl* suggests by its conclusion that the transformation of the Dreamer has been achieved through a spiritual pilgrimage. The pilgrimage transpired in his dream vision as he followed the path through the dreamscape to the stream where he encountered the Pearl-Maiden, talked with her, and then beheld the vision of the Lamb of God in the New Jerusalem. The poet makes clear that such transformation is available to readers of his poem. That is why, at the end of his poem, he invokes the Eucharist, "the form of bread and wine / that the priest shows us each day" (1209–10), the memorial of Christ's sacrifice, and then he prays that this God will grant that all of us become precious pearls for the pleasure of the Prince (1211–12).

With a clear understanding of the plot, date, manuscript, dialect, authorship, sources and analogues, contemplative devotional context, genres, settings, structures, characters, points of view, symbols, themes, theology, and the conclusion of *Pearl*, which has been presented in this introduction, it is possible to consider how to teach the poem. The next section, "Materials for Teaching *Pearl*: Classroom Texts and Instructor's Library," presents the Middle English editions, dual-language editions, and modern English translations of the poem. It also refers to relevant works of literary criticism and theory as well as multimedia resources. The "Materials" section is followed by an overview of the essays; the essays themselves; questions for student reflection, discussion, or writing assignments; reproductions of the manuscript illustrations of *Pearl*; and the list of works cited. As the editors, we welcome our readers to *Approaches to Teaching the Middle English* Pearl, and we hope it will prove useful for years to come.

Part One

MATERIALS

Teachers of the Middle English *Pearl* have an abundant treasure of texts available to them for classroom use. It may seem, at times, that the treasure has been buried in a field, and that the work of digging down to extricate it requires too much effort. It need not be the case. This introduction to the various materials available can serve as a tool to quickly and effectively facilitate the teacher's discovery process. Ideally it will help teachers locate a desirable text of the poem *Pearl*, as well as supplementary texts to help teach it.

Classroom Texts

This section identifies the editions, dual-language edition-translations, and modern English translations of *Pearl* available, as well as the commentaries and anthologies that include the poem or selections from it. It gives suggestions on how these texts might best serve students in courses that have different designs and purposes. Teachers who peruse this section should be able to evaluate the available texts of *Pearl* and choose one (or more) to use in their classes.

Facsimile Editions of Pearl

There are two modern, photographic facsimile editions of *Pearl*. One is in print and the other online. The Folio Society produced its beautiful, color, to-scale facsimile version as part of a two-volume set in 2016 (Pearl *Manuscript*). The facsimile volume is accompanied by a second volume that includes Malcolm Andrew and Ronald Waldron's parallel text, Middle English transcription and prose Modern English translation with accompanying notes. The cost (over five hundred dollars) and the limited print run (only 980 copies) make it an unlikely purchase for students, but university libraries can acquire it so that faculty members and graduate students can study it in place of the original manuscript held by the British Library.

The online facsimile is known as the *Cotton Nero A.x Project*. Edited by Murray McGillivray and Kenna Olsen, it is available at the University of Calgary's Web site (gawain-ms.ca). This edition provides a transcription as well as digital facsimile images of every page of the sole manuscript containing the Middle English poem *Pearl*, including the four illustrations that precede the manuscript. (Analysis of the critical reception of the manuscript illustrations has been well articulated in essays by Jennifer Lee and by Paul Reichardt.) Olsen and McGillivray's online edition and its bibliography are being expanded and updated. The online *Cotton Nero A.x Project* is particularly valuable for courses and assignments that involve students in the study of paleography, codicology, and transcription as well as the reproduction of medieval manuscripts in digital environments. Access to the edition online is free.

Editions of Pearl

There are eleven printed editions of *Pearl*, and three critical editions of the poem are currently regarded as standard editions and widely used in classroom teaching:

> *The Poems of the* Pearl *Manuscript*, edited by Malcolm Andrew and Ronald Waldron, first published in 1978 and in its fifth edition as of 2008
> Pearl, Cleanness, Patience *and* Sir Gawain and the Green Knight (1962, 1976, rev. 1996), edited by J. J. Anderson and A. C. Cawley
> *Pearl* (2001), edited by Sarah Stanbury, published by TEAMS (Teaching Middle English Texts Series) in print and available free online

A fourth edition, *The Works of the Gawain-Poet*: Sir Gawain and the Green Knight, Pearl, Cleanness, *and* Patience (2014), edited by Ad Putter and Myra Stokes, is likely to become another frequently used standard edition. It is available in both print and electronic versions.

Malcolm Andrew and Ronald Waldron's work is the best-known and most widely used edition, as indicated by its multiple reprintings. It begins with a preface, list of abbreviations, select bibliography, an introduction (with sections devoted to each poem in the collection), a note on language and meter, and a note to the text. The text of the poem includes original letters, *thorn* and *yogh*, as well as textual and explanatory footnotes. A glossary is provided at the end of the book along with an appendix of relevant biblical passages from the Latin Vulgate. Andrew and Waldron's edition is suitable for graduate and upper-division undergraduate courses in which *Pearl* is taught in the original Middle English.

J. J. Anderson and A. C. Cawley's effective edition begins with a preface, an introduction (with sections devoted to each poem in the collection), and a select bibliography. The text of *Pearl* has marginal glosses with translations of hard words in a given line, as well as footnotes that give many complete translations of whole lines of the poem. It modernizes the lettering, replacing *thorn* with *th* and *yogh* with *y* or *g* as appropriate. The appendixes include notes on spelling, grammar, and meter. This edition is suitable for graduate or undergraduate courses in which the poem is taught in the original Middle English and the students are working on translating the language into modern English, especially on sight.

Sarah Stanbury's fine edition begins with acknowledgments and an introduction containing sections on metaphor and form, contexts (date, authorship, occasion), courtly economics and the Ricardian court, and notes on the edition; a select bibliography follows the introduction. The text of *Pearl* has marginal glosses that translate hard words in a given line and footnotes that give occasional translations of lines (though many fewer than those found in Anderson and Cawley). The Middle English letters of the poem, *thorn* and *yogh*, are modernized. Following the poem, there is a section of textual and explanatory notes as well as a glossary. Neither the marginal glosses nor the concluding glossary is complete; some readers will need to consult the *Middle English Dictionary*. This edition is suitable for graduate or undergraduate courses whose teachers expect the students to consult outside sources in order to read, understand, and translate *Pearl*. It has the advantage of being available for purchase in print in addition to being free online, where it is easily accessed.

Ad Putter and Myra Stokes's new edition of four poems is available in print and e-book formats. This is the first complete edition of the four poems available in e-book formats. It has an introduction with sections devoted to the poems and the poet, dialect and inflections, alliterative meter, editorial practice, and acknowledgments. The section on editorial practice indicates that *thorn* and *yogh* are replaced by their modern equivalents, and that any given word, spelled variously in the Middle English manuscript, is regularized in this edition. Each of the poems, beginning with *Pearl*, is prefaced by an overview and interpretation of the poem's contents. The edited poem follows: in the e-book version, hard words in individual lines are hyperlinked so that clicking on them takes the reader directly to the definition in the glossary. After the edited poems are the notes on each poem, which explain key terms, ideas, and cruxes in the individual lines. A bibliography of works cited, a list of editorial emendations to individual words in the four poems, the aforementioned glossary, and a list of proper names mentioned in the poems appear at the end of the volume. This edition is clearly targeting undergraduate student readers, though the editors mention that general readers may also be interested in reading *Sir Gawain and the Green Knight* in the Middle English given in their volume.

In addition to these standard, widely accessible editions of *Pearl*, there are several earlier editions. These were edited by Richard Morris (EETS, 1864, rev. 1969, rpt. 1965); Israel Gollancz (1891, rev. 1897, 1921); Charles Osgood (1906); Stanley P. Chase (1932), with members of a Chaucer course at Bowdoin College; E. V. Gordon (1953), with contributions by J. R. R. Tolkien (though he is not credited in the first published edition); and Charles Moorman (1977). Because the copyright has expired and not been renewed, some of these editions are being republished as free e-books or affordable reprints made available through

such venues as Amazon. (For links to these, see medievalpearl.wordpress.com/
pearls-editionstranslations/.) Gollancz's 1891 edition includes his verse translation and, because it is in the public domain, can be downloaded in various forms
from the *Internet Archive* (archive.org) as well as from other sites.

Dual-Language Edition-Translations of Pearl

There are eleven modern, dual-language edition-translations of *Pearl*, prepared
by the following:

Mary Vincent Hillmann (1967)   Victor Watts (2005)
Sara de Ford and her students (1967)   David Gould (2012)
John Crawford, with Andrew Hoyem (1967)   David Williams (2015)
William Vantuono (1984; 1995)   Simon Armitage (2016)
Casey Finch (1993)   Jane Beal
Bill Stanton (1995)

In general, these eleven works are valuable because they provide a Middle English text and a modern English translation in facing-page editions (or, in Crawford's case, an interlinear edition), which may make the meaning of the poem
accessible to nonspecialist readers of the Middle English dialect of *Pearl*. Facing-page editions allow for comparisons to be made between the original and the
translation. Eight of the eleven are stand-alone editions, providing *Pearl* to readers without the other poems attributed to the *Pearl* poet; the three exceptions are
the versions by Finch, Vantuono, and Williams. None of these has emerged as
the standard, dual-language version. But the relation of the Finch version to the
Andrew and Waldron popular edition and the second printing of the Vantuono
version suggest that they are more widely used than the others and the inclusion
of the Williams version in the online component of the *Broadview Anthology of
British Literature: The Medieval Period*, 3rd edition, makes it accessible to all
readers of that excellent anthology.

Casey Finch's dual-language edition makes use of Andrew and Waldron's text
of all four poems of Cotton Nero A.x as well as some of their notes, which are
provided as endnotes rather than footnotes, and their glossary. Clifford Peterson's Middle English edition of *Saint Erkenwald* and his notes are also included.
Finch provides translations of all poems, including *Pearl*. His modern English
Pearl preserves the rhyme scheme and alliteration, but, as translator, he chooses
to render the alliterative line of the poem in iambic tetrameter. In several instances, perhaps as a result of trying to reproduce the complex form of the poem,
the modern English words are not faithful translations of the original Middle
English. This, however, can be readily seen by the teacher familiar with the
Middle English because of the facing-page layout.

William Vantuono's modern English *Pearl* suffers from the same difficulty for similar reasons. Yet like Finch's edition, it has an outstanding critical apparatus. Vantuono first produced it in 1984 with Garland Press in an "omnibus edition" in two volumes, one containing *Pearl* and *Cleanness*, and the other containing *Patience* and *Sir Gawain*. His *Pearl* was then published in 1995 in a stand-alone volume with the University of Notre Dame Press.

This latter version begins with brief acknowledgments, a preface, and an introduction that covers the manuscript, the poet, the audience, *Pearl*, and the theme and structure. There follows a preface to the text, translations, and notes; black-and-white plates reproducing the four illustrations of the poem from the manuscript as well as the first page of the manuscript; and the dual-language translation itself. A little more than two stanzas is printed on each page, and the bottom of the page has glosses of key terms from the Middle English or, occasionally, a literal translation of the phrase where this differs from the modern verse translation. Then comes the "Commentary" section, very detailed textual and explanatory notes tied to line numbers, which contain references to many critical interpretations of the poem by literary scholars. There are appendixes on poetic mastery in *Pearl*, on dialect and language, and on sources and analogues, followed by a list of abbreviations, divided by grammatical and other terms, languages and dialects, parts of the Bible, and periodicals, dictionaries, and serial volumes. There are also two useful bibliographies and a glossary. While this critical apparatus is worth consulting frequently, the infelicities in the translation leave something to be desired.

Vantuono's 1995 translation may be contrasted with Hillmann's translation. Hillmann's dual-language edition, currently out of print, made a significant impression on later editors of the poem, including Vantuono and Stanbury, in whose editions she is quoted often. Her book includes an introduction by Edward Vasta, a preface, a three-page interpretation, and a Middle English text of the poem with a modern English translation. This is followed by a list of abbreviations, a list of textual emendations, and a section of explanatory notes tied to line numbers as well as a bibliography and glossary. Designated a "literal translation" in the table of contents, Hillmann's translation does not seek to preserve the rhyme scheme or alliteration of the original (though there are plenty of rhymes and alliterative phrases that occur without a deliberate attempt to reproduce the poem's form). In this way, her *Pearl* is quite faithful to the meaning of the words, if not to the form of the poem.

Sara de Ford's edition-translation is the only published one that relies on multiple translators. De Ford edited the medieval text and provided the notes while she and her five former students created sections of the translation. Their translation aims to preserve the rhyme scheme. The preface to the book explains this process, as well as the lack of punctuation in the volume's Middle English text (because, they add, the manuscript contains none), and that the notes were synthesized from the glossaries and notes of the separate editions of Osgood, Gordon, and Hillmann; the preface ends by giving a short list of abbreviations. The introduction is a brief two pages. Two stanzas from the poem are given on each subsequent page, with footnotes that are explanatory in some cases and with glosses of individual words in other cases. The book concludes with a selected bibliography. While this little-known, dual-language edition is also out of print (but may be found in a university library), it serves as a case study of what a graduate or undergraduate seminar might be able to accomplish with *Pearl*.

John Crawford's translation with Andrew Hoyem is unique in that it provides the Middle English text, in red, interlineally. The translation is unrhymed. It was originally printed in a limited edition of 225 copies. As a rare, fine-press edition, it is currently for sale only through rare bookstores, for over two hundred dollars a copy. Although it would not make a suitable student text, it is relevant to know of this book's existence for those teachers and students interested in the poem's editorial history and reception.

Bill Stanton, a radio writer in the United Kingdom, created his translation when he was a student at the University of York. It was published online, after 1995, as part of a Web site featuring his other works (including his original poems, plays, and stories and novels, some for children). The menu for the online edition has an introduction followed by the twenty sections of the poem (and so is divided as in the manuscript), a link to the "original text," and another link to the verse translation. The brief introduction identifies the work as nonscholarly, produced to encourage the enjoyment of the reader. Clicking on one of the individual sections of the poem brings up a three-part page: in the left column is the Middle English (two stanzas), in the right column is the modern English verse, and at the bottom is a literal prose translation from the Middle English to the modern English. Clicking on the menu item "Original Text" gives a text of the whole poem in blue; clicking on the blue text reveals it to be a hypertext, which is linked to the verse translation in red. While teachers are unlikely to use this edition-translation, their tech-savvy students are likely to find it when given translation assignments from the Middle English (so teachers are advised to keep an eye out for direct plagiarism from Stanton's work).

Victor Watts's dual-language version was published posthumously as a kind of memorial volume in the translator's honor. There are three introductions, one written by Watts, one by Kathleen Raine, and one by Corinne Saunders. The original text is edited and glossed by David Fuller and Saunders; Watts's translation, called a modernization, is provided on the facing page. Three stanzas are given per page, in small print, with marginal glosses of hard Middle English words on the far right side. According to the section "The Text and Its Modernization," by Saunders, the translation preserves as far as possible the original wording and word order but modern-izes the spelling. This is a limited form of modernization, but the only way in which all the features of the original text's elaborate formal structure, which are so important to its feeling as a poem, can be retained: the alliteration, pat-terns of rhyme, and patterns of linked opening and closing lines by which the stanzas are grouped.   (22)

Like de Ford's version, Watts's is little known, but does provide a good example of one very literal kind of translation, one that teachers or students may practice, and it is unique in its approach among the dual-language editions.

David Gould's version is available in print and e-book formats. It is an excel-lent edition for classrooms in which codicological or paleographic issues will be intensively studied. Called *Pearl of Great Price: A Literary Translation of the Middle English* Pearl, it emphasizes the manuscript context of the poem by reproducing photographic images of the handwritten text from Cotton Nero A.x beside each stanza translated by Gould. There follows a transcription of the text after the presentation of this unique, facing-page, dual-language facsimile-translation. (However, one might wish that the transcription had been paired with the photographic images of the text and the translation given separately because this would allow for easier analysis of the success of Gould's paleog-raphy.) After the transcription, the book provides textual notes, a glossary, a list of abbreviations, a short essay on how to read the manuscript hand, and a works-cited section.

At the beginning of the book Gould provides an insightful preface on his approach to translation, one that gives critical explanations of difficulties the translator of *Pearl* faces. He makes a distinction between "literal" and "liter-ary" translation, explaining that the latter aims to "recreate the poetic effects" (vi) in the target language. There are, of course, drawbacks to both types of translation, but dual-language edition-translations mitigate some of these, and so Gould chose this form for his book, aiming to create a literary translation that is literally accurate. At different points in his preface, Gould compares his translation with two of its most popular precedents, those of Marie Borroff and J. R. R. Tolkien.

Following his successful translation of *Sir Gawain and the Green Knight*, the poet and elected Oxford Professor of Poetry Simon Armitage has translated *Pearl* as well, after being commissioned to do so by Faber and Faber in the United Kingdom and W. W. Norton in the United States. He used the editions of Cawley and Anderson and of Andrew and Waldron for his base text, but the publishers printed Charles Osgood's original edition of the poem, providing it in a parallel column beside Armitage's modern English version (presumably because Osgood's was published in 1908 and is beyond copyright at this point).

Armitage states that he read other editions and translations of the poem by Borroff, Tolkien, Gordon, Draycott, and Vantuono and consulted *A Companion to the Gawain-Poet*, edited by Derek Brewer and Jonathan Gibson. His introduction to the poem is indebted to Tolkien, echoing some aspects of Tolkien's interpretation of the poem quite obviously. Aside from a single textual note on the one line missing from the manuscript copy of *Pearl*, all footnotes concern biblical allusions and quotations. Armitage indicates that these footnotes were provided by James Simpson, a professor of English at Harvard University, who also commented on drafts of the translation. The Armitage translation reads easily, emphasizing four stresses in each line of syntactically normative modern English and retaining alliteration but laying aside the rhyme scheme. This is a translation for general readers and lovers of poetry. Josephine Livingstone's review of it in *The New Yorker* (16 June 2016) certainly has brought the poem to the attention of a very wide audience. Livingstone aptly observes, "The speech of the heart invites translation of many kinds."

Jane Beal has also created a dual-language edition-translation of the poem entitled Pearl: *A Medieval Masterpiece in Middle English and Modern English*. In her translation, she uses a plain style, retaining the alliteration without attempting to keep to a strict meter or rhyme scheme, with the goal of maintaining fidelity to the meaning of the words. She provides a critical introduction that briefly considers the date and provenance of the *Pearl* manuscript; authorship and audience questions; the Ricardian court and West Midlands contexts; the poem's story and symbolism, literary genres and four levels of meaning; design and diction; biblical and liturgical sources; literary sources and analogues, and cruxes and scholarly debates. She also provides helpful advice to readers in brief sections entitled, "The Nature of Translation," "Some Purposes of Translation," and "Making the Most of This Translation." Her translation includes textual and explanatory notes as well as relevant appendixes; a literary sourcebook, biblical source passages, a list of significant liturgical dates, a chart of concatenation words, key terms and study questions, and links to an art sourcebook available at her companion Web site, medieval-pearl.wordpress.com. Her book is specifically designed to aid university faculty members and their students interpreting *Pearl* in its medieval literary and cultural contexts.

Modern English Translations of Pearl

In addition to the eleven dual-language edition-translations, there are fifteen complete, modern English translations of *Pearl* in verse, listed here in chronological order of publication:

George Gordon Coulton (1906)

Sophie Jewett (1908)

S. Weir Mitchell (1908)

Marian Mead (1908)

Jessie Weston (1912)

Ernest J. B. Kirtlan (1918)

Israel Gollancz (1918)

Stanley P. Chase (1932)

Brian Stone (1964)

John Gardner (1965, 1967, 1970, 1975)

Margaret Williams (1967, 1970)

J. R. R. Tolkien (1975)

Marie Borroff (1967, 1977, 2001, 2010, 2011)

Jane Draycott (2011)

Giles Watson (2014)

There are also two in prose, one by Charles Osgood (1907) and another, with minimal editorial apparatus, by Malcolm Andrew and Ronald Waldron. Andrew and Waldron's prose translation was originally included as part of the CD-ROM version of the fifth edition of *The Poems of the* Pearl *Manuscript* in 2007, subsequently printed separately in 2013, and is now included as part of the Folio Society's parallel-text Middle English transcription and Modern English translation volume. There are also numerous partial translations of *Pearl*. The two stand-alone translations most often used in classrooms today are by Borroff and Tolkien, which are, as already mentioned, in verse.

The translation of J. R. R. Tolkien, who was a professor at Oxford University, was published posthumously by his son, Christopher Tolkien, with two other Middle English poems Tolkien had translated: *Sir Gawain and the Green Knight* and *Sir Orfeo*. The book includes brief introductions to the three poems. The one Tolkien wrote for *Pearl* expresses his view that the poem is an elegy on the death of a child, based on a possibly literal dream vision of the poet mourning his daughter's death, one that is best understood not in allegorical terms but in symbolic ones (though Tolkien acknowledges that the poem contains allegorical elements). It is a literary translation that reflects Tolkien's beliefs about the poem's genre and symbolism as well as the relationship between the Dreamer and the Pearl-Maiden. There is no critical apparatus beyond the introduction. Nevertheless, it is a fine translation, rendered alongside two of the most admired medieval English romances; it has been a popular choice for an undergraduate textbook and, of course, for fans of Tolkien.

The translation by Marie Borroff, professor emerita at Yale University, is certainly the most often reprinted and widely read of all the stand-alone modern English translations. It is generally recognized as one of the most accurate literal translations of *Pearl* but also one of the loveliest literary translations. One admirable aspect of Borroff's translation is the way she preserves the ambiguity of certain Middle English words in modern English, allowing the reader to make decisions about meaning rather than supplying it (e.g., translating "faunt" as "maiden child" instead of "infant").

Norton has published Borroff's translation in a stand-alone volume and in collections as part of Borroff's translations of the other poems attributed to the *Pearl* poet. Her most recent set of translations are gathered in *The Gawain Poet: Complete Works* (2011). This contains five poems, the four from Cotton Nero A.x and *Saint Erkenwald*. As in Finch's edition-translation, the inclusion of *Saint Erkenwald* in Borroff's book reflects growing acceptance of Clifford Peterson's argument that *Saint Erkenwald* is part of the *Pearl* poet's canon even though it does not, of course, appear in Cotton Nero A.x. The only oddity is Borroff's editorial organization of the poems, which differs from the manuscript. She presents first *Sir Gawain and the Green Knight*, then *Patience, Cleanness,* and *Pearl,* and finally *Saint Erkenwald.* In this ordering, *Pearl* is deprived of its usual first place.

Borroff provides a critical apparatus with her translation. Her introduction to *Pearl* considers the story of the poem, its symbolism and theme, literary background, design and significance, and her own translation. Her general introduction to the *Complete Works* reviews the manuscripts, subject matter and form of the poems, the history of alliterative poetry generally, and late Middle English alliterative poetry specifically. At the conclusion of both the stand-alone version and the collected works version, she has brief essays on the metrical form of the poem and scansion. Her selected bibliography is quite brief and contains only two citations of critical works on *Pearl* after 2003.

In addition to Tolkien's and Borroff's translations, other translations of *Pearl* have intrinsic value, and it is useful to know something about them because teachers may have reason to assign them and students may consult them independently. The six translations made in the first two decades of the twentieth century reveal the poem's popularity and wide appeal at that time. Five were made by medievalists: Coulton, a historian at Cambridge; Osgood, a professor at Princeton University; Weston, an independent scholar and folklorist famous for her book on Arthurian legend, *From Ritual to Romance* (1920), and its influence on T. S. Eliot; and J. B. Kirtlan, who also translated *Beowulf* and *Sir Gawain and the Green Knight.* Sophie Jewett, affiliated with Wellesley College, was better known as a poet than a medievalist; her translation, in the meter of the original, is elegant. It is worth noting that Gollancz's translation was reprinted in a stand-alone version (without his edition of the Middle English poem) in 1918 on behalf of the British Red Cross, apparently to raise funds to meet human needs at the end of World War I.

S. Weir Mitchell was not a medievalist but a medical doctor, famously associated with the "rest cure" so severely critiqued by Virginia Woolf and by Charlotte Perkins Gilman in her story "The Yellow Wallpaper." He was also a poet (his collected poems appeared in 1914) and a writer of fiction (he produced several historical novels). Mitchell based his translation of *Pearl* on that of Gollancz. Because he was interested primarily in the elegiac sense of the poem, he shortened *Pearl* in his translation, leaving out stanzas 12, 30, 34, 38, 39, 47 and 49–96 because they dealt with, in his words, "uninteresting theological or allegorical material" (Mitchell, foreword [n. pag.]). Only sixty copies of his translation were printed in 1908, but Mitchell's translation is now available in its entirety online, digitized by Google. The translations by Gollancz, Mitchell, and Mead all open with a quatrain that Alfred, Lord Tennyson, wrote about *Pearl*:

> We lost you—for how long a time—
> true *Pearl* of our poetic prime!
> We found you, and you gleam re-set
> in Britain's lyric coronet!

Tennyson's stanza clearly ranks the poem highly, which its early-twentieth-century translators felt to be important.

Two translators, Jessie Weston and Brian Stone, published their versions of *Pearl* along with several other translations of Middle English poetry. In 1912 Weston published her translation with a collection of other alliterative poems she had modernized, including, in the following order: *Sir Gawain and the Green Knight*; *Adventures of Arthur at the Tarn Wadeling*; *Morte Arthure*; *Cleanness*, *Patience*; *Pearl*; *Vision of Piers Plowman* (A text); and a selection from the opening of the *Vision of Piers Plowman* (B text). More than fifty years later, in 1964, Stone would similarly anthologize his translation of *Pearl* in a Penguin Classics edition titled *Medieval English Verse*, which organizes dozens of translations of medieval poems by theme and genre. Stone's anthology includes a number of short essays introducing his translations, including one on *Pearl*. Here he admits, "Although several different approaches to the task of translation were made, and the poem was worked in its entirety in two different modes, it proved impossible to be utterly faithful to the complex form of the original" (136).

Between the publications of Weston's and Stone's translations, Stanley P. Chase crafted a translation that was published in 1932 in New York by Oxford University Press. He dedicated it to his wife, Helen Johnson Chase, who assisted him with the translation. Helen was the daughter of Henry Johnson, who had been the Longfellow Professor of Modern Languages at Bowdoin College from 1882 to 1918, and she had been married to Stanley Chase since 1912. The Chases' translation was intended for a general readership but it was also a companion to Stanley Chase's 1932 edition, compiled collaboratively with his students in a Chaucer course at Bowdoin College, also in 1932. The Chases' translation and edition have been made available online as free e-books.

John Gardner and Margaret Williams created separate translations of the "complete works" of the *Pearl* poet in which they also included *Saint Erkenwald*. Gardner's introduction and commentary focus on the poet, conventions and traditions in the poems, the poet's vision of reality and dramatic sense, the interrelation of the four poems from the same manuscript, and versification

and form. There is a section of notes at the end of his book. Williams's introduction concerns the book and its maker, the manuscript (meaning Cotton Nero
A.x), the language, the alliterative movement, and the author as well as backgrounds of the poems. She has three appendixes—on the manuscript, language,
and prosody—as well as a bibliography, footnotes, and five annotated charts.
The charts may be especially helpful in course manuals or handouts. One of the
charts provides a breakdown of the setting, dramatic structure, keywords, and
action in *Pearl*, along with symbols, themes, and sources—biblical and other.
Both Gardner and Williams attempt to reproduce the alliteration and rhyme
scheme of the original *Pearl* in their translations. However, Borroff's translation
became more popular and has been reprinted more often, while those of Gardner
and Williams have not.

Jane Draycott, a British poet, published her translation of *Pearl* in the Carcanet Oxford Poets series. In her three-paragraph acknowledgments section, she
recognizes the influences of the Andrew and Waldron edition as well as the
translations of Tolkien and Borroff on her work. Bernard O'Donoghue introduces the translation, comparing it with Seamus Heaney's translation of *Beowulf*: "As with Seamus Heaney's *Beowulf*, when the alliteration offers itself in
an unforced modern idiom, Draycott uses it" (8). Draycott's translation is very
free, neither giving a literal translation of the words nor reproducing the literary
form of the poem, but its plain speech makes it accessible as a work of poetry in
the modern age in its own right.

Giles Watson, who has been a secondary teacher and is now a tutor in literary
theory at the University of Western Australia, published his *Pearl: A Translation from the Middle English* in 2014 with several lovely black-and-white plates,
a brief introduction, and a concluding prose summary of the poem. The translation aims to retain some alliteration and the rhyme scheme, and interestingly,
all verbs in the translation are rendered in the present tense. His fifty-seven
footnotes focus primarily on concatenation words but also address wordplay,
biblical allusion, and the like. Watson used Andrew and Waldron's and Anderson and Cawley's editions as the base texts for his translation, but he asserts
that he did not consult any modern translations. His book is available in print
from Lulu Press and online at www.poemhunter.com/poem/pearl-a-translation/.
He has recorded his translation and published it as a video on *YouTube*, and he
has made his color versions of the photographs (included as black-and-white
pictures in his printed book) available on *Flickr*. This multimodal-multimedia
Pearl translation is suitable for secondary students and general readers.

In addition to the modern English translations, *Pearl* has also been translated,
either in whole or in part, into German (trans. Decker, 1916), Frisian (trans.
Kalma, 1938), Italian (trans. Olivero, 1936; Guidi, 1966; Giaccherini, 1989), and
Japanese (trans. Sekigawa, 1952; Miyata, 1954; Terasawa, 1960; and trans. and
ed. Naruse, 1971).

Commentaries

Pearl has inspired writers to create commentaries. The genre of commentary has its roots in extended glosses of the Bible, and because *Pearl* is a poem deeply informed by scripture and shaped by theological complexities, commentaries on it are appropriate. Authors of commentaries follow the form of biblical commentary, examining word by word, line by line, stanza by stanza, or section by section. Three *Pearl* commentaries are available to teachers and students.

Vernard Eller translated the poem and commented on it, stanza by stanza, in *A Pearl. . . for the Brokenhearted* (1983). His commentary gives counsel and encouragement to the grieving. It treats the poem explicitly as a consolation that could comfort Christians if they applied its truths to their lives today. It is available in print, reprint (through Amazon), and online (www.hccentral.com/eller10/).

Jane Zatta's commentary, "*Pearl*: An Introduction" (2000), is on each of the twenty sections of the poem and available online through *ORB: The Online Reference Book for Medieval Studies* (www.the-orb.net/textbooks/anthology/middle enganon/zatta.html). Her commentary begins with a short essay on patterns, forms, and symbolic meaning in the poem. It concludes with brief comments on the dream vision (as a literary genre), the manuscript, some notes, and a select bibliography organized topically.

In a similar but more extended fashion, *Practice and Theory of Commentary*, a 2015 special issue of the literary-critical journal *Glossator*, edited by Nicola Masciandaro and Karl Steel, provides several essays by authors who comment on each of the twenty sections of the poem. These essays provide close readings of the poem with critical references. The special issue is available in print and online and may be useful for students to consult when interpreting cruxes and challenging passages in the poem.

Anthologies

For the most part, the editors of major anthologies that survey British literature choose *Sir Gawain and the Green Knight* as representative of the *Pearl* poet's canon. As a result *Pearl* does not appear in the current printed editions of the commonly used Norton, Broadview, or Longman anthologies. Earlier editions of the Norton do have selections from *Pearl*, and the complete poem does appear in the online supplement to the *Broadview Anthology of British Literature, Vol. III: The Medieval Period*, third edition, published in 2015, as a parallel text edition-translation created by David Williams. Students can read it online or download the PDF file to read on their electronic devices.

Pearl also appears in Middle English in several anthologies of medieval literature including Charles Dunn and Edward Byrnes, *Middle English Literature*

(1973; revised and reprinted 1990), organized chronologically from the twelfth to the fifteenth century; Thomas Garbáty, *Medieval English Literature* (1984), organized by genre (*Pearl* is placed in the category of allegorical and religious verse alongside *Piers Plowman*); and Ann S. Haskell, *A Middle English Anthology* (1969, 1985). *Pearl* also appears in John Conlee's *Middle English Debate Poetry: A Critical Anthology* (1991), though this book is out of print. Selections from the poem appear in anthologies: lines 361–612 in Kenneth Sisam and Tolkien's *A Middle English Reader and Vocabulary* (1921–22, 2005) and in the description of the New Jerusalem in Fernand Mossé's *Handbook of Middle English* (1952, 1968, 1991, 2000). These anthologies are useful for students in seminars who are learning to read and translate Middle English into modern English. Stone's *Medieval English Verse* (1964) is one anthology that presents the poem in modern English.

The Instructor's Library

This section gives an overview of the introductory studies of the *Pearl* poet, the three major critical collections of essays on *Pearl* (and related poems), books and dissertations on *Pearl*, books and essays for teaching critical contexts of *Pearl*, studies of *Pearl* that use the paradigms of critical theory, and bibliographies of *Pearl* and the *Pearl* poet for further reference. In addition, this section identifies some key multimedia resources that could be used for classroom instruction, including audio recordings of *Pearl* and online resources for teaching *Pearl*, as well as some new essays that specifically address how to teach *Pearl*. Although these resources are primarily for the teacher's background knowledge, some of them may be ideal for sharing with students. This section will help the instructor of *Pearl* discern which resources would be valuable for different levels of learners and therefore help the instructor decide how these resources could be used for creative, analytic, or research projects on the poem.

Introductions to the Pearl Poet

Although no one has determined definitively the identity of the *Pearl* poet, literary scholars have written introductions to the poet that include biographical sketches based on the information revealed in the poems of Cotton Nero A.x. Because interpretation of that information varies, so does the life story of the poet as told by different critics. These "biographies" of the unknown poet can amount to a few paragraphs or pages in the introductory material to editions and translations, or they may form longer accounts in essays and books. Three essays examine authorship questions more thoroughly: Andrew's "Theories of Authorship," in Derek Brewer and Jonathan Gibson's *A Companion to the Gawain-Poet* (1997; rpt. 1999); N. S. Thompson's "The Gawain Poet," in his *British Writers: Supplement VII* (2002); and Anthony Edwards's essay, "Authorship of *Pearl*," in this volume. The first might be considered suitable for graduate students, the second for undergraduate students (also available through many libraries in e-format), and the last for teachers of the poem.

Book-length introductions to the *Pearl* poet and his poems include Charles Moorman's *The Pearl-Poet* (1968), Edward Wilson's *The Gawain-Poet* (1976), W. A. Davenport's *The Art of the Gawain-Poet* (1978), Sandra Pierson Prior's *Pearl Poet Revisited* (1994), Ad Putter's *An Introduction to the Gawain-Poet* (1996), J. A. Burrow's *The Gawain Poet* (2001), and John Bowers's *An Introduction to the Gawain Poet* (2012). Henry Savage also wrote an introduction, *The Gawain-Poet: Studies in His Personality and Background* (1956). It is outdated now but notable because it presents an early argument for the inclusion of *Saint Erkenwald* in the *Pearl* poet's canon. Each of these works is intended for the generalist, beginner, or student reader. They provide contextual historical and literary information as well as individual chapters on each of the four poems. Unique among the introductory book-length studies, Bowers discusses *Saint Erkenwald* along with a survey of sources and influences. These introductions would be useful in upper-division undergraduate seminars devoted to the *Pearl* poet.

Critical Collections of Essays

To date there is still only one collection of critical essays exclusively devoted to *Pearl*, John Conley's *The Middle English* Pearl: *Critical Essays* (1970). Conley selected previously published essays on the poem in such a way as to show the development of the debate over the poem's generic status (whether elegy or allegory or other), its theological orientation (orthodox, heterodox, or heretical), and its outstanding literary features: main characters, diction, symbolism, themes, and sources and influences. A valuable essay that has been reprinted in the Conley collection and in Robert Blanch's Sir Gawain *and* Pearl: *Critical Essays* (1966) is A. C. Spearing's "Symbolic and Dramatic Development in *Pearl*."

Two other essay collections consider *Pearl* alongside the four other poems usually attributed to the *Pearl* poet: *Text and Matter: New Critical Perspectives of the* Pearl-*Poet* (1991), edited by Blanch, Miriam Youngerman Miller, and Julian Wasserman, and *A Companion to the Gawain-Poet* (1997; rpt. 1999), edited by Brewer and Gibson (neither of these collections treats *Saint Erkenwald* at much length). The first has five essays on *Pearl* covering such subjects as the Dreamer and the eleventh hour, animal similes, allegory and the four levels of interpretation, *Pearl* as diptych, and courtly love language. The second has essays that frequently deal with multiple poems at once, addressing such topics as the Cotton Nero A.x manuscript, allegory and symbolism, and vernacular theology. Though *A Companion to the Gawain-Poet* demonstrates a marked preference for *Sir Gawain and the Green Knight*, two essays deal only with *Pearl*: Jane Gilbert's "Gender and Sexual Transgression" and Felicity Riddy's "Jewels in *Pearl*." Graduate students regularly consult both collections when studying the *Pearl* poet in seminars. Some instructors will no doubt wish to assign one or the other alongside an edition of the poems.

Critical essay collections on other topics, such as *Ineffability: Naming the Unnamable from Dante to Beckett* (Hawkins and Schotter, 1984), *From Medieval to Medievalism* (Simons, 1992), *Feminist Approaches to the Body in Medieval Literature* (Lomperis and Stanbury, 1993), and *The Art of Vision: Ekphrasis in Medieval Literature and Culture* (Johnston, Knapp, and Rouse, 2015), include at least one essay each on *Pearl* in the context of an overarching theme, indicated by the essay collection title.

Academic Books and Dissertations

The first century or so of scholarship on *Pearl* included the production of four academic monographs on the poem. These books elaborated on the allegorical and symbolic significance of *Pearl*. Robert Garrett argued in *The* Pearl: *An Interpretation* (1918) for the existence of a correspondence between the pearl symbol and the Eucharist. Mary Madeleva, in Pearl: *A Study in Spiritual Dryness* (1925), suggested that the entire poem was a spiritual autobiography by a religious man that drew on the traditions of Christian contemplatives, or mystics. Patricia Kean, in her Pearl: *An Interpretation* (1967), analyzed the poem, the themes of death and rebirth evident in the topoi of the garden, and the way that the central images of the garden are transformed in the earthly paradise and then in the New Jerusalem. Ian Bishop's Pearl *in Its Setting* (1968) presented a masterful allegorical analysis of the poem, arguing that it is, generically, a consolation; that it is important to distinguish between the "allegory of the theologians" and the "allegory of the poets"; and that the liturgy, especially the Mass of Holy Innocents (recognizing the deaths of the infants in Bethlehem ordered by King Herod near the time that Jesus was born), provides a valuable context for interpreting the poem (though subsequent critics have argued for the influence of other liturgical celebrations on the poem).

With the publication of A. C. Spearing's *The Gawain-Poet: A Critical Study* (1970), the landscape of scholarship on *Pearl* changed. Spearing had already argued in his essay "Symbolic and Dramatic Development in *Pearl*" (first published in 1962) that *Pearl* need not be an allegory and that the central symbol, the pearl, undergoes symbolic transformation as the poem progresses. That idea had already begun to influence scholars' interpretations of the poem (clearly evident from how often Spearing is quoted by others), and his book extended his argument more widely at this time, alongside analyses of the other poems attributed to the *Pearl* poet. Essentially, Spearing's book endorsed the common authorship theory, and common authorship of the four poems of the Cotton Nero A.x manuscript came to be accepted among scholars. Therefore it could be said that the book laid the groundwork for subsequent books about *Pearl*, including those published in the 1990s, which would often analyze *Pearl* in relation to *Cleanness, Patience,* and *Sir Gawain and the Green Knight* as well as, occasionally, *Saint Erkenwald.*

The decade of the seventies saw the production of Dennis Moran's *Style and Theology in the Middle English* Pearl: *Patterns of Change and Reconciliation* (1976) and Theodore Bogdanos's 1975 dissertation from the University of California, Berkeley, which was later revised and published as Pearl: *Image of the Ineffable* (1983). These monographs addressed theology expressed through literary form, on the one hand, and symbolism expressed in metaphor and landscape, on the other. Wilson's *The Gawain-Poet* (1976) and W. A. Davenport's *The Art of the Gawain-Poet* (1978) both fully endorsed the common authorship theory by including chapters on all four poems from Cotton Nero A.x, including one each on *Pearl*. Davenport's chapter on *Pearl* argued it could be read in stages—emotional, didactic, and sacramental—and further suggested that the poem combines literal and allegorical modes. By then, scholarship on *Pearl* was no longer so tightly bound to debates about authorship, genre, or theological orthodoxy.

A year before Bogdanos's dissertation appeared, Lynn Staley wrote her Princeton University dissertation (1974), which later became *The Voice of the Gawain-Poet* (1984). Jennifer Lee's research for her 1977 dissertation from the State University of New York, Stony Brook, led to her excellent article "The Illuminating Critic" (1977) on the illustrations of the Cotton Nero A.x manuscript. Lee's work complemented an earlier book on the handwriting of the manuscript: John Cameron McLaughlin's *A Graphemic-Phonemic Study of a Middle English Manuscript* (1963). Thus, matters relating to the manuscript context of the poem, its paleography and illustrations, were being addressed. Meanwhile, new-historicist contexts for the poems were being charted, as in John Burrow's book, *Ricardian Poetry* (1971), which established a collective term for late-fourteenth-century poetry and thereafter influenced the work of John Bowers on *Pearl*.

Jonathan Nicholls's study, *The Matter of Courtesy: Medieval Courtesy Books and the Gawain-Poet*, appeared in 1985. Nicholls placed all four poems in the context of medieval manuals of social instruction in courtesy. He argued that, in the case of *Pearl*, expectations of courtesy are confounded when the Dreamer attempts to enter the Heavenly City, from which he is excluded because he has not yet been invited in. Nicholls's study broke new ground in exploring the contexts of *Pearl* and the other three poems of the *Pearl* manuscript, and it laid the groundwork for fruitful future studies relating *Pearl* to its social milieu.

In the 1990s new books addressed the four poems attributed to the *Pearl* poet and their contexts: Stanbury's *Seeing the* Gawain-*Poet* (1991), Marti's *Body, Heart and Text in the Pearl-Poet* (1991), Blanch and Wasserman's *From* Pearl *to* Gawain: *Forme to Fynisment* (1995), and Prior's *The Fayre Formez of the Pearl Poet* (1996). These scholars accepted common authorship and focused on commonalities between the poems, such as the theme of sight and vision, the intricate connection between the complex structure and themes of the poem, the *Pearl* poet's pervasive recognition of the Creator-God acting in history from its beginnings to its culmination, and the idea of the creative genius of the poet, demonstrated through his use of a variety of literary forms and genres.

The first decade of the twenty-first century saw the production of new work that generally considers *Pearl* in the context of the other poems attributed to the *Pearl* poet. Key studies analyze *Pearl*'s theology, structure, language, and imagination. In *Poetry Does Theology* (2001), Jim Rhodes discusses the *Pearl* poet's development of vernacular theology in his poems in comparison with Chaucer's and Grosseteste's. In *The Numerical Universe of the Gawain-Poet: Beyond Phi* (2002), Edward Condren looks carefully at how phi structures all four poems, including *Pearl*, and, beyond phi, at the poet's fascination for number symbolism and geometrically significant shapes (e.g., the dodecahedron and the sphere in *Pearl* and the pentangle in *Sir Gawain*) in each of his poems.

Like Rhodes, Borroff, in her book *Traditions and Renewals: Chaucer, the Gawain-Poet, and Beyond* (2003), also considers *Pearl* in relation to Chaucer. Of the two chapters dedicated to *Pearl*, one focuses on the "maynful mone" crux and the other on the poem's design. In *Language and Imagination in the Gawain-Poems* (2005), J. J. Anderson examines all four poems, focusing his analysis of *Pearl* on the Dreamer's emotions and the poet's key ideas, as he progresses chronologically through the poem. Anderson examines earth and paradise, emotion and reason, error and correction, redirection, rank and reward, grace and innocence, the spiritual marriage of the Lamb and the Pearl-Maiden, redirection (once again), and the Dreamer's return to earth upon awakening, where, in Anderson's estimation, his grief is not completely assuaged.

The first half of the second decade of the twenty-first century saw the publication of new books on *Pearl*: Piotr Spyra's *The Epistemological Perspective of the Pearl-Poet* (2014) and Cecilia Hatt's *God and the Gawain-Poet* (2015) consider all four poems usually attributed to the *Pearl* poet, devoting a single chapter to *Pearl*. Jane Beal's *The Signifying Power of* Pearl: *Medieval Liter-*

ary and Cultural Contexts for the Transformation of Genre (2017) concerns the dream-vision poem exclusively. The contributions made by these studies are discussed below in the section "Critical Theory."

Since the turn of the twenty-first century, graduate students have been doing very interesting work on *Pearl* as well. A search in *Dissertation Abstracts International* reveals approximately forty dissertations written partially or exclusively on *Pearl*, among them: Elizabeth Schirmer, "Genre Trouble: Spiritual Reading in the Vernacular and the Literary Project of the Pearl-Poet" (U of California, Berkeley, 2001); Heather Maring, "Oral Tradition, Performance, and Ritual in Two Medieval Dream-Visions: *The Dream of the Rood* and *Pearl*" (U of Missouri, Columbia, 2005); Lucy Anderson, "The Architecture of Light: Color and Cathedral as Rhetorical Ductus in the Middle English *Pearl*" (New York U, 2009); and Elizabeth Keim Harper, "Gifts and Economic Exchange in Middle English Religious Writing" (U of North Carolina, Chapel Hill, 2009). Each scholar examines *Pearl* in a different medieval context: reading, performance, architecture, economy. Anderson's work reflects the influence of Ann Meyer while Schirmer's is cited in Seeta Chaganti's *The Medieval Poetics of the Reliquary*; Anderson, Maring, and Harper have since gone on to publish insightful academic articles on *Pearl* that concern the subjects of their doctoral research. Clearly, the poem continues to inspire new interpretations.

Critical Contexts

Like all objects of enduring scholarly investigation, *Pearl* is part of an ongoing discussion about its themes and meaning. A major danger of engaging this discussion with students is the tendency to treat the poem like a puzzle that has one solution, when this very rich poem can be positioned within many critical contexts. The broader literary and linguistic contexts of the alliterative revival and the rise of the vernacular give opportunity to explore the complex form of the poem. Historical realities can generate insight into political issues raised by the poem. Finally, late medieval visual culture provides powerful images and objects for comparison with similar images and objects described within the poem.

Most teachers give some consideration to medieval dream-vision theory and therefore to the dream-vision genre as well as other genres of the poem, especially dialogue or debate. Many contextualize the poem within the medieval Catholic worldview as it is expressed in the poem, through concepts of pilgrimage, death, salvation, apocalypse, heaven, the New Jerusalem, and the symbol of the pearl as well as related Neoplatonic thinking influenced by Augustine and, importantly, the problem of suffering evinced through the Dreamer's experiences of love, loss, and grief. Some also examine the practices of the mystical tradition, or the contemplative life, and the liturgy of the church.

Resources for teaching the poem as dream vision in the context of medieval dream theory are many. Three significant books in this field are Kathryn Lynch's *High Medieval Dream Vision* (1988), J. Stephen Russell's *English Dream Vision* (1988), now available online as a free PDF, and Stephen Kruger's *Dreaming in the Middle Ages* (1992). These secondary sources provide the authors' analyses of the genre and syntheses of material from primary sources.

Primary sources are essential in courses on dream vision. Teachers of *Pearl* can begin with the biblical dream visions (from Genesis, Daniel and other prophetic writings, the Gospels, and Revelation), and dream-vision theories of Augustine and Macrobius, and then give as required reading the *Roman de la Rose*, Boethius's *Consolation of Philosophy*, and Dante's *Vita Nuova* and *Divine Comedy*. Some instructors may wish to teach *Pearl* along with several other canonical, Middle English dream-vision poems: Chaucer's dream visions (especially *The Book of the Duchess* and *The Parliament of Fowls*), William Langland's *Vision of Piers Plowman*, and Gower's *Confessio Amantis*. Visions from the Christian mystical or contemplative tradition may also be included: Julian of Norwich's *Revelations of Divine Love*, Margery Kempe's *Book*, Richard Rolle's *Fire of Love*, and *The Cloud of Unknowing*.

When considering *Pearl* as a poem in the genres of dialogue or debate, John Conlee's *Middle English Debate Poetry: A Critical Anthology* (1991) is a solid, comparative resource. A fine critical study is Thomas Reed's *Middle English Debate Poetry and the Aesthetics of Irresolution* (1990). Theoretical grounding for the debate in *Pearl* can be provided by Stanley Fish's *Self-Consuming Artifacts* (1972).

Since many of today's students lack biblical and medieval cultural literacy, it can be helpful to provide them with primary and secondary source material for understanding the *Pearl* poet's use of scripture as well as his Catholic worldview. Teachers of *Pearl* can assign readings from the Douay-Rheims translation of the Vulgate, including passages from the Gospels (especially the relevant parables, including the Parable of the Pearl of Great Price and the Parable of the Workers in the Vineyard), the Song of Songs, and Revelation. Teachers may also wish to assign portions of Augustine's *De doctrina christiana* ("On Christian Teaching"). E. Ann Matter's *The Voice of My Beloved* (1992) gives an outstanding analysis of the reception of the Song of Songs in the medieval period, as does Ann Astell's *The Song of Songs in the Middle Ages* (1995), which specifically considers *Pearl*. Caroline Walker Bynum's *Holy Feast and Holy Fast* (1987) and *The Resurrection of the Body in Western Christianity* (1995) are excellent resources for graduate study, advanced undergraduates, or for faculty preparing to convey to their students the richness of the medieval cultural beliefs about the Eucharist and death, the afterlife, and resurrection.

William McClung's book *The Architecture of Paradise: Survivals of Eden and Jerusalem* (1983) provides an excellent overview of the medieval conceptualization of Eden and Jerusalem in art, architecture, and literature. Valuable shorter studies concerning the vision of the New Jerusalem and the bleeding Lamb in *Pearl* are Rosalind Field's "The Heavenly Jerusalem in *Pearl*" (1986), Cynthia Kraman's "Body and Soul: *Pearl* and Apocalyptic Literature" (2003), and Hugh White's "Blood in *Pearl*" (1987). In "*Pearl*: Landscape and Vision" (1974), John Finlayson analyzes the Dreamer's progression through the three main landscapes, and he comments on the significance of each landscape. In "Landscape in *Pearl*: The Transformation of Nature" (1981), Elizabeth Petroff considers the liturgical context of the Assumption of the Virgin Mary in relation to her argument that the first landscape, the garden, violates medieval expectations of what a courtly love garden would be like while the dreamscape and the New Jerusalem transform those expectations. In addition to these useful studies, portions of *Mandeville's Travels* can provide an interesting primary source for comparison of landscapes.

The Pearl-Maiden's discourse on the Parable of the Workers in the Vineyard is a sermon. So when studying exegesis and preaching in *Pearl*, Alan Fletcher's *Preaching, Politics and Poetry in Late-Medieval England* (1998) is an insightful resource. Jane Chance has interpreted *Pearl* in the light of the *ars praedicandi* ("art of preaching") in her study, "Allegory and Structure in *Pearl*: The Four Senses of the *Ars praedicandi* and Fourteenth-Century Homiletic Poetry" (1991). Thorough and reliable studies of preaching in the Middle Ages include G. R. Owst, *Preaching in Medieval England* (1926); James J. Murphy, *Rhetoric in the Middle Ages* (1974); B. M. Kienzle, editor of *The Sermon* (2000); as well as Claire Waters, *Angels and Earthly Creatures: Preaching, Performance, and Gender in the Later Middle Ages* (2004), which provides particularly relevant contexts for interpreting the Pearl-Maiden as a female preacher.

The Pearl-Maiden's role, which has often been compared with that of Boethius's Lady Philosophy or Dante's Beatrice, has origins in biblical figures like Wisdom, who in the Old Testament book of Proverbs is personified as a woman. Erich Auerbach's "Figura" (1984) provides a useful starting place for contextualizing interpretation of the figure of the Pearl-Maiden. So does Barbara Newman's critical study *God and the Goddesses: Vision, Poetry and Belief in the Middle Ages* (2005), which concerns the feminine figures of Lady Philosophy, Lady Love, Dame Nature, and Eternal Wisdom. Her essay, "The Artifice of Eternity: Speaking of Heaven in Three Medieval Poems" (2005), specifically interprets *Pearl*.

Scholars of *Pearl* have recognized that the biblical paraphrases and allusions in the poem may be connected to the liturgy of the Mass and the Church's liturgical year, and they have examined whether Bible passages included in the ecclesiastical lectionary that are also included in *Pearl* might have a liturgical context that affects interpretation. Thus Ian Bishop, in Pearl *in Its Setting* (1968), considers the Mass of Holy Innocents important. Other relevant studies include James Earl, "Saint Margaret and the Pearl Maiden" (1972), John Gatta's "Transformation Symbolism and the Liturgy of the Mass in *Pearl*" (1974), and Susan Rastetter's "'Bot Mylde as Maydenes Seme at Mas': The Feast of All Saints and *Pearl*" (1992), based on her dissertation "The Liturgical Background to the Middle English *Pearl*" (1989). In "The Signifying Power of *Pearl*" (2012), Jane Beal connects the liturgy of Septuagesima Sunday, when the "alleluia" was buried in preparation for Lent, with the poem's Paschal imagery and the representation of the Pearl-Maiden as a figure of the Dreamer's joy.

The vernacular and alliterative revival provides critical contexts for understanding the form of *Pearl*, including its interlaced stanzas and overall circularity, evidenced by concatenation, wordplay, and numerology, as well as its alliteration, rhyme, and meter. Studies by Elizabeth Salter ("The Alliterative Revival I") and by Derek Pearsall ("The Origins of the Alliterative Revival"; "The Alliterative Revival: Origins") give general overviews of the alliterative revival. Thorlac Turville-Petre's book, *The Alliterative Revival* (1977), sheds further light.

Historical contexts, like Ricardian poetics and the Lancastrian ascendency, the war with France, the plague, labor shortages, and the Peasants' Revolt, can generate insight into political issues raised by the poem. General introductions to the time period include Barbara Tuchman's *A Distant Mirror: The Calamitous Fourteenth Century* (1978) and Ian Mortimer's *The Time-Traveler's Guide to Medieval England: A Handbook for Visitors to the Fourteenth Century* (2008, 2011); both books are now available in e-book format. For a broader view of fourteenth-century England in a European context, see the sixth volume of *The New Cambridge Medieval History: c. 1300–c. 1415*, edited by Michael Jones.

Helen Barr set a high standard of critique with her second chapter, "*Pearl*: The Jeweller's Tale," in her book *Socioliterary Practice in Late Medieval England* (2001). Other political contexts have been discussed by John Bowers in two essays in 1995, and in two books (*The Politics of* Pearl and *An Introduction to the Gawain Poet*). Alan Fletcher provides an alternative view about the extent to which historical contexts can be used to interpret *Pearl* in his essay "*Pearl* and the Limits of History" (2005).

Iconography and medieval visual culture are two other important contexts for understanding *Pearl*. Art objects like the Wilton Diptych, the Hours of Catherine of Cleaves (with its rosaries and pearl borders), and the tradition of illuminations in manuscripts focusing on the Apocalypse (as well as other types of manuscript illustrations and illuminations), frescoes, and tapestries with imagery from Revelation provide primary source material for cross-genre comparison with *Pearl*. An excellent book providing historical context for understanding images in *Pearl* is Mary Carruthers's *The Craft of Thought: Meditation, Rhetoric, and the Making of Images, 400–1200* (1998) as well as her earlier essay specifically addressing the poem, "Invention, Mnemonics, and Stylistic Ornamentation in *Psychomachia* and *Pearl*" (1995). Other useful studies are Maidie Hilmo, *Medieval Images, Icons, and Illustrated Literary English Texts: From the Ruthwell Cross to the Ellesmere Chaucer* (2004) and Susanna Fein, "Of Judges and Jewelers: *Pearl* and the Life of Saint John" (2014). On the illustrations of *Pearl*, studies by Jennifer Lee (1977), Sarah Horall (1986), and Paul Reichardt (1997) provide insightful analyses.

Critical Theory

The application of theory to the discipline of literature has inspired new interpretations of *Pearl*. Previous generations of medievalists have tended to base their interpretations on philological insight, historical context, and New Critical literary analysis, but medievalists working today, informed by these traditional perspectives, often weave contemporary literary theory into their analyses of medieval poetry as well. Feminist and psychoanalytic approaches predominate in studies of *Pearl* marked by applications of theory. In addition, some scholars extend Bakhtinian dialectical and Marxist or medieval economic views while still others apply new-historicist and material culturist paradigms to *Pearl*. The use of medieval allegoresis has also reemerged as an important interpretive approach. Quite frequently, medievalists combine multiple theoretical approaches in their analyses.

The foremost feminist critic of *Pearl* is Stanbury, whose book *Seeing the Gawain-Poet* (1991) and essay "Feminist Masterplots: The Gaze on the Body of *Pearl*'s Dead Girl" (1994) interrogate the interplay of male gaze and female body in *Pearl*. Stanbury's insights inform several subsequent analyses, which could be characterized as feminist (or perhaps womanist), including Charlotte Gross's "Courtly Language in *Pearl*" (1991), Maria Bullón-Fernández's "'Byyonde the Water': Courtly and Religious Desire in *Pearl*" (1994), Jane Gilbert's "Gender and Sexual Transgression" (1997), Catherine Cox's "*Pearl*'s Precios Pere': Gender, Language, and Difference" (1998), and Jane Beal's "The Pearl-Maiden's Two Lovers." In "*Pearl* and the Flawed Mediation of Grace" (2014), Claude Willan uses a combination of insights from these feminist readings, together with structural-numerical analyses of *Pearl*, to conclude that the flaws in the poem point to the reality of divine grace that goes beyond the power of language to express it. Contemporary feminist theory has been incorporated into literary analyses of *Pearl* as well. To name just two examples: Julia Kristeva's book *Tales of Love* (1987) informs Josephine Bloomfield's "Aristotelian Luminescence, Thomistic Charity: Vision, Reflection, and Self-Love in *Pearl*" (2011) while Luce Irigaray, *This Sex Which Is Not One*, is cited in Willan.

David Aers and Sarah Stanbury have offered psychoanalytic interpretations of the poem. Aers's "The Self Mourning: Reflections on *Pearl*" (1993) focuses on the psychology of the Dreamer (in terms that might be considered Freudian) while Stanbury's "The Body and the City in *Pearl*" (1994) views the city of the New Jerusalem as mother in feminist psychoanalytic terms. Both discuss their own emotive connection to the poem, which is unusual in medieval literary scholarship (though perhaps less so in the case of *Pearl*). Influencing both these readings is Ann Astell. In "Mourning and Marriage in Saint Bernard's *Sermones* and in the *Pearl*," the fifth chapter of her book, *The Song of Songs in the Middle Ages* (1990), Astell gives a Jungian analysis of the poem and argues that *Pearl* evokes the feminine as a "dynamic principle" essential to "a process of spiritual growth" (120). In another vein, George Edmondson produced "*Pearl*: The Shadow of the Object, the Shape of the Law" (2004), which he characterizes as a mid-period Lacanian psychoanalysis.

The conversation between the Pearl-Maiden and the Dreamer, which has been deemed a *debatio* and interpreted in the light of medieval conventions governing that form of discourse, has also been viewed in terms of Bakhtinian dialectic in Jim Rhodes's "The Dreamer Redeemed: Exile and the Kingdom in the Middle English *Pearl*" (1994). Since that conversation involves a retelling of the Parable of the Workers in the Vineyard and refers to all workers being paid the same wage, a penny (traditionally interpreted as representing salvation), Rhodes sees the poet as rooting his considerations firmly in the economic milieu of the fourteenth century (136–38). A decade before Rhodes, Jill Mann, in "Satisfaction and Payment in Middle English Literature" (1983), analyzed the economic implications of the parable in *Pearl* using a Marxist paradigm to facilitate interpretation. Later, Elizabeth Harper, in "*Pearl* in the Context of Fourteenth-Century Gift Economies" (2010), analyzed the poem in relation to medieval gift-exchanges as markers of social hierarchy. Harper's interpretation could also be considered a new-historicist, even material-culturist, approach, inspired in part by the work of John Bowers.

John Bowers has written two seminal essays on *Pearl*: "*Pearl* in its Royal Setting: Ricardian Poetics Revisited" (1995) and "The Politics of *Pearl*" (1995). These take a new-historicist approach to connecting *Pearl* to late-fourteenth-century royalty (e.g., King Richard and his queens, Anne of Bohemia and Isabelle of France) and their display of wealth through bejeweled (indeed, be-pearled) objects, such as the now famous crown of the Princess Blanche. Influenced by J. A. Burrow's work on Ricardian poetry, Bowers in turn has influenced other interpretations of *Pearl* offered by scholars looking at the poem in the context of late medieval material culture. Studies with broadly material culturist implications include Felicity Riddy's "Jewels in *Pearl*" (1997), Heather Maring's "Never-the-Less: Gift-Exchange and the Medieval Dream Vision *Pearl*" (2005), and Seeta Chaganti's "Enshrining Form: *Pearl* as Inscriptional Object and Devotional Event" (95–30), which is a chapter from her book *The Medieval Poetics of the Reliquary* (2008). Riddy considers the material reality of jewels and their influence on the imagery of *Pearl*; Maring, images of surplus and abundance; and Chaganti, the devotional tradition of the reliquary and its relation to the form of *Pearl*.

In her work on the poem, Ann Meyer reflects in deeply meaningful ways on connections between the material culture of the Middle Ages and allegoresis. Meyer's "Taking Allegory Seriously: Ornament as Invitation in *Pearl*" and "'Þe New Cyté o Jerusalem': *Pearl* as Medieval Architecture," chapters from her book, *Medieval Allegory and the Building of the New Jerusalem* (155–86, 137–54), particularly note the remarkable parallels in the symbolic programs of the building of twelfth- and thirteenth-century churches and the form and content of *Pearl*. Meyer's interest in allegory points back to earlier nineteenth- and twentieth-century allegorical interpretations of *Pearl* and to the body of medieval literary interpretation that used the "four-fold method of scriptural interpretation" as its own critical theory for interpreting not only the Bible but also poetry. This approach found an early advocate in D. W. Robertson, who discussed a fourfold meaning in the poem in "The Pearl as Symbol" (1950). Later, Jane Chance (1991) and Jane Beal (2012, 2017) further examined the allegorical significance of the poem from other angles. Even though Meyer, Chance, and Beal, who could be called the new allegorists, differ in their understanding of the allegorical meanings found in the poem, they all agree that *Pearl* conveys an allegorical sense, one that contemporary scholarship has unduly ignored.

Allegorical considerations sometimes figure in studies of *Pearl* that focus on the key concept of ineffability, or the inexpressibility topos: the idea that no language, however beautiful, is sufficient to express the divine realities. The ineffability of the holy, and wholly extraordinary, in *Pearl* is a focus in Theodore Bogdanos's *Pearl: Image of the Ineffable* (1983), which draws insights from Ong, Eliade, and Chenu; J. Allan Mitchell's "The Middle English *Pearl*: Figuring the Unfigurable" (2000); and Justin Jackson's "The Infinite Desire of *Pearl*" (2009), which uses the work of Emmanuel Levinas to provide a theoretical framework for understanding. It becomes clear from these examples that medieval scholars integrate the study of ineffability with contemporary literary theory.

As the foregoing overview suggests, medievalists often synthesize their theoretical approaches to *Pearl*. In studies of the poem, feminist and psychoanalytic approaches interpenetrate; new-historicist and material culturist analyses overlap; interpretations utilizing the concepts of allegory and ineffability converge and diverge. Yet, in general, medieval scholars of *Pearl* rarely (if ever) use theory in ways that would contradict the known historical realities of the Middle Ages, including philological, paleographic, codicological, cultural, historical, and theological contexts. Indeed, they may privilege the use of medieval over modern literary theory in their studies.

This fairly characterizes three recent books on the *Pearl* poet and *Pearl*. Piotr Spyra's *The Epistemological Perspective of the Pearl-Poet* (2014) uses the theological and philosophical ideas of Augustine and Aquinas to frame the *Pearl* poet's ways of knowing. Cecilia Hatt's *God and the Gawain-Poet: Theology and Genre in* Pearl, Cleanness, Patience, *and* Sir Gawain and the Green Knight explores Aquinan incarnational theology in the poet's celebration of embodied human life as divine gift in the four poems of Cotton Nero A.x, identified respectively as courtly dream vision, university-style sermon, comic fable, and courtly romance. Jane Beal's *The Signifying Power of* Pearl*: Medieval Literary and Cultural Contexts for the Transformation of Genre* (2017), posits an interpretive relation between medieval and modern genre theories, arguing that *Pearl* can be understood literally as an elegy, spiritually as an allegory, morally as a consolation, and anagogically as a revelation. Her fifth chapter gives consideration to folktale motifs derived from oral tradition (e.g., parables, fables, and fairy tales) that appear in the poem while her conclusion analyzes psychological theories of grieving and trauma in relation to the poem as well.

Bibliographies

Several bibliographies and bibliographic review essays of *Pearl* scholarship can help teachers and students get a full sense of the quantity of literary critical work that has been published on the poem. René Wellek reviews scholarship on the poem up to 1933, and Lawrence Eldredge surveys scholarship from 1933 to 1975. Charles Russell Courtney provides an annotated bibliography in his 1975 University of Arizona dissertation; Malcolm Andrew subsequently published *The Gawain-Poet: An Annotated Bibliography, 1839–1977.* A partial bibliography to 1988, compiled by Marley Washum, appears online. Michael Foley surveyed *Pearl* criticism in further detail in his 1989 essay, "The *Gawain*-Poet: An Annotated Bibliography," which appeared in *The Chaucer Review.* In 1996 Robert J. Blanch published "The State of *Pearl* Criticism" in the *Chaucer Yearbook.* Murray McGillivray and Kenna L. Olsen, at the University of Calgary, provide a nonannotated online bibliography covering the years 1994–2008. Stanbury's selected bibliography (2001) includes brief annotations; these accompany her print and online edition of *Pearl.* Additional bibliographies can be found in other books and essays published on the poem.

Multimedia Resources

In addition to the multimedia resources that have been discussed, especially the *Cotton Nero A.x Project* online, there is another valuable resource for the teaching of *Pearl*, the Web site *Medieval Pearl* (medievalpearl.wordpress.com). It features a brief biographical introduction to the *Pearl* poet, digital reproductions of the full-color manuscript illustrations of *Pearl* (with commentary), and a page devoted to the many editions and translations of the poem with hyperlinks to the texts wherever they are available online. The site also includes a list of several bibliographies of literary criticism, discussion questions, and a free downloadable *PowerPoint* for teaching, and hyperlinks to recordings of the poem.

At present, there are several partial audio recordings of the poem, but there is only one complete recording in Middle English: the Chaucer Studio's *Pearl*, available on CD, read aloud by Alan Gaylord. There is also a complete recording of Sophie Jewett's modern English translation of *Pearl* available from LibriVox, recorded by Jordan, which can be heard online or downloaded in various formats. This recording is also available on *YouTube* ("*Pearl* Free Audiobook"). Giles Conrad Wilson has recorded his complete modern English translation of the poem, read as a voice-over to film shots of various natural landscapes relevant to *Pearl*, available in a series of clips on *YouTube* as well.

Resources for teaching the language of the poem include the *Middle English Dictionary* (or *MED*), hosted online by the University Michigan (quod.lib.umich.edu/m/med/). Another site is "METRO: Middle English Teaching Resources Online," which features pages on teaching *Pearl* (metro.fas.harvard.edu/icb/icb.do), hosted by Harvard University. The Web site on the history of the English language, *HEL on the Web*, contains a useful bibliography on Middle English with links to several related sites (sites.google.com/site/helontheweb/me).

Pedagogical Studies

In addition to the essays available in this volume, *Approaches to Teaching the Middle English* Pearl, new studies of ways to teach *Pearl* recently have appeared in the online pedagogical journal *The Once and Future Classroom*, which is sponsored by TEAMS and the Medieval Institute of Western Michigan University. The fall 2015 issue includes Kara Crawford's essay "Linking *Pearl* Together," which won the 2015 TEAMS Teaching Prize (K–12), and Sherri Rankin's essay on teaching *Pearl* in the undergraduate classroom by focusing on the poem's connections to the book of Revelation and the concept of apostolic embodiment. The spring 2016 issue includes Jane Beal's essay, "Three Approaches to Teaching *Pearl*: Introduction to Literature, British Literature I, and the Mythology of J. R. R. Tolkien."

As this overview shows, the resources for teaching *Pearl* are extensive. Teachers who know of their existence can familiarize themselves with them and then use them in the classroom for the benefit of their students. In this way, the extraordinarily beautiful poem *Pearl* may become more widely read and better understood in the future.

Part Two

APPROACHES

Introduction to the Essays

Mark Bradshaw Busbee

This volume responds to an MLA survey of college and university teachers, which suggested that the challenges of teaching *Pearl* stem not only from the text's high level of complexity but also from students' limited knowledge of the culture, literature, and history of the late fourteenth century. The nineteen essays published here are therefore meant to help students break through "a wall of forbidding alterity" (a phrase borrowed from John Fleming's essay in this volume). The essays are divided into four sections, three addressing historical, literary and theoretical, and comparative approaches, and a fourth section concerned with specific classroom strategies.

The first section, "Historical Approaches and Contexts," addresses the fundamental cultural barriers students face when learning about the poem's author, language, manuscript context, and audience. In "The Authorship of *Pearl*," Anthony G. Edwards engages the crucial question of who wrote the poem. Students will naturally want to know what scholars have wondered about for generations: is the story inspired by the author's personal experience, and what can we learn about the poem from studying its author's life and times? Edwards offers ways to deflect unanswerable questions about authorship by thinking about the narrative voice and how an image of the character emerges through the narrator's account of what happens. The language of the poem is another cultural barrier. Since the poem is written in a dialect of the North-West Midlands, which differs significantly from the more familiar language of Chaucer's London, students usually encounter the text in the form of a heavily glossed edition, a dual-language edition, or a modern English translation. In "Teaching the Language of *Pearl*," Laura Howes turns these linguistic challenges into opportunities by urging teachers and students to regard the language as a territory for fresh discoveries. Using specific examples of the poem's rich linguistic texture, she lays out various approaches for courses ranging from surveys to graduate-level seminars. Howes's approach to teaching the poem's linguistic artistry provides a segue into the artistry of the material object of the manuscript. In "Teaching *Pearl* in Its Manuscript Context," Murray McGillivray and Kenna L. Olsen explore how digital images enable students to experience the "visual richness and interpenetrating signifying systems" of *Pearl*. To give students hands-on (though virtual) encounters with *Pearl*, the authors describe the Cotton Nero A.x (art. 3) manuscript before discussing how they use its images from the *Cotton Nero A.x Project* in their courses. In "Public *Pearl*," David Coley considers how medieval readers may have used this manuscript. He explains how *Pearl* has traditionally been read as a private experience, a meditation upon loss and grief, but that it has lately been reconsidered as an artistic production bound up in public matters of the court of Richard II. Coley explains how, in his classes, he and his students pursue the question of how such an intimate work might evince a public voice.

Questions about the cultural and historical contexts of *Pearl* set up the literary and theoretical questions taken up in the second section, "Literary and Theoretical Approaches," where essays explore the poem's function as a poem. How, for example, does the poem employ allegory and symbolism? How does its structure affect its meaning, and how do its characters relate to one another? Two essays offer theoretical approaches to *Pearl*, contemplating its participation in late-fourteenth-century ideological systems. In "Teaching the Allegory and Symbolism of *Pearl*," Ann Meyer and Jane Beal frame their approach with key questions about the poem's literary interpretation. They explain medieval practices of interpretation before sharing strategies that might help students appreciate the poem's overlapping layers of meaning. In "Structures of Meaning in *Pearl*," John Fleming points out that, while allegory imposes no particular form on a poem, number symbolism does. Fleming offers a way into the poem's complicated numerical structures by calling upon technical reading skills and by connecting discoveries about patterns with the tradition of scriptural exegesis, which the poet draws on. This approach reveals that the structure of the poem gives meaning to the story it tells and the characters it describes. In "The Relationship between the Pearl-Maiden and the Dreamer," Jane Beal turns her students' attention to those characters. In their analysis of the interpretive crux that is the characters' relationship, Beal and her students study the four *Pearl*-related illustrations from the manuscript as commentary on the action of the plot. Discussions about the illustrations launch the class into analysis of the literal and allegorical elements. In "*Pearl*, Pedagogy, and the Poetics of Enshrinement," Seeta Chaganti frames the poem with ideas about the material culture of shrines and reliquaries. Viewed this way, the poem can be understood to be engaging a "poetics of enshrinement." This theoretical construct serves Chaganti and her students as a pedagogical tool for considering medieval aesthetic culture, concepts of medieval authority, and practices of formalist reading. But whereas Chaganti uses models from material culture, Justin Jackson presents the various Christological lenses that the poet offers his readers. In his essay, "Christological Meditations in the Works of the *Pearl* Poet," Jackson explains Christological hermeneutics and demonstrates how this interpretive disposition influences plot and theme not only for *Pearl* but also for other poems in the manuscript.

Many teachers are like Jackson in that they present *Pearl* as part of preselected groups of texts, depending upon factors such as the purpose and nature of the course, the level of the students, even the length of the course. Attending to this common pedagogical practice, essays in the third section, "Comparative Approaches," treat the poem as inhabiting a web of signifiers: *Pearl* is read as complementing its famous sibling in the manuscript, *Sir Gawain and the Green*

Knight; as drawing meaning from its many sources and analogues; as functioning in a network of contemporaneous Middle English poetry; and as inspiring the creative and scholarly work of the twentieth-century writer, J. R. R. Tolkien. Arthur Bahr shares his experiences teaching *Pearl* alongside the "crowd-pleaser," *Sir Gawain*, in survey courses and seminars. His central questions are how the two poems are related and how, when taught together, they can shed light on each other's thematic-cultural issues and literary-formal concepts. In "Teaching *Pearl* with Its Sources and Analogues" Mark Bradshaw Busbee focuses similarly on the benefits of teaching the poem in a comparative context. He proposes a way that teachers might use (instead of avoiding) the potentially bewildering number and variety of source texts and analogues. First, he offers an approach that hinges on habituating students to highly allusive texts like *Pearl*; then he overviews the principal background texts and analogues to the poem. In "*Pearl* as a Gateway to Middle English Poetry: Comparative Approaches" Elizabeth Harper explains how the poem can be a window into medieval culture for different populations of students. She leverages student successes in understanding *Pearl* against the difficulties they sense in other similarly foreign poems like Chaucer's *Book of the Duchess*. The final essay in this section, "Teaching *Pearl* When Teaching Tolkien," unashamedly announces an effort to draw students to the poem through Tolkien's celebrated modern fiction. John Bowers surveys Tolkien's interest in the poem as well as his unpublished and published editions and translations of *Pearl*, and he discusses how passages in *Lord of the Rings* that were inspired by *Pearl* can provide students with entry points into the poem and a base for comparative analysis.

The final section, "Specific Classroom Contexts," offers models for topical approaches. The essays equip teachers with practical and creative strategies to bring the poem into focus. For William A. Quinn in "The Trope of Translation in *Pearl*," the notion of translation serves as a conceptual frame for understanding deeper levels of exchange within the poem. Quinn wants his students to dig into the poem's emotional substance. He has them analyze how concepts are handled through wordplay, which he frames as "translation." As a result, students become aware of the elusiveness of language when communicating emotion. Heather Maring offers another way to heighten attention to the poem's language, its underlying meanings, and its relation to the ritual of the Mass. Maring's approach leads students to comprehend how a text like *Pearl* inhabited a living rhetorical moment and how performance can bring to the foreground otherwise unnoticed meaning. Eugene Green also wants students to consider the Dreamer and the Pearl-Maiden as speakers, so he trains students to focus on the debate at the center of the poem. The approach offered in "Voicing the Debate" helps students attend to patterns of expression through creative dramatic class activities. Students learn from one another and discover similarities between themselves and their fictional medieval counterparts. In "Teaching *Pearl* and Landscape"

Elizabeth Allen addresses what she sees as the poem's central problem, the complex relation between earthly and heavenly experience. She leads her students to focus on the physical spaces in the poem so that they may recognize how the poem returns the Dreamer (and the audience) to reality at the end to complete the important task of living in a difficult created world. The last two essays in this volume focus on *Pearl* as having special affinities with texts through the ages and being connected through a central religious image with a community of faith. Jane Chance teaches the poem as part of the broader medieval tradition of the dream vision. In her essay, "*Pearl* and Medieval Dream-Vision Traditions in a Graduate Seminar: Genre, Mode, and Gender," she outlines how she first surveys definitions and origins of the genre before examining types of the genre. This groundwork prepares students for an encounter with *Pearl*, which then leads to a study of visionary mystical writings. (Chance also provides a handy "required reading" list for seminars focused on the genre of the dream vision.) And finally, in "*Pearl* and the Bleeding Lamb" Nancy Ciccone relates how she includes the poem in a combined undergraduate and graduate survey course. *Pearl* appears midway through the course, right after *Sir Gawain*; that way, students are prepared to discuss the five wounds of Christ because they have learned about it through discussion of the pentangle in *Sir Gawain*. Her focus on the wound in the vision of the New Jerusalem allows her to elaborate on its significance in the narrative, how it allows the poet to collapse figurative and literal elements, and how, through this image, students can identify the cohesiveness of symbolism throughout the poem.

How readers choose to approach the essays depends entirely on their motives. Teachers new to *Pearl* might begin with "Historical Approaches and Contexts" to ground their understanding of the poem in medieval history and thought before turning directly to discussions of more abstract aspects of the poem. More seasoned teachers or those with specific training in fourteenth-century culture and thought might turn directly to essays focusing on literary or theoretical approaches. Those seeking fresh strategies to replace or supplement what they already know might turn directly to "Specific Classroom Contexts." To assist readers looking for particular ways to approach *Pearl*, we propose below five thematic categories for the essays. But because the essays offer various points of consideration, our categories should by no means be seen as definitive or proscriptive. Readers should feel free to read through the essays according to their needs.

The Text of Pearl *and Its Contexts*

When teaching *Pearl* as part of a course devoted to masterpieces of literature, many instructors will be compelled by a historical organizational method to connect it to its physical and historical circumstances in the late fourteenth century. A number of the essays in this volume touch upon the central question: how can the poem be understood as a product of its culture? Of course, essays in the first section deal with this question. Edwards dislocates from the text the long-running question of the poem's authority. Howes explores the rich variety of the dialect of the poem and demonstrates how its ambiguity can provide ways into its poetic richness. McGillivray and Olsen lead their students into the materiality of the text to help them discover possible answers, and they address aspects of the illustrations accompanying *Pearl*. Finally, Coley urges students to consider how audiences might have received the poem. Essays in other sections also address the question of the poem's connection to its culture. While Busbee situates the poem in the context of its many sources and analogues to see it as existing in a web of connections, Chaganti and Fleming look closely at the shape of the poem, as it follows poetic conventions and creates meaning through its form.

Pearl *in the Company of Other Works*

Many teachers of British literature will be expected to move quickly through a chronological survey leaving them little time to spend on any specific text. Because *Pearl* is so highly allusive and overtly aware of other texts like the Bible and *The Romance of the Rose*, the poem fits into a course of reading that involves a variety of texts from other cultures. Essays by Harper and Busbee provide some ways to put the poem into relation with other Middle English works and within the larger context of its many sources and possible analogues in biblical, classical, and continental literature. Bahr reads *Pearl* and *Sir Gawain* together, while Chaganti reads *Pearl* as participating in important patterns of literacy with other poems in the manuscript. Jackson also pays special attention to the similarities between *Pearl* and the other poems in the manuscript. Chance provides a thorough overview of the tradition of the dream vision, a tradition that brings in many often-taught medieval English masterpieces. Bowers brings *Pearl* into the context of the creative works of J. R. R. Tolkien to give students a way to grapple with its symbolic and stylistic power, as well as many of its themes.

Literary and Rhetorical Aspects of Pearl

More than eight of the essays deal with some technical or rhetorical aspect of the poem. Essays by Harper, Beal, Fleming, Meyer and Beal, and Chance lay out the technical aspects of the genre of the medieval dream vision, while Chaganti offers a new category through which the genre can be understood. Ciccone focuses on a central symbol to consider how *Pearl* employs symbolism. Taken together, these essays create tensions around the technical function of the dream vision. For example, Chance does not limit her reading to medieval texts, applying twenty-first-century surrealism as a theoretical tool, while Chaganti places them fully in the context of literary and cultural practices to understand how they work.

Quinn and Jackson turn from the technical aspects of the poem to the reception of its rhetorical appeal to the individual. For Quinn the poem provides a spiritual exercise for the readers as they experience the event with the Dreamer and translate the literal or carnal symbols into figurative or spiritual ones. Jackson explains how the poem can be read by students as a meditation piece, meant to provide not only final answers but, more important, an event of devotion.

Other essays explore the rhetorical effects of the poem on its readers and listeners. Maring and Green urge students to perform the poem aloud in order to hear meaning that might otherwise be missed in a silent reading. This approach is similar to Coley's method mentioned above, where the rhetorical situation in the historical context is fleshed out, and questions about meaning are attached to questions of audience and purpose. Here rhetoric might shed light on the poem's content, so Busbee approaches the source materials and analogues as interwoven strands of meaning. The texts that lie behind *Pearl*, as well as other literary texts that present similar content, provide the poem with tensions and create shifting meanings in the narrative. More concrete again are the contributions by Fleming and Beal, who return our focus to the workings of the poem. The authors work through the poem's structure and its illustrations to see how it comments on itself and reveals its potential meanings. Structure is as much a part of the rhetorical effect as is the pathos created by human relationships.

Relationships between Form and Content in Pearl

The overriding question inspired by a focus on the poem as a cohesive work of art is this: how does the poem at once proclaim and embody meaning? Genre dictates answers in the case of essays by Chaganti, Chance, and Fleming. For Coley the dual courtly and private contexts coexist. From Meyer and Beal's perspectives, the complexities of the poem's use of symbolism and allegory affect how we understand the genre and meaning of *Pearl*. Chaganti asks students to approach the poem with a "poetics of enshrinement" in mind—a conceptual frame that is adaptable to various perspectives, be they historical or cultural or literary—and, as a result, meaning in the dream vision is shown to relate directly to the nature of the enshrinement. Chance proposes that students consider allegory and how it can affect meaning in the genre while Fleming considers meaning constructed through the poem's structures.

The Religious Message of Pearl

Six of the essays go straight for what is likely the most difficult aspect of *Pearl* for students— its religiosity or spirituality. A good start is the essay by Busbee, who outlines the biblical and classical sources for the poem's religious sentiment, followed by Meyer and Beal, who cover the nature of inherited traditions such as allegoresis and biblical commentary, and then by Jackson, who discusses the poem as a series of meditations on interpretation itself. Jackson addresses the poem's Christology and puts together a way of leading students into appreciation of how medieval Christians may have read the poem. Ciccone offers an approach to these issues by having students focus on one aspect of the Dreamer's vision: the bleeding Lamb.

A Note on Translations of Pearl

When teachers consult a variety of translations, they encounter a variety of opportunities for comparison and refinement of meaning. Therefore, essays in this volume draw upon a variety of translations of *Pearl*, all of which are discussed in the introduction to the "Materials" section. In some cases, authors provide their own translations of key portions of the text. We encourage teachers to explore the many translation options available to locate the one that they find most useful and teachable.

The Authorship of *Pearl*

A. S. G. Edwards

The poems that survive uniquely in British Library MS Cotton Nero A.x—*Pearl, Patience, Cleanness*, and *Sir Gawain and the Green Knight*—all lack crucial contexts potentially relevant to their proper historicization. It is not possible to establish with any degree of precision where, when, and by whom they were written. It is possible to tentatively suggest that they were composed around the middle of the fourteenth century, somewhere in northern(ish) England, possibly somewhere between Staffordshire and Yorkshire. But the most fundamental of these missing contexts, the question of their authorship, has resisted even such a tentative degree of clarification.

And yet authorship is an issue that is likely to come up in classroom discussion. Like all the poems in the Cotton manuscript, *Pearl* lacks the basic context of clear poetic identity. Students will need to be made aware of the interpretative limits that are therefore placed on a poem that has an intensely autobiographical thrust to its narrative. We cannot know how "real" the narrator's grief and loss are or the extent to which they are rooted in authorial experience. All this places some interpretative constraints on the ways it is possible to appropriately respond to the poem. This essay will give an overview of the question of authorship and, in its conclusion, suggest how it might be approached in teaching *Pearl*.

The issue of the impossibility of establishing who wrote *Pearl* cannot be separated from the larger question posed by the Cotton manuscript: were all the poems in this manuscript created by a single author? The assumption that they were all written by one person has been a generally asserted but never conclusively demonstrated view that has shaped much of the history of their literary analysis. Its primary ground is that no other surviving Middle English manuscript contains a collection solely of alliterative verse. It seems to have been largely on this basis that, by and large, critics have taken the question of common authorship as a matter of fact. Hence it has been seen as requiring no further demonstration, but can by itself provide a firm basis on which to build further arguments. As one commentator put it: "In writing this book I have assumed that the four poems were written by one man, and I have ignored the need to demonstrate the idea" (Davenport, *Art* 2).

This recurrent procedural assumption has shaped most writing about these poems. There have been occasional attempts to give the assumption a degree of specificity by attributing a name to this putative single author. But such efforts have not proved very fruitful. Over the past hundred or so years various candidates for single authorship of the Cotton poems (and sometimes other poems as well) have been advanced with varying degrees of implausibility.[1] These names have included Huchoun of the Awle Ryale, Ralph Strode, John Donne, John Prat, John of Erghome, Hugh or John or William Massey, David Rate, and Richard Newton, as well as, less precisely, the author of the alliterative *Wars of Alexander*. None of these candidates have survived more than cursory scrutiny.[2] Indeed, in some instances it is highly unlikely they ever existed. And in others their tenuous biographies cannot be shown to provide any basis for linking them to the Cotton poems.

But even if the specific identity of a single author cannot be established, there have been various attempts to find a methodology, based on some combination of metrical, stylistic, linguistic, and dialectal grounds, that could prove that some or all the poems in the Cotton manuscript were written by a single, albeit unnamed, person. The most significant of these attempts have been recent and have sought to assess the hypothesis of such shared authorship by applying statistical or computer analysis or both to some of the criteria mentioned above. The outcomes of such analyses have not yielded any useful conclusions. For example, the computer analysis of McColly and Weier (1983) provided no clear evidence to support single authorship and McColly (1987) subsequently cast doubt on the validity of the methodology that had been used. Later computer analysis by Cooper and Pearsall (1988) has limited value because it specifically omitted *Pearl* from consideration.

A more complex factor that has sometimes been invoked in support of common authorship for these poems is the perceived existence in all of them of numerological designs. The conception of numerology as a shaping factor in Middle (and Old) English verse has a developed history. And there has been a general acceptance that some aspects of the design of *Pearl* were shaped by numerological considerations.[3] Such arguments have, in recent times, been extended to include both *Cleanness* and *Sir Gawain and the Green Knight*.[4]

There is nothing inherently implausible about numerical design as an aspect of Middle English poetic structure. For example, in his article "Sir Thopas" (1971) John Burrow has brilliantly demonstrated Chaucer's use of numerology in Chaucer's own narrative Sir Thopas in *The Canterbury Tales*. But a possible shared preoccupation with such symbolism does not, in itself, provide evidence for single authorship of a number of poems, especially since the numerological strategies identified in the poems in the Cotton manuscript have generally been peculiar to individual poems, and not identified as some form of shared controlling design in all of them.[5] And the more varied and the more complex the numerological analysis becomes, the greater the difficulty some will find in accepting that there is sufficient shared evidence of a shared design that extends across the four poems to make compelling the likely existence of numerology as demonstration of common authorship.

There is also a fundamental problem with number symbolism that has to do with the realities of manuscript transmission. The poems as they survive in Cotton are clearly not the original manuscript or manuscripts but are copies that survive at (quite probably) a number of stages of scribal copying from the original forms in which they were composed. While it is not clear how many stages of copying are reflected in the various poems as they survive in Cotton Nero A.x, it is clear that to a greater or lesser degree they all have been subject to textual corruption as they passed from scribe to scribe over time through these different stages of transmission. (It is also unclear whether the poems circulated together from the point of their original composition.) The likelihood is that errors will have been introduced through these stages of transmission and obscured or corrupted any original design that depended on precise symmetries. In *Pearl* the stanza comprising lines 901–12 is anomalous since it disrupts the otherwise invariable pattern of five-stanza groups; but it has been seen as necessary to at least some of the arguments about number symbolism and authorial identity (Adam). Also, one line, 472, appears to have been lost in the course of transmission. And at a couple of points within (612–13) and between (720–21) stanza sequences, the other regular pattern of concatenation is disrupted. It is not possible to establish the extent to which the transmission of the poem from copyist to copyist over time and probably from place to place may have obscured crucial aspects of the original form of these poems. But the evidence of *Pearl* does suggest that at least some aspects of its original conception may have become obscured. It may be wise, therefore, to be conscious that such stages of transmission inevitably introduce errors in copying, including omissions and misplacements, and that this element ought to place some constraint on efforts to base interpretation on aspects of numerology that involve the number of lines or the specific placement of images or phrases or other details in the texts, especially if such evidence is to be used as a factor in establishing common authorship.

Another problem with numerology, in *Pearl* and in the other poems, is that different aspects of the poems have been given different weight by different critics according to the symbolic methodology they perceive as being employed within and between or between the various poems in the Cotton manuscript. Some arguments, for example, have emphasized the positioning of decorated initials and the intervals they mark in various poems; others have placed weight on intervals of line numbers; others depend on the existence of narrative number patterning within a poem (like the pentangle and the parallelism of the three hunts and three bedroom scenes in *Sir Gawain and the Green Knight*); while still others have based arguments on more complex mathematical ratios or formulas. The inability to identify any shared numerological design that connects the four poems seems an indication of the failure of such a methodology to provide a convincing basis for determining single authorship. That there is some form of number symbolism in *Pearl* is clearly quite likely. But this does not, of itself, establish shared authorship with the other poems in the Cotton manuscript since such symbolism seems to vary in form and emphasis from poem to poem.

This circumstance points toward another that has to do with the question of poetic identity. While a lot of energy has been expended on attempts to attach a single identity to the entire corpus in the Cotton manuscript, there have not been any sustained attempts to consider the question of possible multiple authorship—that at least some of the poems might be by different authors. The studies by J. W. Clark cited below are an exception to this generalization. *Pearl* is particularly relevant here since it is perhaps the most difficult of the four poems to fit into a hypothesis of single authorship for all the poems. Aspects of its design and style seem to set it apart from the others. Its blend of allegory, elegy, and dream vision, its first-person voice, its use of a rhymed twelve-line stanza divided into five-stanza sections, and the use of concatenation to link both stanzas and sections demonstrate levels of technical sophistication not evident to the same extent or in the same ways in any of the other poems in the manuscript. Such a degree of literary distinctiveness does strengthen the possibility that *Pearl* may have been created by someone other than the author or authors of the rest of the poems in the manuscript. Distinctions based on stylistic criteria (in the broadest sense of the term) are often very slippery and ultimately of indeterminate evidential value. It seems in theory possible, if not likely, that a gifted poet could vary style and technique across his oeuvre, while simultaneously leaving common stylistic "signatures." But assessing such (possibly) shared features of style is difficult. For example, how much weight might be attached to the correspondence between the endings of *Pearl* and *Sir Gawain and the Green Knight*? *Pearl*'s final line, "Ande precious perleȝ vnto his pay" (1212) recalls its opening line, "Perle, pleasaunt to prynces paye" just as the ending of *Sir Gawain* (2524–25) echoes its opening lines. It is a stylistic parallel that cannot be summarily dismissed as probable coincidence especially since it is linked to a further numerical parallel. *Pearl* comprises 101 stanzas while *Sir Gawain* consists of 101 verse paragraphs. But it is hard to know how much significance to attach to such parallels. *Pearl* achieves this number of stanzas only by violating its own formal symmetries through the insertion of the anomalous stanza (discussed above). In contrast to the verse form of *Pearl*, the verse paragraphs in *Sir Gawain* vary in length, and the manuscript does not reveal any structural divisions: the modern presentation of the text divided into four parts is entirely arbitrary. The formal parallels between the two poems are rather less striking than their differences and provide only a small degree of support to a belief that they could have been written by the same author.

It remains possible that some of the four poems could be part of a single corpus, but criteria and methodologies for making such discriminations on the basis of internal evidence have not gained general acceptance. Some analyses have attempted to discriminate language or dialect features between poems in the Cotton manuscript. J. W. Clark in a series of articles in the late 1940s and early 1950s argued that vocabulary provides grounds for believing that the four poems were by different authors.[6] His arguments seem to have been ignored. Recently the assumption that all these poems share a common dialect that can be confidently localized has been challenged (Putter and Stokes, "Linguistic Atlas"). The question awaits further consideration. The relative brevity of some of these poems may limit the possibility of drawing any firm conclusions about such matters. But those arguments are at least suggestive and may place some constraint on less disciplined speculation or overconfident assertion that may come from literary criticism in its search for shared themes or preoccupations as a means of relating these poems to one another.

Any discussion of attributional method and the problems of authorship ultimately involves the question, Why does the issue of authorship matter, especially if no name of any identifiable individual can be credibly attached to any or all four poems in the Cotton manuscript? We have seen already that the assumption of a single author has proved particularly appealing to literary critics. This is doubtless because it offers the possibility of finding a poetic vision that can connect all the poems and can hence form the basis for comprehensive and sustained literary analysis. The single-author assumption is a handy interpretative tool, one that can make differences in form, structure, and technique appear as indications of literary range and breadth of accomplishment. It creates a single poetic presence whose multiplicity of individual achievements commands admiration in a way that would not be possible for a controlling hypothesis of multiple authorship. Perhaps modern literary studies have an investment in the creation and perpetuation of such a figure. The single author provides a substantial corpus and with it a means of manipulating discussion of all four poems in ways that privilege such concepts as coherence of point(s) of view, diversity of poetic achievement, and distinctiveness of original audience to create a fourteenth-century poet of high stature. The existence of more than one poet (or possibly four poets) of varying degrees of individual accomplishment (*Patience* and *Cleanness* have generally attracted less critical attention than the others) is a less attractive prospect to the literary critic looking for a field that has good career prospects. Such elements of academic realpolitik need to be understood.

Students need to be made aware of the extent to which their thinking about questions of authorship can be shaped by such critical stances—and that such stances lack the supporting evidence that would make them a basis for fruitful speculation. In teaching *Pearl* it seems best to deflect unanswerable questions about authorship by thinking instead about what can be inferred about the nature of the narrative voice and even the "character" of the narrator as it emerges through his account of his experiences. Such an approach may help to bring students closer to the emotional and spiritual core of the poem: the poetic enactment of those experiences and the enhanced understanding on the narrator's part that seems to follow from them.

Any discussion of the authorship of *Pearl* can only be inconclusive for the reasons I have tried to explain. However, it needs to be made clear that neither the lack of a named author nor comparison with the other poems in Cotton Nero A.x (whether they are by different authors) affects *Pearl*'s greatness as a poem. As so often with medieval literature, the inability to provide a concrete identity to the author reminds us of how much we cannot know about the contexts for the medieval works we study—and of how little this ultimately matters with the greatest works.

NOTES

[1] I leave aside the question of whether the *Pearl* poet (or poets) might also have written *Saint Erkenwald*; see, most recently, Borroff's "Narrative Artistry," which cites a number of earlier studies on the possible common authorship of *Saint Erkenwald* and the poems of the *Pearl* manuscript. The suggestion made by Henry Bradley that the Middle English romance *The Wars of Alexander* should be added to the *Pearl* poet corpus has not gained any support.

[2] Nearly all these are discussed in the excellent overview by Malcolm Andrew, "Theories" 23–25.

[3] The question is most lucidly discussed by Kean, "Numerical Composition"; see also Coolidge Chapman, as well as Barbara Nolan and David Farley-Hills.

[4] On *Cleanness*, see Donna Crawford; on *Sir Gawain*, see A. Kent Hieatt.

[5] The exception to this generalization is Edward I. Condren, "Numerical Proportion."

[6] See Clark's articles: "Observations"; "*Gawain*-Poet"; "Paraphrases for 'God'"; "On Certain 'Alliterative.'"

Teaching the Language of *Pearl*

Laura L. Howes

The North-West Midlands dialect of *Pearl* presents a series of obstacles to the student new to Middle English. To take the poem's first two lines as an example, most readers will recognize "perle," "plesaunte," "prynces," "paye," "golde," and "clere," as variant spellings of modern English words, in addition to the recognizable prepositions encountered in those lines: "Perle plesaunte, to prynces paye / To clanly clos in gold so clere . . ." (1–2). But "clanly clos" may strike a new student as opaque in meaning, and the grammatical function of "paye" in the first line stumps a student who thinks it might be a verb. Students who come to *Pearl* having studied Chaucer may find their initial assumptions easier to revise as they read along, but these students also will find much that is unfamiliar in vocabulary, syntax, morphology, and orthography. A good glossary becomes a necessary appendage, whether it appears in the back of students' texts or in digital form. A second critical tool would be the open-mindedness advised by the linguist and grammarian Fernand Mossé, when he instructs a new student of Middle English to "[b]ecome as a little child again and read symbol for symbol aloud" (Mossé ix).

The effort required of the student encountering *Pearl*'s Middle English for the first time, however, is repaid many times over. As editors and translators have noted, *Pearl* uses "a dizzying punnology" and "an intricate system of verbal echoes" (Stanbury, "Introduction" 4, 6), marked by "a wide range of metaphorical suggestions and connotations" (Andrew and Waldron, Pearl *Manuscript* [2007] 32) and "verbal extravagance" (Borroff, *Gawain Poet* 122). Indeed, to an extraordinary degree, the message and meanings of the poem link to its intricately patterned use of language. Translations, however skillful, simply cannot capture the way in which a single word or phrase, repeated in different lines and in new contexts, takes on new and deeper meanings, pushing the poetic argument forward, in ways both direct and subtle, echoing—and contrasting with—the sounds and sense of neighboring words in the stanza.

Tackling a sequence in class that repeats a word familiar in modern English, such as "jueler" ("jeweler") in sequence 5, may reveal in detail to the student how repetition plays on the word's connotations, and how the meaning of the word "jueler" evolves as the sequence progresses. The generally accepted meaning of "jueler" ends the first stanza of the sequence, "I haf ben a joylez juelere" (251), as the narrator bemoans the loss of his precious pearl, a gem that he valued above all others. But by the end of the sequence, a "kynde jueler" is juxtaposed to the "joylez juelere," as one who would understand his wider, God-given role in the world, as a Christian soul. And the Pearl-Maiden does criticize his attitude at the start of the next sequence: "I hald þat jueler lyttel to prayse / Þat leuez wel þat he sez wyth yȝe" (301–02); the jeweler who only believes what he can see with his own eyes, the jeweler who is blinded by material reality, lacks true vision and is considered "no kynde jueler" (276) by the Pearl-Maiden. In the course of sequence 5, he is instead instructed that he cannot trust what he sees with his eyes—a maiden in a beautiful valley across a stream from where he stands—and this figure, who seems so near and accessible to him, corrects him. He desires to be a "joyfol jueler" (288) by joining her physically in the space she occupies, but she asserts that "no joyfol jueler" (300) can "passe thys water fre" (299), thus dashing any hopes for physical reunion that he has harbored. The jeweler who felt he owned and lost his gem must come to realize that the gem was never his to begin with. A lesson in re-definition and fundamental re-vision is thus captured in the changing use of "jueler" within this five-stanza passage, from the generally accepted notion of someone who works with gems to set them into precious ornaments for individuals to own or sell to someone who honors true, spiritual beauty, invisible to the human eye and unavailable for personal ownership.

This transformation is also aided by changes to the word "juel" itself in lines 277–78, where the maiden, "þys geste" ("this visitor"), is called a jewel, and her words, "sawez," are also termed jewels, "juelez" (278). Thus, as "jueler" falls away from its literal meaning, so too do "juel" and "juelez" become metaphors for the heavenly figure and her precious words.

Some of this change in meaning may be gleaned from a good translation, of course, as "jueler" and "juel" correspond closely with modern English "jeweler" and "jewel/gem." But when one encounters the adjective "kynde" (276) in the Middle English, a seemingly similar correspondence with modern English "kind" will not work, as it does not capture the full range of the word in Middle English. Variously translated as "proper" (Borroff, *Gawain Poet* 133); "gracious" (Vantuono, *Pearl: An Edition with Verse Translation* 27); and "grateful" (Tolkien, *Sir Gawain* 133; Jewett, *The Pearl* 15), the word defies a simple parallelism with "kind." In Middle English, its range of meanings include "natural," "native" as "in accordance with nature" (*Oxford English Dictionary* I.1.a); "innate," "inherent" (I.1.b); "proper," "appropriate," "fitting" (I.1.c); "belonging to one by right of birth, descent, or inheritance" (I.2.a); and "lawful, rightful" (I.3.a.)—all meanings attested well before the date of *Pearl*. For the student of the language, many of these shades of meaning will figure seamlessly into these lines. That is, the Pearl-Maiden encourages the narrator here to give over his "joylez jueler" status in favor of a role or identity he can be said to have been born with—a native, inborn, inherited aspect of his spiritual nature as a human. She urges him to leave off his cultural role as father-jeweler to the young girl, figured as a gem-pearl, and instead to reanimate his God-given role as a human with a soul and to embrace his inherited membership in the dimensionless and invisible *Civitate Dei* ("the city of God"), to use Saint Augustine's metaphor.

Further, focus on the alliterative pattern of this sequence reveals many words alliterating on the *j* sound ("jueler," "gem," "gentyl," "joyfol," and "joylez"), which makes the nonalliterative "kynde" in line 276 that much more powerful in context.

In an undergraduate survey course, class units devoted to Middle English alliterative verse may include excerpts from the poem, like the sequence discussed above, along with simple translation exercises designed to tease out the myriad meanings of the original lines. A course focused more tightly on Middle English literature may mix Middle English with translated texts. Here, too, an excerpt from *Pearl* may serve to illustrate the rich complexity of the original, particularly when contrasted with two or three translated versions of the same passage. (See, e.g., the translations by Marie Borroff, William Vantuono, J. R. R. Tolkien, and Sophie Jewett. A nonscholarly version by Bill Stanton and the looser, poetic translation by Jane Draycott also provide interesting examples.)

In a graduate-level course or an advanced undergraduate course devoted to the *Pearl* poet, or to Middle English alliterative verse more generally, the poem may be read in its entirety in Middle English over a period of two to five weeks, depending on the students' Middle English skill level and on whether the class has already read texts in this dialect. In a class that is devoted to the study of the language of medieval England and that uses a set of excerpted texts as examples of various dialects and various time periods, a final unit on the *Pearl* poet's language and artistry may reward a semester of language work as an effective culmination.

In any of these classes, from beginner to advanced, a series of translation exercises can demonstrate the myriad decisions necessary to translation, thus alerting the students to the intractable nature of the enterprise. A useful assignment for students divided into small groups is to have them translate together a stanza of the poem and work out among themselves whether they will copy the rhyme scheme, alliteration, and meter of the original work; how loose they will allow themselves to be in their choice of words; and the like. This necessitates their knowing, or figuring out, what the rhyme scheme, alliteration, and meters are, and establishing a good literal translation of their passage as a first stage. If several groups take on the same stanza, the various versions may be shared and discussed: why did one group decide on the words they did, while the other(s) used a different set of associations in their version(s)? Issues that will usually emerge in class include how poetic or how literal a translation might be; whether it is in fact possible to translate the emotive effect of a poem directly; whether fourteenth-century cultural values and assumptions may be represented, as we understand them, or whether a modern rendition of a similar set of values and assumptions can suitably stand for, if not replicate, the original. Awareness of the kinds of decisions made by translators on a word-by-word basis can also inform students' further engagement with Middle English.

This kind of exercise can be expanded to include a comparison of published verse translations, and students may be assigned to compare and contrast two versions of the same passage, or to compare their own versions with a published one. As with the in-class exercise, this individual assignment encourages word-by-word comparisons and judgments about each translator's decisions.

For example, the Middle English word "maskellez"—the repeated word in sequence 13—is translated variously as "immaculate" (Tolkien, *Sir Gawain* 150–52; Borroff, *Gawain Poet* 146–47); "spotless" (Vantuono, Pearl: *An Edition* 59–63); and "unblemished" (Jewett *The* Pearl 29–31). The connotations of these modern English renditions repay attention. "Immaculate," which is etymologically related to "maskellez," both derived from the Latin "immaculatus" ("without stain," "without spots"), also carries with it in modern English a strong theological connotation, as the word is most commonly encountered in the phrase "immaculate conception," referring to Saint Anne's conceiving the Virgin Mary. This choice, then, associates the Pearl-Maiden strongly with the Virgin Mary, her mother, and their state of heavenly perfection. In contrast, the word *spotless* draws on our visual experience, eliciting the image of a perfectly formed and perfectly pure appearance, with the further connotation that, when *spot* is also understood as a moral or ethical defect, the phrase emphasizes both the exterior and interior state of the Pearl-Maiden. The term *unblemished* also brings to mind, first, the appearance of a material object that stands out as being without imperfection, as a piece of fruit is said to be unblemished if it shows no signs of injury or insect infestation. While these explorations may seem beside the point to some students, others enjoy considering the range of possible connotations in such a translation exercise and will engage more deeply with the poem through this kind of detailed analysis.

Instructors will also want to point out in this sequence the importance of the alliteration in the concluding line: "A makelez may and maskellez" (line 780), which resounds with alliterative force, and which Tolkien translates as "A matchless maid immaculate" (*Sir Gawain*, 151) and Borroff as "A matchless maid and immaculate" (*Gawain Poet* 147). A further note of interest is that *maskellez* is a word found only here, in this poem, in this sequence.

At a more advanced level, study of the language of *Pearl* will engage more profoundly with the poem's dialect and use of alliterative poetic language. First, students of the language will note that dialectal markers in *Pearl* include -es and -ez/-eȝ endings for many third-person singular present indicative verbs (see "berez," "passez," and "cortez" in lines 746–53); present participles ending in -ande (as in "wyschande" in line 14); and third-person plural pronouns: "þay" (lines 1113, 1120, 1146); "her" (1108) and "hem" (788). If students have already studied Chaucer's language, these markers may be contrasted with southern British forms: -eth for third-person singular present indicative verbs and -yng/-ing for present participles. The third-person plural pronouns in Chaucer show Scandinavian influence, as the earlier southern nominative forms of "hy/hi/ho/heo" have become, in Chaucer's dialect, "they/thei."

The extensive vocabulary of the *Pearl* poet, with many synonyms for recurrent concepts, is a function of the alliterative forms used by the poet in all four (or five) of his poems (Borroff, "Narrative Artistry"). Following E. V. Gordon, who found several parallels between the *Pearl* poet's vocabulary and terms still in use in mid-twentieth-century North-West dialects, particularly in Cheshire, Lancastershire, Yorkshire, and Shropshire, an interesting exercise may be to research topological terms used in *Pearl*. Many are still in use in northern dialects and place-names, including "bonk," "schore," "huyle/hylle," and "greue" (Gordon li–lii). Additionally, the several terms for *stream* used in the poem point to the necessity of synonyms in the alliterative tradition. Students may compare the following lines and the terms in each for *stream/current/sea/watercourse*, all derived from Old English words:

Doun after a *strem* þat dryȝly halez	(line 125)
Byȝonde þe *broke*, by slente oþer slade	(141)
He lauez Hys gyftez as water of dyche,	
Oþer *gotez* of golf þat neuer charde.	(607–08)
Bow vp towarde þys *bornez* heued.	(974; emphasis added)

As can be seen in these lines, "strem" is not needed for the alliteration of line 125, but "broke," "gotez," and "bornez" all figure into their lines' alliterative patterns, allowing the poet to say much more about this stream than he could have done using only one or two words for it. Our modern vocabulary is also enriched with several words for *stream*, derived from Old English *stream*, such as *river* and *brook*, derived respectively from Anglo-Norman *rivere* and Old English *bróc*.

In addition to the vocabulary that is particular to the North-West Midlands and derived from indigenous Old English terms, we encounter several words borrowed from Romance and Scandinavian languages, some added into the spoken language before the fourteenth century, and others added during the late fourteenth century, when this poet was writing. A quick perusal of just one column from Gordon's glossary for this poem (122) reveals the following examples. From Old Norse, we get "blunt" (meaning "stunned"), "bolleȝ" ("tree-trunks"), "bolne" ("swell"), "bone" ("petition," "prayer"), and "bonk" ("shore," "bank"). From Old French, we find "blwe" ("blue,") "boffeteȝ" ("buffets"), "bonerte" ("beatitude"), "borde" ("jest"), "bornyst" ("polished"); and from Anglo-French: "boyeȝ" ("ruffians"), "bostwys" ("massive," "rough"). This small sampling gives a hint of the richness of the *Pearl* poet's vocabulary. He drew not only from the spoken language of his home, showing influence from Scandinavia and Norman French, but also from literary Middle English, Anglo-Norman, Old

French, and Old Norse sources—drawing alliterative vocabulary from many linguistic strands into his work.

A useful exercise would be to have students analyze several lines of the poem etymologically, noting the origin of each word, as recorded in the *Oxford English Dictionary* online, for example. Using this readily available resource may help students understand the ways in which our modern English is derived from many sources. Some words used by the *Pearl* poet are now obsolete, of course; but many others are still in use, with different spellings or different meanings or both attached.

The experience of reading the poem entirely in Middle English, or only a small part of it in Middle English, is to engage in a study of linguistic artistry at the very highest level. The original language of the poem conveys much of its subtextual meaning, as discussed above. Connotative meanings, etymological linkings, and the play of puns all contribute to the poetic intricacy of one of the finest Middle English poems, bar none.

Teaching *Pearl* in Its Manuscript Context

Murray McGillivray and Kenna L. Olsen

The imaging revolution of the last twenty years has dramatically altered the world for teachers and researchers of medieval literary texts. Previously all but a privileged few well-funded scholars were reduced to reading these texts in printed editions, especially in North America, and students, particularly, were often completely unaware of the complex vehicle of communication that is the medieval manuscript. Thanks to digital images of manuscripts and the databases that serve them to the Web, the visual richness and interpenetrating signifying systems of these early handwritten books have recently become available in slowly increasing numbers to students and scholars who live far from the depositories that hold them. As teachers of *Pearl*, we are among the first to be able to deploy high-resolution color images of the original manuscript of our literary text in our classrooms.

British Library MS Cotton Nero A.x (art. 3) is the sole surviving copy of *Pearl*, as well as of *Sir Gawain and the Green Knight, Cleanness*, and *Patience*. Written on parchment in a script based on textura, or Gothic script, but influenced by late medieval cursive scripts, the manuscript features unusual brightly colored full-page illustrations of its four poems, including four illustrations of *Pearl*. Although the ink has faded, the handwriting is relatively easy to read with some practice and instruction, especially as seen in the high-resolution images recently published on the Web by the *Cotton Nero A.x Project* at Gawain-ms.ca (McGillivray) and with the help of the "Cotton Nero A.x. Project's Transcription Policy" (Olsen and McGillivray). Students who spend some time with the manuscript in the online photographic facsimile can learn many things about medieval manuscript culture in a hands-on (though virtual) way, and they can reach a new understanding of the processes, decisions, alterations, and even misunderstandings that underlie the critical edition or translation of *Pearl* they are reading. As co-investigators in the *Cotton Nero A.x Project*, we were able to use the manuscript images in our classrooms for some months prior to their release to the general public in summer 2012, and we report here on some classroom uses and student projects that have proved to be particularly valuable ways to teach *Pearl* in its manuscript context.

General Classroom Use of Manuscript Images

Between the two of us, we have accumulated experience in teaching this manuscript in different institutions (a major research university and a four-year teaching-focused undergraduate university) and at different levels, from an undergraduate period survey to a graduate class entirely on *Pearl* and its companion poems in Cotton Nero A.x. In all these teaching situations, we found great educational value in the simple projection of images of the manuscript for discussion. The printed edition that the students have been reading (and this would be even more true of a translation) is strikingly different in appearance from the manuscript, and this prompts many questions. In the original manuscript, for example, the poem is not written out with space between visually discrete stanzas; instead, other indications of stanza boundaries are used (such as capital letters, some ornamented, and the pairs of marginal slanting lines called paraphs). How does that change the reading experience? And there is no punctuation in the manuscript, no periods, commas, quotation marks, or question marks—all these were supplied by the editor of the reading edition. What would it be like to read *Pearl* without that help? It might be more confusing, but does it give the reader more power to interpret the text?

With a little more preparation, the teacher can project a page of *Pearl* in the students' reading edition that is known to have been emended by an editor. Students, with some help if this is their first contact with the manuscript, can spell out a few lines or a whole stanza and then compare that classroom-produced manuscript transcription with the edited text. Just to realize that an edited text may often not follow the punctuation or format of the manuscript original and that it can also be altered textually by the editor in greater or lesser ways can be a valuable experience. Classroom discussion can also focus on the particular emendation. Does it make sense? What kind of sense did the original manuscript reading make? What presumptions underlie such bold editorial intervention? What does it do to our reading of the printed edition when we realize that we may not be looking at what the editor first saw?

It is also useful to pause while an image of a manuscript page is on the screen to describe how the manuscript culture of the later Middle Ages was strikingly different from even later print culture, let alone our current Internet culture. The process of preparation of parchment from animal skin by flaying, scraping, drying, and smoothing can be described; and the engagement of multiple craftspeople in the work of manuscript production can be recounted, from the scribe who wrote the main text to the rubrisher who then drew the ornamental initials to the illustrator and finally the binder. Students can think about what difficulties this elaborate and costly process of reproduction of a text would have posed for the dissemination of a literary work; what the value of a book would have been in such a culture; what the introduction of copying mistakes or intentional and meaningful enthusiastic changes by the scribe would have done to the text in transmission. These questions about manuscript culture will naturally have their place in a separate medieval literature course, but they might be particularly valuable to bring up, for example, in a British Literature survey, when *Pearl* represents the whole medieval period.

The Illustrations as Early Commentary

The four illustrations of *Pearl* are a "remediation," or transfer between different media, from the original text into the form of two-dimensional colored images (Appendix 2 at the end of the volume). As such, they can give some insight into how the illustrator, who must have been a close contemporary of the author, understood the poem. In the first illustration, (fig. 1), the Dreamer, having fallen asleep beside a large dark shape that may represent a grave-mound, lies with closed eyes among stylized trees, his hood blown dramatically to the right and a strange blue and white path with scalloped edges extending upward from his head, perhaps indicating the departure of his soul into the dream. In the second, (fig. 2), the same figure, face mostly missing due to degradation of the surface of the manuscript leaf, stands surrounded by stylized trees beside a blue stream with a large fish in it and points with one hand at the fish and with the other upward. In the third illustration, (fig. 3), the Dreamer again stands amid foliage beside a stream, this time showing three fish, but opposite him on the farther bank is the Pearl-Maiden, a full-grown woman in white wearing a belted high-necked gown, possibly decorated with pearls on the placket up by her neck, and an elaborate gold crown. The Dreamer again points with both hands, fingers now directed at the Pearl-Maiden herself in what could be exposition or accusation; she raises both palms toward him in response in what would seem to be a sign of rejection, refusal, or pacification. In the final illustration, (fig. 4), the Dreamer appears to kneel with joined hands at lower left, while the Pearl-Maiden, standing inside the stone wall of the New Jerusalem across the stream at top right gestures toward herself with one hand and toward him with the other. Besides its surrounding wall, the Heavenly City in which she stands has as main architectural features a small round crenellated tower ornamented with a cross-shaped arrow slit and a large half-timbered building with an arched roof.

Students who have read *Pearl* find the illustrations quite interesting. Classroom discussion can circle around a number of topics proposed by the instructor. What particular moments of the story are depicted here? Why has the illustrator chosen these particular moments? What do the attitudes of the figures tell us about their relationship? What do their gestures indicate? Do these depictions match the images presented in the poem? Can you detect the illustrator's own interpretation of the Pearl Maiden or of the Dreamer, or of the relationship between them, in his drawing them? How? In general, students in our experience will only briefly be constrained by an attempt to focus on the illustrations, as the reaction of an early reader to the poem, and will instead have numerous questions, interpretations, and comments about these pictures, both in relation to the poem and as independent visual objects redolent of medieval culture. Although neither of us has done this, we can also see interesting essays coming out of a set essay topic that asked students to make this kind of comparison between images and text of *Pearl*.

Transcription and Editorial Projects

We believe that students can learn a great deal very quickly by "getting their hands dirty" with real-world projects that involve them in manipulating medieval text in a professional or scholarly manner. The Cotton Nero A.x images do not exactly seat the student in the British Library Reading Room with a magnifying glass, but they come close, and this opens the way for a variety of student projects that can work through the processes of professional practice with manuscript texts, from transcription through editing, glossing, annotation, and even publication.

We mentioned above the possibility of engaging an entire class in a brief transcription from the manuscript. A slight variation that can be a classroom activity or a take-home project depending on the length of the assigned text is to give individual students or small groups a section of the poem to transcribe. A transcription protocol needs to be given to the students, along with some graphic representation of the letters of the medieval alphabet (and other signs, or glyphs) they will be working with. Both of these are handily supplied by the "Cotton Nero A.x. Project Transcription Policy" (gawain-ms.ca, publications tab), though instructors may well wish to emend that document to eliminate some of its complexity for their students, especially in a nonmedieval course. This simple exercise of struggling through the identification and correct transcription of medieval letters, we have found, brings home the nature of manuscript text and manuscript culture more efficiently and more effectively than any lecture could.

At the other extreme from a mere transcription, students could be asked, and this might be a major course final project, to take a section of text (e.g., a sequence of stanzas of *Pearl* sharing a concatenation word) and work through the whole process from transcription, proofing, and checking to word-by-word glossing of the text with the aid of the *Middle English Dictionary*, through punctuating, consideration of possible emendation to authoring of textual and explanatory notes and finally to publication as a Web page, for example. Murray McGillivray assigned such a project to teams of three or four students in a joint undergraduate-graduate course with considerable success. The variety of skills that students learn, quite a few of which (proofing, punctuation, Web publication) they can clearly identify as career-related, and the sheer fun of being in charge of a project so practical and so closely engaged with the medieval text in its manuscript matrix makes this a memorable student favorite.

Transcription and Edition Project: Case Study

Because we have experimented with several ways of engaging students in projects that involve transcription or editing from manuscript of the poems of Cotton Nero A.x, we know that the possibilities are quite diverse and we expect that teachers can bring many other innovations to this general idea. To give a concrete idea of the way such projects can work in classes, however, we thought it useful to choose one implementation as a case study, so we selected a specialized senior *Pearl* poet course taught by Kenna L. Olsen at Mount Royal University (see appendix at the end of this essay).

After a translation assignment, students were asked to consider a passage of *Pearl* in its manuscript context and to provide the following: a codicological description of the folios under consideration; a transcription of a passage corresponding to the assigned folios; and a critical edition of the passage transcribed. The twenty-five-student class was divided into seminar groups based on the schedule. Groups of two to four are ideal. Students were then directed to the manuscript images provided on the *Cotton Nero A.x Project*'s Web site and assigned a sequence of folios (the number again will vary according to class size and need, but it is best if each seminar group has the opportunity to consider examples that include illuminated capitals and "regular" text as part of their assignment). Students were also directed to the "Cotton Nero A.x Transcription Policy." Instruction on codicological considerations and terminology (such as the state of a folio, appearance or lack of decorated initials, catchwords, pagination, and signs of correction or erasure) were included during class time, as were the fundamentals of transcription and principles of diplomatic versus critical editions (see the assignment at the end of this essay for a description of the task). Students then prepared their literary discussion, transcription, and critical edition for class presentation. Following the presentation, the class transitioned from seminar presentation to discussion as a whole class, where students were asked to identify and perhaps comment on the differences between their classmates' critical edition, that of their textbook (Andrew and Waldron), and those of previous editors (as evidenced in the textual notes of Andrew and Waldron). For instance, in referring to the sample result given in the assignment sheet (see the assignment below), the sample critical edition retains the manuscript reading, where Andrew and Waldron emend "spenned" to "penned." Students evaluate Andrew and Waldron's explanation, "that the poet usually avoids identical rhyme, [and] it is likely that this was the original reading" (57n53 [2007]), by comparing this stanza with others. After consulting the glossary, students engaged in a discussion on the intricacies of the words' differing meanings (a change from "clasped," implying loss, to "imprisoned"), involving rigorous debate about the merits and possible justifications of each reading. Additionally, students learned that the textual notes of a critical edition record previous editorial treatment. In this case, students could see that Andrew and Waldron accept the emendation first suggested by Ferdinand Holthausen.

This assignment, then, accomplishes many tasks: it asks English majors to explicate a short literary passage; it introduces students to a medieval text in its manuscript context; it introduces codicology and paleography as foundational skills; it introduces students to the intricacies of textual editing, such as different types of editions, how to read textual notes and reconstruct a text, and invites them to consider the role of editor. Students tend to become so fascinated by the realities of editors disagreeing with one another or choosing to ignore a manuscript reading (both as evidenced in textual notes) that they often ask to pursue the topic of editing further. When this happens, I often assign a traditional essay that asks students to respond to the following statement: "Editors have a responsibility to clearly identify their editorial practices and editorial emendations." Students can respond by researching themselves 1) *Pearl*'s manuscript reading (or readings) by accessing the digital images and 2) the past editorial treatment of the reading(s) in question.

APPENDIX: Sample Assignment for a Junior (Third-Year) or Senior (Fourth-Year) Class

Note that this assignment builds on an earlier translation from the Middle English assignment and is a group assignment for two to four students. The actual assignment sheet is presented here.

Seminar Assignment

Objective

The purpose of this assignment is to encourage each student to think about a specific text (or textual passage) in its manuscript context and about the different approaches we might take in its analysis. Students will learn basic transcription skills, codicological description, and the fundamentals of textual editing. Merit is based on evidence of careful reading, thorough and thoughtful engagement with the text and the manuscript context, and clear articulation of presentation choices. Please do not use outside sources; I'm interested in what you see and how you handle the material. Seminars should be planned as initial presentations but be designed to sustain the entire course of the class. All members of the group must present.

Resources

> Assigned manuscript images and transcription policy from *Cotton Nero A.x Project* Web site (gawain-ms.ca/)
> Junicode font (available at junicode.sourceforge.net/)
> Sample results and directions (see below)
> Text of the poem (Andrew and Waldron's 2007 edition)

Directions

For your seminar presentation, you should include the following in the order described here.

1. First present an aspect of, or an approach to, your text (or part of the text) that you find interesting or helpful, referring liberally to specific passages from the text to illustrate your points (please note citations so that we can locate the passages during your presentation). The presentation should further our understanding of a significant aspect of the assigned reading by offering a thematic, contextual, intertextual, stylistic, structural, or other approach to the work as a whole, or to one or more of its key themes, episodes, motifs, or characters.
2. Present a correct transcription (using the *Cotton Nero A.x Project*'s transcription policy as a guide, and Junicode as the font for displaying your transcription). Then present a critical edition based on your transcription.
3. Be prepared to discuss your own critical edition, how it differs from or is the same as Andrew and Waldron's, and discuss the passage's past editorial treatment (as recorded in Andrew and Waldron).

Remember that your transcription should be an exact replica (as far as the Junicode font will allow) of what you see in the manuscript. For instance, your transcription must record whether letters are joined, whether an abbreviation mark is present, and it must correctly distinguish between different types of letterforms. For your critical edition, you may choose to incorporate punctuation, capitalization, or word spacing different from what appears in the manuscript. Be sure you can articulate the reasons behind your choices. Remember to expand your abbreviations by underlining.

Sample transcription and editing results for *Pearl* folio 39v, lines 13–17 (your chosen passage should be approximately 10 lines):

Transcription (diplomatic edition) of lines 13–17

> Bifoɹe þat ſpot my honde I ſpēnd
> foɹ care ful colde þat to me caȝt
> a deuely dele in my hert dēned
> þaȝ reſoū ſette my ſeluen ſaȝt
> I playned my perle þᵗ þᵒ watȝ ſpēned

Critical edition of lines 13–17

> Bifore þat spot my honde I spennd
> For care ful colde þat to me caȝt.
> A deuely dele in my hert dennd,

Þaȝ resoun̲ sette myseluen saȝt.
I playned my perle þat̲ þer̲ watz spen̲ned.

Points to consider for class discussion

The critical edition presented here includes punctuation different from Andrew and Waldron's. At line 17 of 39v (line 53 of the poem), the critical edition here retains the manuscript reading, "spenned," while Andrew and Waldron (after Holthausen; see Andrew and Waldron 57) emend to "penned."

Public *Pearl*

David Coley

The title of this chapter—Public *Pearl*—is intentionally counterintuitive. After all, for most of its critical history *Pearl* has been apprehended either as a sustained elegy on the loss of a child or as a sophisticated allegory of Christian salvation, a narrowly courtly or exclusively spiritual work. The former interpretation, voiced by Richard Morris in the inaugural publication of the Early English Text Society, regards the poet as "[giving] expression to his own sorrow for the loss of his infant child, a girl of two years old" (Morris xi). Compelling to professional scholars and students alike, Morris's elegiac reading has proved tenacious, and while critics have repeatedly refined it (we are now, e.g., less apt than Morris to ascribe the poem's central loss to the poet himself), we continue to read and teach the poem as a searing meditation on grief, one that bears stately comparison to Milton's "Lycidas" or Shelley's "Adonaïs." The latter interpretation of *Pearl* as an allegory of Christian soteriology finds its most energetic expression in D. W. Robertson's "The Pearl as a Symbol," which subjects the poem's central image to the fourfold exegesis usually reserved for biblical scripture. In Robertson's reading, the Dreamer's lost pearl ascends through the literal, allegorical, and tropological levels to reach its apotheosis in the anagogical, becoming by turns a gem, the innocent on Earth, the penitent soul, and the reward of eternal life ("Pearl" 160).

More recent scholarship on *Pearl* has departed from the moribund elegy-allegory debate, but ironically, even as it has broadened our understanding of the poem's cultural and textual contexts, it has also tended to enclose *Pearl* in ever more insular spheres: courtliness, occasionality, individuality, even psychological interiority. John Bowers's groundbreaking work on *Pearl* and the Ricardian court situates the poem in "a complex network that embraced the king's chamber, the royal household, the council, the offices of state, the chief law courts, even the Parliament" (Bowers, *"Pearl* in Its Royal Setting" 112). Even within this broad political nexus, however, the *Pearl* that Bowers describes remains a fundamentally inward-looking work, its intricate symbology thoroughly imbricated with the self-referential displays of authority adopted by Richard II in the 1380s and 1390s, its dialect and poetics so readily associated with Ricardian power that the poem was ultimately to be suppressed, along with other artistic products of Richard's Cheshire-oriented court, by an insecure Lancastrian dynasty looking to secure its power base in London (*"Pearl* in Its Royal Setting" 154–55). Lynn Staley likewise sees *Pearl* as a court-oriented text, reading it not as an elegy on the death of a young girl but rather as an occasional poem commemorating the entry into a nunnery of Isabel, third daughter of Thomas of Woodstock (84). From a markedly different scholarly direction, psychoanalytically inflected criticism has moved the poem from the court and the occasion to the still narrower confines of the individual psyche. David Aers, who detects a whiff of religious heterodoxy about the poem, regards *Pearl* foremost as a work that treats "loss and the self in mourning" (55). George Edmondson, too, understands the poem as "forever circling around a lost object that can neither be forgotten, because it embodies the trauma of lack, nor directly recuperated, because it also embodies a residue of impossible enjoyment" (40).

Whatever *Pearl* is—elegy, allegory, livery badge, courtly prize, symptom—its fractious critical history seems at least to agree on what it is *not*, namely a "public poem," one that, in the influential definition developed by Anne Middleton, projects "a 'common voice' to serve the 'common good'" (95). This is not to say that *Pearl* performs no ideological work. Rather, it is to suggest that such work is almost always understood as decisively introspective. When considered within such critical confines, *Pearl* becomes, at its most expansive, a poem that reflects the glory of the royal affinity through a web of images and rhetorical postures meaningful only to a select few. At its narrowest, the poem plumbs the psychic depths of one individual's mourning, offering obscure spiritual counsel and psychological insight in equal measure. Moreover, with its absolutist theology and its pervasive language of *fin'amor*, the poem can hardly be described as charting "a course between the rigorous absolutes of religious rule on the one hand, and, on the other, the rhetorical hyperboles and emotional vanities of the courtly style" (Middleton 95). If anything, its twinned elegiac and allegorical modes drive *Pearl* across these two poles rather than between them. Nor is *Pearl* a poem that "speaks 'as if' to the entire community . . . rather than 'as if' to a coterie or patron" (98), nor is its hypermetaphoric poetic voice one that we would classify as "common" (96). Indeed, *Pearl* would seem to be disqualified from consideration as "public" on any number of grounds: its filigreed style and poetics; its rarified courtly audience; its investment in aristocratic luxury; its stringent adherence to Christian soteriology; its meditative, even mystical spiritual epistemology. How could such an intimate work evince a public voice?

In several of my third- and fourth-year classes, my students and I have pursued precisely that question to surprisingly productive ends, exploring the ways that *Pearl*, even as a self-evidently courtly production, might perform some of the "mediating and meliorative" cultural work imagined by Middleton as the province of public poetry, how the poem might, among other things, "justif[y] itself within society . . . as a moral force, in essentially public terms" (104). There are, as I see it, two immediate pedagogical advantages to such a contrarian approach. First, reading *Pearl* as a public work places it in productive contact with important fourteenth- and fifteenth-century works more obviously and more robustly engaged with their contemporary political and social world, works from which the poem is too often bracketed: *Piers Plowman*, the alliterative *Wynnere and Wastoure*, and Hoccleve's *Regement of Princes*, to name a few.

In my classes on *Pearl*, I find the prologue to the *Confessio Amantis* particularly useful in spurring discussion, as Gower's discussion of a world undone by mutability offers several compelling entry points into the *Pearl* poet's own upending of established social norms. Lamenting the corruption of his own age, Gower writes longingly of an idealized past:

> The word was lich to the conceite
> Withoute semblant of deceite.
> Tho was ther unenvied love,
> Tho was the vertu sett above
> And vice was put under fote.
> Now stant the crop under the rote.
> The world is changed overal,
> And therof most in special
> That love is falle into discord.   (prologue, lines 113–21)

Here, in Gower's straightforward and hortative verse, we encounter the extroverted voice so conspicuously lacking in the courtly *Pearl*. Here, too, we hear the address to a heterogeneous audience that Gower seems determined "to respect, to bring to mutual awareness, and to resolve into common understanding . . . about our common condition" (Middleton 98). What is often striking to students, however, is how closely Gower's "public" plaint that the root of the tree now stands over its top resonates with the seemingly narrower concerns staged in *Pearl*. The pointed reversal in social order that Gower decries finds a counterpart in the social location of *Pearl*'s heavenly Maiden, who "cowþez neuer God nauþer plese ne pray, / Ne neuer nawþer Pater ne Crede" (lines 484–85) but who nonetheless instructs the older Dreamer, her earthly father, in Christian lore. So too does Gower's claim that "love is falle into discord"—a lament that speaks both to a crisis in the outwardly directed love "that issues in acts of social amelioration" (Middleton 97) and to the power of such "common love" (97) to heal the rifts in Gower's riven society—gesture toward the kind of love that *Pearl*'s Dreamer strives to reclaim with his apotheosized daughter and that he finally manifests when he participates in the communal sacrament of the Eucharist in the poem's final stanza. Perhaps most evocative is Gower's desire for a language in which "the word [is] lich to the conceite." *Pearl*, I would contend, is a poem that seeks a similar kind of language, deploying its layered "punnology" (the phrase is Sylvia Tomasch's) and intricate poetics to develop a vernacular laden, even overflowing, with significance. *Pearl*'s language is, in this sense, almost Adamic. Through it, the poem itself, as many readers have pointed out, effectively becomes a pearl in its translucence, its circularity, its near flawlessness. The words of the poem, like the words of Gower's unspecified but Edenic past, are in this way the very thing that they describe.

This emphasis on language gestures toward the second pedagogical advantage of considering *Pearl* a public poem: it forces students to consider an increased range of semantic possibilities for the poem's vibrant and polysemous vocabulary. Dealing with the poem's language is of critical importance in teaching *Pearl* and is fundamental to any understanding of the poem. Sylvia Tomasch's "A *Pearl* Punnology" and Sarah Stanbury's introduction to the TEAMS edition of the poem both offer excellent analyses of the *Pearl* poet's linguistic strategies that reveal how the poem "with extraordinary facility rewrites the definitions of the poem's central terms" (Stanbury, "Introduction" 4). But like similar analyses, both of these discussions assume a more limited range of semantic play than the poem may actually exhibit, a range implicitly circumscribed by the poem's own putative insularity. Tomasch, for example, painstakingly traces the poet's development of the word *spot* throughout the poem, but she focuses on only two of the word's potential meanings—"place" and "blemish" (11)—and thus limits the kinds of development that the word (and the poem) can sustain. In my work on *Pearl*, which attempts to position the poem in the context of the plague pandemic that ravaged England throughout the waning Middle Ages, the term *spot*, along with other keywords such as *bolne*, *bele*, and *moul*, takes on the additional meanings of "plague sore" and "bubo," senses that both draw from and open *Pearl* up to the consideration of a national cataclysm (Coley 219–24). Read with such senses in mind, *Pearl* thus becomes a poem that still functions in the allegorical and elegiac modes that critics have traditionally described but that also reaches outward, offering an elegy not only for a single loss but for the losses of a nation beset by a grievous pandemic, allegorizing not only the progress of a single soul toward the heavenly city but also the progress of countless souls after four decades of pestilence. Such a turn from the personal to the communal—from the individual to the common—necessarily begins at the level of the word in *Pearl*, with the careful punning and wordplay that the poet uses to develop meaning in his work.

My research aside, I have found that reimagining the parameters of *Pearl*'s language in these ways can also be productive in the classroom. In a recent fourth-year seminar on the poems of the Cotton Nero A.x manuscript, I asked my class to focus on the twelfth stanza group (lines 661–720), and particularly on the link word for that group, *ryȝt*. Using the *Middle English Dictionary* definitions for both "right" and "rīte" as a guide, the class divided into several groups, each responsible for considering two of the definitions highlighted by the *Middle English Dictionary*. Many of these definitions, of course, confirmed or extended traditional understandings of the poem: when we considered *ryȝt* as denoting "that which is morally right" or "that which is just" ("Right," defs. 1, 2), for example, we understood the line "Þe innocent is ay saf by *ryȝt*" as supporting the inherent righteousness of the Pearl-Maiden's claim to her heavenly status, a reaffirmation of the primacy of innocence in the divine hierarchy of the New Jerusalem. Likewise, when considering *ry3t* as referring to a "formal religious act or service, ritual, ceremony; a religious procedure or observance" ("Rīte," def. 1), we saw the word as foreshadowing, if obliquely, the celebration of the Eucharist in which the Dreamer participates at the poem's close.

But other definitions of *ry3t* pushed against these more traditional readings. Paramount among them, the explicitly legal senses of *right* as "a rule of conduct, a law; also, the law of a land" ("Right," def. 3) and as "a just claim, an entitlement; a legal or moral right" ("Right," def. 5) led many students to consider how *Pearl* might engage in those questions of right rule and governance more openly queried in the works of Langland and Gower. Particularly when coupled with the Pearl-Maiden's almost sociological discussion of the Heavenly City in the latter half of the poem, the broad social questions implied in stanza group twelve—What should a vassal expect from his or her lord? What responsibilities do the two have to one another?—seemed to many students to suggest something of a *speculum principum*. *Pearl* thus became a work whose didactic impulse was directed not only to the individual penitent or the mourner but also more broadly to the apparatus of the state and to its citizens. One particularly ambitious student eventually wrote a final research paper on just this issue, reading *Pearl* as a poetic conduct manual for Cheshire expatriates in Richard II's retinue. Informed largely by the works of John Bowers ("*Pearl* in Its Royal Setting") and Michael Bennett ("Community, Class, and Careerism") and augmented by our in-class discussions, this student argued on semantic and dialectical grounds that *Pearl*'s central conceit of an outsider-dreamer looking into a privileged city mirrored the experience of Richard's own retinue of Cheshiremen looking into the courtly world of London from a position of regionally marked social inferiority. The reading turned on a macaronic pun that the student and I identified in the first and final lines of the poem: "prynces paye" (1) came to mean not only "God's pleasure" in the redeemed soul but also "Prince's country" (Old French *pais*), the unfamiliar land into which Richard's Cheshiremen were forced to assimilate.

By contextualizing *Pearl* with contemporary works and by bringing a wider interpretive schema to the poem's polysemous language, what I ultimately attempt to do in discussing the "public-ness" of *Pearl* with my classes is both to de-center the work and to demystify it, to dislodge it from its rarified courtly milieu and also to provide the tools necessary for students to position it within the broader cultural sweep of fourteenth- and fifteenth-century England. *Pearl* can be an intimidating poem for students approaching it for the first time, largely because many undergraduates (and indeed some graduate students as well) still regard it as the work influentially described by Charles Muscatine over forty years ago as "so completely poetry, [a work] of art, and so little history" (88).

Compounded by the self-evident challenges offered by the poem's dialect, the frustratingly indirect way that the poet creates meaning, and the difficulty that students often have with the poem's slow pace and dialogue-based plot, *Pearl*'s apparent aloofness from the tumult of the fourteenth century can render the work all but unapproachable to students. (*Sir Gawain and the Green Knight*—with its robust hunt scenes, recourse to clearly articulated chivalric values, and easily tracked narrative—tends to be a much easier sell for most students.) Grounding *Pearl* in a broader cultural context and then using the idea of the poem's public voice as a central point of discussion can, in my experience, help students locate a point of entry into a work that may seem impenetrable, especially compared with more commonly taught Middle English works such as *Sir Gawain* and *The Canterbury Tales*.

What I want to insist on here, however—and what I insist on to my students as well—is that such a "public" approach to *Pearl* should in no way replace other critical insights into the poem as a meditation on personal loss, as a work of Christian didacticism, as a courtly commission, or as an aesthetic poetic object without parallel. These established critical frames are central to our understanding of *Pearl*, and to ignore them would be to do a great disservice to the work and also to provide an incomplete picture of its many poetic facets. But *Pearl* is a capacious piece of literature, and the very additive properties that propel its richly suggestive language can be extended to the poem as a whole. How, we might ask our students, can a poem that seems so focused on the salvation of the individual soul also be directed to a communal end, toward a regional or even national "vision of communal harmony" (Middleton 114)? How can the sophisticated punning, intricate poetics, and rich wordplay that make the poem both so rewarding and so frustrating also be commensurate with "the characteristic embodied voice of Ricardian public poetry," whose "social tone . . . is that of an observant and enlightened citizen among peers" (114)? How can the difficult and sometimes caustic dialectic between the heavenly Pearl-Maiden and the earthbound Dreamer also impress upon a late medieval reader a "new importance to secular life, the civic virtues, and communal service" (95)? The keyword, both in the sentences above and in the classroom itself, is *also*.

Indeed, we might ultimately find ourselves answering these questions in the negative, arguing that *Pearl* is finally a work less interested in the commune than in the individual within it, less interested in the Dreamer's perilously human world of "civic virtues" than in the celestial absolutes described by the uncompromising figure of the Pearl-Maiden. At the very least, however, the notion that Middle English poetry can contain the activist ethos ascribed to it by Middleton is a useful heuristic for students struggling with *Pearl*'s hyper-metaphoric language and intimidatingly austere theology. More positively, I have found that discussing the public voice in *Pearl* can give students a new way to articulate (and in some cases reconcile) the turbulent contradictions that seethe beneath the poem's seemingly placid surface: the struggle that the poem stages between submission to God and human desire; the inherent contingencies of knowledge implied by the Dreamer's uncertain vision; the well-rehearsed debate between the elegiac and allegorical frames of the poem itself. Such tensions, articulated more broadly, have to do with the expectations of the individual within society, the way that we mourn, the way that we know what we know, and the way that we reconcile ourselves to the will of a power greater than ourselves (even if doing so runs against our own individual desires and impulses). If *Pearl* is a poem that addresses such tensions, then it is also a poem that, by necessity, strives for a public voice. What is most fascinating about this tightly constructed poem, I think, is considering how it strives for that voice even against the contours of its own rigid and uncompromising poetic form, against the crenellations of its hermetic and semimystical theology, and against its removed courtly pedigree.

NOTE

My thanks to Geoffrey Morrison of Simon Fraser University for allowing me to discuss his fine paper "Repetition, Ritual, and Link-Words in *Pearl*: An Expatriate Poetics?" in this essay.

Teaching the Allegory and Symbolism of *Pearl*

Ann Meyer and Jane Beal

When teachers are considering the pedagogical ramifications of trying to teach the allegory and symbolism of the exquisitely beautiful fourteenth-century dream-vision poem called *Pearl*, key questions emerge:

> How can a teacher help students perceive *Pearl*'s multiple layers of meaning?
>
> What is medieval allegory? How can a teacher explain *Pearl*'s allegorical sense to students?
>
> Within the complex process of interpretation demanded by *Pearl*'s multivalent verse, what key symbols do students need to understand in order to read the poem well?

Teaching *Pearl's* Genres and the Four Levels of Scriptural Interpretation

One way to introduce students to *Pearl*'s multiple layers of meaning is to introduce them to the genres with which the poem has been associated in literary criticism. Another way is to teach how medieval students and scholars read scripture (as well as poetry) for its fourfold meaning. By providing these two contexts, the teacher gives students interpretive tools from both modern scholarship and the medieval past.

Pearl is a dream vision that shares characteristics with elegies, allegories, consolations, and revelations (Beal, *Signifying Power* 7–10). An elegy might be defined as a poem memorializing a beloved person who has died, and an allegory is a narrative with more than one level of meaning, literally and spiritually. A consolation (*consolatio*) is a poem that attempts to comfort the lyric speaker and, by extension, those sharing in the speaker's experience through reading. A revelation (*revelatio*) records a prophetic vision (or audition) of truth shown (or spoken) by God to a human being about the present or the future. Examples of revelations abound in both prose and poetry, not only in the canonical scriptures but also in visions recorded by medieval contemplatives and by the poets influenced by the contemplative, visionary, mystical tradition.

In the Middle Ages theologians read sacred scripture for four simultaneously present levels of meaning in the text: literal, allegorical, moral, and anagogical. The literal meaning concerned the historical sense of the text. The allegorical meaning concerned spiritual matters. The moral sense, sometimes also known as the tropological sense, showed how readers should apply to their own lives what they learned from the text. The anagogical sense revealed eschatological aspects of the future as understood in the Christian worldview (e.g., the Second Coming of Christ, the Last Judgment, heaven, the afterlife, eternity). These levels of meanings are readily summed up in a Latin phrase: "Litera gesta docet, quod credas allegoria, / moralis quid agas, quo tendas anagogia" ("The literal sense teaches deeds, allegory what you believe, the moral what you are doing, the anagogical where you are going").

When university scholars, often theologians in training (priests and monks), had learned this method of interpretation, they applied it not only to their interpretation of scripture but also to their interpretation of classical literature, as a means of redeeming classical works for Christian use. The method also produced diverse retellings of classical myths and Christian commentaries on them; these retellings found allegorical, spiritual truths in the myths despite their original secular sense. New poems in the vernacular languages of England and Europe were often translations of the Judeo-Christian Bible and stories from that Greco-Roman past or amalgamations of these two traditions.

Most interesting, poets composing in the vernacular languages could anticipate that their readers might apply this layered approach as well. The *Pearl* poet seems to have expected his readers to approach his poem literally as an elegy, spiritually as an allegory, morally as a consolation, and anagogically as a revelation.

Teachers can explain this information on genre and the four levels of meaning in a lecture. It may help to have a brief discussion before the lecture begins, asking those students who have read the poem (in part or whole) what they believe is happening, literally, in the plot of *Pearl* and what aspects of the poem seem to be nonliteral, spiritual, or suggestive of another layer of meaning. Students often perceive that *Pearl* is operating on more than one level of signification, even if they do not yet have the critical, scholarly, and medieval literary background to fully understand how it is done. Asking them questions first can provoke curiosity about the wider medieval world of which *Pearl* was a part. This kind of dialogue presents the opportunity to invite students into a deeper understanding of allegory and allegoresis.

Teaching Medieval Allegory and Pearl's Allegorical Meaning

Pearl is identified correctly as a dream vision: the poem begins with an account of a man falling asleep; it progresses with a narrative of his dream, including a vision of the New Jerusalem; the poem ends soon after the man wakes up. One must also note that the poem draws upon other forms of medieval literary expression—not only elegy, allegory, consolation, and revelation but also homily, hagiography, and courtly romance. *Pearl* is a careful synthesis of genres, yet the poet chose dream vision as the form best suited to ideas he wished to convey and responses he wished to elicit from his audience.

The dream vision encourages participation in the allegorical process. For the medieval artist, the supreme model for this genre is the last book of the New Testament, the Apocalypse (the Revelation to John). Biblical dreams often unveil or reveal divinity.

Medieval audiences of *Pearl* would have recognized a dream as a liminal space between wakefulness and the divine world. It is in a dream, for example, that Jacob sees a ladder stretching from earth to heaven, upon which angels ascend and descend. It is in a dream that John is shown visions of the Last Judgment and the Heavenly Jerusalem. Medieval audiences would have understood the dream as akin to an otherworldly journey (like Dante's pilgrimage through hell, purgatory, and paradise). Indeed, dreaming is like stepping over the threshold of a Gothic church: the entrance to space specifically crafted to be a symbol of the New Jerusalem. Passages from liturgies for the dedication of medieval churches make clear this relation between church building and its signification of heaven on earth (C. Wilson 8; Meyer 69–97).

Before Jacob goes to sleep, sees his vision, and hears God, he lays his head on a rock. To understand the allegorical craft of *Pearl* with its multiple meanings of the pearl as object, we may turn to the medieval interpretation of Jacob's rock or stone pillow. A medieval Christian audience understood the rock as signifying Christ, the head of humankind, Saint Paul's mystical vision, the church, the Incarnation, the pilgrim's progress from ascent to total trust in God, and the mystical journey from the temporal to the eternal (Jeffrey 388). After his dream, Jacob anointed the rock, identifying it as a sacred place, a place where God is present. With this act Jacob offers more allegorical possibilities for the stone pillow. Augustine, Bede, and Bonaventura suggest that it is a figure of other sacred edifices in the Bible: for example, the Ark of the Covenant, Solomon's Temple, the city of Jerusalem, the human body as temple, the anagogical crown of them all, and the description of the New Jerusalem in the closing chapters of the Revelation to John. The fact that *Pearl*, too, ends with a vision within a dream, in which the Dreamer beholds the New Jerusalem, is profoundly significant.

Recognized as a masterpiece of late medieval literature, *Pearl* offers superb opportunities to introduce students to a complex, sophisticated tradition of allegorical craft and interpretation. Advanced students familiar with the allegorical tradition can study how the poem engages theology, biblical exegesis, mysticism, and the symbolic programs of medieval art and architecture. At the heart of the relation between *Pearl* and other medieval literary and cultural achievements is the author's understanding of the image as a location for spiritual transformation.

But should allegory itself be understood as a genre in the case of *Pearl*? On the surface the answer seems obvious—yes, it should be—but the question is complicated by deeper contexts of medieval expression and interpretation. Other terms may seem to be used interchangeably with allegory: *metaphor, figure*, or *sign*, for example. In their study of *Pearl* and allegory, students will require, therefore, a discussion of relevant terminology.

The word *allegory* combines the Greek *allos* ("other") and *agoreuein* ("to speak"). The meaning conveyed by the Greek, *allegoria*, then, is "to speak otherwise," "to say other things." The single use of the word (as a participle) *allêgoroumena* in the New Testament appears in Paul's Letter to the Galatians (4.24) to designate the relation between Old and New Covenants. Other uses of the word and its related forms appear in writings of major theologians in the medieval West. Augustine, for example, cites Paul's Letter to the Galatians and glosses it with the phrase "quae sunt aliud ex alio significantia" ("which things signify one thing by another"; *De Trinitate* 15.9; see also *Civitate Dei* 15.18–19). Ancient and medieval writers used *allegory* and its related verbal and adjectival forms in conjunction with, and often as a substitution for, a whole range of terms to designate identical or closely related meanings. These terms include *symbolon* ("symbol"), *figura* ("figure"), *signum* ("sign"), *imago* ("image"), *eikon* ("icon"), and *aenigma* ("enigma"). Augustine shows great flexibility in his use of *allegoria* and *figura* in biblical exegesis, not wishing to distinguish these terms from the Pauline *typos* (*figura* in 1 Corinthians 10.6) and *typikôs* (*figura* in 1 Corinthians 10.11) or from *similitude, umbra, sacramentum, mysteria*, and *imago*.

Students must also be aware that the term *allegory* has often been used to designate a technique or system of interpretation. Medieval theologians conceived of a multileveled system of biblical exegesis, with terms such as *literal, typological, tropological*, and *anagogical* serving as specific designations for different levels of meaning. Thomas Aquinas offers an excellent summary of this interpretation in his *Summa Theologica*: "Whether in Holy Scripture a word may have several meanings" (question 1, article 10).

Not without a great deal of subsequent response from literary critics, Dante famously adapted the allegorical system used by the theologians to discuss ways of reading his own poetry. In book 2 of *Convivio*, for example, Dante describes four levels of meaning: 1) the literal, "which does not extend beyond the letter of the fictive discourse"; 2) the allegorical, which is "hidden under the cloak of fables, a truth disguised under a beautiful lie"; 3) the moral, which "teachers should seek out with most diligence when going through texts, because of its usefulness to them and to their pupils"; and 4) the anagogical, which is the "sense beyond . . . when a spiritual interpretation is to be given a test which . . . represents the supreme things belonging to eternal glory by means of the things it represents."

Students might understand the *Pearl* poet's interest in allegory not by definitions and terminology used in the poem itself, but by recognizing ways the poet engages in the activity and display of medieval allegory. The poet demonstrates through his craft a sophisticated familiarity with the ramifications of medieval discussions on allegoresis, such as those cited by Augustine, Aquinas, and Dante. When students discuss the genre of *Pearl*, therefore, they need to perceive allegory as an activity rather than a form.

Using a symbolic program similar to what we find in great Gothic accomplishments—number symbolism, iconographic imagery, biblical references, liturgy and sacramental activity, structural symmetries, and geometrical combinations of the circular and the vertical—the poet engages in allegorical craft to communicate to an audience that he assumes to be familiar with allegorical interpretation. Allegory may be understood in *Pearl*, then, as corresponding activities of creativity and interpretation. Experiencing *Pearl* as an allegory is a process, a movement of mind and soul that began with the artist's inspiration and that he expressed through words as images meant to move the audience to increased spiritual awareness. Just before the Dreamer wakes, he is shown an image of the New Jerusalem. Yet sustained revelation (for the Dreamer or for the audience) is not the goal of the allegorical poem; learning and love for God is. The poem ends with an activity of intimacy with the divine that may be repeated on earth in the form of the sacrament of the Eucharist.

Furthermore, the symbolic program of *Pearl* is evidence of a poet immersed in the visual and intellectual traditions of late medieval Western Europe, including, specifically, architectural achievements. When contextualizing the poem's symbolism, teachers would be justified, therefore, in showing slides of the Sainte-Chapelle in Paris. Showing such slides is a useful way to demonstrate how the poem takes part of a developed allegorical tradition that uses symbols to convey complex layers of meaning.

To explore the medieval architectural analogy, note that *Pearl* is more like Louis IX's royal Sainte-Chapelle—a superb jewel of the late Gothic flamboyant style—than the massive Gothic cathedrals in Paris, Chartres, Lincoln, or York. This analogy will help students appreciate the late medieval commitment to the potential artistic virtuosity of smaller spaces and forms and how the *Pearl* poet responds to that commitment. Other examples of this late medieval interest in what art historians have called micro-architecture can be observed in images of private chapels and in embellished devotional objects such as reliquaries, altarpieces, and illuminated manuscripts.

The analogy between *Pearl* and late medieval private chapels is quite useful in discussions of allegory and symbolism because it allows students to see how relations among different medieval forms of expression extend beyond surface similarities. The more one understands *Pearl* as allegorical craft that uses images as symbols, the more one imagines the poet giving shape to light and color in order to lead his audience along a path of spiritual transformation. One appreciates more fully that the author of *Pearl* chose words for his art of Gothic revelation, just as architects used stone and glass.

Teaching Key Images as Symbols in Pearl

Within the extraordinary structure of *Pearl*, crafted so exquisitely that it has been compared to a crown, a reliquary, and a cathedral (Bishop; Chaganti; Meyer), are many vivid images that serve a symbolic function. The imagery and symbolism of the poem are associated with the three dominant colors, the three major landscapes, and the three major characters of the poem. To continue the architectural comparison, if *Pearl* is like a cathedral, its images are like stained-glass windows: light shines through them, illuminating their many possible symbolic interpretations.

Pearl is a poem suffused with light that particularly shines on three symbolic colors: white, gold, and red. The whiteness of the symbolic pearl, and the Pearl-Maiden, naturally stands for purity; the gold associated with the Maiden and the New Jerusalem, for holiness; and the red, pouring forth from the Lamb's wounded side, for the passion of Christ and its redemptive power. The poet makes vivid use of other colors as well: black in the earthly garden (or burial ground), blue and silver (associated with the extraordinary trees) in the paradisial landscape of the dream vision. But the foremost colors of the poem are white, gold, and red. This can be seen also in the manuscript illustrations in which, strikingly, the Dreamer is dressed in red and the Maiden is dressed in white, bringing to mind the scriptural verse: "Though your sins be as red as scarlet, they shall be white as snow" (Isa. 1.18).

The three major landscapes of the poem are themselves richly symbolic. The garden at the beginning is reminiscent of the *hortus conclusus* ("enclosed garden") of the Song of Solomon, which was later associated with the Virgin Mary. It has both sacred and secular connotations, especially when considered in the tradition of courtly romance literature. The paradisial landscape of the dream vision is suggestive of Eden, the medieval English imaginative conception of the Far East (especially India, which is mentioned at line 76), and key literary precursors, like the garden with its stream near the top of the purgatorial mountain in Dante's *Divine Comedy*, in which Dante, the dreamer-pilgrim, encounters Matilda. The New Jerusalem, which the Dreamer sees in a vision within his dream, invokes the entire symbolic network of biblical precedent, including Pauline rabbinic midrash on Isaiah, Jeremiah, and Genesis (in Romans 11 and Galatians 4.21–31), Hebrews 12.22, and John's Revelation 3 and 21, as well as Augustinian theology and the tradition of medieval Apocalypse manuscript illustrations. Each of these three landscapes contains features that are themselves symbols in miniature: the plants in the earthly garden (such as the gromwell, for example, with white nutlets that look so much like pearls), the stream in the paradisial landscape of the dream vision, and the gates of pearl in the New Jerusalem.

Interestingly, each of the main characters of *Pearl* dominates one of the landscapes: the Dreamer in the garden, the Maiden in the paradisial dreamscape, and the Lamb in the New Jerusalem. At different points on his spiritual journey, the Dreamer is connected with animal imagery and symbolism. The poet compares the Dreamer to a mild hawk (line 184), a startled doe (345–48), and a dazed quail (1085). The Maiden is connected not only to the central symbol of the poem, the pearl, but also to the flower (962) and the rose (269–70), which is appropriate to her depiction as a beloved courtly lady. Christ is depicted as the bleeding Lamb (1135–37) and invoked in the poem's closing allusions to the Eucharist (1209–10), which, teachers can explain to students unfamiliar with medieval Catholic theology, is Christ's body, broken for the salvation of humanity.

The central symbol of the poem is, of course, the pearl. The symbolic pearl undergoes transformation as the poem progresses. As A. C. Spearing has observed, the symbol develops just as the narrative does, from a lost gemstone to the Pearl-Maiden to the kingdom of heaven itself (Spearing, "Symbolic and Dramatic Development" 1–12). Just as in the Parable of the Pearl of Great Price, the pearl stands for the kingdom of heaven: to obtain it is to enjoy salvation and redemption forever.

In an undergraduate classroom, one straightforward way to help students discern the imagery and symbolic value of *Pearl* is to divide the students into small groups, assign to each group one of these five categories (color, landscape,

Dreamer, Maiden, Christ) along with key lines or passages (previously identified by the instructor), and ask students to discuss and then report back to the class on what they have discovered on these questions:

> What symbolic images (or qualities) are associated with colors, landscapes, and characters (Dreamer, Maiden, and Christ) in *Pearl*?
> Is there a pattern of development in these symbolic images?
> What is the significance of this complex symbolism in relation to the themes of the poem?

The teacher can either begin or end with reflection on the central symbol, the pearl, or interweave key thoughts into the classroom discussion. Using *Power-Point*, *Prezi*, or another type of presentation technology, the instructor may also wish to project images from the *Pearl* manuscript as well as other medieval manuscripts and architectural structures to reinforce student understanding of symbolism in the poem.

The poet's "pearl" can be understood allegorically as gemstone, Maiden, New Jerusalem, the poem itself, and the audience of the poem for the pearl is an invitation, transfiguration, location, and occasion for revelation. In teaching *Pearl*, whether referring to Jacob's rock or the poet's gemstone, multiple meanings are not mutually exclusive. Rather, many meanings are both correct and simultaneous. For an audience to engage in the process of interpretation, then, is to participate in the divine visions of dreamers themselves. The reader as allegorical interpreter is the soul always in motion on spiritual pilgrimage.

This emphasis on simultaneous layers of meaning, together with sustained movement of the mind and soul through interpretation, is a key element of allegorical sophistication. It is akin to liturgical process and symbolism: procession, gesture, prayer and song, responsive attentiveness, participation with all the senses, in silence and in physical communication on a journey of spiritual renewal and transformation. While some readers may be inclined to associate allegory with abstract thought through personification, this association is wholly inaccurate in complex medieval allegory. A character named Avarice, or Greed, does not require interpretation. Personification of an idea requires little reflection on the meaning to be conveyed. Complex allegory, however, similar to the one we see in *Pearl*, requires the reader to participate as pilgrim, as dreamer in constant movement toward beatitude.

Lingering at one level of the process—at one of the rungs on Jacob's ladder —is stagnation. Stagnation relates to iconoclasm; it is complacency to reside at a particular level of meaning that is in itself inadequate as an expression of the divine. The apocalyptic, paradisial landscape of the dream, the earthly realm of possible unveiling, must be one that is always in flux: it requires the activity of interpretive journey. The goal of complex allegory in this tradition is divine revelation, the beatific vision, a glimpse of the light and love of God.

NOTE

Our thanks to Geoffrey Morrison of Simon Fraser University for allowing us to discuss his fine paper "Repetition, Ritual, and Link-Words in *Pearl*: An Expatriate Poetics?" in this essay.

Structures of Meaning in *Pearl*

John V. Fleming

The Middle English *Pearl* is one of the most beautiful poems in our literature, but the contemporary student is likely to be precluded from its easy appreciation by several daunting problems. Its language is very difficult—considerably more difficult than that of Chaucer. It is full of unfamiliar dialect words, often chosen to satisfy the technical requirements of alliteration. Its narrative element is slight and its precise subject matter—concerning which even medievalists are by no means of one mind—often elusive. The poem is intimately related to, and founded upon, several biblical texts and especially to the twenty-first chapter of the Apocalypse, among the least accessible of scriptural books, which few students will ever have read. The poet holds many complex and precise medieval theological ideas. Some of these he expounds, but many he simply assumes. Only the learned among his contemporary audience could possibly have followed him confidently. Today's American undergraduate faces a wall of forbidding alterity.

Under these circumstances some preliminary study of the poem's *structure* may offer a convenient way into it. In general the best preparation for reading difficult poetry is having read a number of difficult poems beforehand. My own experience regarding the *Pearl*, however, is that the engineer is often better placed than the literature major. For however dark and speculative may be the *meanings* to be drawn from the text, the poet manifestly advances them in a form that practically cries out for the sort of technical analysis that will be congenial to students with mathematical aptitude, to those with some formal training in musical theory, and to those interested in games and puzzles based in cybernetic code. The most obvious features of the poem's structure, easily observable to even the most inexperienced student of medieval poetry, are the numerical *regularity* of its individual stanzas (twelve lines each), the conspicuous *irregularity* of its number of stanzas (101), and the highly suggestive link words used to suture the stanzas together. A teacher may or may not want to push a student in one or another direction in the *interpretation* of these phenomena. Simply pointing out their existence provides an excellent pedagogical entry to the poem.

All poetry deserves as much autonomy as it can convincingly claim. One should be wary of trying to impose upon it some a priori, universalizing theory. At the same time, however, it would be foolish when approaching the question of the structure of the *Pearl* to eschew the useful suggestions of cultural context literary tradition. *Pearl* is in the first place an *allegory*. The "story" of the poem—a narrator lost a pearl in a garden and then talks about it and to it (or her) at great length—is not the "meaning" of the poem. Allegory, as defined by one standard medieval authority, is *alieniloquium*: saying one thing to mean another. The figure of the pearl "means" something other than a dense, spherical concretion reflexively formed within the shell of a living oyster and regarded as a gem. Some interpreters of the poem think its primary meaning is the narrator's dead young daughter, whom he laments. Others think it must mean something more abstract—the primal innocence of humanity lost in the Garden of Eden, perhaps. It could "mean" both of these things, of course, and more besides, even as the poet develops his ideas, whatever they may be, with such literal details as the beauty, luster, roundness, and extraordinary value of an actual pearl.

One text of undoubted relevance in equating the pearl with the highest spiritual good is Matthew 13.45, "The kingdom of heaven is like a merchant in search of fine pearls; on finding one pearl of great value [*una pretiosa margarita*] he went and sold all that he had and bought it." The modern English connotations of *jeweler* stress craftsmanship. The best translation of Middle English *jueler* is "trader in jewels." Hence we have in a scriptural text that is very frequently commented upon in the Middle Ages and, taken as a homiletic theme, an explicit grounding for the poem's two *dramatis personae*: the jeweler and the jewel that is the object of his attention.

The mode of allegory imposes no particular *structure* on a poem, but it does encourage us to be receptive to the possibility of recurrent allegorical techniques solidly identified in other medieval works. With regard to *Pearl*, it may suggest at least a useful structural pattern. Many medieval allegories are first-person narratives in which the narrator, beginning in a despairing and unenlightened state, undergoes through one or more interlocutors a process of education that leaves him enlightened, joyous, and purposeful. Two such very famous books— both of which have been convincingly linked with *Pearl*—are *The Consolation of Philosophy* by Boethius and Dante's *Divine Comedy*.

Our approach to *Pearl* may be illuminated by commonplaces of medieval literary tradition broadly conceived, but there is also a specific local context of crucial importance. The *Pearl* exists in a unique manuscript—Cotton Nero A. x, in the British Library. There it is in the company of several other excellent alliterative poems, also unique, which like the *Pearl* have been assigned names by modern scholars. Three of these—*Patience*, *Cleanness* (also called *Purity*), and *Sir Gawain and the Green Knight*—are, along with the *Pearl* itself, usually believed to be the work of a single author, often called the *Gawain* poet or the *Pearl* poet. Each of these poems has its uniqueness, but they do reveal a common artistic core reflecting what most scholars take to be the signature of a single creator.

The two other major *overtly* religious poems of the *Pearl* poet, *Patience* and *Cleanness*, are like *Pearl* closely linked to specific and identifiable scriptural texts. They also show evidence of what in the Middle Ages often accompanied biblical text: commonplace associations from the vast body of allegorical exegesis that was the principal fruit of biblical study in that age. A prominent theme in allegorical exegesis was number symbolism.

Sir Gawain and the Green Knight is a secular poem in the sense that its hero is a familiar figure in Arthurian romance. The folkloristic quest he pursues—he is seeking the remote habitation of a mysterious green knight, where he has every reason to expect to find death—is not biblical. But Christian and biblical themes are everywhere in the poem, which is replete with symbolism of various kinds. This conspicuously includes number symbolism, especially symbolism relating to the number *five*. There are many suggestions that the number *five* is thematically and *structurally* significant. Gawain's mystical sign is the pentangle (the "endless knot" in the form of a five-pointed star). The poem's stanzas each have twenty-five—the square of five—lines. Of particular interest for *Pearl* is that *Sir Gawain* is also composed of one hundred and one stanzas.

As we shall see, this peculiar number is almost certainly related to the learned scriptural exegesis on which the poet draws. If we look at the poems of this manuscript as a group, we do indeed see the evidence of a serious theological education. But we find no less evidence of his familiarity with some of the greatest of his vernacular poetic predecessors. The textual echoes of the *Divine Comedy* adduced by the learned editors of the *Pearl* are so numerous as to strongly suggest the poet's familiarity with Dante's poem. In *Cleanness* he alludes by name to Jean de Meun and the *Roman de la Rose*, of which there are also clear textual reminiscences in *Pearl*.

The manuscript itself gives some clear indication of obviously intended patterns of formal division. The first of these, signaled by the distribution of twenty calligraphically prominent decorated majuscule initial letters, establishes twenty subdivisions of the text. Nineteen of these consist of five twelve-line stanzas, or sixty lines each. There is one anomaly, necessitated by the poet's possibly puzzling decision to have a *hundred and one* stanzas rather than an even hundred. One subdivision (the fifteenth, stanzas 71–76, lines 841–912) has *six* stanzas.

Within the twenty textual divisions initiated by the majuscule letters there are certain clear patterns of verbal repetitions or keywords that help a reader discern the flow of the argument. For example, the first line of the first stanza is "Perle plesaunte to prynces paye . . . " and its twelfth line is "Of þat pryuy perle withouten spot." The key idea of the stanza, repeated fugally in each of the following four stanzas of the first division is "pearl without spot"—the immaculate "Pearl-Maiden." We note, however, that "spot" usually means "blemish" (*macula*) but sometimes has the quite different meaning of "place" (*locus*). The keywords of the twenty sections are:

1. *perle, spot*
2. *dubbement* (and variants), meaning "adorned"
3. *more, more and more*
4. *precious, perles,* and *pyȝte* (and variants), "set" or "adorned" [with jewels]
5. *juel, jueler* ("jewel," "jeweler" [the narrator who has lost the jewel])
6. *deme* (and variants), from Old English *deman* ("judge," "deem," "doom")
7. *bliss* and *ground of all my blisse*
8. *Quen of cortaysye* (and variants) "The Queen of Courtesy," "the Virgin Mary"
9. *date* ("end" or "goal"; as "appointed time" date in the modern sense)
10. *þe more*
11. *the grace of God is great enough* (with slight variants)
12. *innocence, innocent*
13. *makel[l]eȝ* ("spotless") several times with *perle*
14. *Jerusalem*
15. *lesse, never, never þe lesse*
16. *with-outen mote* ("blemish"); in one stanza simply *mote*
17. *apostel John* often with *Apocalyppce*
18. *mone* ("moon") sometimes with *sun*
19. *delyt*; usually *gret delyt* ("great delight")
20. *pay[e]*; usually *prynces paye*

The keywords unify the stanzas within each of the twenty subdivisions. They also, by concatenation, link each subdivision with the one immediately following it. Thus the final word in the first section (60) is the keyword, *spot*. The same word is the first noun in the first line of section (line 61).

Like several other aspects of the poem, the keywords or link words have been much discussed, and most commentators agree that they provide generally accurate suggestions concerning the themes and subject matter dealt with in any particular grouping of stanzas. One obviously relevant theme is the relation of loss and gain, less and more.

There are two anomalies that in a poem so carefully constructed can hardly be accidental and that therefore invite explanation. (1) The poet obviously found it important that there be 101 stanzas in the whole poem. His decision precluded the possibility of the tidiness of an even century uniformly divided into twenty subdivisions of five stanzas apiece. The necessarily "extra" stanza is assigned to the fifteenth group. The keywords of this group point to plenitude, and the first of its stanzas actually preserves the proverb "The more the merrier." This group uniquely has *seventy-two* lines and includes the *seventy-second* stanza, which Israel Gollancz, responding to earlier suggestions, skeptically allowed "may represent a discarded stanza that has been against the poet's intention copied by the first copyist" (Gollancz 157). (2) There is no verbal concatenation linking the twelfth and thirteenth sections—at lines 720–21.

We are likely to think of number symbolism as something so artificial and extrinsic as to mean little more than precious decoration; but that is very far from the typical thought of Antiquity, the Middle Ages, and the Renaissance. It was an ancient Greek philosopher, Pythagoras, who declared *number* to be the fundamental building block of the universe. Christian exegetes endlessly expounded the Hellenistic scriptural verse that held that God has laid out "all things in number, weight, and measure" (Wisd. 11.20), terms that also became fundamental in the vocabulary of musical theory. The artists—verbal, pictorial, or architectural—were responding to a sacramental view of reality according to which, in Saint Paul's words, the invisible things of God were made known in His visible creation. In other words the numerological poet was not, from his own point of view, dealing in an extrinsic and artificially imposed device. Rather, he was like the sculptor who sees his task as releasing the form imprisoned in the marble block.

To be a realistic artist demanded the depiction of what was *really*, and not just phenomenally, there: harmony, the silent music of the spheres. The fundamental numerical harmonic ratio was that of the diapason, 2:1, which in theological terms characterized the hypostatic union in Christ, wherein divinity and humanity joined in a single unity. As we shall see, the *Pearl* poet's choice of the *twelve*-line stanza reflects the duodecimal architecture of the heavenly Jerusalem, but he has constructed the stanzas in two metrically identifiable divisions of *eight* and *four*. In creating the anomalous section 15 with its *six* stanzas, the intellectual caesura at 4:2 punctuates the description of the "new song" sung before the throne of God.

There have been several numerological studies of the poem, of which in this essay I touch on but three. *Pearl* follows the typical comic plot of many medieval allegories dealing with the "education of the narrator," of which the *Consolation of Philosophy* is the typifying text. The narrator begins in dejection and despair at the loss of the pearl; he is instructed at length by the *Pearl* girl; finally, in a state of incremental enlightenment, he describes the beauty of the heavenly Jerusalem, ending in a state of religious exaltation. Approximately equal passages of the poem are devoted to each of the three stages. In an article written nearly eighty years ago, Coolidge Chapman argued that this structure was a response to Dante's numerological interests in the *Divine Comedy* with its tripartite schema of Hell: Purgatory: Heaven. Dante resolved the problem of his "extra" canto by placing it at the very beginning of the poem. According to Chapman the first section of the *Pearl* consists of the first thirty-three stanzas, the second section of the next thirty-two, and the third of the next thirty-four. The final two "extra" stanzas make up a kind of summary coda at the end of the whole poem. Though the argument is not entirely convincing, the characterization of the poem's three movements is hard to fault, and many of Chapman's incidental numerological observations are acute.

Maren-Sofie Røstvig, the most committed of the numerologists, seems to have been unaware of Chapman's essay. She suggests an alternative two-part structure, with the division point coming at the end of the sixtieth stanza between the twelfth and thirteenth larger divisions. Røstvig's theory is that the unique and therefore conspicuous absence of verbal concatenation here signals a definitive thematic transition, also numerologically suggested by the relation of the *twelve* divisions in the first part (twelve being the number of months, and therefore of human calendrical time) and the *eight* divisions of the second (eight being the mythic and reduplicative number of the ages of the world. This hypothesis is weakened, in my view, by the proposed division at lines 721–22 coming in the middle of a continuous speech.

The suggestion of numerological structural patterns is always strengthened by explicit textual reference to the numbers involved. In *Sir Gawain and the Green Knight* repeated textual references to the number *five* practically require the reader to consider that number in terms of theme and structure. In *Pearl* the corresponding number is *twelve*. The textually obvious source is the duodecimal theme in the architecture of the New Jerusalem of the Apocalypse, and the 144,000 (12 x 12 x 100) virgins, among whom is the pearl-girl, who adore the Lamb (Rev. 14). This book of the Bible is itself manifestly constructed on numerological principles, as medieval exegetes recognized. It is this obvious and textually explicit scriptural element that differentiates the *Pearl* from the large number of other medieval English twelve-line stanzas cataloged by Susanna Greer Fein ("Twelve-Line Stanza Forms").

The most conspicuous numerological features of *Pearl* have to do with the numbers *twelve* (the number of lines in each stanza) and the number of stanzas: *one hundred and one*. This means, happily, that the total number of lines is the reduplicative 1212, the elements of the diapason. But what of the 101 stanzas? Some scholars have so much wanted the poem to have an even 100 that they have been willing to impute a glaring mistake either to the poet or to his copyist. Their view cannot be accepted, unless we are willing to offer the same hypothesis concerning *Sir Gawain and the Green Knight*, which also has 101 stanzas. To paraphrase Oscar Wilde, to miscount the number of stanzas in one poem would be carelessness; to make the same blunder in a second poem, disqualifying innumeracy. The most committed of the numerological critics, Røstvig, writes: "We must take our stand on the fact that the poem totals 101 stanzas, neither more nor less, and that this is the only possible number for the particular poem in view of its subject matter" (328).

Røstvig believes that the primary significance of the number is culmination or consummation: one century finished and another begun. That the poem's end is in its beginning is textually demonstrable:

> Perle plesaunte to prynces paye . . .   (1)
> And precious perles unto his pay   (1212)

Like the pearl, praised in the poem as *endeleʒ rounde* (738), the poem itself has a perfect circularity.

There is also an exegetical explanation linked to several of the poem's principal themes, especially that of loss trumped by paradoxical gain. More than thirty years ago, I published an essay drawing attention to the exegetical tradition of the parable *Exiit qui seminat* 'A sower went out to sow' beginning at Matthew 3.3. (This is the same chapter in which "the pearl of great price" later appears.) The seeds that fell in unsuitable places failed to germinate or soon withered; but some fell on "good soil" and brought forth its increase of grain—some a hundredfold, some sixty, and some thirty (*aliud centesimum, aliud sexagesimum, aliud tricesimum*). The hundredfold increase is called the *centuplum* in another famous text: Jesus's consolatory saying that "everyone who has left houses or brothers or sisters or father or mother or children or fields for my name's sake will receive a hundredfold, and inherit eternal life" (Matt. 19.29).

I adduced as a structural parallel to the *Pearl* the *Arbor vitae* of Ubertino da Casale, a complex fourteenth-century work of ascetic theology replete with number symbolism distributed throughout 101 chapters, but I do not suggest this Franciscan work as a textual source. It is, however, possible to identify the wellspring of most medieval exegesis of *Exiit qui seminat* and of the concept of the *centuplum* in the early Judeo-Christian sermon "De centesima, sexagesima, tricesima" sometimes attributed (erroneously) to Saint Cyprian. Jean Daniélou has demonstrated the wide influence in the early church of this anonymous work produced within an early apocalyptic community (*origins* 59–92). The three gradations of increase are there applied to the rewards of martyrs (line 100), virgins (60), and the faithful, just 30. As martyrdom became mere literary memory, the schema evolved, and it was virginity that gained the centuple. In whatever specific form, however, it is this pattern of thought that lies behind various tripartite schemes of the virtuous life in the Middle Ages—such as the Dowel, Dobet, and Dobest of *Piers Plowman*. In many monastic texts, the hundredfold increase characterizes the virgins, as it does in *Pearl*.

That the poet intentionally exploits such exegetical-theological ideas is highly probable, but they are unlikely to mean much to an undergraduate. Any intelligent student, on the other hand, can appreciate the justice of Røstvig's observation that "the poet was a careful craftsman who was fascinated by the use of formal devices with symbolic implications ..." (328). The two most obvious such devices are the thematically suggestive patterns of the divisional key-words and the mathematical ratios. Once students grasp the fundamentals of the poet's mathematical procedures, they are likely to set off in search of others on their own. In other words, paying close attention to artifice may encourage a kind of close reading that sidesteps some of the poem's intellectual "otherness."

The Relationship between the Pearl-Maiden and the Dreamer

Jane Beal

In classes that I have taught on *Pearl*,[1] four questions generally shape classroom discussions:

> How is the symbol of the pearl transformed throughout the poem?
> What is the nature of the relationship between the Pearl-Maiden and the Dreamer?
> How might we interpret this poem literally, allegorically, morally, and anagogically?
> Is the Dreamer consoled at the end of the poem? If so, how? If not, why not?

The second question, focused on the nature of the relationship between the Pearl-Maiden and the Dreamer, presents nothing less than an interpretive crux. It is also clearly related to the other three questions because the Pearl-Maiden is one manifestation of the poem's pearl symbolism; her character has literal and spiritual dimensions; and the nature of her relationship to the Dreamer has a direct bearing on the kind of consolation he needs and whether he actually receives it.

In order to invite new readers of *Pearl* into a deeper understanding of these interrelated questions, I first decide which text of the poem (Middle English edition, dual-language edition, or stand-alone, modern English translation) to assign depending on the anticipated needs of my students in the level of the course I am teaching. Before we discuss *Pearl* in class, I provide students with a detailed list of questions on *Pearl* in a course manual or online (medievalpearl.wordpress .com/teaching/), which they are supposed to review in conjunction with their at-home reading to help them be prepared. (See the study questions I have provided in the appendix at the end of the volume.) I like to begin by sharing the four illustrations of *Pearl* from the manuscript, projected on-screen in all their glorious color at the front of the classroom;[2] this visual text of the poem gives us the only late medieval commentary on *Pearl*. We are then ready to consider the modern literary-critical reception of the poem and to develop our own views of the nature of the relationship between the Pearl-Maiden and the Dreamer.

Choosing a Text of Pearl

It is important to recognize that most modern editions, translations, online summaries, and literary-critical books and essays do not present the nature of the relationship between the Pearl-Maiden and the Dreamer as an interpretive crux. Instead, these works default to a commonly accepted belief, namely, that the Pearl-Maiden is the Dreamer's daughter who died at two years of age. While this is one possibility, it is not the only one.

As Ian Bishop observes in Pearl *in Its Setting*, the Pearl-Maiden "may have been a godchild, a grandchild, or even a younger sister" (8). All we can know from line 233 of the poem is that she is nearer to him than an aunt or niece (and so, necessarily, is neither his aunt nor his niece). This nearness, however, may refer to physical proximity, family kinship, or emotional intimacy. At least two scholars have suggested that the Pearl-Maiden might have been the Dreamer's beloved (Carson; Beal, "The Pearl-Maiden"). Yet understanding the Pearl-Maiden in these female roles can only apply in the case of a literal interpretation. Spiritual, allegorical, and metaphorical interpretations of her role have also been suggested. As William Henry Schofield once wrote, the poem lacks "any statement of the poet on which to build the prevalent notion that 'the Pearl' . . . is his own child. Never once does he refer to her as such, nor does she a single time refer to him as father" (158).

So how is this wide range of interpretive possibility foreclosed in editions and translations of the poem—and why? This is certainly an important question to ask of students when dealing with textual issues—one of many questions that can point their attention to interpretive cruxes. I encourage making comparisons between editions and translations as I assign stanzas to translate from *Pearl* so students can understand, from experience, just how hard it can be to render Middle English accurately in modern English. At the same time, I find it valuable to give students the history behind this particular crux.

Seeing the Pearl-Maiden and the Dreamer in the narrowly defined relationship of father and daughter began with Richard Morris who, in 1864, edited the poem for the Early English Text Society and offered his interpretation. Morris wrote, "The author evidently gives expression to his own sorrow for the loss of his infant child, a girl of two years old" (qtd. in Conlee, *Middle English Debate Poetry* 3). Many subsequent editors and translators have followed suit in their introductions and prefaces, giving this reading of the poem as their own, including the two translators of the most popular, modern English-only texts: Marie Borroff and J. R. R. Tolkien.

Borroff's translation, more than many others, attempts to maintain the poem's ambiguity about the relationship when representing it in modern English, but she writes in her preface of the "dead infant" (x) and of "the feelings of a father for his lost infant daughter" (xvi). Tolkien acknowledges the existence of the debate between elegiac and allegorical interpretations (10), but he asserts his own view, "The depth of sorrow portrayed for a child so young belongs rather to parenthood ..." (17), and he calls the Dreamer "the father of her body" (17). In lesser-known translations, like those of Victor Watts (2005) and Jane Draycott

(2013), the situation is the same. In the introduction to Draycott's translation, Bernard O'Donoghue claims, "The poem is a religious dream vision, but it is also an elegy for a dead two-year-old daughter by a father sorrowing in . . . 'his prison of sorrow'" (9). The back of the book cover to the Watts translation states: "*Pearl* is one of the greatest English medieval poems, a dream vision that is both a profoundly personal elegy for the Dreamer's lost daughter and a subtle theological debate. . . ."

Similar sentiments are expressed in dual-language editions. In William Vantuono's case, the poet is not considered co-identifiable with the Dreamer, but despite this difference the Pearl-Maiden is still considered the Dreamer's daughter:

> It is conceivable, then, that *Pearl* was written for a nobleman who had lost a young daughter, a man who is perhaps the poet's patron. The father, in grieving over the death of his daughter, questions the ways of God, and this prompts the poet to put himself in the father's place to console him and to attempt to bring him to an understanding of the Lord's ways.   (Pearl: *An Edition* xxiii)

Although he does not call the Dreamer her father, Casey Finch calls the Pearl-Maiden a "little girl" (36). His edition draws on the Middle English version of Malcolm Andrew and Ronald Waldron (reproducing its Middle English text and notes), and these earlier editors see a father-daughter relationship between the Dreamer and the Pearl-Maiden. In their 1978 standard edition of all four poems, Andrew and Waldron write that the pearl is used metaphorically "by the narrator for his dead child" (33). (While still holding to this view in the fifth edition, they acknowledge other possibilities.)

While, like Finch, editors A. C. Cawley and J. J. Anderson do not identify the Dreamer as father outright, they do write of "the loss of a beloved child" (ix), "the loss of a child who was dear to him [the Dreamer]" (x), and "the dead child" (xi), and they compare the poem to the *Olympia* Eclogue in which Boccaccio mourns the death of his five-year-old daughter, Violente; they further consider the possibility that the poet "was recording an actual vision that he had experienced" (xi). Likewise, Sarah Stanbury's introduction to the TEAMS text, intended for undergraduates, declares "[t]hat pearl, we find out, is also a girl, the narrator's two-year-old daughter" (4). Even Ad Putter and Myra Stokes, who could have presented a more complex view of the matter, express a similar view in the most recent critical edition (2014).

Further examples could be given from a number of other translations and editions of *Pearl*. However, only one, Mary Vincent Hillmann's, clearly states in Edward Vasta's introduction that "the relationship between the dreamer and the maiden is not easily defined" (ix). Sister Hillmann herself views the relationship as allegorical. Her 1961 edition, however, is out of print.

Simply stated, nearly all translations or editions of the poem available to new readers of the poem suggest, either directly or indirectly, that the Pearl-Maiden is the Dreamer's daughter. The authority of editors and translators, who are perceived by students as expert interpreters, thus provides a father-daughter reading of the relationship between the Pearl-Maiden and the Dreamer that new readers often simply accept and assume. Why would they question it when the text their professor assigned endorses it?[3]

This situation means that any teacher of the poem will necessarily be faced with a number of students who assume a father-daughter relationship between the two protagonists of this poem. This number grows when students read on-line summaries from *Wikipedia* and other sites. When trying to consider the complexities of the relationship, the teacher will then be working against that assumption—if, indeed, the teacher chooses to address the issue at all. For the teachers themselves were once new readers of *Pearl* who encountered the poem in these very same translations and editions, and their understanding may have been shaped thereby. Yet there are ways to overcome, or work through, this assumption: analysis of the four manuscript illustrations of *Pearl* and consideration of the literary-critical perspectives in *Pearl* scholarship open up the interpretive possibilities.

Using the Four Manuscript Illustrations to Begin Classroom Discussion

The four *Pearl*-related manuscript illustrations are not interspersed throughout the poem; rather, they preface it. A late medieval English reader holding the manuscript and turning the pages in order would therefore see the images first, and perhaps meditate on them. Situated as they are, the miniature paintings may make an impression on a reader emotively and hint at major plot developments in the poem to come—perhaps even pique the reader's curiosity about the characters and the situations they are in. The questions that arise in readers' minds can compel them forward into the text of the poem much as a hook pulls a fish through the water.

As already mentioned, the illustrations constitute the only late medieval commentary on the poem. The manuscript did not circulate widely and has very little marginalia; because it was not rediscovered and published until the nineteenth century, little commentary on it was made before then. So what story do the illustrations tell? What snapshots from the plot of the poem do they provide? Do they give any insight into the relationship between two of the three major characters in the poem?

My students and I have observed that in the first illustration, we see a garden setting with the Dreamer dressed in a loose-fitting, red robe with large sleeves;

he has a blond beard and wavy hair. Foliage surrounds him. He is asleep in the garden beside a darkened patch that looks like a human body lying on its side, back to the Dreamer, and we see that the Dreamer's hands are reaching out toward the lower back of this body (almost as if the two of them were in a spooning position). The pearlescent white flowers growing out of the dark patch also draw the attention of our eyes. The blue hood, with liripipe floating upward through the trees toward the sky as if on the wind, may be the illustrator's way of envisioning line 161: "my spirit sprang into space." Certainly there is tension between the hands reaching downward toward the mound and the thin liripipe disappearing upward while the thicker part, the medieval hood with face opening turned up and five dagging settles flying out, is pulled sideways. Between the Dreamer's hands is what appears to be a large white pearl falling toward the ground.

The second illustration, which depicts the Dreamer standing beside a stream and pointing directly over a dark bush (the same color as the dark mound in the previous illustration) at a fish within it, makes us wonder aloud about whether the image of the fish should be interpreted naturalistically, allegorically, or psychologically. In nature, it would not be unusual for a man to see a fish in a stream. However, the poem itself makes no mention of any fish, but instead emphasizes the bejeweled bed of the river when the Dreamer reaches it. Interpreted allegorically, medieval Christian iconography has a long tradition of representing the fish as a symbol for Christ. Yet we know that the Dreamer is estranged from Christ for most of the poem—and the fish in this stream does not look like the traditional *ichthus*.[4] Perhaps viewers are meant to think of Peter, whom Jesus promised to make a "fisher of men" (Matt. 4.18–19), or of medieval astrology and the twelfth sign of the zodiac, Pisces, associated with water and the beginning of spring (February and March).[5] Is it acceptable to speculate, from the perspective of psychological or feminist literary criticism, that the fish might be a phallic or fertility symbol? All three interpretations may overlap, and others may be possible.[6] Whatever the case may be, the fact that the picture shows the Dreamer pointing at this fish so dramatically suggests that the illustrator wanted to provoke viewers to ask questions and seek the full meaning.

The third illustration represents the Dreamer on one side of the stream and the golden-crowned Pearl-Maiden on the other. The dark color associated with the mound in the first illustration and the bush in the second has entirely disappeared. Instead there is a five-pointed, star-shaped flower at the Dreamer's feet with a pearlescent white center. The Dreamer and the Pearl-Maiden contrast with one another: he in his red robe and she in a high-necked white one, gathered at the waist.[7] This dress is a "sideless surcoat":

> a specific form of aristocratic dress . . . which was worn to distinguish royalty during ceremonial occasions, was portrayed by artists as a costume for brides,

and was featured in funeral effigies from the mid-fourteenth-century through the fifteenth century. The symbolic and semantic content of this garment style would have been clear to the poem's late-fourteenth century readers, allowing the poet to visually underscore the Pearl-Maiden's existence as a departed soul, and her newly elevated status as a Queen of Heaven and Bride of Christ, prior to the dialogue that explicates the details to the grief stricken and oblivious Dreamer.   (Jack 67)

In this illustration, unlike in the poet's description, her blond hair is braided.[8] The two figures seem to be having a conversation with their hands. The Dreamer reaches out to the Pearl-Maiden, pointing at her, while she holds up the palms of both of her hands as if to ask him to halt or stop. Is this a pose that courtly lovers might take, the entreating lover and the sovereign beloved? Viewers may notice that while the Pearl-Maiden is crowned, the Dreamer is not: the crown is a symbol that implies her higher rank and authority.

Then we notice that three fish are depicted in the stream, one swimming in the opposite direction of the other two. What do these fish represent? Is this Trinitarian symbolism? Or might the three fish correspond to the three characters of the poem, the Dreamer, the Pearl-Maiden, and the Lamb? The Pearl-Maiden and her lord, the Lamb, may very well be "swimming in the same direction," but the Dreamer's conversation with the Pearl-Maiden in the poem suggests he is "swimming against the current." This interpretation may be reinforced by the fact that the gazes of the Dreamer and the Pearl-Maiden do not meet; each is looking away from the other. But the Dreamer's pointing finger is just over the nose of the fish in the middle, between the other two fish, and if we follow the arc of his finger pointing across the stream to the body of the Pearl-Maiden, we find that its trajectory ends, not at the Pearl-Maiden's face or heart, but at the *mons Veneris*, which is modestly concealed by the Pearl-Maiden's white robes.

The fourth illustration shows the Dreamer and the golden-crowned Pearl-Maiden still on opposite sides of the stream, but now the Pearl-Maiden is removed behind a crenellated castle wall decorated with eight crosses, a tower beside her, and a small building behind her, painted red, white, and blue. It may represent her "bower": the red door to it appears to be open slightly.

The conversation of the speaking hands continues, as the Dreamer reaches up to her and turns his face upward at a painfully awkward angle to look at her. She, meanwhile, is holding one hand to her heart while the other one is extended downward to the Dreamer in the position a lady might assume for a suitor to take it and kiss it. The stream now has only two fish in it, which are much enlarged and looking somewhat ominous, again facing each other so that at least one of them is working against the current. Meanwhile, the dark color associated with the mound and the bush in the first and second illustrations, absent in the third, has reappeared in a low dark bush near the Dreamer's feet. Is this representative of the memory (and the threat) of death?

It can be interesting to contrast the fourteenth-century illustrations from the manuscript with the modern illustration on the front cover of the CD for the Chaucer Studio's recording of the *Pearl* poem. The latter is of a very childlike young girl with a round face and blond hair who could easily be two years old. The Maiden shown in the manuscript illustrations is quite different: older, taller, dressed like a noblewoman.

While scholarship on these illustrations has primarily been concerned with evaluating their quality, whether crude or sophisticated (Lee, "Illuminating Critic"; Reichardt), my classroom discussion tends to focus on the visual interpretation of their meaning in relation to the settings, characters, and themes of the poem. Definitive decisions about what these illustrations are meant to convey are not possible, but the questions and possibilities they raise are certainly tantalizing. I have noticed that once the students see the illustrations and think carefully about them, they are rarely able to believe that the illustrations represent a relationship between a father and his two-year-old daughter. If the only contemporary commentator on the poem, the illustrator, did not apparently think that this was the nature of the relationship between the Pearl-Maiden and the Dreamer, should we?

A medieval reader glancing at these illustrations would not suppose that the Dreamer is speaking as a father to his daughter. Instead, the man's lower position in relation to the woman's elevated one might suggest a submissive lover conversing with his lady. The iconography of the Pearl-Maiden's crowned head and castle home, the Dreamer's outstretched hands, and the garden setting all suggest *amour courtois*.[9] This is not the only possible interpretation of the poem, and modern critics might well disagree with the illustrator's understanding of it. Yet it seems, to borrow a phrase from Charlotte Gross's essay on courtly language, that the illustrations evoke "the invariable triad of the courtly love-lyric: a lady identified with ideal perfection, a lover who aspires to and is ennobled by that perfection, and the inviolable distance separating the two" (83).

Deepening Discussion through Consideration of Literary-Critical Perspectives

Literary-critical scholarship on *Pearl*, in contrast to the modern editorial tradition, does more to acknowledge the wide range of possible ways to interpret the nature of the relationship between the Dreamer and the Pearl-Maiden. I find it useful to divide the possibilities into two categories, literal and allegorical, and to cite a selection of scholars who have made a strong case for a particular interpretation. A simple chart included in a handout or projected in a *PowerPoint* slide can convey the information. Students in an upper-division or graduate course who have read some of the criticism of the poem may be able to fill in the chart themselves and compare and contrast critical opinion that way. It is then possible to discuss with the students the relationship between the Dreamer and the Pearl-Maiden, and even to have them take and defend certain positions with textual evidence for the sake of argument.

Literal Interpretations

- A father mourning the death of his daughter (Morris)
- A man grieving the death of his godchild, grandchild, or younger sister (Bishop, Pearl *in Its Setting*)
- A poet sympathizing with a patron who is father to a young girl (such as Isabel, daughter of Thomas of Woodstock, brother of John of Gaunt) who was sent by a noble family to a religious house (like the house of Minoresses in London) and who consequently "died to the world" and "married Christ" through monastic enclosure (Staley, "*Pearl* and the Contingencies of Love and Piety")
- A poet of the Ricardian court honoring Anne of Bohemia (Bowers, *Politics of* Pearl)
- A jeweler related to an infant-transformed-into-a-woman who is like the virgin martyr Saint Margaret of Antioch (Earl)
- A lover mourning his beloved who died before their love could be consummated (Carson; Beal "Pearl-Maiden's Two Lovers")

Allegorical Interpretations of the Pearl-Maiden

- Maidenhood or virginity (Schofield, "Symbolism, Allegory and Auto-biography in the *Pearl*")
- The Dreamer's own soul (Madeleva)
- The Dreamer's own soul in mystical union with Christ (Hillmann's introduction to her edition, *The* Pearl)
- The Dreamer's regenerate soul, eternal life, or beatitude, or all three (Hamilton, "The Meaning of the Middle English *Pearl*" and Higgs, "Progress of the Dreamer in *Pearl*")
- The Dreamer's lost innocence or the innocence of childhood (Cawley and Anderson's introduction to their edition of *Pearl*; Robertson, "The Pearl as a Symbol")
- The Dreamer's "alleluia" or his joy in salvation (Beal, "Signifying Power of *Pearl*")

After that discussion, I do share my own view with students, namely that several interpretations can coexist without contradiction when we consider how medieval readers historically interpreted scripture and classical texts in four interrelated ways. Literally the Pearl-Maiden could be the Dreamer's beloved whose death he mourns. Allegorically she could represent his "alleluia" or the figure of joy in the salvation that he has lost but needs to regain along with his hope in the Resurrection celebrated at Easter. Morally she has much in common with female personifications of Wisdom (Proverbs), Philosophy (Boethius), and Blessedness and Joy (like Beatrice in Dante's *Divine Comedy*), especially in her desire to provide consolation to the Dreamer in his sorrow. Finally, anagogically she claims to be the Bride of Christ, and her words show that she is inviting the Dreamer, her spiritual brother, to enter into a deeper understanding of relationship with Christ and the experience of eternal life.

NOTES

[1] Over the past twelve years, the classes in which I have taught *Pearl* have included literary survey and special topics courses for undergraduates, such as Introduction to Literature, Literature of the Western World, Classical and Early British Literature, British Literature I, Poetry Seminar, Spiritual Autobiography, and the Mythology of J. R. R. Tolkien. I have also incorporated the study of *Pearl* in creative writing classes as well as in History of the English Language. I have discussed my pedagogical views in other essays on teaching *Pearl*, including "Three Approaches to Teaching *Pearl*: Introduction to Literature, British Literature I, and the Mythology of J. R. R. Tolkien."

[2] These illustrations are available at the end of the volume; facsimile versions (in color) are available online at the *Cotton Nero A.x Project*, which is hosted by the University of Calgary (gawain.ucalgary.ca), and digital copies (slightly cropped and color-enhanced versions) are available at *Medieval Pearl* (medievalpearl.wordpress.com).

[3] In the past few years, I have preferred to use my own modern language translation of the poem, which presents in the introduction the relationship between the Dreamer and the Pearl-Maiden as a crux with many possible interpretations. My translation also contains same-page annotations on the poem to facilitate the new readers' perceptions of the interpretive possibilities of the poem. I have made this available to my students in electronic format so that students can read it on their laptops, tablets, or smartphones. I plan to make it available to a wider public in due course.

[4] Unlike the fish drawn in the stream in the manuscript illustrations of *Pearl*, an *ichthus* is not realistic or naturalistic; it consists of two curved lines that meet at the point of the "nose" of the fish and cross each other at the "tail." It is purely symbolic.

[5] The symbol for Pisces is, however, two fish connected to each other and pulling in different directions, which the *Pearl* manuscript illustrator does not depict.

[6] It is possible that the illustrator is referring obliquely to the Parable of the Seine Net, which, in Matthew 13, directly follows the Parable of the Treasure Hidden in the Field and the Parable of the Pearl of Great Price. In the Parable of the Seine Net, the net represents death and the fish represent human beings; when fish are caught, they are sorted by the angels, who keep the good fish and throw the bad back into the sea: a picture of the Last Judg-

ment. Thus, the Parable of the Seine Net has eschatological implications consonant with the ending of *Pearl*, which focuses on the Second Coming of Christ and on the New Jerusalem.

[7] The color of their clothing is symbolic and can be interpreted in the light of the two biblical verses, from Isaiah and Revelation respectively: "Though your sins be as red as scarlet, I will make them as white as snow" (Isa. 1.18) and "These are they who came out of great tribulation, and have washed their robes, and made them white in the blood of the Lamb" (Rev. 7.14). On color symbolism in *Pearl*, see Blanch, "Color Symbolism"; White.

[8] Note that the *Pearl* poet describes the Pearl-Maiden's hair as free-flowing, not braided (lines 213–14). That she is depicted with braided hair in the illustrations contrasts with Lee's claim that the illustrator is consistently faithful to the text of the poems he illustrates. For a discussion of the possible significance of the Pearl-Maiden's hairstyle, see Lucas.

[9] For the image of a lover's outstretched hand in a garden setting, compare the illustrations from the *Pearl* manuscript with an image of two lovers playing a game in the Luttrell Psalter (folio 76v), reproduced in Backhouse 47.

Pearl, Pedagogy, and the Poetics of Enshrinement

Seeta Chaganti

Pearl participates in what I have termed elsewhere a medieval poetics of enshrinement.[1] Informed by its engagement with the material culture of shrines
and reliquaries, *Pearl* offers an understanding of poetic form as enshrinement,
a dialectical dynamic between container and contained, in the manner of a reliquary that contains a saint's body and is in turn contained by the presence,
narrative, and ceremonial constitution of that saint. In this essay I consider the
poetics of enshrinement as a pedagogical tool. Just as *Pearl*'s language performs a constant oscillation between container and contained, so we might teach
the relation between *Pearl* and the other poems attributed to its author as one
of enshrinement, in which the texts contain and are contained by one another.
These poems are *Cleanness, Patience,* and *Sir Gawain and the Green Knight,*
which all accompany *Pearl* in British Library MS Cotton Nero A.x; and *Saint
Erkenwald,* found in British Library MS Harley 2250. *Saint Erkenwald*'s location in a different manuscript has historically undermined the certainty of its
shared authorship with these other poems. I teach it with the others, however,
because the powerful images of enshrinement in all five poems can generate
conversations not only about how they are related but also about the meaning
of textual relations. Teaching *Pearl* through a discourse of enshrinement can
thus accomplish several useful pedagogical goals. First, it communicates to students an important aspect of medieval aesthetic culture. Second, focusing on a
shared device like enshrinement raises helpful questions for students about the
principles underlying the comparison of these texts: does making such comparisons depend on the establishment of a common historical author? What other
pedagogical value might lie in reading them together? Finally, and perhaps most
crucially, this approach to teaching the poem foregrounds the activity of formalist reading, making the *Pearl* poet's oeuvre a useful training ground in this skill
for students of literature from any period.

I introduce *Pearl, Cleanness, Patience, Sir Gawain,* and *Saint Erkenwald* to
students by suggesting that enshrinement describes the structure of these poems' interdependence. To make this point, I choose not to read each entire poem
in sequence during the course. Rather, for the first three class meetings, I create a concatenated pattern of poetic openings. In the first meeting, we discuss
the beginning of one pair of poems; in the second meeting, another pair; and in
the third, we pair the fifth poem's opening with that of a poem we have already
looked at. This structure allows for a great deal of flexibility: a teacher might
foreground particular ideas or themes, or adapt to student need, by adjusting the

arrangement of the poems. My technique also creates a pedagogical dynamic that, from the beginning, construes the poems as existing in relation to each other.

I will begin here with a couple of examples of such pairings. One might start discussing the *Pearl* poet by pairing the first stanza of *Pearl* with the first nineteen lines of *Sir Gawain*. As an introduction to this body of work, such a pairing might appeal to students who would find *Sir Gawain* more accessible in subject matter and therefore more reassuring than the other poems. One could compare the stanzaic structure of *Pearl* with that of the bob and wheel in *Sir Gawain* and ask students about the effects of these highly elaborate rhyme schemes: how they resemble each other and how they differ. The different components of *Pearl*'s stanza form—its twelve-line ballade rhyme scheme, its use of concatenation between stanzas, its refrains, its alliteration—are not unique to this poem (Fein, "Twelve-Line Stanza Forms"). But *Pearl*'s combination of these elements is certainly remarkable and deserves students' focus. Pairing the poem's stanzaic form with another verse structure that might also be novel for students but is simpler, like the bob and wheel, can help them arrive at insights about early poetic form. Beginning with the first stanza of *Pearl* is additionally useful because its opening lines introduce concepts like personification and allegory. The stanza initiates questions about what levels of allegorical meaning the loss of a pearl in a garden might have, and the ambiguously apostrophic move of the opening line allows questions about who or what is being addressed, where agency and sentience lie.

Students also benefit from beginning with *Pearl* and *Sir Gawain* because these poems can provide a framing context for a pairing such as *Cleanness* and *Patience*, texts whose difficulty and unfamiliarity might make them daunting to approach on their own. Engaging in a discussion of allegory and personification in *Pearl* will prepare students to think about the presentation of feminized abstract concepts in *Patience* and *Cleanness* (for a discussion of such female personifications, see, e.g., Newman, *God and the Goddesses* 2–24). Alternatively, more advanced students might find the initial pairing of *Pearl* and *Cleanness* more thought provoking, since this configuration would allow them to compare the vocabularies of cleanness and purity in both texts' opening (such as "thay in clannes clos" in *Cleanness* [line 13] and "clanly clos" in *Pearl* [2]). Students might also consider *Cleanness*'s "fayre formez" (3), which will resonate in many ways with *Pearl* (on the meaning of this phrase, see Prior, *Fayre Formez* 4–7). In addition, the opportunity to decide which of these texts should pair with *Saint Erkenwald* allows for a creative but textually grounded way to begin discussing the question of this poem's relation to the others (a question to which I shall return).

However these pairings are arranged, what becomes evident in using this strategy is these poems' suggestively complex network of enshrining contexts for one another. They can be understood as containing one another's interests and stakes while being contained by them. Moving at a relatively rapid pace through all the poems before settling into one at greater depth communicates the message that each poem must be seen as constitutive of and constituted by the entire network. In response to the framing imagery apparent in *Pearl* and the other poems, we might say that each text frames and is framed by the others through its language and themes.

Once students have a feel for this enshrining and interrelated dynamic across the poems, one might explore images of enshrinement within *Pearl* to understand visual images of enclosure through the poem's formal expression of enshrining acts. *Pearl* is a useful place to begin thinking about enshrinement, and this poem also demonstrates enshrinement's relevance as a method of reading and as an aspect of medieval aesthetics and material culture. My work on this topic sees late medieval reliquaries as modeling the acts of enshrinement found in the formal characteristics and imagery of *Pearl* (Chaganti 95–129). An image in *Pearl* that can generate conversation about the poem's relation to this aspect of material culture occurs in the description of the heavenly Jerusalem. The dreamer's account is based on Revelation, as his reference to John reminds the reader:

> As John hym wrytez ȝet more I syȝe
> Vch pane of that place had thre ȝates,
> So twelue in poursent I con asspye,
> The portalez pyked of rych platez,
> And vch ȝate of a Margery,
> A parfit perle that neuer fatez.
> Vichon in scrypture a name con plye
> Of Israel barnez, folewande her datez. (lines 1033–40)

> As John wrote, yet more I saw
> each wall of that place had three gates,
> so I saw twelve in the enclosing wall,
> the gateways adorned with rich metal plate,
> and each gate [made of/adorned with] a pearl,[2]
> a precious pearl that never fades.
> Each one contained an inscribed name
> of the sons of Israel, corresponding to their dates.

The motif of inscription is useful to track in this passage because it demonstrates an effect of layered enshrinement. This effect allows students to think about the nature of the borders between visual and verbal culture. In what sense, for instance, is the poem an inscription of the same kind as the inscriptions found on these gates? Do these types of inscription exist on the same or different onto-logical planes? What is their spatial and conceptual relation to one another? To what extent are the inscribed biblical names on the wall ultimately a framing or enclosing context for the whole poem in its capacity as spiritual allegory?[3] And if the passage creates syntactic ambiguity between the gate consisting of pearls and the gate decorated with pearls, does this verbal ambiguity enshrine that of the Pearl-Maiden, a resident of this city who is herself a "perle . . . in perlez pyȝt [decorated]" (241), creating multiple and intersecting acts of enshrinement?

One might also wish to supplement such a line of questioning with other cultural and artistic contexts, including illuminated manuscript frontispieces that draw on reliquary imagery (Stahl 205–32) resonant with *Pearl*; apocalypse manuscripts that have been read in conjunction with *Pearl*'s depiction of the heavenly Jerusalem as a jeweled city (Stanbury, *Seeing the* Gawain-*Poet* 12–41; Whitaker 183–96); jewelry (Riddy 143–55); and late medieval ornamental and architectural practices that inform the poem's allegorical and eschatological programs (Meyer, "Þe New Cyté" [*Medieval Allegory* 137–86]). Numerous possible questions emerge from such material. What, for instance, does it mean to think of the poem—or the relations among poems—as architectural or material? What can we learn about how the stanzaic form of the poem operates by comparing it to objects, illustrations, or buildings? What problems emerge in trying to compare visual and verbal forms of expression? How might aspects of the poem address or respond to these?

Moving back outward from *Pearl*, one can use enshrinement as a point of reference through which to articulate similarities and differences among the rest of the poems. *Cleanness*'s pearl reference at lines 1065–72, for instance, invites comparisons with *Pearl*. Both texts also challenge readers to understand whether they are seeing nature as artifice or artifice as nature, as in the jeweled birds and blossoms of *Cleanness* (1463–67) and the evocative stanza describing the river beginning at line 109 of *Pearl*. Because it places in an earthly setting the celestial imagery of *Pearl*'s heavenly Jerusalem, *Cleanness*'s banquet (loosely based on Daniel 5.1–20) also suggests itself as a moment of comparison. Here the speaker imagines the feast table as an "avter" (1451, 1477) and produces a serialized description of decorative gemstones (1468–76) that could be set beside the catalog of gems starting at line 997 in *Pearl*. But having established these basic similarities, students can move on to consider what happens to the enshrining structure, so evident in *Pearl*, when this imagery migrates to *Cleanness*. Do *Cleanness*'s references to rich materials without enshrining form suggest Belshazzar's problematic excess, a lack of the decorous containment that, in *Pearl*'s heavenly Jerusalem, speaks to moral integrity? There are other ways as well for students to think about the importance of the enshrining dynamic as distinct in *Pearl*. To what extent, for example, does the enshrining dynamic of *Pearl* speak to the nature of mental process? Because the poem announces itself to be a dream vision, it raises questions about space and location—the location of the dream vision inside or outside the dreamer's mind.[4] The formal enshrinements of *Pearl*, highlighted by their contrast to the form of *Cleanness*, provide a template for perceiving the cognitive activity of the dreamer as framed by and framing his mind and mental space. Furthermore, one might ask what emerges in the contrast between the enshrinement of exquisite artifice, on the one hand, and images of organic, even repellent, enclosure, on the other, such as Jonah's experience inside the whale in *Patience* (273–340). When is enclosure sanctuary and when is it prison? How does the shift between nature and artifice change the dynamics of enshrinement in these poems?

One might, at the same time, consider images of enclosure and sacred enshrinement that express themselves more consistently across the poems in the group. Perhaps most striking is the entombed judge in *Saint Erkenwald*. Students might investigate the meaning of *Pearl*'s desire for bodily integrity and perfection as filtered through the pagan judge's miraculously intact entombed body in *Saint Erkenwald*. This reading could also be triangulated with other hagiographic narratives about St. Erkenwald's ability to heal and make whole those who appealed to his body in the tomb (Whatley 133, 155). Specific details of the physical elements of enclosure, like *Saint Erkenwald*'s indecipherable "bordure embelicit wyt brʒt gold letters" (line 51) framing the judge, can help students think further about the role of inscription in objects of enshrinement like the heavenly Jerusalem. Through these images of inscription emerge further questions concerning the difference between acts of reading and acts of looking. Engaging in these comparative readings teases out the implications of form and imagery in particular enshrining moments within texts. It also reinforces the extent to which *Pearl* contextualizes and exists within the contexts of the other poems.

Enshrinement—whether asserted in individual poems' imagery or in their relation to each other—can also inflect discussions of the poems' authorship. In particular, the question of *Saint Erkenwald*'s relation to the four poems in Cotton Nero A.x has produced a broad range of opinion. Following early-twentieth-century arguments for common authorship (Savage, *St. Erkenwald* liii–lxv) or at least hypotheses that the *Erkenwald* author was a "disciple who very closely caught the style of his master" (Gollancz, *St. Erkenwald* lvii), Benson uses linguistically based evidence such as vocabulary (lines 395–96, 404) and alliterative formulas and conventions (396–403) to unbuckle what might have seemed an ineluctable link between *Saint Erkenwald* and the other poems. Throughout the twentieth century, counterarguments resoldering *Saint Erkenwald* to the other poems range from the anagrammatic (Peterson 53) to the thematic, invoking, for instance, the shared presence of the supernatural and imaginative (McAlindon 475). Contemporary scholarship continues to reflect a divide. While Bowers's book-length introduction to the *Pearl* poet includes *Saint Erken-*

wald in the poet's oeuvre (*Introduction* xi), Putter's does not (2). Articulating unresolved issues of authorship through the language of enshrinement leads to productive lines of inquiry. Students could, for example, be encouraged to think about how including or excluding *Saint Erkenwald* affects their perception of the poet's aesthetics or agenda. Do the Old Testament narratives of *Patience* and *Cleanness*, for instance, function to enclose and contextualize devotionally the more localized English saint's miracle of *Saint Erkenwald*? Or vice versa? How do the uncanny and marvelous elements of *Sir Gawain* and *Saint Erkenwald* frame each other in their shared nationalist context? If, as noted above, *Pearl* and *Saint Erkenwald* display in common an emphatic interest in enshrinement, what might this help us to understand or even conjecture about their author? It is, at the same time, important to ask students to consider the possibility that such commonalities reflect not the tastes and preferences of a single author but rather more expansive cultural conventions. And if this is the case, one might then ask students: when does the comparative reading of anonymous texts require a presumption of shared authorship and when does it not? Following this train of thought might allow students to develop a more general understanding of medieval authorship as a phenomenon distinct from authorship in other periods.[5] For this reason, juxtaposing these poems also holds a pedagogical value existing independently of the attempt to regain access to a historically specific author, or even workshop, producing these texts. Reading the poems together, having to tolerate their shared anonymity, can acclimate students to the kinds of networks of textuality, sometimes tethered to personal authorship but sometimes not, that characterized medieval literate culture (see, e.g., Hanna, *Pursuing History* 70–77).

Lest this conception of ambiguously authored voices, communicating in a complex network, prove dauntingly abstract or esoteric for some students, one can use enshrinement to explicate this idea and render it concrete. I illustrate this point through *Saint Erkenwald*'s unique representation of communication among its characters. Readings of the poem tend to focus on interlocution between pairs, particularly that of the pagan judge and the saint (Chism 61; Burrow, "Thinking in Poetry"). But the poem's invocation of ceremonial contexts, like the Mass, complicates its vectors of communication. A medieval priest's bodily participation in the Mass negotiates a discourse that triangulates him with God and the people (Graves 308). Erkenwald's initial address to the judge occurs within the immediate context of a High Mass: "the byschop hym shope solemply to synge the heghe masse" (line 129). When this service ends, Erkenwald passes to the tomb as the aristocratic congregation bows in their places. If the multidirectional orientations of the bishop's body during the Mass orchestrate the audience's involvement with him, then his repositioning immediately following the Mass might participate in this same dynamic. Erkenwald's body in ritualized motion continues to negotiate, as it did during the Mass, a larger set of interactive trajectories involving the divinity whom he supplicates, the miraculous judge figure, and the audience surrounding and watching him. Thus: how many are speaking? Who is really speaking to whom here? Who is listening? To what extent is the performance of the Mass an enclosing frame for all these interactions? To what extent are the illegibly inscribed characters surrounding the pagan judge, enclosed in his tomb, participating in other layers of inscription and communication in this moment? In the classroom, such inquiry into *Saint Erkenwald* might allegorize for students the subtle, not always visible, but highly complex ways in which the different texts and discourses of the *Pearl* poet speak to, across, and around each other, like the border of letters surrounding the tomb.[6] Through motifs of enshrinement and network, I attempt to consider authorship by moving beyond its negation or death in the old-fashioned Barthesian sense (Barthes 142–48). Rather, I propose using the formal, imagistic, and thematic relations among these texts to loosen our investment in historically identifiable authorship; doing so appropriately reflects some fundamental characteristics of medieval textual culture and might thus convey more accurately to students the nature of medieval authorship.

I conclude by asserting that *Pearl* is not only a fruitful but also a necessary and foundational text for students to engage as part of the important process of training in close reading. Readers of this essay will no doubt notice that I have eschewed discussion of chivalry, ethics, courage, courtliness, mourning, or any of the other mainstays that often make the events and characters in *Pearl* and the other texts "relatable" to students. Instead, I hope that some of the suggestions in this piece will showcase *Pearl*'s potential as a text through which to explore modes of close formalist reading. Doing so will mean, of course, resisting student desire for reassuringly tidy numerological readings in favor of formalist interpretation that accommodates more suggestive ambiguity and troubling irresolution. The questions I have posed about *Pearl* and the other poems are designed to work against the idea that a highly formalized text like *Pearl* contains codes and patterns that lead a reader toward a key that unlocks one correct understanding of the text. I think that *Pearl* offers many more suggestive and usefully open-ended ways to perceive the work of literary form. I deploy the poetics of enshrinement as a means into this type of reading because its material basis allows students to grasp an aspect of the text and generate multidimensional conversations about objects and poetry. But it is really only a starting point from which *Pearl* encourages us to think about the meaning of literary and poetic form. For this reason, teaching *Pearl* and the other works of the *Pearl* poet can form an integral part of a larger literature curriculum. The challenge of close reading *Pearl* can train students to be their most inventive and insightful formalist selves when they interpret later English and American poetic texts.

NOTES

[1] Chaganti 19–45.

[2] Gould (175) and Borroff (*Gawain Poet* 156) take this line to mean that the whole gate is made of pearl; however, Finch's translation takes a parallel construction to be implied between lines 1036 and 1037, so that the word "pyked" ("adorned") should be understood as the verb in line 1037 (93). The source in Revelation appears to represent the gates as made of pearl: "And the twelve gates are twelve pearls, one to each: and every several gate was of one several pearl" (*Douay-Rheims Bible*, Revelation 21.21), "et duodecim portae duodecim margaritae sunt per singulas et singulae portae erant ex singulis margaritis" (*Vulgate Bible*, Revelation 21.21). But the interaction between the *Pearl* poet's creative vision and his source leaves room for deliberate ambiguity between pearl as decoration and pearl as content, an ambiguity that reflects the poetics of enshrinement.

[3] For a brief review of critical debate over *Pearl*'s allegorical or elegiac nature, see J. A. Mitchell 86–87.

[4] For additional discussion of this question about mental vision, see Newman, "What Did It Mean" 1–43. For a discussion of imagined and envisioned worlds in medieval texts from the perspective of media theory and virtuality, see Rust 1–30.

[5] For students new to the particularities of medieval poetic authorship, see Olson's "Making and Poetry," a valuable resource.

[6] Sanok sees *Pearl*'s conversation between the Dreamer and the Maiden as allegorizing different kinds of narrative discourses (181); thus, the process of studying these texts might involve various ways of interpreting character interaction as allegorically representative of more abstract literary phenomena.

Christological Meditations in
the Works of the *Pearl* Poet

J. A. Jackson

In teaching the poems of the *Pearl* poet, one is often struck by the overt religiosity and even piety of the poems. In many ways, this can make teaching the poems difficult since not all students will share the poet's Catholicism or even his Christianity. Nevertheless, to avoid the religious dimension of the poems would be, somehow, doing violence to the poems themselves, to avoid our part in a conversation the poet has tried to begin with the reader. In order to engage the theological and poetic dimensions of these four poems, I should like to focus on the poet's sense of Christological poetics, the way he offers his readers various Christological lenses through which to read his poetry. In short, the poems' theological meditations are less an object of study than they are an aesthetic and a hermeneutical disposition of the poems themselves. These Christological lenses, of course, act as the very foundation for medieval biblical hermeneutics with their foundation in typology and in their employment of history, allegory, tropology, and anagogy.[1] Teaching this fourfold method of reading can be a daunting task to the teacher of medieval poetry, but I would like to submit that we can allow these four poems to be our teacher in this regard. We should be aware of and sensitive to the various Christological meditations throughout—some overt, some subtle. My students often feel as if a whole universe has opened up to them when I point out that the poetry attempts in many places to incarnate the Christological reflections found in its lines. While we need not focus on specific fourfold readings of the poems themselves (though this is often valuable), we can certainly follow the ways in which images of Christ (as the Lamb, through various Eucharistic imagery, through baptismal imagery, and seen in the rupturing of finite, historical time) help us situate ourselves inside the poems so that we are enabled to read along with them in manifold ways—theologically, ethically, and existentially.

Christological hermeneutics, one can argue, is just the way the New Testament understood itself in relation to the Old Testament.[2] When our students blush and wonder whether English professors just "make things up" with regard to our reading practices, we should agree with a vengeance when it comes to medieval biblical narrative. Why? Because the New Testament, through its employment of typological readings, finds Christ everywhere in the Old Testament and appears to be "making it up" as the writers find convenient. But if their premise was that scripture was inspired by the Holy Spirit who announces the coming of the Son of God, it would make perfect sense that scripture always speaks of Christ.[3] The teacher should then be prepared to talk about the manifold ways scripture was so understood—both biblically (Jonah as a prefiguration of Christ; the Suffering Servant of Isaiah as Christ; Elijah as a prefiguration of John the Baptist; the Flood and the crossing of the Red Sea as prefigurations of baptism in the church, etc.) and in the exegesis developed in the early church. Jean Daniélou's *From Shadows to Reality* and Henri de Lubac's *Medieval Exegesis* will help ground the instructor's discussions. Again, the point here is not to be rigid or prescriptive in our readings; in fact, Christological hermeneutics has a tendency to open things up, to offer us grounding so that we can ask serious theological questions without going astray. It is as Saint Augustine says in his commentary on the commandment in Genesis "to be fruitful and multiply" (*Confessions* 13.24): because we find a single truth expressed in manifold ways, we should then interpret a single expression in different ways. And yet I would like to emphasize again that we allow *our poems* to guide us. We simply need to be alert to the poetics already at play in the poems, to the manner in which our poems give us different narratives under the guise of single expression, and then proceed from there. In short, we can learn to read these poems if we allow them to teach us how to read biblically.

Perhaps the most immediate example of the way in which a poem stages for us its own Christological hermeneutics can be found in *Pearl*, section 16. This section introduces the reader to a hermeneutical shift within the poem, as the Maiden attempts to explain the "two" Jerusalems of scripture. The poem openly meditates upon the double meaning of Jerusalem, rendering it through a historical understanding (the historical city, outside of which Christ is crucified; lines 937–38), an allegorical one (the fallen world that was tending toward decay and death, until Christ atones for it; 941–42), and finally the movement to the eschatological or anagogic vision (the New Jerusalem, the Kingdom, the ever-moving liturgical procession). Section 16 of *Pearl* offers one of the most succinct examples of medieval biblical hermeneutics a student will find. If one is at a loss about how to teach medieval typological/allegorical readings, I would suggest that we let *Pearl* be our guide. The fourfold method employed by the poem is not an end in and of itself, and it is important that our students understand this. The poem is just announcing its hermeneutical position; this, it turns out, has been its hermeneutical position all along since the invocation "withouten spot" in the first stanza group. Section 16 simultaneously recalls the difficulty of static, rigid one-dimensional understanding of "spot" in the first stanza group by making explicit that Jerusalem occupies "of motez two" (949), two places, and that this assertion of a word ("spot," "mote") signifying two realities simultaneously would be quite natural.[4]

When we move to section 19 of *Pearl*, the reader witnesses in the liturgical procession of the brides of the Lamb the culmination of and the final answer to the Dreamer's theological discourse with the Pearl-Maiden. The Lamb here, of course, is the same Lamb as in Saint John's Revelation—the slain Christ. All the Dreamer's previous theological discussions, misunderstandings, and frustrations get reread and filtered through the vision of the Lamb and the brides' relationship to Him. Once the class arrives at section 19 of *Pearl*, I like to reorient the students' attention to the various places in the text where we have seen previous misunderstandings. Now that we have a nondidactic response to the Dreamer's quandaries in the form of the Lamb and the procession, I like to reread the previous difficulties.

For example, the Dreamer misunderstands the Maiden's exalted position as Queen and believes she has misspoken and usurped Mary's role. In turn, she gently explains that all who enter the Kingdom are kings and queens, and yet in achieving such a vaulted status, they deprive no one of their own exalted position; all are not only not deprived of joy, each queen and king feels greater joy at the throngs who arrive (lines 444–55); the Maiden then repeats this teaching just before the vision of the Lamb (842–53). This image of appropriated bliss—where each bride/queen/king is happier because of the happiness of the other bride, queen, or king, where every experience of bliss saturates and exponentially increases every other blissful experience—finds its fulfillment in the Dreamer's vision of the Lamb, in his concise observation: "Hundreth þouwsandez I wot were there, / And alle in sute her liueréz wasse. / Tor to knaw the gladdest chere" ("A hundred thousand I know were there, / And their garments were all alike. / It was difficult to know who was the happiest"; 1107–09). In other words, the vision is an experience of the Lamb, a mystical vision, which becomes supra-rational, so that the previous contradictions are overcome, not by rational means, but simply by experience, by knowledge through the *spiritus intellectus*. This single vision enables the Dreamer, even if only momentarily, to overcome the difficulties of the Maiden's retelling of the Parable of the Workers in the Vineyard. The vision acts as a fulfillment of the Maiden's teachings. This fulfillment, however, then makes the Dreamer's act of crossing the river even more problematic. It is a great joy to take the students through the various readings of his act: is it one of rebellion? Love? If of love, for whom? The Lamb? The Maiden? Can we now fully distinguish between the two since the poem makes their relationship so intimate?

The first time I taught an undergraduate seminar on the *Pearl* poet, I began with *Cleanness*, and I found it to be a very hard poem to teach (though I love the poem dearly)—hard because its narrative structure is so opaque, hard because it focuses so much on apocalyptic biblical narrative, hard because we witness "innocents" drown in the flood, and cries for mercy are seemingly ignored in the flood and in Sodom and Gomorrah. However, between the Genesis accounts and the retelling of Belshazzar's satanic feast, the reader is offered a meditation on the Incarnation of Christ and the effects on his creation. Starting at line 1057, interestingly with an invocation of *The Romance of the Rose*, the reader is encouraged to take up a life in imitation of Christ. The poem makes clear the reasons for this imitation of Christ: that through various sacraments instituted by Christ—baptism, communion, penance—one could participate in, indeed be wholly interpenetrated by, the cleanness of Christ himself. In a limited manner, the poem offers its own brief *cur deus homo* ("why God became a man"; lines 1089–116): He comes to heal the sick, to drive out corruption and death (bodily and spiritual) so that each one who comes in contact with Christ through the sacraments "tyd tourned to hele" ("quickly became healthy"; 1099). And yet we can still go further: Christ stands here not only to disapprove of the "unclean" characters we witness beforehand and to give us a positive model to imitate (though this is certainly part of it) but to be our hermeneutic guide through which we return to those previous scenes.

One of the Gospel scenes the poet decides to recount is instructive; the road to Emmaus is the typological hermeneutic par excellence in scripture. On the road to Emmaus, Christ himself instructs his disciples on how to read scripture (meaning the Old Testament). They are to read it through a Christological lens: "And beginning at Moses and all the prophets, he expounded to them in all the scriptures the things that were concerning him" (Luke 24.27). For biblical commentary, the Road to Emmaus, then, offered the church two main hermeneutical positions: 1) when one read the Old Testament, one was to look for Christological types—prefigurations of the coming of Christ (and therefore also of Mary and the church); 2) that because the disciples remained blind to Christ's exegetical lesson on the Road to Emmaus until they broke bread, and because this breaking of bread was understood as a Eucharistic symbol, the act of properly reading scripture depended on two mutually reciprocal mysteries: Christ's institution of the Eucharist and the way in which one reads most clearly from within this communal act; that is to say, participation in the Eucharist was the hermeneutical gesture par excellence precisely because it was the foremost Christological position, where he abides in the communicant and vice versa. There is an intimate connection between the act of communion and the act of reading itself—to see Christ from within a Christological lens, the Eucharist.

So when we turn back to the Old Testament story and the harrowing destruction of the cities, we are now struck by what appears at first to be a throwaway anachronistic line: just as the fire and brimstone rain down on the cities so that there is no escape, the people cry out in a "ʒomerly ʒarm" ("miserable cry"), cries so loud that they "clatered the cloudes" ("rattled the clouds"), "that Kryst myʒt haf rawthe" (line 972). This final line must give us pause; I find it best, if one is not teaching from the Middle English, to write this line in the original on the board so students can see it clearly and wrestle with the theological and ethical difficulties. It is an extrabiblical detail, wherein the poet, in classic medieval typological fashion, has found Christ in the Old Testament. But he has placed the name of Christ in the mouths of those about to be destroyed. We can ask, "Now what?" One could go in a number of directions: the time of repentance has passed and there is nothing else the people of Sodom can do; this is a re-minder to the readers that death and judgment will come like a thief in the night so one must always be prepared (e.g., through penance); or, perhaps, the reader is supposed to see himself in those crying out so that Christ may have mercy. I do not want to close off the readings here because Christological readings are supposed to be fruitful, to point to Christ in manifold ways. This begins even at the level of translation, where everything turns on the word "my3t haf rawthe." Is this "might have pity/mercy"? Or are we going to be so bold to posit "was able to have mercy"? We must ask our students to wrestle with the implica-tions and the ramifications of both, reminding them that the poet is not con-cerned only, or primarily, with a literal/historical reading of the poem, but with a moral and ethical one as well, which includes the role and spiritual condition of the reader.

We witness the same thing in the Flood episode. Instead of offering us an alle-gorical reading of the Flood as baptism (and certainly a viable and fruitful read-ing in *Cleanness*)—common in traditional typological/allegorical readings—our poet hyperliteralizes the event by adding extrabiblical details. In short, what do we do with lines 378–402? These are not the giants of old, those who we are told love violence so that "And ay þe biggest in bale þe best watz holden" ("And always the most violent were held as the best"; 276). These hell-bent men seem to be long gone when we see only one hundred lines later women and children scurrying up the hills to escape the flood waters, when we are told that the beasts roar out to God (clearly a metonym for the humans' cries), and finally when we see friend embracing friend to die in each other's arms. When I encounter this passage with my students, I simply ask how they respond viscerally. What has the poet done to us by changing these biblical details? Do we respond with hor-ror? With a sense of justice? With "rawthe" ("pity")? If the latter, do we risk be-ing more merciful than God here? Does the hyperliteralized narrative not seem to provoke such a reading? After all, where in Genesis do we see women and children drowning in the flood? These are tough questions no doubt, but ones that the poem raises, but it raises them precisely because of where we actually began this reading—with the poet's meditation on Christ. In other words, the poem has promised us mercy, a desire to heal and cleanse, and has asked us to go back and find Christ in these Old Testament scenes. So where is he? Should we be so bold and perhaps offer our own pity for these women and children, persons who most certainly are not the violent members of the antediluvian community of which the poet speaks? Are *we* that imitative ethical, merciful Christological voice in the poem?

If our students find themselves pitted against God—whether they enjoy this hermeneutical position or not—they should know that they may have already been situated right alongside God in their apparent "opposition." Indeed, the women and children in the flood scene from *Cleanness* beautifully echo the

God of *Patience* when He confronts Jonah in response to Jonah's anger. In lines 509–19, God asks Jonah how he could even consider destroying the people of Nineveh since they have now turned to him with cries of repentance. Even more to the point, the city is filled with men and women with no theological discernment, who cannot judge their left hand from their right. Even worse, there are breast-feeding babies who have never committed any evil. And let us not forget the beasts that are not even able to sin. So it could be that our poet has struck a Marcionite chord and has created "two Gods" for his two poems; perhaps he has drawn a clear line between the God of mercy and the God of judgment and is working through each of these faces of God. Perhaps. The students can have fun fleshing this out. But perhaps another way we can provoke them is by trying to have them reconcile these two positions.

Perhaps what is most playful about *Patience* is that it takes Jonah, a clear typological prefiguration of Christ (Christ himself invokes Jonah as a type of Christ in Matthew 12.40), and renders him most un-Christ-like. The extra-biblical markers throughout the poem highlight for its readers what has always seemed a bit of an exegetical quandary: how is Jonah in his reluctance to preach to the Ninevites anything *at all* like Christ, who teaches that the Gentiles have a place in the Israel to come. The poet utilizes Jonah's disdain for suffering—again, a most un-Christ-like characteristic—to mark Jonah as the antitype. In lines 92–95, the poet gives us Jonah's monologue: he resents this God who seems to be far away and so without any concern for his creation that God would not grieve at all if Jonah found himself in Nineveh, "dispoyled, / On rode rwly torent with rybaudes mony" ("stripped naked, / On a cross, pitifully torn apart with many villains"; 94–95). I like to show students the exegetical game at play here: by inserting these extrabiblical details, the poet offers us a Jonah who is not Christ-like specifically because he rejects the very suffering on the cross that Christ will accept. But the poet is not yet done. No sooner do we see a distancing between Jonah and Christ—though no doubt this is a distancing that brings to the fore a Christocentric meditation on suffering—than the poet inserts imagery connecting Jonah to Christ: when Jonah sleeps in the ship to Tarshish, the narrator calls on the Devil (Ragnel) to rouse Jonah out of his slumber (188); when Jonah sits in the whale's stomach, the narrator praises God who "Warded þis wrech man in warlowes guttez . . . þat stank as þe deuel" ("Protected the wretched man in the Devil's gut . . . which stank like the devil"; 258, 274). So now the poet is playing off the "Days of Jonah" in Matthew 12.40 where Christ refers to himself in the tomb for three days, harrowing hell, just as Jonah lay in the belly of the great fish. In this way, it appears that Jonah is in fact playing the typological role of Christ here in the devil's belly.

Jonah comes to inhabit, then, two Christological positions in two modes: if Jonah is a type of Christ, and he is, then his un-Christ-like positions ought to be startling for the reader, so much so that the antitype becomes a model for the reader. Jonah admits as much in lines 416–20 where he tells God that he knows how long God abides "lur" ("injury"), how "late" is God's "vengaunce," and how gracious is God's mercy; Jonah, however, rejects all of this. He announces the truth to God only to willfully ignore or, even worse, resent his own teaching about God's mercy. God then takes up the task of teaching Jonah about "pacience," about long-suffering founded on compassion. This is, of course, the divine position of this poem, but if we ask our students to return to *Cleanness* and put these two in dialogue, then we also get to ask what it would mean to read *Cleanness* from the position of *Patience*. Do we then choose which God we like best? What if we propose, just for fun, that the hermeneutical position of *Patience* was always already the position of *Cleanness* because of the advent of Christ in the poem itself, the interruption of violence (from the human community and from God) by Christ who enters the world to heal the suffering (physical and spiritual)?

For Christian theology and hermeneutics, the Incarnation of God ruptures the temporal realm, which allows us to read from multiple vantage points simultaneously, to read eschatologically, as it were; in the famous medieval formula, one must always remember the final things. Reading from the "final things" offers the reader a way to read history as well—past, present, and the already-not-yet future. *Sir Gawain and the Green Knight* takes up this sense of eschatological time in the form of chivalric romance. Cyclical time seems to invade the poem: the prologue to the poem recounts the cyclical history of Britain, where the nation finds itself always vacillating between "both blysse and blunder"; Gawain must meet the Green Knight in a full year's time to receive his reciprocal stroke; at the beginning of fit 2, the poet recounts for us how season leads to season and that time marches on, humans often unaware; and finally, as if time has sped up, Gawain must wait three days in Bertilak's castle, three days in which he seems to have lost sense of his own mortality, of time itself, until the final day, marked fittingly enough with a cock crowing. Time in its various forms then has a sense of doom and renewal (from winter to summer), joy and disaster (from feasting to Bertilak's castle to meeting the Green Knight)—in short, "boþe blysse and blunder" (line 18).

The poem incarnates this sense of cyclical time, as if this is the way of the world, when at the very end it returns to the beginning of the poem, when it recounts for us once again the first line of the poem, "After þe sege and þe assaute watz sesed at Troye" ("After the siege and the assault had ceased at Troy"; line 2525). After Gawain's shame, his blunder, we are set in motion once again. The history of Britain marches on as it always has, except this time the poet strikes a pious note: he invokes Christ and brings him into human history and asks that he bring us to His "blysse." Granted, this may be a simple invocation, a pious gesture for a poem composed for Christmastide. But this invocation also seems to repeat a pattern throughout the poem with regard to history, to time itself:

that there are moments that rupture finite time, that make it wholly uncyclical, unrepeatable. The narrator says explicitly: "Þe forme to þe fynisment foldez ful selden" ("the beginning and the end very seldom match"; 498). So time may move on, and things may appear to be as they always have been, but the poem makes sure that the narrative exceeds itself, that it ends not where it began, that there is often something disruptive about living in the world, that it is unpredictable, full of mystery. It remembers the final things.

This interruption of the way of the world is portrayed perfectly when Gawain, after one full year, has returned to the Green Knight. His journey returns him to where he was one full year ago: a game of stroke for stroke, except the roles and place, of course, have been reversed. In perfect reciprocity, the Green Knight finally delivers his stroke: "Þe scharp schrank to þe flesch þurȝ þe schyre grece . . ." ("the blade sank through the body through the flesh"; 2313). The return blow by the Green Knight, of course, mimics the same blow Gawain delivered to him at Camelot, repeating the very same words: Gawain too used a "scharp" which "schrank þurȝ þe schyire grace" (424–25). What accounts for the difference between the two? In what way can this perfectly reciprocal stroke be so radically different? We see both a fulfilling of the contract and also an interruption of the reciprocal violence begun in Camelot. But how to define such an interrupting force? The lack of a deadly blow can be seen precisely as an excessive gift, an act of mercy that puts a stop to this "gomen," and yet fulfills the letter of the law perfectly. It allows us to come full circle and yet exceed our beginning—or perhaps it allows us to imagine what Gawain's blow at Camelot could have looked like (a simple knick on the neck) had he exercised a modicum of "fraunchyse" or "pité" (651, 653), two of the five chivalric virtues symbolized in the pentangle on his shield. It seems the interruption of blunder is wrought by mercy, by a gift that asks for no reciprocation.

The Christological meditations of these poems, then, shift our focus from theological discussions *about* Christ to hermeneutical discussions about the very act of reading. I have found that this slight shift, from theological to textual, allows the students more room to breathe in and not to fear theological inquiry because it is now text-based, focusing on the poems in front of them. Furthermore, I find that students are less inclined to fear that English professors "make things up" after one demonstrates to them that the act of reading in much of the exegetical history of the West (and of Eastern Christendom, and in the Rabbinic tradition as well) has been to "make it up" (of course we explain that "making it up" takes lots of exegetical grounding). That our poet would not hesitate to employ his own biblical reading in his poetry means that we can follow suit and observe the ways in which his biblical readings spring from his various Christological meditations throughout these poems. Rather than finding theological or religious or pious shackles, the students may find this polysemous approach rewarding and quite liberating.

NOTES

[1] There is a lot of overlap among these various modes of reading and often no clear-cut distinction, for example, between typology and allegory, or even between a historical reading and a tropological one (see Young, esp. 161–212).

[2] I use the designation *Old Testament* throughout this essay when referring to the Hebrew Bible read through a Christological lens.

[3] I should note that a statement such as this would be uncontroversial, though certainly arguable, at Hillsdale College, where I teach. Hillsdale College is a nonsectarian Christian institution, and the vast majority of our students are Christian and come to the school already familiar with biblical texts and with Western theological traditions.

[4] Unless otherwise noted, all translations are my own. All references come from Andrew and Waldron, *Poems of the* Pearl *Manuscript* (2007).

Teaching *Pearl* with *Sir Gawain and the Green Knight*

Arthur Bahr

As a widely anthologized, relatively short, crowd-pleasing text, *Sir Gawain and the Green Knight* often finds its way into introductory British literature survey classes. Here I offer some suggestions for teaching *Pearl* in such contexts, considering first thematic-cultural issues, then literary-formal ones.

At the thematic-cultural level, juxtaposing *Pearl* with *Sir Gawain* as works almost certainly by the same author shows that religious devotion, as expressed in the former, is wholly compatible with the wit, vivacity, and sheer fun of the latter. Medievalists may find that proposition self-evident, but many undergraduates have only a crude understanding of medieval Europe's religiosity (e.g., in the Dark Ages people didn't think for themselves, and they burned lots of witches), and in some survey classes, piety is the implicitly unsavory other against which medieval literature is defined into "fun" relatability, whether through the pagan heroism of *Beowulf,* the scurrilous humor of Chaucer's Miller, or the brilliant irreverence of the Wife of Bath. *Pearl* shows that such a dismissive attitude is unjustified, both historically and today. The story of *Pearl* is relatable at some moments and alien at others; this tension between the wholly strange and the tantalizingly familiar (a version of which is also experienced, within the poem, by the Dreamer himself) can be presented as one aspect of what makes studying the distant past difficult and rewarding—and, indeed, rewarding because difficult.

Instructors might ask students (in class, not in essays; answers are too temptingly Google-able for the latter) how and whether the two poems seem related, despite their obvious and important differences. Some answers might include delight in verbal play and repartee (*Pearl*'s central debate and its punning concatenation words; the bedroom banter between Gawain and Lady Bertilak); concern for agreements and keeping one's word (the Dreamer's implicit agreement, later violated, not to cross the stream that separates him from the Pearl-Maiden; the beheading and exchange of winnings games in *Sir Gawain*); alien systems of value and exchange (the Parable of the Workers in the Vineyard in *Pearl* and heavenly economics more broadly; the apparent incommensurability of various exchanges in *Sir Gawain*); the passage of ordinary, mortal time and its relation to larger temporal systems (in *Pearl*, evocations first of the harvest and later of the time beyond time of John's Revelation; in *Sir Gawain*, the beautiful "passing of the seasons" opening to fit 2 and the poem's framing allusions to epic, national, and chivalric time); and the motif of circularity visible, among other ways, in the poet's decision to end each poem with a line nearly identical to its opening.

One similarity between the poems that students are unlikely to notice on their own is that both have 101 stanzas and an apparently numerologically significant total number of lines: 1212 for *Pearl* (although see below for a potential complication), which evokes the centrality of twelve to the architecture of the Heavenly Jerusalem; 2530 for *Sir Gawain*, which can be construed as many permutations of five ($500 \times 500 = 2500 + 5 \times 5 = 2525 + 5 = 2530$), the number central to the imagery and symbolism of Gawain's knighthood. Any skepticism in the classroom, about the latter suggestion especially, can be leveraged into a frank, more literary-critical discussion of the extent to which both poems—*Sir Gawain*, perhaps, more than *Pearl*—resist definitive, settled interpretation. The numerology of *Sir Gawain*, for example, would be easier to feel sure of if the poem had only 2525 lines; that would make it obviously parallel to *Pearl*'s 1212. The extrusion of the final bob and wheel also means that, properly speaking, *Sir Gawain* does *not* end with a version of its opening line, as do *Pearl* and *Patience*. This formal contrast can be related to the issue of thematic closure: are we any more confident of the Dreamer's having "learned something" from his adventure than we are of Gawain's? Does the presence of characters besides Gawain and the Green Knight in their poem—in contrast with *Pearl*, which features just the Dreamer and the Pearl-Maiden—affect our answer to that question? And in what sense are any of these textual constructs "characters," anyway? (This last question is a perennial one for contemporary readers of medieval literature; Chaucer's texts could be used for comparison.)

As the foregoing suggests, juxtaposing *Pearl* with *Sir Gawain* can produce compelling discussions even if the class is reading them entirely in translation.

If time and level allow some degree of engagement with the original, of course, the possibilities multiply. If the poems are part of a class that includes Chaucer's easier Middle English, instructors might assign that first, then use Sarah Stanbury's student edition of *Pearl* (which is free online) to have students work their way through just one section of the poem. *Sir Gawain* poses considerably more challenges in the original (chiefly of vocabulary), but a highly glossed version of the first two stanzas should prove manageable. (I have always simply produced my own version of these stanzas for this purpose.) Students should hear these comparative passages read aloud and, ideally, learn how to declaim them. The measured cadence and lush rhymes of *Pearl* contrast viscerally with the exuberance of *Sir Gawain*, its rhythmic irregularities and changeups, and this aural contrast suggests thematic ones as well: for example, motifs of roundness and enclosure in *Pearl* as against *Sir Gawain*'s unmistakably propulsive drive but uncertain endings (how long will this line or stanza be? how and where will Gawain end up?). Lest this distinction result in reinforcing simplistic contrasts between "religious" and "secular" texts, it is worth noting that the final image of both poems is one of sacred roundness: the elevated Host in *Pearl* (line 1209) and the Crown of Thorns in *Sir Gawain* (2529).

I would not have students in introductory classes read even heavily glossed excerpts before they have read the poems in translation, however; the texts themselves are sufficiently (brilliantly) strange that, if linguistic difficulty is added to the mix at the same time, the class may simply tune out. To get around this, one strategy would be to read the opening stanzas of each poem, out loud and in the original, at the end of the meeting before the class reads *Pearl* in translation (it sounds sufficiently weird and beautiful that it should whet their appetites), then spend a session on it, another on *Sir Gawain*, and a third comparing the two, for which they would read a few stanzas of each in the (heavily glossed) original. Of course, three class sessions are not enough to do full justice to either poem, much less both, but such a unit would usefully counterbalance the *Canterbury Tales*, which often dominates the medieval portion of British literature survey courses.

Teaching Pearl *with* Sir Gawain *in Middle English in Seminars*

My experience teaching *Pearl* and *Sir Gawain* in Middle English suggests that, except in extremely specialized contexts (a roomful of students who are not just English majors but also avowed medievalists, such as one might expect in a graduate seminar), treating these poems as most of us treat Chaucer—here's a (lightly) glossed text; just read it until you get it—does not work. (It is not clear to me that this strategy works particularly well with Chaucer either, but that is a subject for another volume.) The language in *Pearl* and *Sir Gawain* is simply too difficult, yet simultaneously fundamental to the experience of the poet's texts. This is especially true of *Pearl*, whose plot sounds threadbare set against its poetry. I begin this section by outlining ways of making linguistic experience central to students' apprehension of both poems, assuming a relatively small class (twenty or fewer students) with a significant proportion of English or humanities majors, most having perhaps little or no background in medieval literature or culture. I conclude with suggestions for using *Pearl* and *Sir Gawain* as occasions for more theoretical readings and discussions. For both purposes, I recommend using the standard scholarly edition of Malcolm Andrew and Ronald Waldron.

I suggest having students come prepared to translate the day's reading as if they were taking a class in Old English or Latin. Be forthright about the amount of work involved in really understanding the poems, and give students a concrete method: they should read out loud first, then look up words in the glossary (writing the meanings in the margin, or they'll forget), then read through again for comprehension, and finally (after a pause of at least an hour or two to clear their minds) reread for literary appreciation. (Instructors will understand that such a process will often be more ideal than reality.) During translation in class, correct mistakes and flag interesting words, images, or syntactic structures that merit literary-critical discussion. Challenge students who produce overly literal, word-for-word translations to explain what the lines' sense actually is; likewise, push those who rely wholesale on the frequent, sometimes overly helpful translations at the bottom of the page to explain the relation between the editors' version and the Middle English. When translation is on the agenda, try to ensure that each student gets the opportunity to translate at least one stanza or two per class period.

When teaching *Pearl*, I go through one section of the poem this way before moving to literary-critical discussion; for *Sir Gawain*, whose structure is less regular, the number of stanzas one translates at a time may vary a bit. To make sure students have something to say when we get to discussion, I ask them to be prepared with at least one comment or question about the relation of the language to the story of the poem. (This also prevents them from focusing too exclusively on the mechanics of translation.) They might bring up diction, syntax, tone, sound, rhythm, or cadence, or metaphor, image, or simile. (That is not a complete list, of course. Hopefully, they already have such weapons in their interpretive arsenal, but a list with brief definitions would probably be worth providing anyway.) My goal in the literary-critical discussions is to reinforce the extent to which slow, careful attention to language opens up forms of meaning and beauty that would otherwise be inaccessible. It is worth emphasizing that this lesson equally applies to much later literature. For example, the poetry of Elizabeth Bishop yields something like its full interpretive resonance only when we refuse to take the superficial easiness of its plainspoken style as an excuse to read quickly. The enforced gradualism of a first engagement with *Pearl* and *Sir Gawain* in their difficult Middle English, in other words, may reinforce the value of slowness as one component of a more broadly applicable practice of close reading.

I would read *Pearl* before *Sir Gawain* in almost any pedagogical context that includes their original language because *Pearl* is shorter and linguistically easier. That said, translating the first few stanzas of each poem (five of *Pearl*, three or four of *Sir Gawain*) in the same class, even going back and forth between poems, may help the literary effects of their distinctive forms emerge with particular force: *Pearl*'s metrical regularity, rhyme, concatenation, and consistent though not uniform alliteration, versus *Sir Gawain*'s often craggy, bristling texture in the strophes, which contrasts strikingly with the abbreviated rhythm and strict rhyme of its bobs and wheels. This exercise also highlights the poet's remarkable linguistic range, specifically the contrast between *Pearl*'s more Romance-based diction and the more Germanic (Old English and Old Norse) word hoard of *Sir Gawain*. That contrast is not universal, and line 11 of *Pearl* is worth highlighting in this context: "I dewyne, fordolked of luf-daungere." The contrast between the emphatically Germanic *fordolked* and the French diction that predominated early in the stanza (e.g., *plesaunte, oryent, araye, gaye, erbere*) is part of what makes this line rhetorically and emotionally powerful. Its final word, *luf-daungere*, is a Franco-Germanic compound and thus an apt enactment of the poet's linguistic hybridity. The word also offers an early opportunity to discuss aristocratic and courtly-love vocabulary, which governs a number of *Pearl*'s concatenation words (e.g., *cortaysye, blysse, delyt*) and will recur—very differently inflected—in the bedroom-temptation scenes of *Sir Gawain*. It might even be worth having students flip ahead to line 1247 of *Sir Gawain*, in which Gawain responds to one of Lady Bertilak's many advances: "To be plesaunce of your prys; hit were a pure joye." The congruence of this diction with much of *Pearl*'s first stanza and its contrast with *Sir Gawain*'s opening (e.g., "Þe borȝ brittened and brent to brondez and aksez"; 2) should forcefully strike even students who are new to Middle English—again, especially if read aloud.

Clearly, working through either poem in this way is extremely labor-intensive. *Pearl* is sufficiently short and lapidary in its wordplay that I find it worth that investment; students can be reassured that it does indeed become easier and faster with practice. *Sir Gawain*, on the other hand, is just enough longer than *Pearl* and just enough harder in its vocabulary that reading only key scenes in the original works as well, relying on one or more of many fine translations (see esp. those of Armitage; Borroff; Merwin) for the rest of the poem. This informed work with translations could also serve as the basis of discussion and one or more assignments. In assigning passages of *Sir Gawain* to be read in Middle English, I generally choose from among lines 1–36 (the introduction), lines 130–490 (the arrival of the Green Knight, his challenge, and its immediate aftermath), lines 491–536 (fit 2's "passage of seasons" portion), lines 619–67 (Gawain's shield and its symbolism), lines 1046–1125 (the establishment of Gawain's pact with Bertilak), lines 1178–1318 (the first bedroom scene), lines 1468–1559 (the second bedroom scene; note that this one, unlike the first, does not correspond to the poem's stanza breaks), lines 1733–1892 (the third bedroom scene), and lines 2160–2530 (the denouement). Assigning all these scenes would bring the time spent with *Sir Gawain*'s Middle English into near alignment with that of *Pearl*, which seems appropriate to the poems' literary merits and also frees up time in the syllabus for different kinds of work.

There are plenty of worthy ways to spend that time, of course, since aspects of *Pearl* and *Sir Gawain* other than their language invite discussion. As anonymous, untitled texts that survive in a single, not particularly deluxe manuscript, for example, they can spark broader theoretical discussions about the nature of authorship, what can be known of the past, and the construction (social and physical) of literary value. In particular, the poems offer a nicely concrete way of thinking through two foundational essays in literary theory: Michel Foucault's "What Is an Author?" and Roland Barthes's "Death of the Author." After reading one or both essays in the context of *Pearl* and *Sir Gawain*, students might address what justifies and is at stake in the nearly universal belief that the same singular person is responsible for creating *Pearl*, *Sir Gawain*, and the two other, unjustly neglected poems of Cotton Nero A.x. If we decide that we are indeed dealing with a single author, what are the stakes of deciding to call him the *Pearl* poet as opposed to the *Gawain* poet, or vice versa? Is it appropriate that he has never (to my knowledge) been called either the *Cleanness* or the *Patience* poet or, that "he" is universally assumed to be male? What interpretive avenues might be opened up if we took contrarian or agnostic positions on any of these questions, and how do any of them intersect, pragmatically, with the more linguistically and poetically grounded issues raised earlier?

One way of thus reading "against the grain" that unites practical and theoretical concerns would be to return to the total number of lines in *Pearl*, discussed briefly above. In spite of the poem's highly ornate form, line 472 does not appear in the sole surviving manuscript, but all editors and nearly all critics have assumed this omission to be the product of scribal error during transcription, and so the poem is treated as having 1212 lines. David Carlson, however, has made the compelling argument that such formal imperfections in *Pearl* constitute a subtle assertion of authorial humility, the poet's recognition that unlike the structures of the Heavenly Jerusalem described in the poem, his are earthly and so must remain in some measure flawed. This argument cannot be proven, since we lack any other copies against which to compare the one that survives, and that fact might inspire discussion of the burden of proof on which literary criticism should operate—even, more fundamentally, what the purpose of literary criticism is—as distinct from that of other, more quantifiably verifiable forms of scholarship.

The material uniqueness of *Pearl* and *Sir Gawain* can lead to other kinds of theoretical discussion, too. Here I find Walter Benjamin's "The Work of Art in the Age of Mechanical Reproduction" especially helpful for the contrast that it draws between then-novel forms of art like photography or film and older, hand-produced genres like painting and (though Benjamin does not address the medieval in depth) manuscripts. It took centuries, after all, for the poems of Cotton Nero A.x to be mechanically reproduced in modern editions, and if its poems were ever reproduced by hand in other manuscripts, they do not survive. Benjamin's concept of the aura, meanwhile, usefully foregrounds the question of artistic value (something that students will hopefully have acquired practical experience with, and appetite for, through the intensive linguistic work they have already done with the poems), while the fact that he treats mostly non-textual forms of art raises the question of how *literary* value might ebb and flow differently from that of other, more purely visual artistic modes. Benjamin's essay is also helpful for its insistence on the centrality of the material and the historical to these issues. How, instructors might ask, can we recover for (or discover in) *Pearl* and *Sir Gawain* as they survive today a version of their historically contingent "aura" when so little about their historical contexts is conclusively knowable? How should extrapoetic elements of the poems' situation in Cotton Nero A.x, such as the famous addition of the motto of the Order of the Garter to the end of *Sir Gawain*, or the illustrations of scenes from both texts, or even the layout of the pages, affect our reading of them? (The recent publication online of *The Cotton Nero A.x Project*, a free, high-quality facsimile of the entire manuscript, offers an excellent way into such questions.)

Another essay by Benjamin, "The Task of the Translator," would help link the students' intense engagement with the practical difficulties of the *Pearl* poet's Middle English to broader theoretical questions of the sort outlined above, which are comparably difficult although in different ways. Even instructors who are working only with the original might have students compare two or three different translations of a key scene from *Sir Gawain* and discuss what features of the poem each translator manages to convey. (This exercise works well in a range of pedagogical scenarios, including informal discussion, oral presentation, and written essay.) The intricacy of *Pearl*'s form more adamantly resists translation, which is surely the principal reason many fewer have been published. Instructors might ask students which of that poem's many formal features (rhyme scheme, meter, concatenation, alliteration) they would prioritize in a translation and why, then challenge them to produce a translation of just one stanza along with an explanation of their creative and practical choices. Remind students that translation is not only verbal; it has physical and cultural dimensions, too, as its etymology suggests. A good final assignment linking *Pearl* and *Sir Gawain* might be to reflect on the many forms of translation each student has witnessed and participated in during the semester and to articulate in response their own notion of "the task(s) of the translator."

Teaching *Pearl* with
Its Sources and Analogues

Mark Bradshaw Busbee

Traditional pedagogy for *Pearl* might follow the advice of D. W. Robertson, Jr., who urges teachers of advanced courses on medieval literature to place texts "in a cultural tradition that extends from classical antiquity through the early decades of the eighteenth century" ("Context" 129). Even teachers who do not feel compelled to teach *Pearl* within the strict context of the Western cultural tradition would agree that students simply cannot fully comprehend a poem like *Pearl* without some encounter with its sources and analogues. Background texts can lead readers, like the Dreamer in the poem being led by his dream, into "a place of freedom or expansiveness" (Stanbury, "Introduction" 1). The problem is that expansiveness, however liberating it may be, can also overwhelm readers and overshadow the poem. The linear plot, interlocking stanzas, and alliterative rhythms of *Pearl* draw in readers, but the sources and analogues of the poem can perplex and pull them from the central story line. This chapter therefore has a dual purpose: first, to offer an approach that mitigates the intimidating idea of "source study" and transforms reader discomfort into interpretive opportunity; and second, to provide instructors with a survey of prominent sources and significant analogues.

Students in my undergraduate medieval survey courses at a midsize regional university typically had little experience reading highly allusive poetry; as a result, when they encountered *Pearl*, they were limited to a superficial reading of the poem's story line. To help them explore the sophisticated network of sources and analogues, I developed a three-step approach that begins with careful reading of the poem, followed by strategies for identifying and categorizing sources and analogues, and finishes with analyses of its intertextuality. First, students discover background texts within the poem's framework through an initial complete reading in translation, preferably a translation with unobtrusive notes and commentary. (I have found Brian Stone's translation in *Medieval English Verse* particularly useful in introductory survey courses because it relegates commentary to an introduction to the poem and relies on an accessible translation, unencumbered by heavy notation.) Students read the poem while answering questions about plot, character, and theme—to prevent early entanglement in the poem's dense web of allusions. Then they compare *Pearl* with other crossover analogues they know, like *Alice's Adventures in Wonderland* or *A Wrinkle in Time*, where unsettled or unhappy characters journey into parallel worlds and experience healing, growth, or consolation.

With a sense of the poem's basics and of some modern analogues, students move to step two, where they find allusions woven into the fabric of *Pearl* that they might have missed. They reread, this time while listing A) obvious allusions, B) implied allusions, and C) possible allusions (ones they think, but aren't sure, the poet is making). As a class-made list of allusion types A, B, and C materializes, connections become clearer. Students begin to see how the poem works within and against a number of influences and literary parallels and to understand that the poet does not feel what Harold Bloom calls "anxiety of influence." They perceive then that the poet's intention is to draw readers into a shared experience by engaging established cultural traditions. Discussion further facilitates a move from discovery of allusions to their categorization and identification as sources and analogues.[1] I explain that a source is a work that the poet used directly; that close analogues are texts we think the author probably knew but that we cannot call direct sources, judging by the date of the analogue, along with the plot and characterization details; and that distant analogues are ones the poet could hardly have known, judging by the date, the language, and the absence of specific similarities. Allusions identified fit sometimes closely within these different types of sources and analogues. For example, students often discover that A allusions are frequently what we would call sources, while B allusions are usually sources or close analogues, and C allusions are close or distant analogues.

Equipped with terms for the subtexts that they discover, students are ready for step three, where they focus on how the poem is enriched by (and enriches) its sources and analogues. In introductory survey courses, I generally try not to rely too heavily on literary theory during class discussion, but in order to give students a way to think about the relation between texts and subtexts, I have found Julia Kristeva's explanation of intertextuality and transposition particularly useful:

> The term *inter-textuality* denotes th[e] transposition of one (or several) sign system(s) into another; but since this term has often been understood in the banal sense of "study of sources," we prefer the term *transposition* because it specifies that the passage from one signifying system to another demands new articulation.   (*Revolution* 59–60)

To make constructive use of sources and analogues, students must see *Pearl*, its sources, and its analogues not as works isolated from one another, but participating in a fluid exchange of meaning. Rather than conduct a "study of sources" to understand how the *Pearl* poet "uses" disparate elements from *The Inferno* or Revelation or *The Romance of the Rose*, students should consider how the poem is a mosaic of concepts and assumptions transposed from biblical, literary, and even folk traditions.

Of course, seeing *Pearl* as a mosaic of influences and having something to say about it are two different things entirely, so, in order to demonstrate the critical approach, I lead students through a sample analysis of the intertextuality of the first section of the poem. They have already labeled the passages. They now know, for example, that the garden setting (which they usually identify as an A allusion) likely draws upon biblical sources like the Garden of Eden and the garden in Song of Songs; they are also aware that the message about life coming out of death (which they usually label a B allusion) has its basis in the New Testament (John 12.24–25; 1 Cor. 15.35–38; Heb. 10.14). They usually suspect obscure allusions (C allusions) behind the symbolism of the pearl, the grief of the narrator, the onslaught of sleep, and the poet's emphasis on flowers. They struggle to characterize the narrator's feelings for his lost beloved; they have read the entire poem, so they feel sure that it is his lost daughter but, now, returning to the first section, they perceive the tension between the Dreamer's conflicting roles as grieving father and as pining lover.

When students recognize how coexisting ideas transposed from source texts create thematic tension, they are ready to engage the intertextuality of the poem. The last step is to ask them the following questions (or similar ones) about how transposed ideas alter the poem: What is the relation of the source text to the poem? What set of assumptions might this text bring into the poem? How does its presence alter how readers might understand the action? A different line of inquiry focuses on the background interplay of the source materials: Where are allusions in conflict? What is the middle way between the implications of religious sources, on the one hand, and secular source materials, on the other?

The biggest challenge for instructors who are new to *Pearl* is gaining some basic knowledge of the poem's many varied sources and analogues. I offer the following overview as an introduction to those subtexts. Though brief, and in many ways superficial, I believe it should assist instructors with the approach I provide above.

The principal and most conspicuous source for *Pearl* is the Bible.[2] Special influence comes from the New Testament books of Matthew, which contains the Parable of the Workers in the Vineyard (Matt. 20.1–16), and Revelation (Apocalypse in the Vulgate), which depicts the New Jerusalem. All Gospels figure briefly in references to Jesus's Crucifixion (Matt. 26.67; Mark 14.65; Luke 22.64) and baptism (Matt. 3.13; Mark 1.4–9; Luke 3.3), his bidding the children to come to him (Matt. 19.13–15; Mark 10.13–16; Luke 18.15–17), and his Sermon on the Mount (Matt. 5.3–10), while the Epistles (1 and 2 Cor.; Heb.; and 1 Peter) serve to emphasize or reinforce the messages in the Gospels and Revelation. The allusions enrich ideas about the quality of knowledge in heaven (1 Cor. 13.11–12), the significance of the New Jerusalem (Heb. 12.22), and Jesus's role as the Lamb of Jerusalem (John 1.29, 36; 1 Pet.1.14). Gospels and Epistles together underpin the consolatory theme of the necessity of death for rebirth

(John 12.24–25; 1 Cor. 15.35–38; Heb. 10.14). Old Testament books, like the Song of Songs, Isaiah, Psalms, and Daniel, inform and complicate events and references by providing traditional subthemes. Dream interpretations by Joseph (Gen. 40) and Daniel (Dan. 4) are exemplars for how dreams can be mined for meaning. Song of Songs reframes the relationship between the Dreamer and the Pearl-Maiden as one based on desire, while working in support of the imagery in Revelation of the Pearl-Maiden as the bride of the Lamb. Ezekiel and Psalms complement overt allusions and provide subthemes to the theological debate. (The Dreamer, e.g., refers to Psalms 142.2 to suggest that no man is justified before God.)

Patristic writings underlie the poem's treatment of theological matters such as the differences between earthly and heavenly existence, the nature of dreams, the quality of sin and forgiveness, and the nature of the afterlife. If we assume that the poet could read Latin, then the writings of Saint Augustine of Hippo, particularly *De civitate Dei* (*City of God*), may have informed the poem's image of the deceased infant as a grown woman (22.14) and the recurring theme of the distinction between the earthly and heavenly Jerusalem. Augustine's *De genesi ad litteram: The Literal Meaning of Genesis* explains the type of vision in which another spirit mingles with the spirit of a man during a vision to manifest special knowledge. How to receive salvation is also a topic in "A Treatise on the Merits and Forgiveness of Sins, and on the Baptism of Infants" (*De peccatorum meritis et remissione et de baptismo parvulorum*). And his "Sermon 87" asks questions about the Parable of the Workers in the Vineyard and may therefore have inspired the Dreamer's questions following the maiden's retelling of the parable.[3] Thomas Aquinas's *Summa* may have been the poet's source for the writings of Augustine, as well as those of Plotinus (on holy Jerusalem, see Meyer, *Medieval Allegory* 140), Pseudo-Dionysius (on love as a unitive force), Macrobius (on the purity of the soul), and Boethius (on the nature of the Trinity)—all of which are close analogues to *Pearl*.[4]

The *Pearl* poet may have drawn upon other patristic sources, such as the *Glossa ordinaria* and the writings of Bede, John of Salisbury, Bonaventura of Bagnoregio, Bruno of Astensis, and Albert the Great. The poem symbolically equates the penny with salvation and states that "the Maiden has received her 'penny'" (Andrew and Waldron [1978] 80n; lines 569–88). This symbolism can be tracked back to the *Glossa ordinaria*, which was an assembly of glosses from theologians like Augustine, Jerome, and Bede, printed in the margins of the Vulgate Bible.[5] Bede's commentary on Revelation devotes its final section to an exposition of the pearl symbol, and his "Vision of Dryhten" tells the story of Dryhten's after-death, angel-guided journey to the gates of heaven. The others, however, are likely close analogues. In *Policraticus* 6.24, John of Salisbury employs the analogy of the human body and its limbs to explain that state organization is modeled on the hierarchy of heaven and earth; the Pearl-Maiden also uses this analogy, but to different ends. *The Mystical Vine*, a work attributed to Bonaventura, relates different kinds of flowers to virtues.[6] In the third stanza of the poem, the poet similarly discusses the idea of blossoms of immortality springing from mortality. Bruno of Astensis may have furnished the poet with a means of classifying the various brides in the celestial procession, while *In Praise of the Blessed Virgin*—often attributed to Albert the Great—with its description of Mary, may have provided a model for the Pearl-Maiden's adornment in pearls. These, too, might rightly be regarded as either close or distant analogues.[7]

A few lapidaries and texts in the liturgical, hymn, and lyric traditions have traditionally been identified as source materials because they provide symbolic and sometimes spiritual interpretations of elements in the poem. *Pearl*'s first line ("Perle, pleasuante to prynces paye") echoes a common formula in medieval verse lapidaries, found in texts like Marbodus of Rennes's *Book of Stones or Gems*, which is generally regarded as the basis for all medieval lapidaries,[8] and Albert the Great's *Book of Minerals*. Later, at line 39, the phrase "high season" appears. Commonly translated as "holy days," the phrase connects the poem with the liturgy of the transfiguration of Christ, the assumption of the Virgin, and Lammas. The end of the poem connects to the liturgy of the feast of All Saints on 1 November, which included readings from Revelation. Susan Rastetter ("'Bot Mylde'") proposes that a text in *The Saurum Breviary* concerns themes in *Pearl*, such as the absence of anger and envy in the New Jerusalem. At the end of the poem, the Dreamer mentions the Eucharist as a source of solace, which has aroused critical attention. However, we cannot know if the poet consciously drew upon the liturgy in writing *Pearl*; he more likely drew these details from his lived experience. Similarly uncertain is the influence of hundreds of hymns and lyrics praising the Virgin Mary, dating from this period; all relate to the poem at some level, and scholars have noted that the Pearl-Maiden is a kind of lesser Mary. Two hymns—"A Song of Great Sweetness to His Daintiest Dam" and the Harley Lyric on the five joys of the Virgin—bear affinities to *Pearl*; the Five Joys because of its use of the phrase "luf-longing" ("love-longing"; 1152) as a term of religious devotion for the Virgin Mary rather than sexual desire. The influence of liturgy and hymnody is uncertain, but we can assume that the *Pearl* poet may have heard the liturgy in church weekly throughout the year; therefore, it likely made a deep impression on his thinking through regular access.

Although the poet may have had less access to literary texts from the Continent, many scholars have observed that *Pearl* draws upon established rhetorical and literary patterns of the continental literary tradition. The poet demonstrates attention to Matthew of Vendôme's *Ars versificatoria* by establishing overarching tone through his opening description.[9] More significantly, *Pearl* fits squarely within the dream-vision tradition, which began with the sixth book of Cicero's *De re publica*. Cicero tells how Scipio, the Roman consul of conquered North Africa, dreams that his adopted grandfather Africanus talks with him about how to rule effectively. Responsible for the preservation and elevation of Cicero's story, Macrobius's *Commentary on the Dream of Scipio* explains the nature and meaning of the five types of dreams: the enigmatic dream (*oneiros* in Greek and *somnium* in Latin); the prophetic vision (*horama* in Greek and *visio* in Latin); the oracular dream (*chrematismos* in Greek, *oraculum* in Latin); the nightmare (*enypnion* in Greek and *insomnium* in Latin); and the apparition (*phantasma* in Greek and *visum* in Latin). Boethius's *Consolation of Philosophy* and Alain de Lille's *De planctu naturae* (*The Complaint of Nature*) employ the plot structure in Cicero's story and the theory in Macrobius's commentary. In both, the troubled protagonist has a vision wherein an allegorical figure (Lady Philosophy in *Consolation* and Nature in *De planctu*) consoles him through dialogue. Plot and dialogue, particularly between Lady Philosophy and Boethius about differences between true and false happiness, served the poet as models in *Pearl*.

Prominent continental medieval literary sources for *Pearl* that follow the underlying structure provided by Boethius and Alain de Lille are Boccaccio's *Olympia*, Dante's *Divine Comedy*, and by *Le Roman de la Rose* (*The Romance of the Rose*). Boccaccio's *Olympia* is a Latin eclogue written to commemorate the death of the author's daughter. The many resemblances in characterization, plot, theme, and tone position it as a possible source. (See Gollancz [1921] for a translation.) Boccaccio's narrator falls into a grief-induced sleep, dreams of his daughter as a holy figure, is invited to look upon the Kingdom of God, tries to enter but fails, says goodbye to his daughter, and then awakes much happier for her. Problems arise for the status of *Olympia* as a source, however: some deem it unlikely that the *Pearl* poet had access to a copy of the poem. The influence of Dante's *Divine Comedy* is more certain in its modeling of the journey motif, which is not present in Boethius's, Alain de Lille's, or Boccaccio's visions. In the *Inferno*, Dante dreams he enters into a wilderness in a dream journey; in *Purgatorio*, he encounters an exotic river in a terrestrial paradise, where he stops to cleanse himself before journeying into paradise; and in *Paradiso*, he meets his beloved Beatrice who shows him a vision and, later, he sees a heavenly procession. In *Pearl*, similar events occur in the same order.

The Romance of the Rose is another source because the *Pearl* poet uses language drawn from the romance (e.g., "luf-daungere" ["aloofness" or "distance of the beloved"] at line 11) and the Pearl-Maiden quotes the romance (lines 750–56). More generally, both poems employ symbols of perfection at their center. Compared with the rose, the pearl is perfect: it is round, which invokes ideas of enclosure and wholeness, and it is white, which recalls purity. In the fifth section of *Pearl*, the Pearl-Maiden compares the profane rose and the divine pearl:

> You lost a rose that grew in the ground:
> A flower that fails and is not renewed,
> But such is the coffer closing it round,
> With the worth of a pearl it is now imbued.
> (lines 269–72; Borroff, *Gawain Poet* 132)

The rose transforms into a pearl possibly to suggest how profane love becomes sacred. In *Pearl*, profane love is the earthly soul's attempt to grasp at what can be achieved only by transcending the physical world. The narrator himself, still mortal, illustrates how impossible it is to understand divine love while in the profane world. As in *The Romance of the Rose*, the Dreamer's quest moves from natural imagistic narrative to philosophical debate. As the poem progresses, the vision and dialogue resolve complications caused by the confluence of paternal, sexual, and sacred love.

The wider range of Middle English literature reveals a number of literary analogues. Contemporaries of the *Pearl* poet—other so-called Ricardian poets: Chaucer, Gower, and Langland—share indebtedness to the continental models of *The Divine Comedy* and *The Romance of the Rose*, but the status of their writings as source texts is uncertain. In Gower's *Confessio Amantis*, Amans (Lover) enters a dream dialogue with Genius about the overarching theme of love, and in Langland's *Piers Plowman*, the dull-witted dreamer encounters allegorical figures who guide him on his journey. Like the poet in *Pearl* (and John of Salisbury), Gower uses the body metaphor to explain social and spiritual hierarchies (Prologus 152–53). Chaucer's *The Legend of Good Women* contemplates paradise, while *The Book of the Duchess* invokes praise language resembling the *Pearl* poet's.

Analogues in medieval English romance and philosophical literature reveal how *Pearl* participates in broader cultural traditions. Sudden sleep of the Dreamer echoes a stock event of grail legends and saints' lives; the exotic river resembles the ones in romances like *Floris et Blancheflor* (where it poses danger to the maiden); the Pearl-Maiden's removal of her crown as a show of humility resembles an act of the king in *Awntyrs off Arthur*; and the Pearl-Maiden's costume is described in language similar to that of *Winner and Waster* (and Boethius's *Consolation* and Alain de Lille's *De planctu*). *Pearl* also engages a major convention in the tradition of medieval literature: the visions of paradise. *Mandeville's Travels* conveys information about some of the places and events in the Old Testament, including Earthly Paradise. The traveler, like the Dreamer in *Pearl*, is separated from Paradise by a river and can only observe its grandiosity and wonder from a distance. The traveler explains, "No mortelle man . . . may approche to that place withouten specyalle grace of God, so that of that place I can sey you no more. And therfore I schalle holde me stille and retornen to that that I haue seen" (Seymour 222).

A vision of paradise is, according to W. A. Davenport (*Medieval Narrative* 186), a central theme of medieval imaginative fiction in English legend and folklore. One of the "most popular and elaborate texts in the medieval genre of the visionary infernal literature" (Easting, *Visions* 43), the late-twelfth-century *Visio Tnugdall* (The Vision of Tundale), demonstrates possible influence on *Pearl*. The Irishman Tundale has an out-of-body experience and, afterward, offers what is the most detailed imagining of heaven before Dante. The poet tells us that "Tundale had delyte greytt / Of the syghtt of that fayr seytt" (lines 2253–54) and, like Mandeville, Tundale wanted to see more. He says,

> Y have seyn y-nogh
> Dere lorde Y pray the of thy grace
> Leyt me not owt of thys place
> For Y wold never owt of this place wendo
> But dwell here owttyn ende.   (Turnbull 2262–66)

> I have seen enough.
> Dear Lord, I pray Thee of Thy grace
> Let me not out of this place
> For I would never out of this place go
> But dwell here without end.

The guiding angel tells him that he cannot but that he should hold in his thought and not forget what he has seen. "St. Patrick's Purgatory," told in the late-twelfth-century Latin prose *Tractatus de purgatoria Sancti Patricii*, tells a similar story of a man brought to see Earthly Paradise. The story, appearing in the Auchinleck manuscript, offers elaborate description of the Earthly Paradise and its precious stones. What is most relevant to *Pearl* in this account, however, is the doctrinal detail provided about the swift purgation from sin of a young child and the lengthy processes needed for an old man:

> Þe child þat was yborn toniȝt,
> Er Þe soule be hider ydiȝt,
> Þe pain schal ouerfle.
> Strong & heui is it þan,
> Here to com þe old man,
> Þat long in sinne haþ be.   (Burnley and Wiggins 995–1000)

> The child that was born tonight,
> Before the soul hastens to flight,
> The pain shall quickly flee.

Strong and heavy it is then,
Here to come to the old man,
That long in sin had been

Analogues like this one, which engage folk ideas about sin and salvation, reframe once again how we might read *Pearl*.

This far-from-comprehensive overview omits possible sources and analogues in art (from manuscript illustrations to stained-glass windows), and it does not consider possible modern analogues, such as the works of Milton, Shakespeare, or even Hawthorne. These are rich areas of investigation and should be explored for their ability to shed further light on what is a multifaceted, highly allusive poem.

NOTES

[1] The categories I use are adapted from Beidler.

[2] Borroff offers translations of key biblical sources, and William Vantuono's Pearl: *An Edition* (178–80) includes a valuable chart, adapted from Osgood ([1906] 98–100) and Gordon (165–67), of places where biblical allusions are made in the poem. Malcolm Andrew and Ronald Waldron provide the Latin text of key passages in the appendix of their translation, *The Poems of the* Pearl *Manuscript*.

[3] Origen's "Commentary on the Gospel of Matthew" is also commonly considered a source because the poet seems to have the Pearl-Maiden paraphrase it in her retelling of the Parable of the Vineyard.

[4] See Meyer, *Medieval Allegory*, for how *Pearl* might have drawn directly or indirectly on Plotinus (140) and demonstrated knowledge of Pseudo-Dionysius (71–76).

[5] See Migne, "Walafridi strabi," col. 876. Migne attributes the text (and the passage in question) to the Carolingian scholar and poet Walafrid Strabo. Scholars now regard the text as a compilation assembled in the twelfth century and not the work of one person.

[6] See Bonaventura, "Vitis mystica." The work was once confidently attributed to Bonaventura, but now his authorship is widely questioned. The work is a sort of dialogue containing a collection of passages from the Church Fathers about the Passion.

[7] See Borgnet, *Opera omnia*, vol. 36, for a Latin text of *De laudibus beatae Mariae Virginis*, which some believe has been falsely attributed to Albert the Great. A product of the mid-thirteenth century, this work proved hugely influential in Marian scholarship.

[8] See Migne, vol. 171.

[9] See Copeland and Sluiter for a discussion of *Ars versificatoria*.

Pearl as a Gateway into Middle English Poetry: Comparative Approaches

Elizabeth Harper

I taught *Pearl* as part of an upper-division Middle English survey course at a regional comprehensive university in the South. My students, mostly English majors, came to class with a wide range of orientations and skill levels. They also came to class from a fairly homogeneous cultural background: white, with mostly rural or small-town origins and a cultural backdrop of low-church evangelical Protestantism. My goals for the course were simple. First, I wanted my students to understand the culture of medieval England as sharing common experiences and existential questions with our own (and, with some variance, every culture). Second, I wanted them to learn about the historical and cultural context of the texts. On a broader level, I hoped to help my students understand how culture shapes texts and how texts shape culture. Ultimately, of course, I wanted my students to understand *themselves* as culturally situated. And at base, if I am honest, I wanted them to love the Middle Ages, in something like the way that Nicholas Watson advocates in his 1999 essay "Desire for the Past": to recognize these voices from the past as other selves, other "I"s, and to read their writings not just as objects of analysis but as persons speaking from across the gulf of time, geographic distance, and cultural change.

My students started out in one of three positions relative to these goals. First, those who had never encountered medieval literature tended to expect that the readings would be inaccessible to them. This expectation took a number of forms. Some used the word *hard* (in a language and style that they found off-putting or difficult to understand). Others used the word *boring*, meaning that they thought the texts would not meet their expectations for narrative and poetic enjoyment. Still others thought the texts were so old as to be irrelevant to their academic and personal interests because they dealt with topics and situations that they did not understand or care about. All three of these expectations signaled to me that students recognized linguistic, cultural, and psychological distance between themselves and the literature of the Middle Ages.

Second, a vocal minority of students was excited to read medieval literature for a paradoxically related reason: the strangeness of the Middle Ages was precisely what excited them. Unlike the first group, many of these students had already read some medieval texts; they had experienced the distance between themselves and the text as a positive thing. The archaic language, fantastic images, unfamiliar class system, and highborn protagonists appealed mightily to them. The challenge I faced with these students was how best to complicate their fantasies; the task was made easier by the fact that they were already highly motivated.

A third tendency among some students was to ignore difference and simply approach the texts ahistorically, as if no distance lay between themselves and the characters in the text. These were the students who attacked theological points in the texts using evangelical Protestant arguments or diagnosed Julian of Norwich as mentally ill because she claimed to experience visions. Paradoxically, failing to recognize difference created the widest gaps between themselves and the text: after finding their expectations frustrated, they were most likely to judge a text a failure.

In teaching my medieval survey course, then, I had to help all three categories of student learn how to negotiate both sameness and difference. My central argument in this essay is that we can use *Pearl* to help make this happen for our students. *Pearl* can serve as an entry into Middle English literature by giving students a point of emotional connection between themselves and this apparently alien past culture. I start by describing my own experiences teaching *Pearl* as "gateway." I then describe several possible directions to take in teaching it with other Middle English texts. My goal in this essay is not to exhaust every possible approach, but to offer up some discussion questions, activities, and productive ways to compare *Pearl* with other Middle English poems.

Reading *Pearl* as an undergraduate, I myself came away mystified and slightly bored. The extended theological arguments struck me as dry and arcane, and I was eager to get to *Sir Gawain and the Green Knight*, which better met my preconceived ideas about the exotic, fantastic Middle Ages. As a faculty member, I wanted to avoid replicating this experience for my students. I started out very simply, borrowing a strategy from Professor Lesley Allen of Greenville College, in Illinois. During our first day reading *Pearl*, I asked my students to write for five minutes about grieving in their own culture. For guidance I gave them several different questions. How does our culture handle the loss of a loved one? What sorts of feelings do we have, and for how long? What do people say to someone who is grieving? What are you NOT supposed to say to someone who is grieving? I wanted students to connect the subject matter of *Pearl* with what they already knew about this topic. I also hoped that they could articulate and examine their preexisting assumptions in order to better understand how a medieval reader's response to the poem might differ from their own.

The students in my class did all this and more. They started by describing the social scripts that work—"I'm so sorry for your loss"—and the scripts that do not—"I understand, don't cry, she or he is out of pain or in a better place or with God." Some of them discussed the American resistance to thinking about death. Others mentioned the assumption that "normal" people do not show grief in public. I intended to use this outline to contrast with medieval rituals of mourning. However, what surprised me most was how personally many of my students responded. One student talked about the death of his mother from a debilitating disease when he was still in high school; four years later, he still grieved her loss. Another student expressed her rage at hearing from well-meaning friends, "Your mother has gone to a better place," with the implication that she herself must not mourn. Students then began to compare their own experiences with the perspectives on mourning voiced by the characters in *Pearl*. One student, whose father had died from cancer earlier in the semester, said that more than anything else, she just wanted to see his face again and hear his voice. She said that the Dreamer's intense reaction to seeing the Maiden seemed not just realistic but totally justified.

Thus, with almost no guidance from me, the class overcame a persistent problem in *Pearl* scholarship, which is the tendency to assume what A. C. Spearing has called "an attitude of patronizing superiority toward the poem's first person" (*Textual Subjectivity* 164). My grieving students recognized a parallel to their own experience in this alien poem. Their vocal identification then allowed other students to do the same. And, having empathized with the Dreamer, the class was then much more prepared to recognize his perspective as understandable. Even though the poem itself obviously criticizes the Dreamer's emotions, the point of the poem is that they are totally understandable. The heavenly perspective of the Maiden must be identified as strange, counterintuitive, and perhaps even unnatural, if the poem is to be anything other than a platitude. Only by empathizing with the mourner's grief can the audience actually understand what the Maiden is offering in her discourse. (In this way the poem works rather as Stanley Fish argued, in *Surprised by Sin*, that *Paradise Lost* works, by luring readers into committing the sins that it aims to correct.) This identification then allowed my students to see value in the poem as a whole, and they eagerly engaged in debates about its structure and meaning. At the end of the course, several named *Pearl* as the work they would remember longest from their reading.

This approach to *Pearl* has further dividends in the classroom. Cognitive scientists have long understood that students master new ideas faster when they are able to map them onto their existing frameworks of knowledge, which then in turn expand and alter to accommodate the new information (Rumelhart). Students who can empathize with *Pearl* are drawing not just on their classroom knowledge of medieval literature but also on their own experiences and—as in the case of my mourning students—deeply held emotions. As a result, they will make stronger, more personal connections, and they will see more clearly the importance of the text and the problems it raises. As instructors, we can then draw on these connections to help students extend their interest in *Pearl* to other Middle English texts.

In the next section, I suggest three possible ways to talk about *Pearl* in conjunction with other Middle English texts. In each I supply a brief discussion of the texts together, followed by a set of discussion questions. My experience is that class discussion goes best when students have either written about the texts beforehand or had some time to discuss the questions with a small group before interacting directly with me. The questions I supply here could also be adapted as writing prompts for essay exams or research papers.

The Book of the Duchess

One way to teach *Pearl* is to set it alongside Chaucer's *Book of the Duchess.* *The Book of the Duchess* is relatively short, written in fairly accessible Middle English, and depicts a situation of mourning. In contrast to *Pearl*, however, *The Book of the Duchess* portrays a highly conventional love relationship, and the grief it portrays can seem formal and alien to students. Comparing the two poems using one or more of the questions below reveal to them that the cultural constructs we typically use to discuss Middle English literature are not unitary—that, in fact, they contain many contradictory possible lines of development. For example, both poems borrow elements extensively from the *Roman de la Rose* (Gordon; Vantuono; K. Taylor; Diekstra; Shoaf; Finlayson). Yet they do so in wildly divergent ways. *The Book of the Duchess* is concerned with a secular, erotic sphere of discourse and provides a secular consolation, the consolation of memory. *Pearl*, on the other hand, is planted firmly in a theological and sacramental sphere, explicitly rejects the possibility of any kind of possession of the love object, and offers a determinedly theological resolution to grief. Examining these differences can help students understand the tensions between different elements of medieval culture.

1. You might use this comparison to assess the claims of A. C. Spearing in *Textual Subjectivity* (2005) that the *Pearl* poet does not always use the device of a narrator, imagined as a developed particular point of view. Ask students to examine the perspective from which each poem is told. The "I" in *The Book of the Duchess* seems to be much less central to the problem of the poem. He is an observer rather than a participant. In contrast, the "I" in *Pearl* is both the teller of the tale and a participant in the debate. How does this difference change how readers approach the central concerns of each poem?
2. In *The Book of the Duchess*, the Man in Black is made into an ideal figure and his claims are shown to be justified; in *Pearl*, the Dreamer's laments—very much in the same vein—also appear idealized at first, but diverge further and further from an inhumanly heavenly standard. Chaucer's Man in Black claims that Love taught him (lines 789–91)—but love is what the Dreamer in *Pearl* must unlearn or at least direct toward a different object. How would you characterize these two different takes on consolation?

3. In *The Book of the Duchess*, White never appears, but her appearance and behavior are described in detail in lines 817–1041 and 1052–87. Ask students to compare this description with the description of the Pearl-Maiden in lines 162–240. What do the two descriptions have in common? What details differ, and why might this be? Students will probably register that both descriptions use conventional terms to describe their subjects, but that the conventions seem to have allegorical or symbolic meaning in *Pearl*. You might point their attention to the gestures as well: ask them to notice when the maiden removes her crown and when she places it back on her head.

4. Direct students' attention to the descriptive passages in each poem. What is the setting of each poem like (lines 291–442 in *The Book of the Duchess*; 61–160 in *Pearl*)? Consider geography, flora and fauna, and ordering. To what extent do the details of the setting seem to have further symbolic meaning? Students can then consider how setting interacts with other literary elements to produce each poem's characteristic mood and style.

Capgrave's Life of Saint Katherine

A second way to read *Pearl* is to read it in conjunction with John Capgrave's *Life of Saint Katherine*, either in Karen Winstead's TEAMS edition or in her translation published by Notre Dame. Saint Katherine was among the most popular of saints in medieval England; her story was noteworthy not only because of her gruesome martyrdom but also because she was a learned woman who converted fifty pagan philosophers while avoiding marriage to a pagan king. Her story is an important challenge to medieval prescriptive statements about womanly meekness and submission, which students may be inclined to take at face value. It goes without saying that the author of *Pearl* knew some version of Katherine's vita; he certainly drew on the iconography of female saints in his description of the Pearl-Maiden at lines 162–240, while his interpretation of the Parable of the Workers in the Vineyard seems to include a consideration of martyr-like suffering. The Pearl-Maiden also speaks with extraordinary power and authority. Teaching these two texts in conjunction, you might ask students to consider how each fictional character makes claims to various types of authority against the counterclaims of male figures. (You could also extend the comparison to the Wife of Bath, another fictional woman whose voice is so loud, authoritative, and unapologetic that students are sometimes seduced into mistaking it for the voice of a historic woman.) Students then could transfer these concerns into reading fifteenth-century texts such as *The Book of Margery Kempe* and the *Shewings* of Julian of Norwich.

1. Ask your students to look at online images of Saint Katherine painted in English parish churches (sets of images are available at www.visitchurches .org.uk/wallpaintings/ and www.paintedchurch.org/sainintr.htm). What are the physical features and gestures of Katherine in these images? How do these images compare with the Pearl-Maiden as she is described in the poem?

2. Trace the language of purity in each text. How is purity conceptualized in each of these texts? What are the shared concerns surrounding female sexuality and virginity?

3. Look closely at book 2 of *The Life of Saint Katherine* and outline the claims made by the so-called Marriage Parliament about why Katherine should be married. Can the concerns surrounding Katherine's unmarried state shed any light on the claims that the Pearl-Maiden makes about her identity and celestial status as a result of her marriage to the Lamb? How closely does Katherine's mystical marriage to Christ conform to the Pearl-Maiden's marriage to Christ?

4. What kind of authority, according to these two texts, is it proper for a woman to hold? You might think first and foremost of spiritual authority, but pay attention also to political, familial, and even rhetorical authority (which each woman claims through her vigorous debating skills).

Wynnere and Wastoure

Lastly, students can benefit from connecting *Pearl* with a larger literary context by reading it alongside *Wynnere and Wastoure*, which students will probably want to read in John Gardner's modernization (Alliterative Morte) or in Warren Ginsberg's well-annotated TEAMS edition. The two poems are connected through the genres of dream vision and debate, but present quite different thematic concerns. You can use *Wynnere and Wastoure* to show that alliterative poetry typically dealt with public actions and counsel to rulers (Hanna, "Alliterative Poetry"; Trigg xxii–xxvii). Students will benefit from working in groups to analyze the arguments of each character or even from writing a collaborative conclusion for the poem based on their reading of those arguments. Class discussion can then focus on one or more of the following questions:

1. Many Middle English debate poems are constructed in such a way as to leave the outcome undecided. While the characters within the poem may proclaim a winner, the text itself encourages its audience to judge for themselves. The audience is not necessarily being asked to concur with the judgment rendered in the text or even to side unequivocally with one party in the debate. Most of the scholars writing on *Wynnere and*

Wastoure since the 1970s have taken up some version of this argument (Bestul; Harrington; Reed). You can then ask students to judge for themselves, either individually or in groups: Is there an obvious victor in the debate within each poem? If so, who is it, and by what standard does this character win? To what extent is each character invested with narrative authority? This could include invoking theological or political authorities; it could also stand on reasoning alone; or you could decide this based on the narrative resolution to the poem. Does the debate raise questions that it does not answer? Do the differing resolutions to the two debates suggest different orientations toward the poems' audiences? What might be the uses of such irresolution?

2. *Pearl* uses alliteration but has a strict structure of rhyming stanzas and concatenation. In this way, it differs from the other poems in MS Cotton Nero A.x, which are all written in alliterative long lines. Do the preoccupations of alliterative poetry, as represented in *Wynnere and Wastoure*, carry into *Pearl* as well? If so, how?

3. Several scholars have tried, not wholly successfully, to connect the Parable of the Workers in the Vineyard within *Pearl* to later fourteenth-century efforts to control the wages of agricultural laborers (Watkins; Bowers, *Politics of* Pearl 46–49). Having read *Wynnere and Wastoure*, which is obviously topical, your students will be better prepared to assess the topicality of *Pearl*. You might ask students to locate which social spheres are encompassed within each poem: Who is present? Who is absent? Whose interests are opposed to each other? Who is the understood audience of each of these poems? Is *Pearl* topical in the same way that *Wynnere and Wastoure* is topical?

4. The alliterative effects in *Pearl* combine with its highly structured stanzas and concatenation to make the poem into a highly ornamented, precious object, a *juel* in the Middle English sense (Bishop 30; Riddy 147–48; Harper, "Pearl" 423). Questions of exchange are central to each poem, and each poem foregrounds the question of value and the proper use of wealth. How does the perspective on riches differ between the two poems? Can either shed light on the other?

In conclusion, I'd like to return to the three groups of students I described at the start of this essay. I have described the comparative method as a basic tool in reaching each of these three groups. For each group the tool does different work. Students belonging to the first group, who assumed that medieval literature is irredeemably other, benefit from comparing some element of their own culture with what they see in *Pearl* (or whatever historically distant text you are asking them to consider). They are then able to recognize that the text has something to say to them, and they are more motivated to face the difficulties that discouraged them. Students from the second group—students attracted to the strangeness of the Middle Ages—start out in a stronger place than the others. For them the challenge is moving from the realm of fantasy, a refuge from their own historical circumstances, into a better understanding of medieval English culture in all its complexity. Reading *Pearl* in better literary context will help them understand the cultural work it performs. Students in the third group benefit from the same exercise, but for a different reason. These students become more aware that they themselves and the text they are reading are products of particular historical moments. While it is unlikely that they will let go of their own presuppositions entirely, they can be taught to approach the text with a degree of intellectual humility, and be more ready to hear what the text has to say.

Teaching *Pearl*
When Teaching Tolkien

John M. Bowers

If courses on Middle English literature have decreased in number in recent years, courses on J. R. R. Tolkien have proliferated and increased in the wake of Peter Jackson's film adaptations. As a result, *Pearl* in Tolkien's affordable paperback translation can now be included in courses devoted principally to *The Hobbit* and *The Lord of the Rings*. Tolkien edited and translated *Pearl*, and he assimilated its materials into his fantasy fiction. His creative works, therefore, offer students fresh access and teachers innovative approaches to *Pearl*, albeit against the grain of traditional pedagogy and in an entirely different context. Establishing a clear and valid connection is key to any inquiry into a medieval text through a modern author or modern work. Tolkien's scholarship on *Pearl* and his creative assimilation of it establish that connection and provide students with both a point of entry for understanding and an avenue for close interpretation.

A good place to begin making connections between Tolkien and *Pearl* is Scull and Hammond's two-volume *Companion and Guide*, which documents Tolkien's career in great detail. He first encountered *Pearl* as a teenager at King Edward's School in Birmingham and studied it closely as an undergraduate at Oxford. Tolkien considered himself a native of the North-West Midlands, where *Pearl* is thought to have been composed, and he would come to champion literature in its regional dialect (Carpenter, *Biography* 43). As a young lecturer at Leeds, he began teaching the poem, and shortly thereafter, his first major publication was the glossary for Kenneth Sisam's 1921 *Fourteenth Century Verse and Prose* with selections from *Pearl* now available in reprint as *A Middle English Reader and Vocabulary* (Sisam and Tolkien). In 1924 while reading examination papers on *Pearl*, Tolkien started a poem entitled *The Nameless Land* with the alliterating twelve-line stanzas, complicated rhyme scheme, and even imagery from *Pearl*. The poem might be used as a comparison piece to provide students a first opportunity to analyze Tolkien's early engagement looking forward to the Elvish realm of Lothlórien:

> There lingering lights do golden lie
>   On grass more green than in gardens here,
> On trees more tall that touch the sky
>   With silver leaves a-swinging clear:
> By magic dewed they may not die
>   Where fades nor falls the endless year,

Where ageless afternoon goes by
   O'er mead and mound and silent mere.
There draws no dusk of evening near,
   Where voices move in veiléd choir,
Or shrill in sudden singing clear.
And the woods are filled with wandering fire.   (*Lost Road* 109–10)

Tolkien would continue teaching the *Pearl* poet throughout his years at Oxford. The distinguished medievalist Derek Brewer recalled attending these classes in the 1940s: "Tolkien himself lectured on the poem to a small group of devotees, confining himself entirely to textual cruces (often forgetting to tell us which line he was discussing), and doing obscure (to me) battle with some mysterious entity, prophetically as it may now seem, called something like 'Gollancz'" (Brewer and Gibson 2). Students might be surprised to learn that Tolkien was not an outstanding teacher even by his own estimation. "My ineffectiveness as a lecturer was already well known," he would recall in his "Valedictory Address" in 1959; "I would always rather try to wring the juice out of a single sentence, or explore the implications of one word" (224). Thus through his emphasis on cruxes, ones he doubtless read in his copy of Israel Gollancz's 1921 edition of *Pearl*, students are provided with a useful connection point between the poem and his encounters with its words and images as a teacher, scholar, and creative writer. By bringing together passages from Gollancz's edition with corresponding selections from Sisam's reader and Tolkien's own translation, students can access the very set of interpretive cruxes that Tolkien and his students likely analyzed.

    Another useful critical tool is Tolkien's contribution to the edition of *Pearl* that was much on his mind while he worked on *The Hobbit* and *The Lord of the Rings*. The student edition of *Sir Gawain and the Green Knight* (1925), which Tolkien coedited with his friend E. V. Gordon, proved so successful that Oxford University Press asked Tolkien and Gordon to prepare a similar teaching text of *Pearl*. The project dragged on fitfully over the next three decades. Gordon completed his portion of the work in 1937, but he doubted that Tolkien would have the time to complete his part. Tolkien had other demanding duties: as professor of Anglo-Saxon, he was expected to publish on works like *Beowulf* and had just gotten into print his "*Beowulf*: The Monsters and the Critics," still the most influential article ever published on the poem. He had also seen *The Hobbit* through press.

    Gordon died in the following year, and Tolkien felt an even greater obligation to complete their *Pearl* edition. Yet distraction piled upon distraction with the outbreak of World War II and with his own labors on *The Lord of the Rings*. In 1944 he lamented, "[P]osthumous work on *Pearl* I undertook, as a duty to a dead friend and pupil, to put in order; and have failed to do my duty" (Carpenter,

Letters 114). Ida Gordon, his coeditor's widow, eventually completed the edition, and Tolkien helped with a revised introduction, glossary, notes on languages, and other advice on textual emendations and even punctuation. Still the edition did not appear until 1953, the year before *The Fellowship of the Ring*. Tolkien declined to have his name appear on the title page—though gladly accepting a payment of 50 pounds from the publisher.

Appearing when it did nearly concurrently with *The Fellowship of the Ring*, Gordon's *Pearl* edition offers unique opportunities for students to engage the poem with Tolkien's creative work in mind. The introduction's "Form and Purpose" (xi–xix) stands as Tolkien's anonymous contribution, though it did not remain anonymous after his son Christopher Tolkien included it in his father's translation of *Pearl* (10–19). Here Tolkien wrestles with a question that still bedevils students—whether the dream vision's symbolic elements turned *Pearl* into an allegory of salvation. In the foreword to the 1965 edition of *The Lord of the Rings*, Tolkien wrote, "I cordially dislike allegory in all its manifestations, and always have done so since I grew old and wary enough to detect its presence" (*Fellowship* 7). It requires no stretch of the imagination for students to appreciate how Tolkien's attitude toward allegory arose when working on the *Pearl* edition:

> The opening stanzas of the poem, where the pearl slips from the poet's hand through the grass to the ground, is an allegory in little of the child's death and burial. But an allegorical description of an event does not make the event itself allegorical. And this initial use is only one of many applications of the pearl symbol, intelligible if the reference of the poem is personal, incoherent if one seeks for total allegory.   (Gordon, *Pearl* xii)

Here Tolkien identifies an experience of personal loss that the poet diligently concealed within a symbolic narrative, again in ways comparable to Tolkien's own practice of incorporating personal experiences into his novels but rendering them as fiction, not offered as invitations for biographical and historical readings. His *Rings*' "Foreword" expressed irritation that readers were interpreting "The Scouring of the Shire" as an allegory of postwar England. Fiercely rejecting allegorical readings of his own work, he wrote, "I much prefer history, true or feigned" (*Fellowship* 7)—a statement recalling his earlier insistence on the strictly literary rather than biographical reading of *Pearl*. "A feigned elegy remains an elegy," he said, "and feigned or unfeigned, it must stand or fall by its art" (Gordon, *Pearl* xvi).

In "Form and Purpose," Tolkien discusses the dream-vision genre, stating that "to some that slept blessed faces appeared and prophetic voices spoke" (xv). Here students might recall Frodo's prophetic dreams on two successive nights in the house of Tom Bombadil, the first showing him Gandalf trapped on the top of a tower and rescued by an eagle and the second, much further off in time, his own eventual arrival at the Undying Lands (*Fellowship* 138, 146). While dreaming, Frodo briefly glimpses an otherworldly paradise, much like the Dreamer of *Pearl*, before awakening to the present world's challenges. Passages like these redirect attention from what is familiar (Frodo's prophetic dream about Gandalf and his vision of the Undying Lands) to what would otherwise be foreign (the Dreamer's oracular dream about the *Pearl* Queen and his vision of paradise).

Perhaps the best way to gain insight into a foreign-language text is by translating it, and in 1926 after accepting the job of editing *Pearl*, Tolkien completed his own poetic rendering of the work. Christopher Tolkien quoted his father thus: "These translations were first made long ago for [my] own instruction, since a translator must first try to discover as precisely as he can what his original means" (Tolkien, trans. vii). About the scholarly underpinnings of his modern version, Tolkien himself wrote, "I have, of course, had to do an enormous amount of editorial work, unshown, in order to arrive at a version; and I have, as I think, made important discoveries with regard to certain words, and some passages" (Carpenter, *Letters* 364).

In part because of its own complicated history, this translation of *Pearl* also offers opportunities for comparative analysis with the original. Its prospects for publication dogged Tolkien for the remainder of his life. The decade of the 1960s found him still wrestling with the "apparently insoluble metrical problems" that had "disappeared under the weight of the War and *The Lord of the Rings*," but he still thought his efforts were worthwhile. He wrote that the translation "has moments of poignancy; and though it may in our view be absurdly complex in technical form, the poet surmounts his own obstacles on the whole with success" (Carpenter, *Letters* 317). Two years after his death, his *Pearl* translation was published along with *Gawain* and *Sir Orfeo*, now in a paperback reasonably priced for classroom use.

A comparison of the opening stanza's two versions, medieval and modern, shows Tolkien's virtuoso skill at maintaining the original versification. Here is the original:

> Perle, plesaunte to prynces paye
> To clanly clos in golde so clere,
> Oute of oryent, I hardyly saye,
> Ne proued I neuer her precios pere.
> So rounde, so reken in vche araye,
> So small, so smoþe her sydeȝ were,
> Quere-so-euer I jugged gemmeȝ gaye,
> I sette hyr sengeley in synglere.
> Allas! I leste hyr in on erbere;

Þurȝ gresse to grounde hit fro me yot.
I dewyne, fordolked of luf-daungere
Of þat pryuy perle wythouten spot.   (Gordon, *Pearl* 1)

And here is Tolkien's translation, which maintains the elaborate rhyme scheme of *abababbcbc* in stanzas of twelve octosyllabic lines:

Pearl of delight that a prince doth please
To grace in gold enclosed so clear,
I vow that from over orient seas
Never proved I any in price her peer.
So round, so radiant ranged by these,
So fine, so smooth did her sides appear
That ever in judging gems that please
Her only alone I deemed as dear.
Alas! I lost her in garden near:
Through grass to the ground from me it shot;
I pine now oppressed by love-wound drear
For the pearl, mine own, without spot.   (Tolkien, trans. 123)

The translation brings us full circle from his first effort in 1924 of imitating the style and content of *Pearl*. Here we see Tolkien making deliberate interpretative decisions that may have been informed by his creative work. The phrase "in gold enclosed" translates the original "clos in golde," making clear the pearl had been set in a piece of gold jewelry, perhaps a ring. In another noteworthy departure from the original, Tolkien does not keep the word *precios* in the fourth line to describe what has been lost. Students will doubtless recall that Tolkien had created another piece of lost jewelry—the Ring—and another character griev-ing obsessively over its loss with the term "my precious"—Gollum—so that the omission looks almost like an unconscious repression.

Lost jewels stand at the heart of Tolkien's whole mythology, beginning with *The Hobbit*. Lost when Smaug captured the Lonely Mountain—and lost a second time when Bilbo pocketed it from the dragon's hoard—the large white gem, the Arken-stone, "shone like silver in the firelight" (208). Tolkien based the gemstone's name on the Old English *eorcnanstan* meaning "precious stone," and the Old Mercian *Rushworth Gospels* used the word specifically when Christ spoke of the Pearl of Great Price—"þa ænne ercnastan diorwyrðe" ("the one precious gemstone"; Gil-liver et al. 90). In Tolkien's philological imagination, the lost Arkenstone was also a lost pearl, and the biblical language of the Pearl of Great Price echoes unmistak-ably in Thorin's obsessive declaration: "to me it is beyond price" (240). The jewel is placed upon the Dwarf king's chest when he dies, much as the "perle of prys" graces the breast of the dead Pearl Queen (line 746).

In the 1930s, while working on *The Hobbit*, Tolkien also used the Old English *eorcanstanas* to refer to the Silmarils, which were lost at the beginning of *The Silmarillion*. Like the Pearl, each gem was in some sense both *alive* and *sacred* (*Silmarillion* 59). Other pearls were used to pay the Dwarves for their labors, the most magnificent one called Nimphelos. "One there was as great as a dove's egg," Tolkien wrote, "and its sheen was as starlight on the foam of the sea." The Dwarves considered it their Pearl of Great Price, as it were, and "prized it above a mountain of wealth" (84).

Galadriel possesses her own precious jewel set in one of the Three Rings of the Elves. Nenya was adorned with a "white stone," and its name derived from the Quenya *nén* meaning "water," possibly suggesting a pearl which, unique among gemstones, has its origins in water. When first spotting it, Frodo stared at her ring much as the Dreamer stared at the dazzling gemstone worn as a badge by the Pearl Queen. Galadriel will take this jewel on her own passage to the Undying Lands: "On her finger was Nenya, the ring wrought of *mithril*, that bore a single white stone flickering like a frosty star" (*Return* 308).

Students might be encouraged to identify other similarities between Galadriel and the Pearl Queen. The Lady of Lothlórien is "clad wholly in white" with her long free-flowing hair "of deep gold," her look "grave and beautiful" (*Fellowship* 369). Here Tolkien recalls *Pearl*'s description of the Pearl Queen "in linen robe of glistening white" with hair "as shredded sheen of gold," her face "grave for duke or earl" (Tolkien, trans. 130–31). Galadriel's gemlike identity also possibly carries over from the Pearl Queen. Tolkien writes "the Lady Galadriel is above all the jewels that lie beneath the earth" (*Fellowship* 371). Principally she serves the same function of consoling grief after a death—Gandalf's fall in the Mines of Moria—and to advise on ways forward after a devastating loss.

Much like the landscape of *Pearl*, Lothlórien unfolds as an earthly paradise suffused with elegiac sadness. Legolas sings of the lost maiden Nimrodel with her long hair and white mantle, again like the Pearl Queen, until his voice falters in sorrow (*Fellowship* 353–55). Later the Elves inspire Frodo to turn his own mourning into poetic elegy (374–75). The Tolkien scholar Tom Shippey has noted other parallels in *The Road to Middle-Earth*:

> With *Pearl* in mind, one might easily conclude that the stretch between the two rivers is a sort of "earthly Paradise" for Frodo and the others, though one still capable of violation and invasion from the outside world. The "Naith" of Lórien, though, across the second river, is Heaven; the company undergoes a kind of death in getting there, while there is a feeling of significance in the fact they may not touch the water, not even to have their "stains" washed away. A determined allegorist (or mythiciser) might go on to identify the Nimrodel with baptism, the Silverlode with death. (218)

To take the connection between *Lord of the Rings* and *Pearl* further, we might see the city of Caras Galadhon, which stands at Lothlórien's center, as an Elvish version of the New Jerusalem. The *Pearl* poet's description of crystal cliffs amid a landscape of indigo trees with silver leaves (Tolkien, trans. 126) resembles the Celtic otherworld such as the fairyland of the fourteenth-century *Sir Orfeo* that Tolkien already recalled when creating the realm of the Wood-elves in *The Hobbit*. By allowing inspiration for Lothlórien to flow from medieval texts, Tolkien gives his readers what he typically imagined as the lost Celtic originals lurking behind *Pearl* as well as *Sir Orfeo*.

Though Tolkien discouraged biographical readings of his own works, his 1934 article "Chaucer as a Philologist" acknowledged the interplay. Tolkien wrote, "The chance events of the actual lives of authors get caught up into their books, but usually they are strangely changed and intricately woven anew one with another, or with other contents of the mind" (55). Subtle guidance might enable students to see a poignant parallel emerge between *Pearl* and Tolkien's life at a crucial point when working on both his Oxford edition and *Lord of the Rings*.

After his friend Gordon died, Tolkien refocused on editing an elegy about grieving a death, entering into a paradisiac landscape, and encountering a lady who provides consolation in the tradition of Lady Philosophy from Boethius's *Consolation of Philosophy* with its lessons on providence and free will. Similarly in chapters 5–8 of book 2 of *Fellowship of the Ring*, Gandalf has fallen into shadow and apparently died. Frodo and his friends next find themselves in the enchanted realm of Lothlórien where they grieve his loss. As a literary descendant of the Pearl Queen as well as Lady Philosophy, Galadriel consoles Frodo with her Mirror's visions of what might (or might not) come to pass in time. Her Mirror resembles nothing more than a baptismal font, recalling how doctrinal questions in *Pearl* center steadily upon baptism (Bowers, *Politics* 50–56).

Fairies tended to imprison mortals like Queen Heurodis in *Sir Orfeo* and the Dwarves in *The Hobbit*, but Galadriel readily frees Frodo so he can continue his quest—much as Ida Gordon, by taking over the editorial work, freed Tolkien to continue writing about Frodo's quest. Christopher Tolkien traces the composition of these chapters in his *History of* The Lord of the Rings (2: 190–294), so students can appreciate parallels between *Pearl*'s action and Tolkien's biography during the years 1938 to 1942, as well as between the contents of *Pearl* and these elegiac chapters of *Fellowship of the Ring*.

Long before Tolkien moved to Merton College in 1945, T. S. Eliot had pursued graduate study there while at Oxford, later publishing his essay "Tradition and the Individual Talent" in which he wrote about changes in the literary canon: "The existing monuments form an ideal order among themselves, which is modified by the introduction of the new (the really new) work of art among them" (956–57). *The Lord of the Rings* represents exactly such a really new work that modifies the existing monuments. Before Tolkien, *Pearl* was known to literary historians as well as students reading for their English degrees at universities like Oxford. After Tolkien, *Pearl* along with *Beowulf, Gawain*, and a host of other medieval texts gained far greater prominence in the English literary tradition. Now *Pearl* can be taught successfully and more frequently, though differently, within these new pedagogical contexts, in courses with titles such as Tolkien and Medieval Literature—and my own well-enrolled, frequently taught class, Tolkien, Scholar and Storyteller.

The Trope of Translation in *Pearl*

William A. Quinn

The hardest thing to teach about *Pearl* is its emotional substance, its "whole force and poignancy" (Spearing, *Gawain-Poet* 137). The conspicuous artistry of *Pearl*—that is, everything formal and superficial and ephemeral about the sensory exercise of reading—is easy to admire. But the full potential of its emotional impact is pedagogically difficult to suggest. Modern students do sympathize with the narrator's initial grief for his dead daughter. But few readily feel the peculiar passion of the ghostly conversation that follows. For many, making sense of the original poetic language is hardly so difficult as converting its religious discourse into personal relevance. The most fundamental challenge confronting the modern student, then, is essentially identical to that of the sad Dreamer: an informed response requires a radical translation of one's normal or natural or mundane point of view into a transcendent vision—or, at least, into a recollection of a temporary glimpse of such a perspective.

I therefore teach *Pearl* primarily as a sequence of acts of translation that exemplify how "to love spiritually" is synonymous with "to use language properly" (Johnson, 166). The term *translation* needs to be put through its semantic paces. The first meaning of *translate* given in the *Middle English Dictionary* is "to relocate" (s.v., *translaten* v., def. 1a); the etymological sense of "carrying across" (from Latin *trans* and *fero, ferre, tuli, latus*) can refer to the transferal of a saint's relics (def. c) as well as to the conveyance of a soul into heaven (def. 3b); it is cognate to *metaphor*. The *Middle English Dictionary* actually lists our now most common use of *translate* last: "To translate (poetry, a book, etc.) from one language into another" (def. 6a). The reader's first task of translating *Pearl* into modern English reifies what should be a transformative (def. 4) experience.[1]

The seemingly inexhaustible, sometimes inexplicable wordplay of *Pearl* provides more than sufficient practice in glossing. Concatenated words, in particular, seem predestined by stanzaic design to require serial redefinition. In retrospect, "þe laste" rhyme word "schal be þe first . . . / And þe fyrst þe laste" (lines 570–71), but the poem's final use of "paye" transforms its initial significance ("worldly treasure") into the free gift of Christ's ransom.[2] The intervening emotional transitions of the narrator as reader of his own dream are easy enough to map, starting with his natural (and so easy to comprehend) reaction to loss, a grief that incapacitates the very faculty of comprehension: "A deuely dele in my hert denned, / Þaʒ resoun sette myseluen saʒt" (51–52). After sliding into sleep (59), the Dreamer's mood quickly changes from stupid amazement— "More meruayle con my dom adaunt" (157)—to abashed joy (171–74) to stupefied "drede" (181). The still-pensive Dreamer claims to be healed of his former pain by the simple apparition of the "sade" ("dignified"; 211), sober (256), imperturbable Maiden—"My grete dystresse þou al todrawez" (280). But his presumptuous, because premature, request to traverse the dividing "wawez" ("waves" and "woes"; 287) sounds ludicrous or insane to the saint—" 'Wy borde ʒe men? So mad ʒe be!' " (290). That her exclamation refers to "you men" in the plural indicates that the Dreamer's leaping to such a false conclusion represents a common trespass. He promptly jumps to another erroneous assumption. He thinks that the Maiden's "uncompromising severity"[3] means that he has been sentenced "To dol agayn" (326). His feelings recycle through confusion, a foolish desire for immediate rapture, followed by frustrated humiliation still driven by desire (963–34), then renewed amazement (1081), and vicarious celebration of "gret delyt" (1105) before waking to the poem's tonally much-debated resolution. It is both the pathos and the bathos of the dream itself that often get lost in translation.

The Dreamer has claimed he did not intend to "debate" (390) with the Maiden—that is, with God. This disclaimer is either bemused or disingenuous (and amusing). At first, the Dreamer resists correction by his own, now very magisterial daughter, which entails accepting "a double inversion of earthly hierarchies" (Spearing, *Textual Subjectivity* 163). His humiliation will eventually be translated into sincere humility, but this transformation is hardly easy. The Dreamer must first be schooled in the celestial significance of certain words, notably: "right," "innocent," "Jerusalem," and—first and last—"pearl" itself. The semantic tension between "the Dreamer's materialism and the spiritual nature of the world in which he finds himself is a central motive of the whole poem" (Spearing, *Medieval Dream Poetry* 119). The "debate" between father and daughter generates little real dialogue, however; it sounds more like "the dynamic juxtaposition of two conflicting first persons, each vying for a position at the center of the poem" (Blanch and Wasserman 140).

Echoing Jesus's rebuke of Thomas, a skeptic who only "leuez wel þat he sez wyth yȝe" (302) and not the Creed's affirmation that God created all things invisible as well (see Colossians 1.16), the Maiden mocks the Dreamer who believes only what he sees. The Dreamer's skepticism (his desire for empirical proof in the midst of a vision) is merely "a poynt of sorquydryȝe . . . To leue no tale be true to tryȝe / Bot þat hys one skyl may dem" (lines 309–12). Nevertheless, the Dreamer remains "impossibly literal-minded" (Spearing, "Symbolic and Dramatic Development" 111) regarding what true translation requires for some time. The Maiden challenges the presumption of humans to comprehend God's words (line 314). Human verbiage also often occludes the honest significance of human feelings; for example, the Dreamer needs to recognize that his prolonged grieving is not only pointless but an expression of anger (343). All apologies to the contrary, the Dreamer does "speke errour" (422, 471). His misperception of the Maiden as the Blessed Virgin Mary (423), for example, imaged as the *unique* phoenix, initiates a series of false lexical assumptions. J. Stephen Russell discusses the Dreamer's "mistaken predication" of "maskellez" and "makelez" (780) based on "the dangerous similarity of the two words" (Russell 171). The Maiden's immediate concern is to correct the Dreamer's alliterative wordplay and reserve the epithet "matchless" for Mary as in "I syng of a myden þat is makeles" (Boffey and Edwards 1367).

The Maiden's allusion to Paul's metaphor of the Mystical Body of Christ—explicitly annotated by the Maiden herself as an allusion (line 457)—requires that the Dreamer understand "membrez" (458) to mean "courtiers" of Christ rather than bodily "limbs." But the empiricist, literalist Dreamer is distracted from rejoicing in his daughter's sanctified success; his objections derive from a strictly legalistic interpretation of justice—that is, a mistranslation of "right." It is the Dreamer's failure to translate Scripture fruitfully that delays his spiritual growth.

The Dreamer's translation of "ryȝt" (496, 580, 591, 665, and the concatenating word throughout section 12) in terms of the "sothfol gospel" (498) is hampered first by a sublunary sense of "property" (446) and then by a naive understanding of the word "innocent" (625). The Dreamer initially objects to the "fre" (481) economy of heaven. The Maiden must remind the Dreamer of the anagogic "trawþe" (495) rightly explained. It is the emotion invested in the following discourse about the proper parameters of translating the implicit teachings of scripture—the critical contest for control of right reading—that students often fail to appreciate.

The Maiden rebukes the Dreamer's (and so any reader's) continued resistance to correction as wrongheaded or stiff-necked nonsense: "Me þynk þy tale vnresounable . . . Oþer holy wryt is bot a fable" (590–92). The Maiden's rebuttal is (conventionally) pericoptic; she illuminates the efficacy of the sacrament of baptism (moral level) by recalling the revelation (mystical level) of Christ's "bote" (645) redeeming Adam's "byte" (640). Adam is identified as our "forme fader" (639), to be translated as both "first" and "prototypical" father. The blood and water that ran from the side of the Christ on the cross (646–47) becomes the "welle" (649) of salvation that delivered us from "deth secounde" (652)— the truer, less literal death of damnation. This fountain still flows: "Þe water is baptem, þe soth to telle" (653) washing away (655) sin that drowns (656). True faith guides "Ryȝtwysly quo con rede" (709) such wordplay. A right reading of David and Solomon reveals that both rightly predicted Jesus's supralegal invitation to salvation (719). But no modern reader is born truly "innocent."

The somewhat occluded wordplay of lines 624–26 toys with Pelagianism: "Bot innoghe of grace hatz innocent: / As sone as þay arn borne, by lyne/ In þe water of babtem. . . ." Editorial insertion of a comma in line 626, a mere jot, is crucial to translation. Salvation is a Christian's birthright "by line of descent" (cf. "byrþ-whatez"; 1041), but newborns must be baptized "by line" (in due order) in order to be cleansed of the stain of original sin. This apology for the efficacy of infant baptism was "perhaps sparked by claims that the sacrament was unnecessary" (Bowers, "*Pearl* in Its Royal Setting" 122); if not so translated, the Dreamer (if not the poet) would seem a heretic. But the Maiden transcends such quibbles; her redeemed imagination readily translates the license that Christ granted literal children (line 718) into an analogue for His simile of "ryȝt as a chylde"(723); she appreciates her own translation from babe into bride as an amplification of the Song of Solomon, a transformation of erotic desire into chaste ecstasy. The lyric calls "Cum hyder" (762), but the true meaning of "where?" has yet to be translated.

The Song of Solomon has an extremely controversial history of exegesis, but nothing so contentious as that of the book of Revelation. Translating the implications of Saint John's "gostly drem" (790) into personal significance dominates the rest of *Pearl*. Susanna Fein explores in detail the *Pearl* poet's personal identification with "Saint John, the Divine Jeweler of earthly matter and spiritual worth" ("Of Judges and Jewelers" 42). Again, the Dreamer must learn to renounce his desire to take literal possession "Of Jerusalem I in speche spelle" (793; spoken by the Maiden). The Maiden's subsequent *distinctio* between the Old and New Jerusalem is both belabored and crucial as an exemplary act of translation:

Of motes two to carpe clene,
And Jerusalem hyȝt bothe, nawþeles
Þat nys to yow no more to mene
Bot "ceté of God" oþer "syȝt of pes." (949–52)

Her translation of the city's proper name resurrects its etymology (or "true word"). The Dreamer must also learn that "lamb" means more than merely "mutton." The silent Messiah, as foretold by Isaiah (797), was judged in Jerusalem (804)—actually, historically, literally. John the Baptist's words harmonize with Isaiah's prophecy (819), explicating a "trw recorde" of the Lamb to be fulfilled "Þe þryde tyme" (831–33) in the Apocalypse. Section 15 suggests that, although we cannot duplicate the rhapsody of heaven on earth, "Nowþelese non watz neuer so quoynt . . . Þat of þat songe myȝt singe a poynt" (889–91). *Pearl*'s paraphrasing of the book of Revelation is more than just an act of translation from Latin prose into vernacular verse; it is a demonstration of how to read the spirit rather than the mere letter of the *logos*—in other words, how to translate *Pearl*.

The *Pearl* poet thus repeatedly causes the reader, along with the Dreamer, to make mistakes of translation. Learning the ease of error may be the poem's main lesson. The sequence of re-definitions of "pearl" is the most obvious and significant sequence of opportunities to experience the shame of mistranslating. The first disclosure that "pearl" should be read as a proper name rather than as a common noun is so familiar (and so anticipated) by teachers that it is easy to overlook (when re-re-reading) the importance of its first riddle-like use: "we do not know . . . and cannot guess at the future identification" (Edward Wilson 9). There is no reason not to assume at first sight that the "Perle plesaunte" (line 1) is simply a lost gemstone (6).[4] Only dreaming and reading translate the treasure into "A mayden of menske, ful debonere" (162). Even so, the Maiden's identity is initially suppressed and clarified only gradually—"I knew her wel, I hade sen hyr ere . . . On lenghe I loked to hyr þere; / Þe lenger, I knew hyr more and more" (164–68)—and periphrastically, "nerre þen aunt or nece" (233). Indeed, the Maiden is never explicitly identified as the Dreamer's daughter to the reader. Alternative identifications of "pearl" as the Dreamer's dead wife or as his love child or as a personification of his own lost faith are now considered implausible, inadequate, or supplemental (Spearing, *Gawain-Poet* 132–33), but such "mistranslations" clearly demonstrate how unclear the experience of translation can be.

The semantic metamorphoses of "pearl" defy any "synglure" (line 8) translation—indeed, the more, the richer. But the Jeweler needs to radically rethink what he means by "my" when he asks, "Art þou *my* perle þat I haf playned[?]" (242; my italics). In what sense can he possess Pearl? As the Maiden herself says, "Sir, ȝe haf your tale mysetente, / To say *your* perle is al awaye" (257–58; my italics). The buried coffin is really a jewel box; the gravesite, a *locus amoenus* ("a pleasant place") and *hortus conclusus* ("an enclosed garden") imaging Heaven (260); the lost jewel, a seed-pearl that has flowered (Kean, The *Pearl* 78). The Dreamer's misguided sense of "loss" has misled the reader, too: "For dyne of doel of lurez lesse / Ofte mony mon forgos þe mo" (lines 339–40).

The infant Pearl's appearance as an adult saint especially baffles the Dreamer (and many students). He requires some explanation of her translation from a supposed innocence "ful ȝong and tender of age" (412) to immortal life as an adult "quene in blysse" (415). The complimentary diction of the Dreamer appropriates the language of the *Roman de la Rose* (906), as if the Bride of Christ were an *amour de loin* ("love afar"). Such courtesy may indicate some progress from cupidity to charity, perhaps, but the Dreamer's "own inappropriate use of courtly language betrays his spiritual misorientation" (Gross 82)—that is, his confusing *signum translatum* ("figurative significance"—i.e., the spirit intended) with *signum proprium* ("literal significance" —i.e. the image presented). Pearl also has been taken to signify "Koyntyse" (line 690), translating *Sapientia* found in the Wisdom of Solomon (Borroff, *Traditions and Renewals* 151), though the personification is here transgendered as "He"—Christ. Pearl wears "þe perle of prys" (746), a familiar phrasing for faith, readily footnoted (see Matt.). But after the poem's reiteration of the parable's metaphor (729–39), the dream represents this "fayre fygure" (line 747) as real, substantial, like one of many adorning the Pearl's shining body (193–216). This is the redeemed value of the lost pearl without "spot" (the concatenating word of the first section). This immaculate pearl, as an emblem of undefiled souls "Withouten mote oþer mascle of sulpande synne" (725), overrules mere Fortune (98), conventionally imaged as the spotty moon (1069–70)—the anti-Pearl, as it were.

A perfect pearl on each gate of the Heavenly Jerusalem records "in scrypture" (1039) the name of each son of Israel. Innumerable virgin "ferez" (1150) who share the Pearl's royal habit "Depaynt in perlez" (1102) join the celestial communion as "at mas" (1115). The fleece of the Lamb "As praysed perles His wedez wasse" (1112). Angels sing praises to "þat gay Juelle" (1124). The Dreamer's final consolation is utterly dependent on his ability to embrace all these analogous meanings of "pearl" precisely as consonant, mutually confirming translations. But the Dreamer's transitional rapture is still encumbered by carnal language: "For luf-longyng in gret delyt" (1152).

The final translation of "pearl" awaits his awakening to mundane consciousness. The poet asks us to look at the Eucharist, "þat in þe forme of bred and wyn / Þe preste vus schewez vch a daye" (1209–10). The most miraculous act of translation is the miraculous transubstantiation presented as a quotidian and "homly" (1211) gift, anticipated by the "pené" (510) given to the workers in the vineyard "identified by the patristic writers with the 'daily bread' asked for in the Lord's Prayer" (Borroff, *Traditions and Renewals* 118).[5]

As an effort to translate the ineffable mystery of the Incarnation or the Real Presence into human terms, "*Pearl* is essentially a failure" (Bogdanos 146). Ultimately, fully "crossing the river" (143, 1151, 1160) can be translated only by or as "death." For example, Sandra Pierson Prior insists that the Dreamer falls short of complete transformation, but she also observes that the final focus of the poem is "the sacrament, the fairest *forme* available in this world" (*Fayre formez* 186). The inexplicably literal transformation that occurs with the words of consecration can translate "vus" (i.e., the poem's readers) into "precious perlez" too as co-communicants of the Mystical Body of Christ (1211–12). Robert Max Garrett stresses, "The great danger . . . is not exaggeration, but understatement . . ."; the Eucharist achieves "the actual oneness of the whole Church" (15), bridging the otherwise impassable boundary prior to death between the church militant and the church triumphant. Translating *Pearl* should itself thus provide an experience analogous to the reception of communion: "In this 'vus' . . . the poet and his imagined audience merge without distinction to form the congregation" (Putter 15).[6] The poem's extravagant formality is merely a monstrance displayed to allow the opportunity for such a communal experience of reading. This "eþe" ("easy"; 1202) perception is very hard to teach, however.

NOTES

[1] The *Oxford English Dictionary* identifies this meaning as "The chief current sense, s.v. "translate v.," def. 2 2a. The *Revised Medieval Latin Word-List* does not include this sense of "translat/io." The *Oxford Latin Dictionary, s.v.* "translatio, -onis, f." gives several definitions that share a common sense of "transferal" prior to the "translation (from one language to another)," def. 4c.

[2] The poem's own circularity mirrors darkly "the 'endeles rounde' of the pearl, which in turn, as Pearl herself says, 'I lyke the reme of hevenesse clere'" (Burrow, *Ricardian Poetry* 65–66).

[3] J. A. Burrow compares the Maiden's scorn to the *pietade acerba* ("harsh [maternal] pity") of Beatrice in Dante's *Purgatorio* canto 30, lines 79–81 (*Gawain-Poet* 9).

[4] This follows the instructions of Andrew and Waldron (1978), that description of the jewel "clearly" anticipates identification with the Maiden (53n5f).

[5] In addition to affirming the legitimacy of infant baptism, the *Pearl* affirms a completely orthodox understanding of the Eucharist. Explications of the poem's Eucharistic subtext include studies by John Gatta, Jr., Laurence Eldredge, Robert W. Ackerman, and Heather Phillips.

[6] This concluding communion is in clear contradistinction to "the Pearl-Maiden's usage" that had so separated "the exclusive 'us' in heaven, as opposed to 'you' on earth" (Putter 179).

Performing *Pearl*

Heather Maring

In the courses on medieval literature that I teach at a large public university, I assign undergraduate students sections of *Pearl* to enact in performances; I assign graduate students vocalizations—well-considered reading aloud. While some students initially deem performance (or anything outside the university triad of read-discuss-write) to be superfluous, they eventually recognize the value of performing *Pearl*. For, in addition to being a creative and interpretive activity that engages them deeply with the poem's circumstances and argument, performing also attunes them to features of the poem that would otherwise remain mute or muffled when reading the poem silently. Depending on the type and size of the course, I ask students to create individual or group performances, simple vocalizations, or more elaborate stagings of *Pearl*, and they work with the poem in translation or in Middle English. When performing *Pearl*, students learn that giving voice and listening to *Pearl* brings them closer to the creative medium (or one of the media) that the poem ostensibly inhabited in various ways in late medieval England. Some teachers of *Pearl* may find verisimilitude for its own sake to be suspect, but even the most ardent anti-re-creationist will discover that by asking students to speak, hear, and imaginatively create performances of *Pearl*, they become more cognizant of the meaningfulness of the poem's elaborate arrangement of rhymes, alliteration, and verbal echo, of contextual frames, and of the tones conveyed in the conversation between the Dreamer and the Maiden. Performance of *Pearl* may also be used to teach the poem's relation to the ritual recurrences of the Mass.[1] I will say more about these specific foci after I address the manner in which I prepare students for performances and the performance assignments themselves.

Student Performances

Performing *Pearl* in the classroom transforms how students engage with and interpret this poem. Such an approach has pedagogical value, in part, because performances roughly simulate the relations that audiences of the late fourteenth century had with written verbal art. In the attempt to take the position of such an audience, students ideally move away from a provincial "now-centric" frame of reference and hear what *Pearl* has to offer according to a poetic system that coordinates acoustic and performative features as well as visual ones. Nancy Mason Bradbury's description of the various incarnations of medieval romances could apply just as easily to the dream vision *Pearl* (which is, of course, housed in the same manuscript as *Cleanness*, *Patience*, and the romance *Sir Gawain and the Green Knight*). Bradbury writes: "A given story might in the course of its career be read privately by an educated individual, read aloud from manuscripts by members of the household to their social equals, and both read aloud and recited from memory by professional performers" (20–21). Some people in the Middle Ages may have read silently to themselves, as most scholars and students do today, but it was more likely that a solitary reader would have voiced *Pearl* aloud during reading. Hence, medieval verse, in general, was designed for the medium of the voice, in relation to what Paul Zumthor has called *vocalité*, the notion that texts manifest themselves fully when voiced.[2] Joyce Coleman has demonstrated that aristocratic audiences in the late medieval period enjoyed verse read publically by a prelector because public readings created opportunities for discussion, reflection, and "achieving very sophisticated sociopolitical goals" (97; see also 85–86 and 143). Because *Pearl* addresses the desires of "princes" and describes the individual's internalization of devotion (a trend in aristocratic circles during the late fourteenth century; see Garrison 299–302), some have surmised that *Pearl* was directed to an aristocratic audience. Felicity Riddy has asserted on the basis of the description of the Dreamer's rhetorical stance (as jeweler) and the description of the Maiden's luxurious clothing that "*Pearl* is positioned at the meeting point of aristocratic and urban values, which sanction acquisitiveness: the desire to own beautiful things, the taste to recognize and commission them, the leisure to enjoy them, the money to buy them, the skill, training, and capital to make them" (150). Therefore, it may be reasonable to imagine broader audiences, including educated and highly skilled craftsmen tangential to courtly life.

Two distinct but similar uses of the term *performance* have been nurtured in medieval studies. The term *performance* in this essay and in the assignments that I describe refers to the generally familiar notion of text made audible in the medium of the human voice and made unique or unrepeatable by the experience of being present—rather than, say, the manner in which a text engages in the praxis of specific cultural issues, such as kingship or grief. Presenting a text aloud or in performance makes a priority of the embodied enactment of verse for audiences—audiences that may range in size from a multitude to the solitary reader reading aloud—and draws attention to meanings conveyed by embedding the language of *Pearl* within specific performance contexts, where setting, body language, vocalization style, and audience reaction all matter. This approach to performance is informed by scholarship in the fields of oral tradition, folklore, theater, anthropology, and the ethnography of reading. In *Verbal Art in Performance*, Richard Bauman writes that paralinguistic features, such as tone, rhythm, speed, silence, gesture, music, and so on, *as well as* spoken words constitute the meaning(s) of a poem that lives in performance. By silently reading written text that was once part of a culture of oralization (or *vocalité*), students may miss "the emergent structure of the performance event itself," shaped by the speaker and his or her relationship with an in situ audience, that suggests interpretive frames for what is being verbalized (41). When I teach *Pearl* using the medium of performance, my goal is to treat the written poem as a textualized referent to meaningful, aesthetic events.

The assignment to "perform" *Pearl* is an attempt to engage the vocal, aural, and interactive dimensions of medieval verbal art. Undergraduates create multidimensional performances of two to three sections of *Pearl*, sometimes individually and sometimes in small groups. These performances incorporate what they have learned about medieval English culture, specifically, and oral-performative traditions, generally. Essays and book chapters on medieval reading practices can give students the historical and cultural background necessary to practice vocalizations of the poem that move beyond stilted classroom recitations and contemporary adaptations uploaded as *YouTube* posts (both of which have their virtues). Some essays that I have assigned for discussion before the creation of performances include John Miles Foley's "Third Word: Being There: Performance Theory" and "Fourth Word: Verbal Art on Its Own Terms: Ethnopoetics" in *How to Read an Oral Poem*; Benjamin Bagby's *"Beowulf*, the Edda, and the Performance of Medieval Epic: Notes from the Workshop of a Reconstructed 'Singer of Tales'"; Anne Azéma's "'Une aventure vous dirai': Performing Medieval Narrative"; Bradbury's "Orality, Literacy, and Middle English Romance" in *Writing Aloud*; Evelyn Birge Vitz's "Modalities of Performance: Romance as Recited, Sung and Played; Romance as Read"; and Linda Marie Zaerr's *"The Weddynge of Sir Gawen and Dame Ragnell*: Performance and Intertextuality in Middle English Popular Romance."[3] The readings by Foley establish a broad comparative frame of reference for thinking about how oral traditions—as they intersect with the practice of writing—emerge and have been studied in various cultures. Bradbury's essay provides a snapshot of reading and performance practices in late medieval England; Vitz's does the same for medieval France, supplying a resource for comparison. The remaining essays guide students through the process of (re)constructing performances of works of medieval verbal art. Alongside the essays by Bagby and by Zaerr we watch these authors' respective performances of *Beowulf* and *The Weddynge*. We also watch performances on the enormously useful site created by Vitz and Lawrence, *Performing Medieval Narrative*, so that we can discuss the justifications for various performance choices, as well as the broader issues that arise when creating performances, such as the desire for an elusive authenticity and the ethical imperative, as described by Foley, to "make the effort to speak and hear the right language as fluently as we can manage, even if that effort entails a degree of culture shock" (20).[4]

Following the discussion of these readings, students immerse themselves in *Pearl*, reading Marie Borroff's 2001 translation (in most undergraduate classes) and listening to Alan T. Gaylord's vocalization of the poem in Middle English (available for download from the *Chaucer Studio*). Listening to Gaylord's reading before creating performances does run the risk of modeling a specific style of vocalization that may undermine the creativity of students, but the unfamiliarity of most undergraduates with *Pearl*'s dialect of Middle English usually prevents them from hearing Gaylord's reading as the best and only way to read the poem. To further impress upon the students the possibility of various performances, I focus on two segments of Gaylord's reading and ask that they imagine alternative ways of voicing the text that can be justified either by features of the poem itself or by an imagined performance context. This exercise serves as a warm-up for the performances that students will create for the subsequent class. In the process of sharing ideas, some students become aware of new creative interpretations; others realize that their interpretive freedom has the constraint of internal and external evidence.

Undergraduates then stage the poem with one or two speakers, focusing on how tone of voice and emphasis in a reading may shift the way that audiences hear a poem. Performers may also introduce music at appropriate moments, create gestures based on those found in medieval paintings, such as those in Cotton Nero A.x, and include some or all of the classroom in processions. In a small class of 8 to 20 students, every student performs in front of the class. They describe in advance the kind of performance context that they imagine: for instance, a professional reader before an aristocratic court; a reader with a small, intimate audience; a reader voicing the text to himself or herself; or a troupe of minstrels performing for a court or a less elite audience. After each performance, the audience writes down feedback that I then collect and incorporate into subsequent discussions. In a larger classroom with 20 to 40 members, students may upload filmed performances to *Blackboard* or work in groups of 4 to 5 to create longer performances. Using the *Blackboard* route, I have instituted an anonymous voting procedure, with relative success. I invite the students with the most admired performances to re-create them in class while the remaining students engage in a detailed feedback process.

Because graduate students are less comfortable with full-scale performances and typically arrive in the classroom with a fair understanding of medieval notions of authorship and aurality, I ask that they practice voicing two to three sections of the Middle English *Pearl*. They are encouraged to record themselves before class in order to work out the kinds of choices that they wish to make with regard to tone, pacing, degree of emphasis on metrical and structural features, silences, speaking versus singing, use of gesture (or not), and so on. When framed as an interpretive exercise, their voiced renditions of the poem can spark heated discussions. Their performances may be coordinated with complementary readings on *Pearl* that address poetics, ritual, the role of the gaze, manuscript culture, debate verse, cruxes, and so on.

Grading rubrics help students understand the expectations for their performances. Because I teach in an English department, I emphasize that talent and polish matter less than what they learn and are able to verbalize in writing about their process of performing *Pearl*. In short papers, both undergraduates and graduate students justify their performance choices based on what they have learned about performance practices (extrinsic circumstances) and their interpretations of the poem informed by close reading (intrinsic details). This concluding reflection paper is a vital aspect of the assignment, facilitating analytical engagement with both the written poem and its performed versions.

Some Pearls of Performance

The performance assignments previously described in the essay could be (and have been) adapted to a wide variety of Middle English poems. For further ideas, I strongly recommend Vitz and Lawrence's "Teaching Tips" at *Performing Medieval Narrative*. What, then, about performance is especially relevant to *Pearl*? I find that the medium of performance sheds light on the manner in which *Pearl*'s poetic structure reinforces or extends the poem's themes and on significant performance-like events within the poem, such as falling prostrate, the dialogue between the Dreamer and the Maiden, and the heavenly procession. I briefly address these topics here.

When students silently read *Pearl*, in Middle English or in a translation that preserves the poetic structure, they notice the poem's rhyme scheme, alliteration, and the recurring phrases—those that link the stanzas internal to a section and those that join section to section. Yet many report that reading *Pearl* aloud and listening to others read transforms their understanding of the poem's strict poetic structure. The near symmetry of sounds at myriad levels, within lines, from line to line, stanza to stanza, section to section, and encircling the poem, dazzles the ear. The poem's concatenating phrases also grow more audible, in the intellectual sense, with respect to their shifting usage. For example, one may observe that the verb "deme" in section 6 means not just "judge," but also "censure," "ordain," and "condemn," depending on its usage. In the dialogue between the Maiden and the Dreamer, the Maiden attempts to wrest this verb from the province of the failing, foreshortened judgment of humanity to the domain of God (she concludes the section at line 360 with "Al lys in Hym to dyȝt and deme"). But the erring, self-regarding Dreamer then narrates himself in the position of judge at the beginning of a new section, "Thenne demed I to þat damyselle . . ." (361). The relation between the shifting uses of concatenating words and the themes of the poem has certainly been noticed by readers, but my students report having a greater appreciation for the "playing out" of these themes through poetic structure when they engage in the poem's performance as either actors or audience.

Listening for poetic structure also makes more noticeable the one moment where the system of concatenation pauses, at the beginning of canto 13, by not echoing the word "ryȝt" ("right") from canto 12. Barbara Newman proposes in "The Artifice of Eternity" that instead of being an instance of scribal error, the omission could align with other instances of numerological symbolism in *Pearl*,

> to create a chiastic pattern: the last eight cantos recount a vision of the twelve-gated city, while the first twelve introduce the poem's setting in August, the eighth month of the year, and treat the theology of baptism, a sacrament linked with the eighth day of the octagonal font.   (8)

When a student notices the missing word (usually by reading a footnote because most editions change the manuscript's "Jesus" to "Ryȝt"), the moment may inspire two types of discussion. The first focuses on what the presence of the name "Jesus" may mean in this context. Does it exceed "rightfully" the poet's artificial pattern of concatenations? Does it epitomize "Ryȝt" and hence one should hear "Jesus" and "Ryȝt" simultaneously? Is the moment a gesture to an etymological interpretation of the name "Jesus," as Andrew and Waldron (2008) seem to hint (87–88, note to lines 721–23)? Can we connect the intervention of the word "Jesus" to the issue of divine presence and absence potentially posed by the Mass? The variation from the basic pattern of concatenation also inspires a more general discussion of the ways in which *Pearl* exacts the attention of the sensory faculties. The lack of concatenation is audible, but most can only connect it to broad numerological patterns by engaging in sight-based activities, such as reviewing, that are associated with reading habits in a chirographic culture (see Ong 99–101, 103–04). The poem, though interwoven from start to finish with details that engage the visual and aural senses ("Delyt me drof in yȝe and ere"; 1153), nevertheless narrates a shift in emphasis from sound to sight—in the poem's arc from dialogue between the Dreamer and the Maiden to the Dreamer's gaze on the celestial city upon a hill. Students may connect this shift in emphasis to medieval hierarchies of the senses, which value seeing above hearing. The close attention that *Pearl* requires for a listener to *hear* its many interlayered acoustic patterns and to *envision* precisely the dress of the Pearl-Maiden, the liminal meeting space in which they debate, the Lamb, and the twelve lapidary foundations of the heavenly Jerusalem may lead some students to report that in the acts of listening and reading they have been moved sensually (or "performatively") up the hierarchy of the senses, with its concomitant ways of knowing.

By creating performances of *Pearl*, students become sensitive to the poem's representations of significant performative acts. In the first canto when the Dreamer laments the loss of his pearl, he uses common tropes that introduce visionary experience: description of his anguish ("Þat dotz bot þrych my hert þrange, / My breste in bale bot bolne and bele"; 17–18) and falling prostrate ("I felle vpon þat floury flaȝt"; 57). Students enacting or voicing this moment tend to associate the Dreamer's fall with an excessive, overly theatrical despair. Although the Dreamer's overwhelming grief and need for consolation motivate the poem's narrative, another perspective on this particular event warrants discussion. Students may be guided to understand that the Dreamer's prostration upon the grave is a moment ripe with visionary potential, as educated medieval audiences familiar with these tropes would have understood. The solitary demonstration of grief and falling prostrate are practices that signify the *compunctio cordis* ("compunction of the heart") initiating the Dreamer's visionary journey. Mary Carruthers describes the phase of *compunctio cordis*, marked by weeping or grief and lying down, as a spiritually meditative state that "became a standard posture in the Middle Ages for all kinds of invention" (175; see 171–82).

Performing the dialogue between the Dreamer and the Pearl-Maiden can make students aware that different expectations about the roles of each figure and about tone of voice can result in divergent interpretations of *Pearl*. By voicing the dialogue, they quickly grasp the inversion of authority that one typically finds in a parent-child relationship; here the child teaches a supplicant father. Once students understand that the Dreamer makes basic theological mistakes in his questions and assertions, they tend to characterize him as someone dopey and naive. Such an interpretation may be juxtaposed with Jennifer Garrison's interpretation, in which she argues that the Dreamer speaks from a vantage of tremendous pain and of a desire to be in the presence of the Pearl-Maiden. She argues that his failures of understanding are driven by his lack of emotional containment, rather than an absurd degree of naïveté about Christian cosmology. A third possible interpretation of the Dreamer's mistakes relates to generic presentation of these figures for the sake of a pedagogical dialogue. From this point of view the Dreamer strikes a stance of naïveté for the express purpose of eliciting the Maiden's instruction. Students attempt to depict in their performances of *Pearl* one interpretation or another of the Dreamer's state of mind and motivation. Such readings change the way that they voice his lines and also the way that they interpret the end of the poem.

In undergraduate classes, staging the heavenly procession of virgins led by Christ-as-Lamb can occasion more merriment than solemnity. Even so, an embodied enactment of *Pearl*'s procession impresses with its symbolic and ritualistic grandeur. The maidens' calm, joyful movements contrast with the Dreamer's internal agitation and his inability to set himself in motion toward Christ without being cast back into his waking self. In discussion of this event, I direct attention to the parallel, terrestrial ritual of receiving the Eucharist to which the Dreamer alludes in the final stanza. Garrison, finding that concerns with the Mass recur throughout *Pearl*, claims that the poem's central argument is "that repeated participation in the liturgy is the only way for him [the Dreamer] to reform" (320). Students, referring to their experiences of *Pearl* through the medium of performance, can interrogate this idea from the position of reader-actors who have given voice to the poem's ritual-like recurring poetic structure.

In conclusion I want to address the benefits of teaching *Pearl* in performance, using the rubric of "goals, objectives, and outcomes," which some educators include in their teaching plans. By assigning sections of *Pearl* for performance, I am able to meet several goals that I have when I teach medieval verse: developing a repertoire of interpretative approaches that heed the aesthetics of various kinds of medieval verse; encouraging close reading; improving interpretive skills (expressed in discussion, performance, and writing); fostering a better understanding of vernacular medieval literature; and helping students hear and give voice to verbal art presumably designed for aurality. These goals may be achieved by employing the objectives described in the first part of this essay: developing knowledge of basic external circumstances (setting, audience, customs) and internal evidence (through close readings of *Pearl*); creating performances or vocalizations of *Pearl*; preparing carefully considered feedback for other student performances; and writing analytical papers that justify specific performance choices. Some outcomes of performing *Pearl* include the opportunity to hear *Pearl*, rather than read it silently, just as medieval audiences presumably did; hearing what can be missed when reading silently; greater attention to the acoustic construction of *Pearl*; justifying performance choices through consideration of external and internal factors; and exploration of thematic concerns of *Pearl*, such as those described in the second part of this essay.

Describing *Pearl* alongside Dante's *Paradiso* and Heinrich Frauenlob's *Marienleich*, Newman pays homage to their verbal design: "the poems, like heavens themselves, are works of consummate artfulness. . . . These poems are characterized by an intensely self-conscious style that carries poetic language to its limits, achieving a brilliant, glossy finish that makes opacity itself a translucence" ("Artifice of Eternity" 2). Student performances and vocalizations of *Pearl*, in contrast, can be messy, down-to-earth events that sunder *Pearl* in pieces. Yet, performances and vocalization may also do homage, whether tentative, clumsy, sure, or polished; these acts make the translucent beauty of *Pearl* legible and audible, its chiming song "ful lufly dere" (880).

NOTES

[1] Vis-à-vis ardent skepticism toward oral performance, Betsy Bowden writes (tongue in cheek): "Even with indirect evidence from documents that take for granted that people speak, an unbeliever can never be finally convinced by irrefutable evidence that anybody said anything out loud before Thomas Edison did in 1877 in Menlo Park, New Jersey" (13).

[2] *Vocalité* may also refer to a (now mostly lost) tradition of vocal styles that suit specific genres and performance contexts.

[3]For further bibliography, see Vitz and Lawrence.

[4]I believe that "authenticity" is a red herring because oral-connected stories may be told and retold in a highly adaptable and flexible manner (see Lord; Ong; John Miles Foley). With respect to medieval texts that partake in hybrid oral and written paradigms, the idea of an authentic or "original" text matters less than the citation of specific authors for the authority that they exert in the textual tradition (see Clanchy; Amodio). Knowing that authenticity is not only impossible, but also a mistake, students agonize less over the question of whether "this is how it was done" and engage more with what the generic, lexical, and metrical features of the text suggest.

Voicing the Debate

Eugene Green

The long section of debate in *Pearl* offers students an unusual opportunity to consider that medieval and modern temperaments and voices have unexpected similarities. The possibility of such similarities is noteworthy since instructors ordinarily find undergraduate students unconvinced by Middle English debates that, like *Pearl*, engage a troubled man and a self-assured woman. To suggest parallels in *The Consolation of Philosophy* or *Troilus and Criseyde* or else Boccaccio's eclogue on Olympia requires a trust in critics' discernment hard to develop during undergraduate classroom hours.[1] Yet students' actual experiences and likely familiarity with Woody Allen and Penelope Cruz or with Hedda Gabler and Ejlert Lövoborg or Nora and Torvald Hemler encourage unexpected linkages. Comparing and contrasting the debate in *Pearl* to modern film and drama gain strength, moreover, through the recognition and the exercise of the voice as an emotional and intellectual instrument. Of course, instructors do well to discuss first whether the debaters in *Pearl* are contrastively troubled and self-assured and thereby elicit students' views on how gauging the temperament is conducive to dramatic reading. Since students are probably familiar with Allen's reputation (*Annie Hall* will stir curiosity, if not immediate recall), his troubled preoccupations offer comparison with those of *Pearl*'s Dreamer. Likewise, Penelope Cruz's vibrancy, as in *Vicky Cristina Barcelona*, may suggest an affinity with the Maiden's affective appearance in *Pearl*. Moreover, Allen's and Cruz's modes of expression— his continual displeasures, her energetic responsiveness—provide a focus for classroom commentary on the Dreamer and the Maiden as speakers. A readiness, then, to elicit students' first views requires some discussion of linkages between temperament and voice. Inasmuch as the already proposed comparisons on temperament are provisional, they tacitly presuppose as well that classroom discussions will produce intriguing alternatives. Very likely, too, such discussions may benefit from students and instructors listening to one another as they individually give voice to the Dreamer and the Maiden in debate. The analysis below on giving voice to the debate takes as a premise that the *Pearl* poet's linguistic and rhetorical practices lend themselves to constructing a framework useful to students. Hardly rigid, this framework encourages students to attend to patterns of expression in the debate and to experiment with voicing them. Although such attention and experimenting are likely to produce variety, the interplay between the poet's practices and students' inferences promises mutual classroom insights. These insights on voicing may offer, too, a more fully informed appreciation of the Dreamer's and the Maiden's temperaments. In the light of this reciprocal process, the suggestions that follow now, briefly on temperament, more fully on voicing the debate, aim to heighten classroom experience.

If temperament manifests itself by the content of one's heart and mind and by one's manner of expression, then *Pearl*'s poet invests in his characters a rich diversity. For students to appreciate this diversity, a class lecture or two on the allusions to biblical texts in the poem is a preparatory step toward imagining the qualities of the debaters' temperaments. (A review of E. V. Gordon's list, which lays out the poem's biblical sources, reassures readers that both the Dreamer and the Maiden do use biblical allusion frequently.)[2] The difference in their practice is that during the debate, the Maiden quotes and paraphrases biblical lines repeatedly, whereas the Dreamer's utterances contain but three allusions. In the sections of *Pearl* preceding and following the debate, however, the Dreamer's familiarity with the Bible is abundantly evident (five in 1–4, nearly forty in 17–20). This disparity in the Dreamer's and the Maiden's enlisting biblical support during the debate provides, then, an opening for students in their approach to questions of temperament and voice.

Since the Maiden's utterances continually display biblical reference, a likely strategy is to begin discussion with an example of her practice. Stanza 15, fit 3, offers, for instance, an opportunity to appreciate the Maiden's temperament as she speaks of the heavenly virgins:

Lest les þou leue my tale farande,
In Appocalyppece is wryten in wro:
"I seghe," says John, " þe Loumbe hym stande
On þe mount of Syon ful þryuen and þro,
And with hym maydenneȝ an hundreþe þowsande,
And fowre and forty þowsande mo.
On alle her forhedeȝ wryten I fande
Þe Lombeȝ nome, hys Fadereȝ also.
A hue from heuen I herde þoo,
Lyk flodeȝ fele laden runnen on resse,
And as þunder þroweȝ in torreȝ blo,
Þat lote, I leue, watȝ neuer þe les.   (867–76)

A discussion of this stanza will doubtless elicit different views, yet providing students with a framework of pertinent features may help them review and strengthen their arguments. To begin, students need to know that the stanza alludes to Apocalypse 14.1–4 on John's seeing the virgins singing. In this regard, the Maiden's naming John as her source (a feature of recurrent practice, especially from section 8 onward) invites comment on her inclination to identify authority.

A second feature characteristic of this stanza and others is the Maiden's rec-ognizing how willingly the Dreamer accepts her account of her status and life in heaven. Her supposing in lines 865–66 that he harbors some skepticism opens a perspective on her sense of his temperament and on how she should choose and mold her words. Her attending to his skepticism and to a way to respond implies a third feature of the framework: both debaters manifest through their voices an awareness of mostly unharmonious temperaments.

This third feature, as applied to the Maiden's stanza, reveals that she para-phrases John, whose authority helps her confront the Dreamer's resistance to her status as a wife of the Lamb. Her paraphrase, moreover, bears comparison with the original, at least to determine whether her words are merely a transla-tion or to indicate a distinctive trait associated with temperament. The Latin of Apocalypse 14.2 includes two images on the voices of the virgins:

> Et audivi vocem de cælo, tamquam vocem aquarum multarum, et tamquam vocem tonitrui magni: et vocem, quam audivi, sicut citharœdorum citharizan-tium in citharis suis.

> And I heard a voice from heaven, as if it were the voice of many waters, and as the voice of great thunder, and I heard a voice as if it were the harping of harpers on their harps.

The Maiden's paraphrase omits the image of the harpers at their instruments, yet it enlarges the images of a voice like many waters and great thunder with dy-namic force. The waters race torrentially; the thunder reverberates against dark hills. A study of this imagery prompts a heightened awareness of the Maiden's temperament and voice. Thus, the framework includes as a fourth feature the images that the debaters produce in responding to each other.

The images likening the voices from heaven to rapids and thunderclaps fol-low in the stanza the image of the virgins' foreheads stamped like a tattoo. Also found in Apocalypse 14, this image lends itself to analysis of temperament and voice, but also to judgments of significance. How valuable is the image of holy names tattooed on foreheads for unveiling qualities of temperament and voice? Put in relation to waters rushing and thunder rolling, what does the image of tat-toos contribute? In responding to questions like these, students recognize read-ily that their identifying contours of voice and temperament depends necessarily on indispensable judgments. This fifth feature of the framework—the audience as participants—discloses, as well, how closely related temperaments and voices past and current often are. To recover plausibly the dynamics of the Dreamer and the Maiden's exchanges is surely an act of the engaged imagination.

A sixth feature in the proposed framework concerns the possible continuities of voice and temperament between adjacent stanzas. One example has to suffice here. Stanza 15.4 includes two lines bound closely to 15.3: "A note ful nwe I herde hem warpe, / To lysten þat watȝ ful lufly dere" (879–80).

The Maiden's pleasure in the virgins' voices emphasizes her continuing delight. Further, since she is the Lamb's spouse, much of her joy in heaven is to join them—wives together, singing and listening. These lines are self-reflective as well as expressive.

Finally, the framework so far developed admits of an additional feature, this one bearing on the issues that the Maiden and the Dreamer debate. If one stanza in the Maiden's debate with the Dreamer welcomes attending to her temperament and close listening to her voice, her engagement with him elsewhere may differ. Thus the seventh feature of the framework relates temperament and voice to the issues contested. These issues include the possibility of reunion, the Maiden's status as heavenly queen, God's granting souls salvation, and the distinctions between worldly and divine generosity. To sample how these issues in the debate influence voice and temperament, one stanza—8.1 related to the Maiden's status as queen—is representative here. The Dreamer says:

"Blysful," quod I, "may þys be trwe?
Dyspleseȝ not if I speke errour.
Art þou þe queen of heueneȝ blew?
Þat al þys worlde schal do honour?
We leuen on Marye þat grace of grewe,
Þat her a barne of vyrgyn flour:
Þe croune fro hyr quo moȝt remwe
Bot ho hir passed in sum fauour?
Now, for synglerty o hyr dousour,
We calle hyr Fenyx of Arraby,
Þat freles fleȝe of hyr fasor,
Lyk to þe Quen of cortaysye."   (421–32)

Keeping to the framework proposed, the first feature to consider is the Dreamer's allusion to the "Fenyx of Arraby," found, too, in *The Book of the Duchess*. Although the *Pearl* poet was apparently familiar with secular and clerical medieval texts, modern associations with the Phoenix are strongest with the city and science fiction—so the Dreamer's use of the name needs explaining. Beryl Rowland connects the allusion to Christ's Second Coming to the Knight's recalling faire White's singular virtues and beauty and to Mary's immaculate blessedness (*Blind Beasts* 44–45).

The Dreamer in *Pearl* holds to the traditional view of Mary, immaculate from her birth, the embodiment of divine grace. His venerating Mary speaks as well to his temperament—orthodox in his love, a medieval attachment worthwhile to find in modern experience. Yet the voicing of this attachment to Mary occurs in the same stanza that presents the Dreamer's questioning the Maiden's status as a queen in heaven. Why does the poet juxtapose clashes between belief and skepticism in the Dreamer's temperament?

Just as the Maiden counters in 15.3 the Dreamer's skepticism, so his veneration of Mary does not exclude a further purpose. Suppose that the allusion to the Phoenix also carries with it the Dreamer's intent to discredit the Maiden's claim that she is heavenly queen. How does the Dreamer voice at the same time these contradictory purposes—to venerate and to discredit? Evidence for such a disparate linkage, moreover, is again evident in lines 433–34: "'Cortayse Quen', þenne sayde þat gaye, / Knelande to grounde, folde vp hyr face . . .'" Only here in the debate does the Maiden turn away from the Dreamer to kneel and raise her face in loving submission. Is her gesture, too, a doubling of purpose—a dismissal of his innuendo as well as an act of veneration?

If both Dreamer and Maiden express veneration and innuendo, then the poem may show how their debate presents their juxtaposed stances, whether through images or other rhetorical devices. The lines in 8.1 preceding the Dreamer's allusion to the Phoenix comprise mostly three rhetorical questions (421, 423–24, 426–27), the first two alone directed at the Maiden. The arrangement of this sequence of questions awaiting no reply, however, possibly anticipates the innuendo found in the Dreamer's and the Maiden's focus on Mary. If a question has no reply, does the absence of one suggest in itself that the speaker already knows or believes what it should be? In the Dreamer's asking the Maiden to affirm again her marriage to the Lamb and to say that she is the queen of heaven, his questions already imply his disbelief. One may well consider whether the Dreamer is insinuating as well as asking. If so, then his insinuations dramatically anticipate the innuendo of the stanza's closing lines. The third question, too, expressed just before the Dreamer speaks of Mary's divine attributes, rhetorically also harbors his disbelieving that the Maiden has married the Lamb. How can one conceive, as the images in his questions imply, of Christians honoring the Maiden as queen, of anyone removing Mary's crown?

At the heart of the stanza (line 425), too, the Dreamer's sentence has an inclusive *we* (repeated in line 430) for its subject, incorporating all Christians. Nowhere else in the debate does this widely inclusive *we* recur in his utterances. Staged before a listening audience, the occurrence in *Pearl* of his inclusive *we* argues the Dreamer's appeal for orthodox support. Modern readers have the opportunity, like the *Pearl* poet's contemporaries, to treat separately the beliefs that his inclusive *we* affirms and his own use of the pronoun. Listening to the Dreamer's voice is not a straightforward exercise.

So far, the analysis presented of temperament and voice has omitted the phonological dimensions of meter, alliteration, and rhyme. Yet the *Pearl* poet's extraordinary design for his stanzas, on examination, provides phonological nuance to complement allusion, imagery, and grammatical properties. As an instance of how his phonological resourcefulness develops matters of temperament and voice in the debate, consider the Maiden's defense of her early deliverance in 10.4:

> Mor haf I of joye and blysse hereinne,
> Of ladyschyp gret and lyueȝ blom,
> Þen alle þe wyȝeȝ in þe worlde myȝt wynne
> By þe way of ryȝt to aske dome.
> Wheþer welnygh now I con bygynne
> In euentyde into þe vyne I come—
> Fyrst of my hyre my Lorde con mynne:
> I watȝ payed anon of al and sum.
> Ȝet oþer þer werne þat toke more tom,
> Þat swange and seat for long ȝore,
> Þat ȝet of hyre noþynk þay nom,
> Paraunter noȝt schal to-ȝere more.   (577–88)

This stanza follows the Maiden's rendering the Parable of the Workers in the Vineyard; its function is to exemplify God's power to grant salvation, no matter how long a person's life. Dead at possibly an unexpected time, the Maiden speaks of her own deliverance in the stanza quoted above, contrasting her early arrival in heaven to the longer duration that most have on earth. A first impression of her recounting her first moments in the afterlife while others must labor long years perhaps suggests that she is plainspoken and composed. Although unmarked by allusion, vivid imagery, and striking rhetorical figures, the stanza nonetheless provides phonological patterns appropriate to the Maiden's speech.

For students the stanza's alliterative patterns are likely to be most noticeable. Yet three lines in all, 579, 585, and 586 (all associated with those longer-lived than the Maiden), contribute to its phonological structure. The *w* of line 579 binds the phrase "wyȝeȝ in þe worlde" to the verb *wynne*; the *t* of line 585 connects the verb *toke* to the object *tom*, and *sw* in line 586 joins two verbs together. Further, these few alliterated words are even so mainly specific to this stanza. The phrase "in þe worlde," occurring once more in the poem, modifies *wyȝeȝ* and conveys only here the wide inclusiveness that heightens through comparison the Maiden's "joye and blysse." The predicate phrase "toke more tom," together with the rhymed "long ȝore" and "to-ȝere more," instances words of time found only in this stanza. Against the timeless celebration of life in heaven, the years of earthly toil paradoxically seem longer. And the paired *swange and swat*, centered on toil, do not occur elsewhere in *Pearl* in combination or separately. If the consensus is that the stanza exemplifies a moderate tone overall, its alliterating three lines, highlighting words of human time and labor, subtly help to connote the burdens before salvation that most earthly life endures.

The stanza's rhymes also function subtly. Except for the rhyming ȝore and to-ȝere more associated with long stretches of time, the final words in the stanza's lines end with alternating vowel and nasal sounds. This alternation *i* / *o*, front and back vowels, and *m* / *n*, bilabial and alveolar nasals, implies a textured backdrop for the stanza's thematic contrasts. No other stanza in *Pearl* instances this pattern of vowel plus nasal rhyme.

In accord with the poem's general pattern of stress, each line in the stanza has four beats. The final beats, too, mark grammatical connections between clusters of lines, grouped by motif.[3] The first cluster (lines 577–80) contrasts the Maiden's benefits in heaven to the benefits of all those who live longer; the second cluster (581–83) recounts her arrival in heaven; the third (584) emphasizes her heavenly recompense; the last (585–88) portrays the toil and travail of others living longer. Demonstrating how the strong stress at the close of each line underscores the stanza's motifs may encourage discussion of how the poet modulates the pace of the Maiden's voice. Does the poet's design suggest a pace sufficient to identify each motif and to enable the Dreamer and the larger audience to appreciate her heavenly joy and bliss? If so, the stanza helps the Maiden's listeners to focus on how she savors step-by-step her attaining heavenly delight, in contrast to earthly experience.

The debate's extensiveness (sections 5 to the first four lines of 17) is a fine opportunity to appreciate the complex temperaments and voices of the Dreamer and the Maiden. The challenge for discussing these aspects of *Pearl* as well as other aspects of the poem lies as much in weighing what to include as in determining the organization of a course as a whole. One possible approach is to combine questions of temperament and voice in particular stanzas with other perspectives on the poem. These voices may resonate particularly well to modern ears. Since the critical literature on *Pearl* is rich with observation, students will find secondary sources helpful in preparing dramatic readings of stanzas in the debate. Parenthetically, close study of the poem's Middle English phonology, though of course advantageous, is not necessary. Shakespeare's lines, on the other hand, work well enough in modern English.

The framework presented above for the first two analyzed stanzas is merely a device. Obviously, it is an organizational tool for this essay yet some of its features are likely to contribute to undergraduate discussions of *Pearl*. As a device, it may help students prepare a dramatic reading in class. As a contribution to undergraduate study of the poem, the framework implicitly invites critical analysis. For instance, it assumes that the Dreamer and Pearl speak to each other in a manner independent of their encounter in a dream. Do voices debating in a dream vision differ significantly from those in other settings? The framework, too, relies on the poet's apportioning, except toward the close of the debate, separate stanzas to the Dreamer and the Maiden as they speak. Such a division, plausible in a dream vision, is unlikely to occur in other poetic structures. Thus it is surely important to consider how the allocation of voices to entire stanzas (for the Maiden, especially, to sequences of stanzas) contributes to dramatic reading.

These caveats aside, the framework for conceiving of the Dreamer and the Maiden's conversation as a dialogue revealing their temperaments and voices is very likely worthwhile for the writing of essays; it encourages close reading and helps students formulate and argue a thesis. The framework, moreover, does not impel students to settle for received opinion. In its best use, the framework encourages dialectic between the language of debate in the *Pearl*, as given to the Dreamer and the Maiden, and students' intuitions on temperament and voice. Such a dialectic brings together *Pearl* as a text extraordinarily open to interpretation and to students' opportunities to respond to the poem's debate in unpredictable ways. Clearly, students and instructors are likely to find the dimensions of temperament and voice in the Dreamer and the Maiden highly variable. Finally if the issues of voicing the debate in *Pearl* prove attractive, then similar or complementary approaches to other Middle English poems may generate sustaining interest.

NOTES

[1] David Aers likens the Dreamer and the Maiden to Troilus and Criseyde (54–73). Jessica Barr discusses an analogy between speakers in the poem and those in Boethius's philosophy (127–8). E. V. Gordon considers the resemblance between Olympia in Boccaccio's eclogue and the Maiden (xxxv).

[2] Gordon's edition of *Pearl* lists the poem's biblical allusions (165–67). Quotations, and section and line numbers from *Pearl*, appearing in the body of this essay, follow Gordon.

[3] In detail, the grammatical connections run as follows: 577–78, initial comparative clause and appositive phrases; 579–80, closing comparative clause and adverbial infinitive phrase of manner; 581–83, adverbial clause of time, parenthetical clause of time, main clause with periodic close; 584, independent sentence; 585–88, main clause and relative clause, second relative clause, third relative clause, and abbreviated, final relative clause.

Teaching *Pearl* and Landscape

Elizabeth Allen

The doctrinal content of *Pearl* can seem deceptively clear and assimilable: instead of mourning the loss of his Maiden, the Dreamer should turn his awareness to heaven, that is, to the maiden's salvation and his own. But to approach *Pearl* through its landscapes is to emphasize the poem's investment in what is earthly—sense-perceptible and time-bound—and to complicate readers' initial assent to the poem's spiritual message. Landscape is an ideal way to approach *Pearl*'s central problem: the complex relation between earthly and heavenly experiences that mirror one another and differ radically.[1] Certainly the poem encourages awareness that salvation transcends earthly experiences of sense perception, desire, loss, and mourning. To achieve transcendence, however, *Pearl* unfolds through three remarkably concrete spaces, mapped in the illustrations that precede the poem in the manuscript: the *erber* ("garden") where the dreamer has lost his pearl and mourns for her; the shining open space of his dreamscape; and the jeweled New Jerusalem with its crenellated walls enclosing the 144,000 virgins and the Lamb. The progress from garden to dreamscape to visionary city leads, however haltingly, toward heaven.[2] As we shall see, the Maiden's Parable of the Workers in the Vineyard abstracts physical space, demonstrating the limits of symbolic landscape as a representation of spiritual reward. Still, attending to landscape establishes readers in the Dreamer's earthly perspective and in the mimetic function of the poem's language. In particular, approaching the poem through its physical spaces discourages condescension toward the Dreamer by emphasizing the complexity of his experiences and the ways in which we see through his eyes. This approach helps explain why, far from simply leaving grief behind, the poem's conclusion returns both Dreamer and audience to the important task of living in the difficult created world.

Teaching the poem in upper-division courses on dream vision or Ricardian poetry, I typically assign the lush translation of Marie Borroff (2001); to demonstrate details of close analysis, I occasionally supplement with Middle English from Malcolm Andrew and Ronald Waldron (*The Poems of the* Pearl *Manuscript* [5th ed.; 2008]) projecting the original language on the computer screen at the front of the room. My students in these lecture-based courses have read Boethius's *Consolation of Philosophy* and excerpts from Guillaume de Lorris and Jean de Meun's *Roman de la Rose*, and they will go on to read Chaucer's *Book of the Duchess*, along with other poems by the *Pearl* poet. Typically, then, students in my courses have the tools with which to recognize the *locus amoenus* ("pleasant place") where the Dreamer loses his pearl. They have also encountered the idea of a providential order inaccessible to human understanding, and I introduce the poem by linking the Pearl-Maiden to Lady Philosophy.

Even in courses without such structuring encounters—such as a lower-division introduction to early literature or a survey of religious literature—landscape helps students picture the unfolding action. By visualizing the action in space, students can explore the symbolic contrasts among the Dreamer's garden, his dreamscape, and heavenly order in the New Jerusalem; and they can also notice that the poem uses such earthly means to gesture toward a vision of salvation. I use the four images that precede the poem in the manuscript to demonstrate the ways in which the poem is structured according to landscape and to provide a foil for the poem's visual descriptions.

Teaching the poem through landscape focuses students' attention immediately on sensory experience, especially sight (a topic Sarah Stanbury explores in *Seeing the* Gawain-*Poet*). The poem begins with the speaker having lost his pearl in the *erber* where the pearl fell away through the grass, an equivocal depiction of earthly landscape. On the one hand, the earth "marrez" (mars) the jewel (23), her color is "clad in clot" (22), her richness runs to rot (26)—language I give in the original to show the Dreamer's vivid visual sense. The images of ugly clothes and ruined wealth suggest not just loss but the bodily decay of the Dreamer's beloved. At the same time, we see the growth of bright flowers and spices that shine brightly in the sun, and the speaker seems to hope that the pearl is like a seed and will grow again: "So semly a sede moʒt fayly not" ("Such a seed could never have come to nought"; 34). In examining what the landscape looks like, we come quickly to the question of the Dreamer's interpretation: is the pearl ruined by clay, or can she grow anew, as a seed? His metaphors shift; his perspective is effortful and questing and makes readers engage in interpretive effort through him. The concatenation word for the poem's first section (rhyming with "clot" and "rot") is "spot": at once the place in the landscape where the speaker recalls his pearl, the site of loss, and an image of earthly imperfection.[3] The Dreamer is enclosed in this spot until, seized by another sensory experience—the spiritually evocative "odour" of 1.58—his spirit springs free of his body.

The change in setting provides an opportunity to demonstrate the links among landscape, mental state, and poetic form. As the dreamer flies from the spot where his pearl rolled away, the poem's concatenation pattern flies free of the word "spot" and enters the world of "adubbemente" (line 72) an order that exceeds the garden.[4] Students quickly see that this new open landscape indicates a shift in the Dreamer's mind: not only is he capable of perceiving different objects but his mind requires a bigger world. While that world is frankly unearthly, its light emphatically brighter than the sun, the spiritual scene is nonetheless detectable only through the resources of physical description. The Dreamer surveys the cloven cliffs and gleaming rocks, indigo tree trunks and silver leaves, the metallic yet organic forms suggesting supernatural experience while using the tools of natural description.[5] Moreover, the sensory excess of the third stanza of the second section encapsulates this use of natural things to point to a more-than-natural order: the fragrance of the fruits fills him like food (87–88) and the birds beat their wings in time to their voices (93–94). These synesthetic excesses point toward heaven, the more-than-earthly.

In the final stanza of section 2, the Dreamer comes to the banks of the stream that was noticeably lacking in the *erber* and sees the gem-filled water there (for a discussion of the river, see Petroff). At this juncture, I sometimes show the first two illustrations from the manuscript. In the first, the Dreamer reclines beside the grave-mound; in the second, he stands beside the river, a more commanding presence (see the manuscript images at the end of the volume). Anticipating the poem's vision of Jerusalem, I point out the river's symbolic link to the water of baptism, though at this stage I tend to remain reticent about the poem's theological lessons. Students are often struck by the prominence of the Dreamer in the illustrations, which enables us to explore the centrality of his perspective. The poem's emphasis on the jewels in the river suggests that the Dreamer's gaze in *Pearl* resembles that of the Dreamer looking into the pool of Narcissus in the *Roman de la Rose*, where the stones in the bottom reflect his eyes in an image of his own desire. In a similarly self-reflexive way, the Dreamer in *Pearl* thinks the beauty of the landscape has entirely banished his mourning, "Fordidden my stresse, dystryed my paynez" ("Conquered my cares, dispelled my pain"; 124).

Of course, the landscape's beauty is not enough. The pictures' awkward forms, with the Dreamer looming so large, often strike students as insufficient to the glory of spiritual vision. The Dreamer has much to learn; he must, in effect, "raise" his gaze upward and learn how to become aware of what lies beyond the river. As much as the gems in the river suggest self-absorption, the poem shows that they also point beyond this human perspective: they reflect other eyes, for they are like the stars that, "quen stroþe-men slepe, / Staren in welkyn in wynter niȝt" ("while men of the marshlands sleep, / Flash in winter from frosty space"; 115–16). Far from mere narcissism, the scope here is ordinary and cosmic at once. The Middle English "staren" indicates the animation of the stars, as they look down from the sky, suggesting a super-human gaze that continues while marsh-men sleep, an arrangement of watching eyes protecting the created world in the cold night. Still, that gaze of watchful care, that protective image, originates with the self-reflexivity of the Dreamer: his gaze into the river at the beautiful gems and the knowledge of his own desire for such beauty is what enables the poem's metaphorical access to a sense of God's presence.

I try to suggest that—for all the corrective theology of the poem's middle—the Dreamer's intense desire for more is, to a great degree, granted and thus provisionally validated in the early sections of the poem. The Dreamer's joy arises from the hope of transcendence, registered through physical movement: at first he looks, his gaze moving from cliffs to forest, and then he begins to walk, and the further he walks, the fairer the landscape grows (103). When he comes to the water, he walks along the banks of the river, and he thinks that paradise must be across it, inspiring his desire to get beyond it (141–42). Accordingly, "ay more and more" provides the concatenation phrase in the third section, indicating both the continued changes available within the dreamscape and the Dreamer's aspiration to heaven.

This close attention to the Dreamer's perspective can prepare students to see the way that the Pearl-Maiden appears in the landscape as if the Dreamer's desire has conjured her. She is produced within his mental world, an aspect of the dreamscape; at the same time she is also his external object, his "more and more." The Maiden appears toward the end of section 3, at the foot of the cliff across the river—for she has "come down to" him—glistening white but more and more familiar the more he looks at her; and for the next two sections the Maiden's description echoes and gives focus to the landscape where she moves. Like the cloven cliffs, she shines sheer (213); like the river, she is full of gems. The Dreamer's gaze narrows to her body and dress, then to her crown, all crusted in pearls, and finally to the single pearl "withouten wemme" (221) set on her breast. This narrowing of perspective paradoxically broadens the Dreamer's sense of the sheer value of the landscape he has entered, for he sees in that single pearl a "more and more," a metonym for all that surrounds it. The single pearl represents all that is implied by the landscape but that remains inaccessible to the human mind: "A mannez dom moȝt driȝly demme / Er mynde moȝt malte in hit mesure" ("A man might ponder long and late / Ere its full worth were well assessed"; 224–25). The pearl encapsulates the way in which the Dreamer has found what he wants and, more profoundly, found how much his desire exceeds his grasp. Pursuing the poem's metonymic ways of gesturing to the transcendent, I reach forward here to the Parable of the Pearl of Great Price, for which the merchant gives all (721–44).[6] The merchant recognizes the worth of the pearl, which also manifests God's answering care for his creatures—a sense of value that pivots on the pearl as symbol for both the value of life and God's gift of salvation.

Despite the Dreamer's slowly expanding understanding of the Maiden's continuing value, he misunderstands her nature when he first sees her. He thinks her movement toward him is a gesture of reunion, her body an earthly presence rather than a spiritually symbolic form. As soon as the Dreamer sees the Maiden, he registers her worth or, in the poem's framing term, her "paye"; but he has still to learn a far more precise awareness of her worth as a concrete, created form and an image of the saved soul. As with the initial discussion of the dreamscape, here too the manuscript illustrations can open up discussion about the meaning of the Dreamer's perspective in the poem. The third illustration in the manuscript shows the Dreamer gesturing toward the Maiden and looking out as though to teach readers her importance, and students readily notice the difference between his authority in the image and his limited perspective in the poem. Although the poem suggests that his perspective is limited, his experience is nonetheless useful, insightful, even exemplary, as the illustration suggests.

In the middle ten sections of the poem (6–15), the landscape recedes into the background as the Pearl-Maiden instructs the dreamer about the nature of heavenly salvation. In teaching, I linger more on the dialogue than space permits here, focusing on the Dreamer's evolving capacities and limitations. But we explore in particular detail the Maiden's retelling of the Parable of the Workers in the Vineyard (Matt. 20.1–16). Here, landscape becomes a surprisingly inert instrument for the work of bodies in time, from sunrise through the heat of the day until dusk falls and night arrives. The workers in the vineyard assume that hours of work provide the framework for the lord's rewards, only to discover that God's rewards are not doled out on the basis of human space or time. Students readily build the analogy between the workers and the Dreamer, who expects heavenly reward to correspond to a soul's struggles on earth. The Dreamer, almost indignant at the salvation of the innocents, believes salvation should be a symmetrical arrangement—"Þou quytez vchon as hys desserte," he insists ("You render to each his just reward"; 595). But the Pearl-Maiden insists that all those in God's kingdom are "payed inlyche," whether they receive little or much. Her parable transforms the earthly notion of payment into the heavenly notion of "satisfaction": salvation is enough for everyone; it is satisfying. The word "paye," as Jill Mann points out in "Satisfaction and Payment in Middle English Literature," implies both monetary payment of debt and satisfaction— the sense of fulfillment, of getting "enough," the concatenation word of section 11. Mann argues that "Once one is satisfied, there is no need for more—indeed, there is no room for its absorption" (25). From this perspective, the question of how long one lived or how hard one worked becomes irrelevant. From the perspective of salvation, differences among earthly experiences no longer matter. Returning now to develop earlier suggestions about the river, we examine how the Maiden illustrates God's gifts in imagery that merges baptismal water with the blood of the Crucifixion: "Ryche blod ran on rode so roghe, / And wynne water; þen, at þat plyt, / Þe grace of God wex gret innoghe" ("Rich blood ran down rood-tree tall / And with it flowed forth water bright: / The grace of God was enough for all"; 645–47). The imagery of water and blood is irrational and unbounded—at once a more abundant image than the river-boundary of the dreamscape and an indication of the sheer alien immeasurability of that abundance.

When the Maiden retells the parable, she counters the lesson of the poem to which I have tried to draw students' attention: that human perception, desire, and loss can point to transcendence. She replaces the stunning experience of the earthly paradise with a vineyard that suppresses physical sensation, spatial experience, and human temporality; she replaces the Dreamer's renewed awareness of God's care with an insistence on the alterity of God's justice. In this way, her theological abstraction reveals the limit of sense perception, of landscape as a heuristic for spiritual truth, and of poetic language more generally for describing the ineffable.

Having portrayed these limits, however, the poem returns—in a striking symmetry—to a fundamentally spatial mode. After the abstract teachings of the middle section, the last five sections describing the New Jerusalem echo the first five by placing the Dreamer in space with renewed vividness and precision. To be sure, he sees from his riverbank not an enhanced "natural" landscape but a frankly artificial city on the other side. It is resolutely spiritual, not physically present but, as in Revelation, lowered from heaven for the sake of the viewer. The Maiden makes a careful distinction between the earthly and the heavenly Jerusalem and warns him he can only look from outside: "Vtwyth to se þat clene cloystor / Þou may, bot inwyth not a fote" ("Behold it from far off you may, / But no man's foot may there alight"; 969–70). But the city is described in intricate physical detail and in the context of the same paradisiac landscape where the entire conversation has occurred. The poem's return to the riverbank reminds us of the way in which space registers the mental capacities of the Dreamer.[7] Indeed, the increasing preciousness of the landscapes—from the ordinary herbs and spices in the *erber* to the silver, gilt, and indigo of the earthly paradise to the pearl- and gem-encrusted city—does not simply show the Dreamer heavenly truths but reflects his increasing capacity to perceive such truths. In teaching the poem, I use the last of the four manuscript illustrations as a foil. Whereas the image shows a perfectly measurable tabernacle and miniature wall, I ask students to picture movement and grandeur: the Dreamer's haste in running upstream to see the vision; the lowering of the city from on high; the twelve foundations of different stones in various colors; the gold streets and parchment-thin walls and gem-built dwellings; the gates, three to a side; the shining and transparent substance of the city; the sheer size of the cubic enclosure (a furlong is about a quarter mile, so each side is 1,500 miles long). The poem has moved from a spot of earth to an enormous heavenly span, and the Dreamer's perspective has broadened to encompass, however momentarily and incompletely, the fullness of that vision.

The source of the city's beauty lies at once in its arrangement and its lack of hierarchy, so it manifests in spatial form the lessons of the Maiden.[8] The description of the city calls attention to its createdness in a rich vocabulary of device, arrangement, measurement, division, and positioning. Everything shines; no one needs the light of the sun or the moon (the concatenation words of section 18) because God is everyone's "lombe-liȝt" ("lamp-light"; 1046). The visual form of the city answers the Dreamer's desire for the symmetrical structure of justice but reconceives symmetry as a sign of divine perfection. The city's enclosure manifests the protective and loving equality of heaven, for the maidens are all dressed alike, all equally glad, not jostling or competing for position (1105–15). If this radiantly shining, radically symmetrical world were a bodily vision, its power would kill the Dreamer (1090–92). Still, the sublunary world so emphatically disavowed provides a visual metaphor for movement within the city:

> Ryʒt as þe maynful mone con rys
> Er þenne þe day-glem dryue al doun,
> So sodanly on a wonder wyse
> I wayz war of a prosessyoun. (1093–96)

> As the great moon begins to shine
> While lingers still the light of day,
> So in those ramparts crystalline
> I saw a procession wend its way.

Borroff's translation here emphasizes the way in which the moon image creates a sense of one reality superimposed upon another, moon upon sunlight—her note calls the city a "kind of hyperspace" (162n11). Described earlier as a cube, the city now appears circular, with the procession of maidens dressed all alike in the pearly garb of his own maiden, moving together through the streets toward the center, led by the Lamb. The streets then contain both the water moving outward toward the river and the maidens moving inward toward the throne of God. The simultaneity of square and circular spaces, the simultaneous absence and presence of the moon, the linked centrifugal and centripetal motion, the doubling of sunlight by the moon—all create a sensory image of the New Jerusalem as, paradoxically, a place beyond human sensory understanding. The image of the moon recalls from section 2 the cosmic protection of the gazing stars, another moment when an image of earthly light suggested both the protective embrace and the sheer magnitude of God's care for the created world—but here, the care is directed to those innocents protected within the city walls. The maidens' movement toward the Lamb concretizes desire and pleasure—"delyt" in God—just as the Dreamer's movement through the earthly paradise of his dreamscape manifested his desire for "more and more." In depicting the virgins' desire as properly—spiritually—directed and satisfied, the poem differentiates the New Jerusalem from the Dreamer's reality. Though he tries, of course, it is impossible for him to cross the river and join the heavenly host.

When, in the poem's conclusion, the Dreamer finds himself back in the *erber*, his perspective is painfully reduced. As we complete the discussion of what the Dreamer sees in the heavenly city, I want students to hold in suspension their judgments about the way that vision ends—and, in particular, to keep resisting the temptation of condescension toward the Dreamer. After all, the Dreamer's view is the lens through which readers experience the poem, and if we detach ourselves from his perspective too easily at the poem's end, we risk giving short shrift to the difficulty of his mourning and the comforts of his vision alike.

The nature and meaning of the Dreamer's failure have long been debated. For some, the Dreamer falls short of the mystical experiences possible in this life; seeking only his own Maiden among those proceeding through the holy streets, he mistakes heavenly desire for "luf-longyng" (1152) and erroneously thinks he can cross the stream (Spearing, *Gawain-Poet* 167–70). For others, even the most imagistic account of heaven must remain an inaccessible ideal and an apocalyptic vision that "stuns human penetration" (Bogdanos 142). But as Barbara Newman points out, the end of the poetic vision does not mean the withdrawal of heaven: "Calling attention to any failure of mimesis forcefully asserts the reality of its object" and challenges us to a "strenuous act of imagination" ("Artifice of Eternity" 10). The resources of language lie in part in the concrete reality of earthly things: the moon as source of light and image of divine care but also of human turbulence; delight as the sign of paradise but also a human emotion; landscape as a supernatural sign and a natural phenomenon. The Dreamer's love-longing is at once what leads him to a vision of the New Jerusalem and what makes him overestimate his capacity to get there. The Dreamer's final enclosure within the earthly *erber* places the reader within the perspective of mourning: by concluding the dream so suddenly, the poet cuts off his readers, too, from heaven. The abrupt way in which the Dreamer now condemns those who strive against God suggests the act of will that is involved in his effort to recontextualize his loss.

As we have seen, the poem gestures to divinity through symmetrical patterning—and as anticlimactic as the ending can seem, it does balance the poem's beginning. *Pearl*'s expanding and increasingly artificial landscapes have set the Dreamer's initial loss within a much larger framework, a world embraced by a caring albeit bracingly distant God, a world echoed in a city of grand and ever-moving delight. What shifts by the end is not only the Dreamer's knowledge of heaven and his beloved daughter's place there, but his capacity—and ours—to know the expansive, heaven-seeking value of creaturely life.

NOTES

[1] On the complex relations between earthly perception and divine truth, I have been particularly influenced by Kean, *The* Pearl; Spearing, *Gawain-Poet* 96–170; Stanbury, *Seeing*; Mann; and Newman, "Artifice."

[2] On representations of paradise, see Pearsall and Salter's magisterial *Landscapes and Seasons of the Medieval World* 56–75.

[3] On the Dreamer's being stuck or "frozen" in his state of mourning, see Aers.

[4] The image of the soul rising above earthly constraints is common in monastic and contemplative writings (Stanbury, *Seeing* 14–16); on sleep as a meditative state, see Spearing, *Gawain-Poet* 107–17.

[5] Stanbury notes that the Dreamer is suddenly "a small figure surrounded by cliffs that rise above him. No longer focusing exclusively or even myopically on mementos of his personal loss, he perceives the relationships and agencies of light" as well as texture and variations in height and directionality (*Seeing* 19).

[6] On the Parable of the Pearl of Great Price, and the symbolism of the pearl, I am indebted to Kean (*The* Pearl 138–61) and Spearing (*Gawain-Poet* 135–52, 159–70). On the pearl's insufficiency, see Riddy.

[7] The city both functions as an object and "constitutes itself through the dreamer's utterance" (Chaganti, *Medieval Poetics* 126).

[8] Stanbury links *Pearl* to visual depictions of the Apocalypse in manuscript illustrations (*Seeing* 21–33).

Pearl and Medieval Dream-Vision Traditions in a Graduate Seminar: Genre, Mode, and Gender

Jane Chance

A complex fourteenth-century poem that shares many features with its anonymous author's other equally complex and unique works (*Sir Gawain and the Green Knight, Cleanness, Patience*, and possibly *Saint Erkenwald*), *Pearl* stands out from the others because of its multifaceted genre(s) and modes. A dream poem, it is framed at the opening by the narrator's description of his despair over the loss of his pearl in the garden and his irrational lapse into sleep (stanzas 1–5, or section 1) and at the end by his abrupt awakening (in the final five stanzas, or section 20). Consisting of three major parts, the visionary portion portrays the Dreamer as a wanderer in a fancifully embellished country in which he sees a young female figure in white, adorned with pearls: the Pearl-Maiden, whom he identifies as his lost pearl (sections 2–4) and with whom he begins a dialogue about loss and consolation that continues until he awakens. During the course of the poem, the Pearl-Maiden instructs the Dreamer in the New Testament Parable of the Workers in the Vineyard (Matt. 20.1–16) and shows him a vision of the heavenly Jerusalem.

In genre and mode, *Pearl* has been defined variously by scholars: as an elegy commemorating the death of a child; as an allegorization of the stages of grief that begins with the loss of the literal pearl; as a quest for the lost pearl / Pearl-Maiden that bears affinities with the medieval romance; as a consolatory mystical vision of the heavenly Jerusalem; and finally, and most important, as a dream vision that encompasses all these genres (elegy, vision, and romance) and modes (elegiac, allegorical, and mystical). The genre of the dream vision in particular attracted the attention of many well-known fourteenth- and fifteenth-century English and French writers. With its nonrealistic setting, disjunctive transitions, bizarre figures—often allegorical or divine—and its emphasis on the affective spiritual tradition and psychological dilemma, the medieval dream vision drew on a tradition of dream prototypes and interpretation in existence since biblical and classical antiquity. Separately, the waking vision came to be privileged in the thirteenth century as part of a tradition of mystical theology in England and on the Continent that grew out of the mendicant movement in which women, especially the religious, embraced visionary writing as a means of voicing their own gendered concerns. For all these reasons, a graduate course in Middle English dream vision might appropriately include this visionary work as an example of how gender intersects with this more courtly and clerical literary genre.

To reflect the medieval dream vision's changing history and direction, the fourteen-week, three-hour-per-week graduate seminar The Medieval Dream and Vision that I taught at Rice University was divided into four major parts, organized chronologically. The first two weeks introduced definitions and origins: what the ancient and medieval dream visions were and what they meant, primarily gleaned from classical and modern literary, religious, and artistic definitions and examples. During weeks three to five, we examined exemplary Anglo-Saxon, medieval Latin, and Old French antecedents and analogues in translation, ranging from the tenth through the thirteenth century. In weeks five to ten, we focused on the Middle English dream vision as treated by major medieval writers, spending a week on the *Pearl*. We concluded, in weeks eleven to thirteen, with the visionary mystical writings of several fourteenth- and fifteenth-century women writers, English and French, and their influence on two late-fifteenth-century Middle English dream visions. Our very last class in the fourteenth week was reserved for the study of two fifteenth-century Chaucerians, English and Scottish.

The seminar placed *Pearl* within all three contexts of genre, mode, and gender. In respect to genre, the *Pearl* lends itself to interpretation as a poem of complaint and loss derived from Latin philosophical and scholastic allegories such as the sixth-century *Consolatio Philosophiae* (*The Consolation of Philosophy*) by Boethius and the twelfth-century *De planctu Naturae* (*The Complaint of Nature*) by Alan of Lille (all texts required for the course, either on paper or on the Web, are listed at the end of the essay under "Assigned Primary and Secondary Reading"). But *Pearl* also belongs to a later medieval vernacular tradition of courtly-love dream vision that is allegorical in mode and nature. Initiated by the thirteenth-century *Roman de la Rose* (*Romance of the Rose*) by Guillaume de Lorris and Jean de Meun this courtly dream-vision tradition was continued in England by (among other poets) Geoffrey Chaucer (1345–1400) in *The Book of the Duchess* and *The Parliament of Fowls* and by John Gower (1330–1408) in the *Confessio Amantis*. Other Middle English dream visions of the same period that could have been included in the course are the anonymous debate poems *Wynnere and Wastoure*, *Parlement of the Thre Ages*, *Death and Life*, and John Clanvowe's *Boke of Cupide* (or *The Cuckoo and the Nightingale*). Finally, given its mystical vision of the heavenly city of Jerusalem drawn from the apocryphal book of Revelation by Saint John, *Pearl* (likely composed sometime between 1360 and 1390) also bears an affinity with the complex tripartite religious and allegorical dream vision of the lives of Dowel, Dobet, and Dobest in *Piers Plowman* by the cleric William Langland (fl. ca. 1330?–ca. 1400?).

The appearance of gender difference in the medieval dream vision coincides with the popularity of the *Romance of the Rose*, beginning with the mystical visions of late medieval Beguines such as the late-thirteenth-century Belgian Marguerite Porete (d. 1310) in her *Miroeur des Ames Simples* ("Mirror of Simple Souls"), the fifteenth-century English anchorite Julian of Norwich (1342–1416?) in her early *Vision* (or later, revised, *Revelations of Divine Love*), and the dreams and visions of the lay preacher Margery Kempe (b. ca. 1373) in her autobiographical *Book*. Concurrently, in 1405 the self-taught French-Italian poet-scholar Christine de Pizan (1360?–1431?) completed two gendered visionary allegories with a strong autobiographical emphasis, *Le Livre de la Cité des Dames* (*The Book of the City of Ladies*) and *Le Livre de l'advision Christine* (*Christine's Vision*).

To examine the influence cast by these seminal dream visions and allegories on late-fifteenth-century poems, seminar participants read the Middle English "The Floure and the Leafe" (1460–80?) and "The Assembly of Ladies" (1470); *The Temple of Glass*, by the English Chaucerian John Lydgate (1371?–1449?); and *The Thrissil and the Rois* and *The Golden Targe* by the Scottish Chaucerian William Dunbar (fl. ca. 1460?–1520?). Other Scottish Chaucerian dream-vision poems could have been added (had we had the time)—for example, Gavin Douglas, *The Palis of Honoure*; King James I, *Kingis Quair*; or John Skelton, *Bouge of Court*.

Given the breadth of the course, the major requirement entailed one original twenty- to twenty-five-page paper; undergraduates taking the course could submit a fifteen- to twenty-page paper. However, there were also ungraded weekly and biweekly one- to two-page position papers in which graduate students could stake a claim to some small question of interest that had arisen in their reading or in response to a question raised in advance of the reading. The underlying purpose of the brief papers was, of course, to allow students early on to hook into a focused and manageable but original topic for the long paper due at course's end.

Crucial, therefore, to an understanding of the complex issues relating to the dream vision was the foundational introduction to the course in the first two weeks. At issue in any study of the medieval dream vision is the nature of poetic identity and how such medieval fiction works, particularly in the earliest philosophical and literary models. Because the medieval dream vision bears affinities with the techniques advocated and illustrated by the much later modern surrealism movement of the twenties and thirties and with modern dream psychology, discussion during the first two weeks ventured into an explanation of allegory and the theorizing of the strangeness of this visionary genre by means of modern filmic and artistic analogues and early medieval dream theory.

In the first week, students were introduced to the French surrealist art of the twenties and thirties and to the translation of dream into visual art by means of automatic writing, accompanied in fiction writing by the stream-of-consciousness narrative technique pioneered by the novelists Virginia Woolf and James Joyce in Great Britain. Two surrealist works helped: the exploration of the process of thinking as "psychic automatism" (or surrealism) in art and dreams, by André Breton in his "Surrealist Manifesto" ([1924]; available online, as were many of the required and recommended texts), and by Luis Buñuel in his sixteen-minute film *Un Chien andalou* (*An Andalusian Dog* [1929]), with its bizarre imagistic juxtapositions—best known is the image of the razor cutting across the open eye. In this respect, the proximity of Rice University to Houston's Menil Museum and the museum's outstanding permanent collection of surreal art by Giorgio de Chirico and René Magritte, among other artists, made a field trip helpful in exploring the variations of the surrealist movement. For any institution situated outside a major urban center, many illustrated collections of surrealist artworks exist, aside from *An Outline of Dada and Surrealism* by Dawn Ades (e.g., books by Whitney Chadwick, Isabelle Dervaux, David Larkin, Jennifer Mundy, and Simon Wilson are listed under "Assigned Reading").

The viewing of "Surrealist Manifesto" and *Un Chien andalou* set up the next segment in the second week—on the biblical, philosophical, and cosmological explanations of the dream in the Middle Ages. Students read contextual literary models, beginning with visionary examples from the Bible—the book of Daniel, the Dream of Nebuchadnezzar, and the book of Revelation—and late antique dream and vision theory found in brief but influential chapters from medieval tractates such as the fourth- to fifth-century *Commentum in Somnium Scipionis* (*Commentary on the Dream of Scipio*; bk. 1, ch. 3) by the Roman North African philosopher Macrobius (fl. ca. 360–435) and the sixth-century visionary allegory *The Consolation of Philosophy* by Boethius of Padua (d. 524; first and last books only). Secondary reading for these introductory two weeks established a broader philosophical and historical context and offered greater detail than what the class could cover in two sessions. For the first week, students read Steven F. Kruger's "Introduction: Modern and Medieval Dreams" (*Dreaming in the Middle Ages* 1–16, 166–75; text and notes) and, for the second week, J. Stephen Russell's "Medieval Dream Authorities" (*English Dream Vision* 50–81, 211–15; text and notes).

Notably, Macrobius's description of the hierarchy of different types of dreams provides keys to their origins, important later to medieval poets and mystics in the formulation of different types of visionary works. These five types of dreams include, in the order prescribed by Macrobius: first, the *somnium*, or enigmatic dream, an illuminating vision with puzzling figures that will serve as the chief paradigm for the late medieval English literary dream vision; second, the *visio*, the prophetic dream itself, as vision of the future, without explicit agency; third, the *oraculum*, or oracular dream, delivered by an angel, oracle, or other messenger from above; fourth, the *insomnium*, or nightmare, caused by mental or physical stress, either worry about the future or fear of an enemy, or a dream caused by indigestion or overeating; and fifth, the *visum*, the apparition, an incubus that often appears between sleeping and waking (Macrobius 1.3.2–4).

Clearly these types of dream vision often overlap in practice, starting with Geoffrey Chaucer, a master at creating a persona in *Book of the Duchess*, whose reading of an anxiety-producing tale about a character's vision of her dead husband (*visum*) in Ovid's *Metamorphoses* triggers what should be a nightmare, an *insomnium*, but is in fact an enigmatic dream (*somnium*) with puzzling allegorical features, including a Black Knight talking to himself. Or, as in the example of *Pearl*, the speaker's mourning the loss of a daughter engenders a dream that could have been produced by mental stress (*insomnium*) but that additionally allows him to encounter a pearl-bedecked maiden in an enigmatic dream (a *somnium*) offering a vision of the future in the heavenly Jerusalem. Because the vision is identifiably both prophetic and oracular, presented by the Maiden as oracle, it is also a *visio* and an *oraculum*.

Some of this overlap is explainable by Macrobius's repositioning of his five types into a moralized cosmic hierarchy that was likely inspired by Vergil's line in the *Aeneid* (6.896): "False are the dreams [*insomnia*] sent by departed spirits to the sky," which Macrobius repeats in his own text (1.3.6). The oracular, prophetic, and enigmatic dreams (*oraculum, visio, somnium*) arrive by angelic messenger or other agency from the heavens, but the negative dreams are clearly marked as having corporeal or infernal origins, namely the *insomnium* and *visum*, with its incubus, or apparition, directed by the underworld. Supplemental reading, for any student interested, was provided by the later medieval work *On Dreams* by Boethius of Dacia.

In contrast to Macrobius's scientific commentary, another late antique primary work assigned for the second week, Boethius's *Consolation of Philosophy*, offers a literary model for later visionary works in its casting of the author as a subject who envisions and of an agent—in this case, the personification of Philosophy—perceived as a goddess who represents the kind of wisdom associated with the Seven Liberal Arts and who appears at a time of deepest despair in counsel to the subject. This prosimetrum, or mixture of prose and poetry, written during Boethius's incarceration and torture for alleged treason against the emperor Theodoric the Great (454–Aug. 526), King of the Ostrogoths, dramatizes his persona's psychological trajectory from despair over the loss of his professional status, health, fame, and wealth to an understanding of what cannot be taken away by the goddess Fortune, that is, wisdom and virtue. This visionary mode contrasts with the dream vision in its incarnation of the oracle as a character who interacts with a persona who is awake: while Boethius may drowse in his lethargy of despair, he does not literally fall asleep. And what he learns during the visionary appearance of the magister-like personification, Philosophia, instructs him morally and allegorically, thereby instituting a model for the appearance of any number of late medieval visionary guides.

In the second part of the course, during the third and fourth weeks, the assigned early medieval literary models mostly serve to illustrate the vision's often-prophetic association with the foundation of an institution, particularly the church, and of the emergence of the vernacular within a nation whose inhabitants could not read or write their native tongue. The earliest vision, in particular, may have been the angelic visitation to the illiterate Whitby lay brother and shepherd Caedmon to bestow on him a sudden miraculous ability to compose in Anglo-Saxon poetry the story of the creation of the world (and the first book of Genesis). The poem was later preserved as "Caedmon's Hymn" and inserted into the *Historia ecclesiastica gentis anglorum* (*History of the English Church and People*; bk. 4, ch. 22), written in Latin by Bede (673–735) and then translated into Anglo-Saxon. In addition, in the Anglo-Saxon poem *The Dream of the Rood* (ca. ninth to tenth century), the Rood appears in a vision to instruct the dreamer in the significance of religious salvation: by means of the cross's warrior-like service to his lord, Jesus Christ, the Rood facilitates Christ's Crucifixion, death, and, therefore, ultimate resurrection. Helpful for context in this segment was Kathryn L. Lynch's "Introduction: The Medieval Vision and Modern Scholarship," in *The High Medieval Dream Vision: Poetry, Philosophy, and Literary Form* (1–20, 201–03; text and notes).

Also for this third week, students read in translation the Latin philosophic vision of Alan of Lille (d. 1202), the prosimetrum *The Complaint of Nature*, in which the personification of Nature complains to the persona about the unmanning of humankind in acts of sodomy and other forms of courtly love that do not advance her mission as perpetuator of humankind, her task set by God. A seminal allegory, it influenced the satiric continuation by Jean de Meun (d. 1305?) of the paradigmatic courtly-love dream-vision allegory of *The Romance of the Rose*, begun by Guillaume de Lorris (fl. 1230). In this dream vision the Philosophy-like and learned personifications Reason, Nature, and Nature's allegorical priest Genius (also the god of human nature and generation) attempt to convince Amant, the Lover, about the dangers of the Garden of Pleasure, or Mirth (named after its guardian, the personification Deduit), in which the Lover lecherously pursues the Rose (the Lady).

In the third part of the course, during weeks five to ten, the focus falls finally on the fourteenth-century Middle English dream visions. Each work illustrates a novel twist in the genre. In week five, Geoffrey Chaucer's *Book of the Duchess* serves as a consolatory dream vision in which a sleepless and anxious dreamer eventually does sleep and consoles a lamenting Black Knight who has lost his beloved Blanche to Fortune in a game of chess. In week six, Chaucer's *Parliament of Fowls* offers both an anticourtly dream vision and a debate, presided over by the goddess Nature. Here, the dreamer witnesses an argument among various types of birds (predatory, worm, seed, and waterfowl) over which courtly suitor an aristocratic *formel* (female) eagle should choose on Valentine's Day, which uses up all the time allotted and leaves none for the inferior species.

In week seven, the dream vision *Pearl* (in modern translation, because of its difficult North-West Midlands dialect) reflects multiple genres and modes, most especially as elegy and as consolatory vision of the Other World. In weeks eight and nine, the B text of Langland's Lollard allegory of *Piers Plowman* (also in translation, because of its length) presents dream visions within a larger framing dream vision, in which a lethargic hermit, Will, learns how to live a better life after meeting the personifications Dowel, Dobet, and Dobest, along with Piers Plowman himself (Jesus Christ in human armor).

In week ten, selections from John Gower's dream vision of the *Confessio Amantis* (the prologue and bks. 1 and 8) establish an analogy between the unhappiness of the courtly lover, Amans, and the crisis in the larger macrocosm of the English kingdom, divided by its various estates. Amans must be confessed of courtly sin by the priest of Venus, Genius (who is a literary descendant of both Alain's and Jean's Genius as priest of Nature) and absolved by the priest's monitory recitation of tales of love from Ovid and other sources, organized more or less by the seven deadly sins. At the end, the mirror of Venus, into which Amans gazes, reflects the aged persona of the author Gower, his own life becoming an extension of the dream (or vice versa). For supplementary reading, students consulted J. Stephen Russell, "Structure," in *The English Dream Vision: Anatomy of a Form* (115–37; ch. 4).

Pearl shares with these other fourteenth-century English dream visions both mode and genre, as discussed above, but *Pearl* adds gender: although the poet is anonymous, the pearl may have been the speaker's lost daughter, who metamorphoses into the dream figure of the wise Pearl-Maiden and steers him to the vision of the Virgin Mary. As head of the troupe of 144,000 virgins in heaven, Mary functions as an intermediary between humankind and the divine—like Boethius's Lady Philosophy or Langland's Lady Holy Church (Truth). The Pearl-Maiden, young but wise, plays an important function in the tradition, which eventually leads in fifteenth-century autobiography and visionary works to the humanization of the Trinity and, therefore, to works by women. The female humanity of the Pearl-Maiden suggests Christine de Pizan's Lady Reason, Lady Justice, and Lady Righteousness in *The Book of the City of Ladies* and a feminized Christ in Julian of Norwich's *A Vision*.

In the fourth part of the course, in weeks eleven and twelve, on gender and theology in the autobiographical fifteenth-century dream vision—notably in prose rather than in poetry or in prosimetrum—works by English and French women writers relate to "god and the goddesses," to appropriate Barbara Newman's phrase from her book, *God and the Goddesses: Vision, Poetry, and Belief in the Middle Ages*. That is, "How did medieval women writers compensate for the patriarchal God of Christianity, aside from reemphasis on Mary as mother of Christ?" Newman's book is useful in making the connection between the mystical visionary tradition and the dream-vision tradition, particularly in regard to the issue of allegorical personifications used for abstracted but gendered female, as a substitute for the feminine in the religious (1–50, 331–43; notes and text). In week eleven, chiefly of interest was anchorite Julian of Norwich, with a videocassette on her life and works being made available ("Julian"), coupled with a brief look at the protofeminist visionary frame of Christine de Pizan's *Book of the City of Ladies* (in translation; bk. 1, chs. 1–2). Following this segment in the twelfth week was Margery Kempe's *Book* (whatever students could finish of it, but especially its first book), for a more focused repositioning of Margery's dreams and visions within what is in fact an autobiography in the third person. Also helpful was a twenty-four-minute video recording, "Margery Kempe."

Close to the end of the course, in week thirteen, in an attempt to trace Christine de Pizan's protofeminist vision in later works, we reexamined courtly love, gender-related habitus, and protofeminism in two short, anonymous English dream visions, "The Floure and the Leafe" and "The Assembly of Ladies." In the final week, we intended to conclude with a parallel reception of Chaucer in a very brief look at fifteenth-century English and Scottish Chaucerians, namely, John Lydgate, in *The Temple of Glass*, and William Dunbar, in *Thrissil and the Rois* and *The Golden Targe*.

Throughout the course, *Pearl* functions almost as a kind of omnibus for the scholastic and courtly dream vision and for the gendered and autobiographical vision—a hinge that manages to link both traditions in one poem.

Assigned Primary and Secondary Reading for the Seminar

Ades, Dawn. *An Outline of Dada and Surrealism*. London: Hayward Gallery; Westerham P, 1978. Print.

Alan of Lille. *The Plaint of Nature*. Trans. James J. Sheridan. Toronto: U of Toronto P, 1980. Print; Web. (older Douglass Moffatt trans.: http://www.fordham.edu/halsall/basis/alain-deplanctu.html.)

"The Assembly of Ladies." *Floure and the Leafe, The Assembly of Ladies, The Isle of Ladies*. Ed. Derek Pearsall. Kalamazoo: Medieval Inst. Pubs., 1990. Print; Web. <http://www.lib.rochester.edu/camelot/teams/assemfrm.htm>. (in Middle English)

Boethius. *De consolatione Philosophiae* (*Consolation of Philosophy*). Trans. Victor Watts. Rev. ed. Harmondsworth: Penguin, 2000. Print; Web. <http://etext.virginia.edu/etcbin/toccer-new?id=BoePhil&images=images/modeng&data=/texts/english/modeng/parsed&tag=public&part=1&division=div>. (older OP translation)

Boethius of Dacia. *On the Supreme Good, On the Eternity of the World, On Dreams*. Trans. John F. Wippel. Toronto: Pontifical Inst. of Medieval Studies, 1987. Print.

Boffey, Julia, ed. *Fifteenth-Century English Dream Visions: An Anthology*. Oxford: Oxford UP, 2003. Print.

Breton, André. "Surrealist Manifesto." 1924. *Manifestoes of Surrealism*. Trans. Richard Seaver and Helen R. Lane. Ann Arbor: U of Michigan P, 1969. Print; Web. <http:// www.tcf.ua.edu/Classes/Jbutler/T340/SurManifesto/ManifestoOfSurrealism.htm>.

Buñuel, Luis. *Un Chien andalou*. 1929. Transflux Films, 2004. Videodisc. (17 min.)

"Caedmon's Hymn." *Ecclesiastical History of the English Church and People*. By Bede. Ed. D. H. Farmer and Ronald E. Latham. Trans. Leo Sherley-Price. 1955. London:

Penguin Classics, 1990. Print; Web. <http://www.heorot.dk/bede-caedmon.html>. (Latin / Anglo-Saxon)

Chadwick, Whitney. *Women Artists and the Surrealist Movement.* New York: Thames and Hudson, 1985. Print.

Chaucer, Geoffrey. *Book of the Duchess* and *Parliament of Fowls. Dream Visions and Other Poems.* Ed. Kathryn Lynch. New York: W. W. Norton, 2006. Print.

———. *The Book of the Duchesse. Poetry Archives.* eMule.com, 1995–2008. Web. 12 May 2017. <http://www.emule.com/poetry/?page=poem&poem=426>.

———. *The Parliament of Fowles. Poetry Archives.* eMule.com, 1995–2008. Web. 12 May 2017. <http://www.emule.com/poetry/?page=poem&poem=428>.

Christine de Pizan. *Book of the City of Ladies.* Trans. Rosalind Brown-Grant. Harmondsworth: Penguin, 2000. Print.

———. *Le Livre de l'advision Christine.* Ed. Christine Reno and Liliane Dulac. Paris: Champion, 2001.

———. *The Vision of Christine.* Trans. Glenda McLeod and Charity Cannon Willard. Woodbridge: Brewer, 2005.

Clanvowe, John. *Boke of Cupide* (or *The Cuckoo and the Nightingale*). Conlee, *Middle English Debate Poetry.*

Conlee, John, ed. *Middle-English Debate Poetry: A Critical Anthology.* East Lansing: Colleagues, 1991. Print.

———. "Death and Life." Conlee, *Middle-English Debate Poetry.*

Dervaux, Isabelle. *Surrealism USA.* New York: National Acad. Museum–Hatje Cantz, 2005. Print.

Douglas, Gavin. *The Palis of Honoure* [Palace of Honour]. Ed. David J. Parkinson. Kalamazoo: Medieval Inst. Pubs., 1992. *TEAMS Middle English Texts.* Web. 7 June 2016. <http://d.lib.rochester.edu/teams/publication/parkinson-douglas-the-palis-of-honoure>.

Dream of the Rood. Ed. and trans. S. A. J. Bradley. *Anglo-Saxon Poetry.* London: Dent, 1982. 158–63. Print; Web. <http://faculty.uca.edu/~jona/texts/rood.htm>.

Dunbar, William. "The Golden Targe." *William Dunbar: The Complete Works.* Ed. John Conlee. Kalamazoo: Medieval Inst. Pubs., 2004. Print; Web. *TEAMS Middle English Texts.* <http://www.lib.rochester.edu/camelot/teams/dunfrm3.htm>.

———. "Thistle and the Rose" ["Thrissil and the Rois"]. *William Dunbar: The Complete Works.* Ed. John Conlee. Kalamazoo: Medieval Inst. Pubs., 2004. Print; Web. *TEAMS Middle English Texts.* <http://www.lib.rochester.edu/camelot/teams/dunfrm2.htm>.

"The Floure and the Leafe." *Floure and the Leafe, The Assembly of Ladies, The Isle of Ladies.* Ed. Derek Pearsall. Kalamazoo: Medieval Inst. Pubs., 1990. *TEAMS Middle English Texts.* Web. 12 May 2017. <http://www.lib.rochester.edu/camelot/teams/flourfrm.htm>. (in Middle English)

Gower, John. *Confessio Amantis.* Ed. Russell Peck. 2nd ed. Vol. 1. Kalamazoo: Medieval Inst. Pubs., 2006. Print; Web. <http://d.lib.rochester.edu/teams/publication/peck-confessio-amantis-volume-1>.

Guillaume de Lorris and Jean de Meun. *The Romance of the Rose*. Trans. Frances Horgan. Oxford: Oxford UP, 1999. Print.

James I of Scotland. *Kingis Quair*. Boffey, *Fifteenth-Century English Dream Visions* 90–152.

Julian of Norwich. *Revelations of Divine Love*. Trans. Elizabeth Spearing. New York: Penguin, 1998. Print. (Another edition available at http://www.lib.rochester.edu/camelot/teams/julianfr.htm; in Middle English)

"Julian of Norwich." New York: Films Media Group, [2006]. Video. (24 min.)

Kempe, Margery. *Book*. Trans. Lynn Staley. New York: Norton, 2001. Print. (Another edition available at http://www.lib.rochester.edu/camelot/teams.kempl frm.htm; in Middle English)

Kruger, Steven F. *Dreaming in the Middle Ages*. Cambridge: Cambridge UP, 1992. Print.

Langland, William. *Piers the Plowman*. Ed. Elizabeth Robertson and Stephen Shepherd. Trans. E. Talbot Donaldson. New York: Norton, 2006. Print. (older edition in Middle English)

Larkin, David, ed. *Magritte*. New York: Ballantine, 1972. Print.

Lydgate, John. *Temple of Glass*. Boffey, *Fifteenth-Century English Dream Visions*.

Lynch, Kathryn L. *The High Medieval Dream Vision: Poetry, Philosophy, and Literary Form*. Stanford: Stanford UP, 1988. Print.

"Margery Kempe." New York: Films Media Group, [2006]. Video. (24 min.)

Mundy, Jennifer. *Surrealism: Desire Unbound*. London: Tate; New York: Metropolitan Museum of Art, 2001. Print.

Newman, Barbara. *God and the Goddesses: Vision, Poetry, and Belief in the Middle Ages*. Philadelphia: U of Pennsylvania P, 2003. Print.

Parlement of the Thre Ages. Conlee, *Middle-English Debate Poetry*.

Pearl. *Pearl, Cleanness, Patience, Sir Gawain and the Green Knight*. Ed. A. C. Cawley and J. J. Anderson. 1962. London: Everyman, 1996. Print; Web. (Another edition available at http://www.hti.umich.edu/cgi/t/text/text-idx?c=cme;idno=Pearl;rgn =div1;view=text;cc=cme;node=Pearl%3A1).

Russell, J. Stephen. *The English Dream Vision: Anatomy of a Form*. Columbus: Ohio State UP, 1988. Print.

Skelton, John. *Bouge of Court*. Boffey, *Fifteenth-Century English Dream Visions* 232–65.

Wilson, Simon. *Surrealist Painting*. London: Phaidon, 1975. Print.

Wynnere and Wastoure. Conlee, *Middle-English Debate Poetry* 63–98.

Recommended Reading for the Seminar

Aristotle. *De insomniis et De divinatione per somnum: A New Edition of the Greek Text with the Latin Translations*. Ed. H. J. Drossart Lulofs. Leiden: Brill, 1947. Print.

———. *De somno et vigilia liber, adiectis veteribus translationibus et Theodori Metochitae commentario*. Ed. H. J. Drossart Lulofs. Leiden: Brill, 1943. Print.

Astell, Ann W. *Political Allegory in Late Medieval England.* Ithaca: Cornell UP, 1999. Print.

———. *The Song of Songs in the Middle Ages.* Ithaca: Cornell UP, 1990. Print.

Bardavío, José M. "Chaucer: Entorno a cuatro Poemas Mayores." *Estudios de filogía inglesa* (1977): 5–17. Print.

Bodenham, C. H. L. "The Nature of the Dream in Late Mediaeval French Literature." *Medium Ævum* 54 (1985): 74–86. Print.

Boethius of Dacia. *On the Supreme Good, On the Eternity of the World, On Dreams.* Trans. J. F. Wippel. Toronto: Pontifical Inst. of Medieval Studies, 1987. Print.

Carty, Carolyn M. "The Role of Medieval Dream Images in Authenticating Ecclesiastical Construction." *Zeitschrift für Kunstgeschichte* 62.1 (1999): 45–90. Print.

Donnelly, C. "Challenging the Conventions of Dream Vision in *The Book of the Duchess.*" *Philological Quarterly* 66 (1987): 421–35. Print.

Enders, Jody. "Memory, Allegory, and the Romance of Rhetoric." *Rereading Allegory: Essays in Memory of Daniel Poirion.* Ed. Sahar Amer and Noah D. Guylin. Spec. issue of *Yale French Studies* 95 (1999): 49–64. Print.

Erickson, Carolly. *The Medieval Vision: Essays in History and Perception.* New York: Oxford UP, 1976. Print.

Fischer, Steve R. *The Complete Medieval Dreambook: A Multilingual, Alphabetical Somnia Danielis Collation.* Berne: Peter Lang, 1982. Print.

Goyne, Jo. "Arthurian Dreams and Medieval Dream Theory." *Medieval Perspectives* 12 (1997): 79–89. Print.

Harbus, Antonina. "Dream and Symbol in *The Dream of the Rood.*" *Nottingham Medieval Studies* 40 (1996): 1–15. Print.

Herzog, M. B. "*The Book of the Duchess*: The Vision of the Artist as a Young Dreamer." *Chaucer Review* 22 (1987–88): 269–81. Print.

Hieatt, Constance B. *The Realism of Dream-Visions: The Poetic Exploitation of the Dream-Experience in Chaucer and His Contemporaries.* Paris: Mouton, 1967. Print.

———. "*Un Autre Forme*: Guillaume de Machaut and the Dream Vision Form." *Chaucer Review* 14 (1979–80): 97–115. Print.

Jauss, Hans Robert. "Theory of Genres and Medieval Literature." *Toward an Aesthetic of Reception.* Trans. Timothy Bahti. Minneapolis: U of Minnesota P, 1982. 76–109, 205–11 [chap. 3, text and notes]. Print. Theory and History of Literature 2.

Keiper, Hugo. "I Wot Myself Best How Y Stonde: Literary Nominalism, Open Textual Form and the Enfranchisement of Individual Perspective in Chaucer's Dream Visions." *Literary Nominalism and the Theory of Rereading Late Medieval Texts: A New Research Paradigm.* Ed. Richard J. Utz. Lewiston: Edwin Mellen, 1995. 205–34. Print.

Kiser, Lisa J. "Sleep, Dreams, and Poetry in Chaucer's *Book of the Duchess.*" *Papers on Language and Literature* 19 (1983): 3–12. Print.

Klitgård, Ebbe. "Chaucer as Performer: Narrative Strategies in the Dream Visions." *Revista canaria de estudios ingleses* 47 (2003): 101–13. Print.

Kreuzer, James R. "The Dreamer in the *Book of the Duchess.*" *PMLA* 66.4 (1951): 543–47. Print.

Kruger, Steven F. "Medical and Moral Authority in the Late Medieval Dream." *Reading Dreams: The Interpretation of Dreams from Chaucer to Shakespeare.* Ed. Peter Brown. Oxford: Oxford UP, 1999. 51–83. Print.

———. "Mirrors and the Trajectory of Vision in *Piers Plowman.*" *Speculum* 66 (1991): 74–95. Print.

McGinn, Bernard. "The Changing Shape of Late Medieval Mysticism." *Church History* 65.2 (1996): 197–219. Print.

Park, Roswell, IV. "The Authority of the Dream: Geoffrey Chaucer's 'Book of the Duchess,' 'Parliament of Fowls,' and 'House of Fame.'" *DAI* 58 (1997): 160A. Print.

Peden, A. M. "Macrobius and Mediaeval Dream Literature." *Medium Ævum* 54 (1985): 59–73. Print.

Schmidt, A. V. C. "The Inner Dreams in *Piers Plowman.*" *Medium Ævum* 55 (1986): 24–40. Print.

Spearing, A. C. *Medieval Dream-Poetry.* Cambridge: Cambridge UP, 1976. Print.

Stakel, Susan L. "Structural Convergence of Pilgrimage and Dream-Vision in Christine de Pizan." *Journeys Toward God: Pilgrimage and Crusade.* Ed. Barbara. N. Sargent-Baur. Kalamazoo: Medieval Inst. Pubs., Western Michigan U, 1992. 195–203. Print. Rpt. of *Studies in Medieval Culture* 30; also in Occasional Studies ser., Medieval and Renaissance Studies Program, U of Pittsburgh 5.

Thundy, Zacharias P. "The Dreame of Chaucer: Boethian Consolation or Political Celebration?" *Carmina Philosophiae* 4 (1995): 91–109. Print.

Vives, Juan Luis. *Somnium et vigilia in Somnium Scipionis.* Ed. E. V. George. Westport: Greenwood: Attic P, 1989. Print.

Watts, William H. "The Medieval Dream Vision as Survey of Medieval Literature." *Studies in Medieval and Renaissance Teaching* 12.2 (2005): 67–94. Print.

Wilson, Edward. "The 'Gostly Drem' in *Pearl.*" *Neuphilologische Mitteilungen* 69 (1968): 90–101. Print.

Windeatt, Barry A. *Chaucer's Dream Poetry: Sources and Analogues.* Woodbridge: Brewer; Totowa: Rowman and Littlefield, 1982. Print.

Winny, James. *Chaucer's Dream-Poems.* London: Chatto and Windus; New York: Barnes and Noble, 1973. Print.

Wolff, Werner. *The Dream, Mirror of Conscience: A History of Dream Interpretation from 2000 B.C. and a New Theory of Dream Synthesis.* Westport: Greenwood, 1972. Print.

Zink, Michel. "The Allegorical Poem as Interior Memoir." *Images of Power: Medieval History/Discourse/Literature.* Ed. Kevin Brownlee and Stephen G. Nichols. New Haven: Yale UP, 1986. 100–26. Print.

Pearl and the Bleeding Lamb

Nancy Ciccone

I teach *Pearl* in a survey course on medieval literature at a public, urban university. The course format is primarily discussion. Between twenty and thirty students enroll at the combined upper division: undergraduate and pre-MA graduate levels. Because students generally struggle with the Middle English language, I allow reference to translations but focus on Middle English in class. I schedule *Pearl* midway through the course immediately following *Sir Gawain* so as to introduce the five wounds of Christ in discussion of the pentangle. When studying *Pearl*, we first outline the changes in the narrator's location. Creating three columns on the board, I label them Garden, Dream, and New Jerusalem, and students report what they found significant in those sections, which I add under the headings. This storyboard allows us to focus on the intricacies of language and poetics without losing track of the overall trajectory. Graduate students are scheduled for five-minute presentations based on scholarly articles and book chapters. I list options and assign them ahead of time. Depending on access through library databases, I select scholarship different from my own perspective so as to augment discussions. Graduate students report at the beginning of each class, and then we focus on the assigned reading for that day. Given the different levels of competency, I obtain the most productive student engagement by treating the narrator as a father whose daughter has died.

My focus on the wound in the Vision of the New Jerusalem allows me to elaborate on its significance in the narrative and to foster interpretations of the conclusion. As a transition into our discussion, I divide students into groups. I then assign to each group a word or an image indicative of the topics I will address. I ask the groups to find as many references as they can to "water," "heart," "spot" and "mot(e)." To save time, I delegate a section of the narrative to each member in each group. A section of the board is reserved for students to note line numbers and a brief reference to context under the assigned heading. In the course of the discussion that follows, I rely on each student to present and contextualize the quotations. I am including some references here in case students miss significant ones.

Christ as a wounded Lamb centers the vision of the New Jerusalem. Most editions note that the image of the Lamb derives from the Gospel attributed to John of Zebedee and from the book of Revelation attributed to John of Patmos. Unlike the other Gospels, John times the Crucifixion with the killing of the Passover lamb and so links the Old and New Testaments.[1] The Lamb, as opposed to Christ's human form, enables the *Pearl* poet to pun on the Lamb's quality as a lamp that brings light to the world ("lombe-ly3t"; Gordon 38; line 1046). According to the Pearl-Maiden, the "thryde tyme" the Lamb is brought to the "spot" of Jerusalem occurs "'in Apokalypeȝ'" (833–34). Her reference to a third time affirms the prophecies of Isaiah and of John the Baptist, who each refer to the Lamb before he occurs in Revelation (830–31).[2] Because few students have read Revelation, I hand out passages for comparison with *Pearl*.[3] Students note the quotations and paraphrasing of Revelation, but also the differences in the description of the Lamb. John vaguely describes the Lamb as having "the marks of slaughter" on him (Rev. 5.6), but the *Pearl* poet specifically locates a wound in the Lamb's side (1137).[4] I download illuminations from Apocalypse manuscripts into a *PowerPoint* presentation to furnish visual comparisons.[5] We look for depictions of the throne and jewels, but we especially note the many images of an intact lamb. Despite their popularity in the Middle Ages, "illustrations showing the Apocalypse Lamb as wounded are not an artistic commonplace" (Field 12). When depicted, the bleeding Lamb usually accompanies the opening of the book with seven seals (Whitaker 189). The illuminations empower students to recognize the poet's context and innovation and to ask, Why emphasize the wound?

Recorded in John's Gospel, the wound results from a centurion piercing the crucified Christ's side (19.34). In the apocryphal Gospel of Nicodemus, the centurion is named Longinus; his spear thrust ensures Christ's death (7.8). The wound becomes known as the fifth wound in distinction from the other four on Christ's hands and feet. As such, it is privileged in a number of ways. Students aware of its significance are invited to share their knowledge. In keeping with Christian tradition, the *Pearl* poet depicts blood and water, symbolic of the human and divine components of Christ, flowing from the wound. Grace issues with the blood and water: "Ryche blod ran on rode so roghe, / And wynne water þen at þat plyt; / Þe grace of God wex gret innoghe" (lines 646–48). The wound, then, generates the entire dream, for when the Dreamer wakes into his dream, he finds his "goste is gon in Godeȝ grace" (63). In other words, God's grace, flowing from the wound, takes up the Dreamer's spirit when he falls asleep. I assign a five-minute writing exercise for students to explore the significance of this connection. To discourage the students' reducing the narrative to a theological formula, I ask them to list some of the Dreamer's responses to this gift of grace and to characterize his descriptions of the landscape.

In *Pearl* the Lamb is first described as flawless: "Þe Lompe þer wythouten spotte blake" (945). But He later displays a gaping wound: "Bot a wounde fyl wyde and weete con wyse" (1135–37). The student group responsible for finding references to "spot" directs us to quotations. The discussion attempts to reconcile the Lamb's spotlessness with his wound and to elaborate on the meanings of "spot." In the first quotation (above, in this paragraph), the Lamb is the sacrificial one taken to the geographic Jerusalem.[6] We map the connotations in order to recognize a shift in narrative. The descriptions of the Lamb collapse the figurative and the literal: He is the flawless animal fit for sacrifice, and He is guiltless of sin. The "spot" of Jerusalem is also transformed into the one without a geographic location. If *Pearl* is an allegory, the vision opens the way for anagogic thinking, which seeks to explain events in terms of the life to come (Clopper 240). I then ask the group responsible for the link word "mot(e)" to discuss its meanings. The polysemy moves through several connotations stemming from the puns on "mot(e)," "spot," "stain" (924, 948, 960, 972) and "walled city" (936–37, 948–49, 973). The pun suggests that the spot on the Lamb's side makes the mystical city possible as it does the grace that issues in the dream. The vision of the New Jerusalem asks the audience, the Dreamer, to step up to the level of Christian faith, a faith beyond empirical evidence. The Lamb's wound becomes a way to deploy the physical world to convey symbolic meaning. We refer to the list of the Dreamer's responses, which students made previously, to note his reliance on materiality. I ask students to locate evidence suggesting that the Dreamer understands the change in the narrative mode, and we attempt to determine the extent of his understanding.

In the New Jerusalem, the wound gushes: "Of His quyte syde his blod outsprent" (1137). The effluence complements the water imagery throughout. We refer to the student-generated references posted on the board. The river, which the Dreamer first sees with its "stremande sterneȝ" at the bottom and the one issuing from the "flet," "floor," of the New Jerusalem, offers the most accessible example (115, 1058). Even the cry from heaven reminds the Dreamer of a rushing river (874). I then focus on the connection between the wound's effluence and the images of baptism as a fountain of grace. The Pearl-Maiden explains that the blood delivers us from Hell: "Þe water is baptem, . . . / . . . that wascheȝ away þe gylteȝ felle," after Adam drowned us in death (651–56). The fifth wound is specifically credited with generating the church and its rites. A thirteenth-century folio from a French moralized Bible depicts the church birthed from the wound alongside an image of Eve emerging from Adam's side (Bynum, *Fragmentation* fig. 3.6 [99]). The juxtaposition of events reminds Christians that the piercing of Christ's side redeems the Fall of mankind. For *Pearl* the wound enables the placement of the baptized Pearl-Maiden by Christ's side. Baptism in turn allows all Christians to receive the Eucharist and so looks forward to the Eucharistic offering at the poem's conclusion (1209–10).[7]

In iconography the fifth wound is singularly transformative. Abstracted, it centers the other four. It may be depicted either as a full-blown rose or as a bleeding heart (Williams, *Five Wounds of Jesus* figs. 9–11 [16–18]). The rose window in many a cathedral emblematizes the Eucharist resulting from the fifth wound and the institution of the church upon which and within which it is founded (Marti 35). The confluence of the heart, the rose, the penny, and the Eucharist allows for a series of transformative images.[8] They simultaneously subsume and multiply meanings. The penny occurs at the heart of the narrative in the Parable of the Workers in the Vineyard, but the image of the rose first occurs when the Pearl-Maiden scolds the jeweler. She reminds him that what he lost was "'bot a rose / Þat flowred and fayled as kynde hyt gef'" (269–70). Mortality subjects her to the processes of nature. When the image recurs, however, he reminds her of *his* mortal nature: "'I am bot mokke and mul among, / And þou so ryche a reken rose" (905–06). Students compare the passages. Pearl remains analogous to a rose in each reference, but the emphasis changes from that which is seasonally ephemeral to that which splendidly endures: "'byde3 here by þys blysful bonc / Þer lyue3 lyste may neuer lose'" (907–08). The shift from the ephemeral to the enduring rose marks a turning point in the narrative in that it structurally occurs in the 101st stanza, the sixth stanza of section 15. In theological terms, the fifth wound creates the second description of the rose because it is both the reminder of mortality and the evidence of everlasting life. In the absence of the wound, the first statement about the ephemeral nature of life is all pre-Christians could say about loss, so that the 101st stanza becomes the turning point to elicit the Dreamer's epiphany.[9] The analogy between the rose and the Pearl-Maiden, however, points to her communion with Christ rather than to his articulation of faith. Although the Dreamer expresses humility, he next asks, "'Haf 3e no wone3 in castel-walle, / Ne maner þer 3e may mete and won?'" (916–18). His question focuses on the Pearl-Maiden's status even as it initiates the Vision of the New Jerusalem. Most students connect the courtliness of his language with his focus on materiality. Attending to this exchange allows me to elaborate on the transformative symbolism of the rose, wound, and penny, and it enables students to note the Dreamer's focus on the Pearl-Maiden, which leads to his attempt to cross the river.

Upon seeing the Lamb, the Dreamer notes the proximity of heart and wound: "Anende hys hert, þur3 hyde torente" (1136). The image alludes to the Cult of the Sacred Heart, popular in Western Europe by the eleventh century (Marti 132). It complements a medieval monastic and cultural movement wherein Christians emphasize Christ's humanity so as to foster affective spirituality. In order to deepen the symbolic meanings, I introduce quotations from various theologians of the time. The Benedictine William of Saint-Thierry (ca. 1080–1148), for example, understands the fifth wound as a pathway that releases the "mysteries of our redemption" and allows us to "enter whole" into Christ (131). William longs "to approach the most holy wound in [Christ's] side, the portal of the ark that is there made, and that not only to put my finger or my whole hand into it, but wholly enter into Jesus' very heart, into the holy of holies, the ark of the covenant, the golden urn, the soul of our humanity that holds within itself the manna of the Godhead" (38). Aelred of Rievaulx, an English Cistercian (1110–67), declares that the blood flowing from the fifth wound becomes "the wine of knowledge of God" for Saint John and remains the milk of humanity to nurture the ordinary Christian (qtd. in Bynum, *Jesus* 123).

Although not the only religious to write of the Sacred Heart, the nuns at the Saxon monastery of Helfta are known for promulgating the cult. The *Herald of*

Divine Love or the *Revelations* records visions, for example, of souls drinking from Christ's heart through the wound in his side. Referring to Gertrude the Great (1256–ca. 1302), Jesus says, "'The union that you see between her heart and my side indicates that she is thus at every moment able to drink from the flood of my divinity'" (qtd. in Bynum, *Jesus* 192). Another vision reports Gertrude claiming she "'seemed to see a ray of light, like an arrow, issue from the wound on the right side of the image which was painted on the book before me'" (Widdowson 99). The wound as light reinforces the *Pearl* poet's pun on *Lamb* and *lamp*. One of the scribes of the *Herald*, Father Faber reports a vision wherein the wound is even an inkwell for Saint John to use for writing in red letters (147). The wound of the dead Christ paradoxically brings forth the life-sustaining material substance for mortals as a mode of transformation to the immortal.

To facilitate insights, I elaborate on the Sacred Heart because the proximity of the wound to the heart fosters its association with compassion and comfort. The Helfta nuns' devotion to the Sacred Heart also accompanies their emphasis on the Eucharist as the means by which they can intimately participate in knowing God. When the Dreamer wakes and takes the sacraments, then he not only joins the Christian community but also symbolically crosses the river, which was not allowed to his dreaming self. He therefore joins Christ and the Pearl-Maiden in the only way available to the living. I depend on the wound's association with comfort to introduce the concept of genre. If a graduate student has already presented on the topic, I encourage that student to lead the discussion. I track student-generated literary examples of elegy and of consolation. We list characteristics of each to determine the ways that each category fulfills and defeats expectations in respect to *Pearl*.

For the Helfta nuns, and specifically Gertrude, the visions of the Sacred Heart further confer the task of mediation on God and their fourteenth-century communities (Bynum, *Jesus* 196–99). In short, their visions grant them voice. Applied to the *Pearl*, this context suggests that the vision of the wound authorizes the Pearl-Maiden to teach the Dreamer in the first place. The mystical body of Christ also awards children a privileged status: as the child is the microcosm of mankind, so the wound is the microcosm of Christianity (Marti 103). Some depictions of the Sacred Heart that enclose the representation of a small child are indicative of Wisdom and Logos (143). In medieval culture, the heart is synecdoche for Christ's body and for all that Christianity encompasses. Among scholars Marti finds the *Pearl* to be "a body structured around the formal and thematic nucleus of the heart—a heart that is literal as well as metaphorical . . ." (83), a heart that spatially and temporally centers the poem in the shape of a pearl (143), which the Pearl-Maidens wear over their hearts. Once students have a sense of the interplay of themes, we refer to the language at the beginning and at the end of *Pearl* and to the ways in which these links structurally imitate the roundness of a pearl.

Whereas the heart of Christ leads to the whole of Christianity, I remind students that the narrative also focuses on the Dreamer's heart. The student group assigned the "heart" at the beginning of class presents quotations in the narrative: the Dreamer's heart stirs at the dream landscape (line 128); the Dreamer is stunned at his first sight of the Pearl-Maiden (174, 176). He apologizes for his speech on the grounds that his "herte waȝ al wyth mysse remorde" (364). Each Christian's heart supposedly contains the spiritual arc of the covenant and joins in turn with Christ's heart-encompassing Christian theology. We discuss how the Dreamer's heart intersects with Christian faith. This discussion tends to disclose student assumptions about the Christian Middle Ages by allowing them to articulate the conflict between faith and grief.

The symbolic meanings of the wound enable its significance to leave the dream and become emblematic of the garden or Eden, "erber grene," at the beginning and emblematic of the Eucharist at the conclusion (line 38). The narrative, however, resists mysticism. Seeing the New Jerusalem, the Dreamer focuses on *his* "lyttel quene" (1147): "Quen I seȝ *my* frely, I wolde be þere" (1155; my emphasis). After waking, he commits Pearl to God: "to God I hit bytaȝte" (1207). Students are tasked with analyzing his emotional state. During student discussion of the conclusion, I introduce Jacques Lacan's concept of anamorphosis, which "presents us with an unreadable image which becomes intelligible as we change the point of view from which we look at it" (Gilbert, *Living Death* 157). One perspective encompasses the Lamb's wound, heart, expressed in theological language and the other a father's grief, heart, expressed in courtly language (187). I ask students to consider whether the narrative bridges these two perspectives. We also consider the extent to which the theological and cultural contexts of the wound affect their interpretations. Students' responses allow me to gauge whether the class discussion has enabled them to grasp the significance of the Pearl-Maiden's teachings and that of the poet's achievements.

NOTES

[1] For the Old Testament sacrificial lamb, see Isaiah: "he is brought as a lamb to the slaughter" (KJV 53.7).

[2] E. V. Gordon names the two prophets (n831). But whereas Isaiah 53.7 refers to the Lamb taken to Jerusalem, John the Baptist, quoted in John's Gospel, does not (1.29). Despite referring to John of Zebedee as an apostle and not a prophet, the poet seems to be referencing the Gospel in which Jesus is the Passover Lamb.

[3] *Gateway Bible* provides an Internet source of different translations.

[4] *Vulgate*: "agnum stantem tanquam occisum" (Rev. 5.6).

[5] Among resources, the online British Library digitalized manuscript division allows capture of these images. Whitaker's article also includes illustrations (figs. 6–10).

[6] For the Old Testament requirement of flawlessness for the sacrificial animal, see Num. 19.2.

[7] The emphasis on baptism in Pearl may be a response to Lollard arguments against its necessity (Bowers, *Politics* 122).

[8] John Gatta, for one, suggests that the transformation of images corresponds to a change within the Dreamer. Following Ackerman, Gatta reads the rose (line 269) as a form of the "peny" in the Vineyard parable and of the Eucharist (line 1209) at the conclusion (254). See Marti for the medieval *Weltbild* of "geometric equivalencies," wherein iconography depicts concentric circles indicating the four wounds to surround the larger fifth wound that encompasses them as a universal center (135).

[9] John Fleming argues for the 101st stanza to indicate the fruitfulness of consolation in its excess (88). Elizabeth Petroff notes the Dreamer's assessment of the landscape to indicate a change in his mood (191). See also John Finlayson regarding the Dreamer's engagement at this point (*Pearl* 325–29).

APPENDIXES

Appendix 1: Study Questions on *Pearl*
Jane Beal

Pearl *1–10 (lines 1–768)*

1. Where does the poem begin? Think of Eden, the Song of Songs, and Mary's womb, all considered types of the *hortus conclusus* ("enclosed garden") in the Middle Ages. What did these gardens contain? What grew in them? What does the garden at the beginning of this poem contain? What is growing in it?

2. The speaker grieves over his lost pearl in the opening lines of the poem. He says, "Allas! I leste hyr in on erbere" ("alas, I lost her in a garden"); she is "clad in clot" ("dressed in dirt"); he observes, "For vch gresse mot grow of graynez dede" ("for each grass must grow of dead grains"). What do these lines suggest has happened?

3. The speaker falls asleep in the garden and has a dream vision. Describe the landscape in his dream. See section 2. How does his vision of this paradisial dreamscape affect the Dreamer emotionally (121–32)? Whom does the Dreamer see here, and what does that person look like (160–66)?

4. How does the Dreamer feel when he sees the Pearl-Maiden (181–88)? Read lines 230–35. What is the relationship between the Dreamer and the Pearl-Maiden? Notice the Dreamer's description of feelings that have moved him

since his separation from the Pearl-Maiden (241–52). Is this lovesickness? Why does he call himself a "joyless jeweler"? What is the significance of such a self-identification? What is the role of a jeweler?

5. How does the Pearl-Maiden see or identify the Dreamer? Allegorically, symbolically, or metaphorically, then, what is the relationship between the Dreamer and the Pearl-Maiden? The Pearl-Maiden says: "For what you lost was but a rose / That flowered and finally failed in time" (269–70). What does a rose often stand for? Is this a (courtly) love story? (Think of the French allegory, the *Roman de la Rose*.)

6. The Pearl-Maiden reproves the Dreamer for calling Fate ("Wyrde"; 273) a "thief" and calls into question the Dreamer's perception of reality (295–300). Why? What do her words suggest about her intentions in coming to meet the Dreamer in this vision? (Think of Boethius and Lady Philosophy in *The Consolation of Philosophy* and of Dante and Beatrice in *The Divine Comedy*.)

7. At line 325, the Dreamer asks, "Do you judge me . . . my sweetheart, to sorrow again?" What does the Dreamer fear may happen next? Why might he feel that way? To whom does the Pearl-Maiden advise the Dreamer to look? At this rebuke, the Dreamer speaks once more of his intense feelings (361–84). What are those feelings? What kind of relationship does he want to have with the Pearl-Maiden?

8. The Dreamer says the Pearl-Maiden is the ground of all his bliss, but who does the Pearl-Maiden say is the ground of her bliss? At the end of section 7, the Pearl-Maiden describes her spiritual marriage to her "Lord the Lamb." Think of the description in the Bible of the marital relationship between God and Israel, as well as of Jesus and the church, Origen's reading of the Song of Songs as an epithalamion describing God's relationship to the individual Christian soul, Bernard of Clairvaux's commentaries on the Song of Songs, and the tradition of mysticism, especially among women like Bridget of Sweden (or, later, Margery Kempe and Teresa of Avila) who experienced visions in their souls of being married to Christ. What kind of intimacy and what kind of authority does such an experience imply?

9. How does the Dreamer react to the news that the Pearl-Maiden is married (421–32)? Who does he call the "Phoenix of Arabia"? Why? Who is the "queen of courtesy" and the "empress of heaven"? What is the Dreamer really arguing about here?

10. Sections 9 and 10 retell Jesus's Parable of the Workers in the Vineyard from the New Testament. What is that parable about, and what is its point? Why does the Pearl-Maiden retell it here? How does the Dreamer respond to

the parable (590–600)? Is the Pearl-Maiden unworthy of her penny? Why not (in her estimation)? What is "great enough" for her to have a place in heaven as a queen?

Pearl *11–20 (lines 769–1212)*

11. Notice the example of the baptized infants. What makes a soul innocent (625–28)? What sin took place in the Garden of Eden that necessitates atonement (637–44)? What is the significance of the Crucifixion and the blood and the water that sprang from Christ's side (645–60)?

12. In section 12, which two types of people does the Pearl-Maiden discuss with interest? Is there a relation between righteousness and innocence? Why do you think the Pearl-Maiden remembers the stories from scripture of how people brought their children to Jesus to be blessed by him (709–20)?

13. In section 13, the Pearl-Maiden remembers the Parable of the Merchant. What is that parable about and what is its point? This parable is the obvious subtext for the entire poem of *Pearl*. In an allegorical reading that takes this parable into account, what might the Pearl-Maiden stand for? Notice how the Pearl-Maiden describes the pearl on her breast given to her by her Lord the Lamb. What idea does this image reinforce?

14. In the second-to-last stanza of section 13, the Pearl-Maiden again describes her spiritual marriage to Christ. What language does she use to describe her bridegroom? How does she understand herself in relation to him?

15. In section 14, the Pearl-Maiden makes several allusions to the book of Revelation (Apocalypse). What keyword is repeated at the end of every stanza in the section? In the second stanza, what are the names that the Pearl-Maiden gives to her lover ("my lemman")? What key event in the life of Jesus is described?

16. The Pearl-Maiden describes how "each soul" can be the Lamb's "worthy wife" (845–46). Again we see the potential for spiritual marriage not only for the Pearl-Maiden but also for the Dreamer (and even for the readers of the poem!). How does this relate to the allegorical sense of the poem? Discuss the "old" and the "new" Jerusalem. If the Pearl-Maiden's soul is with the Lamb, where is her body (see 856)? What is the music like in heaven (see 877–92)? How does the Dreamer respond to these revelations (901–12)? How does he see himself? How does he see her?

17. What does the Dreamer ask for from the Pearl-Maiden? What does he want to see? Where does he want to go (963)? Who does he wish to see there (964)? Where is the focus of his gaze? What does the Pearl-Maiden say in response?

18. The Dreamer calls himself a jeweler. At line 985 he begins to describe the gems of the foundations of the New Jerusalem. Who else is a Jewel or a Jeweler? In section 18, what are the gates of the city made of? Where does the light in the city come from? What tree grows there and how many kinds of fruit does it bear? Compare these lines to Revelation 21.

19. The Dreamer sees a procession of virgins crowned, arrayed in pearls, and dressed in white, which includes his "blysful." Then he sees the Lamb. How many horns does the Lamb have and what are their colors? What kind of clothes does he wear? What kind of wound does he have? The Dreamer's gaze is filled with this wounded Lamb, a Lamb who responds to his pain with joy. How might this speak to the loss that the Dreamer has experienced? What ecstatic emotion does the Dreamer experience in response to what he is seeing? (Notice the keyword repeated at the beginning and end of each stanza.)

20. In section 20, where does the Dreamer most want to be? What happens when he attempts to cross the water? What is the Dreamer's explanation for what happens? What adjectives does the Dreamer use to describe his actions? He calls his dream a "veray avysyoun" (a "true vision"). What does that suggest about his understanding of his experience? the relation between his dream and reality? between earthly and heavenly experiences?

21. What has the Dreamer found the "Prince" to be both day and night? What names does the Dreamer give to the Lover? How has the dream apparently changed his view of God and of the loss of his beloved Pearl-Maiden? Has he reached the stage of grief in which he can relinquish and still remember peacefully?

22. Why does the Dreamer allude to the bread and the wine of the Eucharist in the last stanza of the poem? What is the purpose of the eucharistic rite? What permission might the Eucharist give the Dreamer to remember?

23. What invitation is given in the last two lines of the poem to the readers of the poem? How are we included in the Dreamer's experience? After this poem is read, what range of meanings appear to be signified in the image or signifier "precious pearls"?

24. How might we characterize the genre of this poem?

Dream Vision
Literal sense	Elegy
Allegorical sense	Allegory
Moral sense	Consolation
Anagogical sense	Revelation

25. The overall structure of *Pearl* has been compared to a cathedral, a rose window, a reliquary, a crown, and the microcosm of a human body with a heart at its center as well as a pearl. How do these comparisons enlarge our understanding of the poem and its memorial, cultural, and theological purposes?

26. Consider also the smaller structures of *Pearl*: 1,212 lines, 101 twelve-line stanzas, and 20 sections (each unified by a key concatenation word), which can be studied as a chiastic diptych (10-10) or a triptych (4-12-4). Given medieval number symbolism, how are these numbers and divisions significant? In what ways are the form and content of *Pearl* intimately related?

Appendix 2: Illustrations from the Cotton Nero A.x Manuscript

Fig. 1. The Dreamer resting by a mound. ©The British Library Board, Cotton Nero A.x, art.3, folio 41r

Fig. 2. The Dreamer standing by a stream. ©The British Library Board, Cotton Nero A.x, art.3, folio 41v

Fig. 3. The Dreamer and the Pearl-Maiden. ©The British Library Board, Cotton Nero A.x, art.3, folio 42r

Fig. 4. The Dreamer reaching up and the Pearl-Maiden behind a castle wall. ©The British Library Board, Cotton Nero A.x, art.3, folio 42v

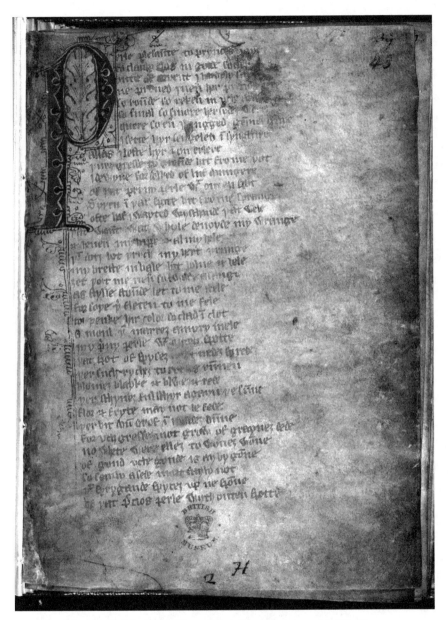

Fig. 5. *Pearl*, lines 1–36. ©The British Library Board, Cotton Nero A.x, art.3, folio 43r

NOTES ON CONTRIBUTORS

Elizabeth Allen is associate professor of English at the University of California, Irvine, and the author of *False Fables and Exemplary Truth in Later Middle English Literature* (2005). She has written essays on Chaucer, Gower, the *Pearl* poet, Matthew Paris, Perkin Warbeck, and episodic narrative; her most recent essay, "Flowing Backward to the Source: Criseyde's Promises and the Ethics of Allusion," appeared in *Speculum* (2013). She is at work on a book project, "Uncertain Refuge: Ideas of Sanctuary in Medieval English Literature."

Arthur Bahr is associate professor of literature at MIT and the author of *Fragments and Assemblages: Forming Compilations of Medieval London* (2013). His research blends formalist and materialist approaches in order to find literary resonance in the physical particularities of medieval books and how those books have survived into the present. He is currently completing a book on the four poems of the *Pearl* manuscript, tentatively titled "Pleasurable Forms and Speculative Histories in the Pages of the Pearl Manuscript."

Jane Beal is an associate professer of English at the University of La Verne in southern California. She is the author of *The Signifying Power of Pearl* (2017), editor and translator of *Pearl: A Medieval Masterpiece in Middle English and Modern English* (in progress), and coeditor, with Mark Bradshaw Busbee, of *Approaches to Teaching the Middle English* Pearl (2017). Among her other books are an academic monograph, *John Trevisa and the English Polychronicon*; an edited collection of essays, *Illuminating Moses: A History of Reception from Exodus to the Renaissance*; and the poetry collections *Sanctuary* and *Rising*. To learn more, see sanctuarypoet.net.

John M. Bowers is an internationally known scholar of medieval English literature with books on Chaucer, Langland, and the *Pearl* poet. Educated at Duke, Virginia, and Oxford, where he was a Rhodes Scholar, he taught at Caltech and Princeton before settling at the University of Nevada, Las Vegas. His work has been supported by fellowships from the National Endowment for the Humanities and the John Simon Guggenheim Foundation; his Great Courses series *The Western Literary Canon in Context* was released by the Teaching Company. His latest book is *An Introduction to the Gawain Poet* (2012). His current project is "Tolkien's Lost Chaucer," based on a long-forgotten book discovered in an Oxford archive.

Mark Bradshaw Busbee is professor and chair of the Department of English at Samford University, where he teaches medieval literature and writing. He is a coeditor for *Grundtvig-Studier*, an international journal published in Copenhagen, Denmark, and a coeditor with Jane Beal of *Translating the Past: Essays on Medieval Literature in Honor of Marijane Osborn*. Busbee has published scholarly essays on Old and Middle English literature as well as on nineteenth-century Scandinavian scholarship on medieval literature. He has taught at the University of California, Davis; Johannes Gutenberg-Universität in Mainz, Germany; and Florida Gulf Coast University in Fort Myers, Florida.

Seeta Chaganti is associate professor of English at the University of California, Davis. She is the author of *Strange Footing: Poetic Form and Dance in the Late Middle Ages* (forthcoming, 2018) and *The Medieval Poetics of the Reliquary* (2008) as well as the editor of the essay collection *Medieval Poetics and Social Practice* (2012). Her essays appear in *PMLA, New Medieval Literatures, Romance Studies, postmedieval, Dance Research Journal, Exemplaria*, and other journals and collections. Chaganti has recently taught courses on Chaucer and the *Pearl* poet as well as on performance, the history of the English language, and medieval and modern theories of form. In 2014 she received UC Davis's Senate Distinguished Teaching Award for undergraduate instruction.

Jane Chance, Andrew W. Mellon Distinguished Professor Emerita in English at Rice University, received an honorary doctorate of letters from Purdue University in 2013. Author of twenty-three books and a hundred articles and reviews on Old and Middle English literature, medieval women, mythography, and medievalism, she has been awarded Guggenheim and NEH fellowships, membership at the Institute for Advanced Study, Princeton, and prizes for her work. Relevant here are *The Genius Figure in Antiquity and the Middle Ages* (1975), *The Mythographic Chaucer: The Fabulation of Sexual Politics* (1996), the coedited *Approaches to Teaching Sir Gawain and the Green Knight* (1986), *Medieval Mythography*, volume 3 of *The Emergence of Italian Humanism, 1321–1475* (2015), and an edition of the Middle English dream vision *Assembly of Gods* (1999).

Nancy Ciccone has published articles on Chaucer's *Troilus* and *Book of the Duchess*, medieval romance, Vergil's *Aeneid*, and Ovid's *Metamorphoses*. Trained in comparative literature, she primarily teaches medieval and classical literatures. She currently chairs the English department at the University of Colorado, Denver, and is working on Saint Cuthbert, "The Body and the Book," and on Chaucer's *Troilus*, "Flying the Coup."

David Coley is associate professor of English Literature at Simon Fraser University. He is the author of *The Wheel of Language: Representing Speech in Middle English Poetry, 1377–1422* (2012), and his articles have appeared in *Studies in the Age of Chaucer, Chaucer Review, Exemplaria, Florilegium*, and *JEGP*. He is currently working on the relation between the fourteenth-century plague pandemic and Middle English poetry, with a specific focus on the poems of MS Cotton Nero A.x.

A. S. G. Edwards is professor of medieval manuscripts in the School of English, University of Kent, at Canterbury and has taught at universities in North America and the United Kingdom. He has published mainly on late medieval and early modern literature; his current research includes a study of attribution in late medieval and early modern literature. He is a Guggenheim Fellow and serves on the editorial boards of several journals and series.

John V. Fleming, Fairchild Professor of English and professor of comparative literature emeritus at Princeton University, is a Fellow of the American Academy of Arts and Letters and a past president of the Medieval Academy of America.

Eugene Green, professor of English emeritus at Boston University, has published *Anglo-Saxon Audiences* and numerous essays on Old English, Middle English, and modern English linguistics and literature. He is currently preparing studies on the passive voice and on expressive verbs in Middle English.

Elizabeth Harper is assistant professor of English at Mercer University and has taught at the University of Central Arkansas. Her publications include *"Pearl* in the Context of Fourteenth-Century Gift Economies" in the *The Chaucer Review* and "'A Tokene and a Book': Reading Images in *Dives and Pauper,"* in *The Yearbook of Langland Studies.*

Laura L. Howes, professor and associate head of the Department of English at the University of Tennessee, Knoxville, is the author of *Chaucer's Gardens and the Language of Convention,* a coeditor with Professor Marie Borroff of the Norton Critical Edition of *Sir Gawain and the Green Knight,* and editor of *Place, Space, and Landscape in Medieval Narrative.* Her work has also been published in *Modern Philology, The Chaucer Review, Studies in Philology, Notes and Queries,* and other journals and essay collections.

J. A. Jackson is professor of English at Hillsdale College in Michigan, where he teaches courses in Old English language and literature, the *Pearl* poet, Chaucer, philosophy and literature, and Dostoevsky. He has published essays on the Old English *Genesis B,* the *Pearl* poet, Julian of Norwich, Emmanuel Levinas, René Girard, Dostoevsky, and on the Revelation to John and apocalyptic hermeneutics. With Ann W. Astell he coedited *Levinas and Medieval Literature: The "Difficult Reading" of English and Rabbinic Texts.*

Heather Maring is assistant professor of English at Arizona State University. Her article, "'Never the Less': Gift-Exchange and the Medieval Dream-Vision *Pearl"* was published in the journal of the *M/MLA.* Her articles on oral-traditional poetics and Old English literature have appeared in *Oral Tradition, English Studies,* and *Studies in Philology.* Her monograph, *Signs that Sing: Hybrid Poetics in Old English Verse,* was published in 2017 with University Press of Florida.

Murray McGillivray teaches Old and Middle English language and literature and digital humanities at the University of Calgary. He is the director of the *Cotton Nero A.x. Project* (www.gawain-MS.ca), which has published an online facsimile of the *Pearl* manuscript with the assistance of the Social Sciences and Humanities Research Council of Canada and the British Library, and he is currently completing new critical editions of its four poems, including coediting *Pearl* with Jenna Stook. His work in digital editions began with his 1997 CD-ROM of Chaucer's *Book of the Duchess* and continues with his current Online Corpus of Old English Poetry (www.oepoetry.ca).

Ann Meyer is a medievalist. She has served as associate professor at Claremont McKenna College and director of the Division of Research Programs for the National Endowment for the Humanities. She currently teaches at Georgetown University. She is the author of *Medieval Allegory and the Building of the New Jerusalem;* her articles and reviews appear in *Studies in Bibliography, Chaucer Review, Medieval Review, Medievalia et Humanistica,* and *The Oxford Encyclopedia of Women in World History.* Her current research focuses on Dante Alighieri's Christian platonism, allegory, and sapiential theology in the *Divine Comedy.*

Kenna L. Olsen is associate professor in the Department of English at Mount Royal University in Calgary, Canada. Her research and teaching interests include Old and Middle English literature and language, the history of the book, vernacular textual and editing studies, and manuscript studies. Her current "Material Girls: Middle English Female Scribes and Their Cultural Agents" (www.material-girls.ca) aims to better determine women's lives in medieval England. She also collaborates on the *Cotton Nero A.x. Project* (www.gawain-ms.ca).

William A. Quinn is distinguished professor in the Department of English at the University of Arkansas and former director of the Medieval and Renaissance Studies Program of Fulbright College. His primary research interests are the history of prosodic theory and performance theory and the interplay of the two.

LIST OF SURVEY PARTICIPANTS

Lesley Allen, *Greenville College*
Fatemeh Azinfar, *Harvard University*
Holly Barbaccia, *Georgetown College*
Candace Barrington, *Central Connecticut State University*
Jane Chance, *Rice University*
Nancy Ciccone, *University of Colorado, Denver*
Rosalind E. Clark, *Saint Mary's College*
David K. Coley, *Simon Fraser University*
Carolyn M. Craft, *Longwood University*
Andrew T. Eichel, *University of Tennessee, Knoxville*
Ruth Evans, *Saint Louis University*
Johanna Fisher, *Canisius College*
John M. Ganim, *University of California, Riverside*
Shannon Gayk, *Indiana University*
Alan T. Gaylord, *Dartmouth College*
Ray Gleason, *Northwestern University*
R. James Goldstein, *Auburn University*
Eugene Green, *Boston University*
Karen Gross, *Lewis and Clarke College*
Julia Bolton Holloway, *University of Colorado, Boulder*
Lisa Horton, *University of Minnesota, Duluth*
Naomi Howell, *Exeter University*
Lisa Lettau, *Western Governors University*
Murray McGillivray, *University of Calgary*
James J. Murphy, *University of California, Davis*
Daniel M. Murtaugh, *Florida Atlantic University*
Marijane Osborn, *University of California, Davis*
Niamh Pattwell, *University College, Dublin*
Julie Paulson, *San Francisco State University*
Oscar Perea-Rodriguez, *University of California, Riverside*
David Andrew Porter, *University of Cambridge*
William A. Quinn, *University of Arkansas*
Michelle M. Sauer, *University of North Dakota*
Elizabeth Schirmer, *New Mexico State University*
Larry J. Swain, *Bemidji State University*
Katherine Terrell, *Hamilton College*
Gary Waller, *Purchase College, State University of New York*
Robin Waugh, *Wilfrid Laurier University*
Miranda Wilcox, *Brigham Young University*

WORKS CITED

Ackerman, Robert W. "The Pearl-Maiden and the Penny." *The Middle English* Pearl: *Critical Essays*. Ed. John Conley. Notre Dame: U of Notre Dame P, 1970. 149–62. Print. Rpt. of "The Pearl-Maiden and the Penny." *Romance Philology* 17 (1963–64): 615–23. Print.

Adam, Katharine L. *The Anomalous Stanza of* Pearl: *Does It Disclose a Six-Hundred-Year-Old Secret?* Fayetteville: Monograph, 1976. Print.

Ades, Dawn. *An Outline of Dada and Surrealism*. London: Hayward Gallery; Westerham, 1978. Print.

Aers, David. "The Self Mourning: Reflections on *Pearl*." *Speculum* 68.1 (1993): 54–73. Print.

Alain de Lille. *The Complaint of Nature*. Trans. Douglas M. Moffat. *Yale Studies in English* 36 (1908). *Internet Medieval Sourcebook*. 1996. Web. 17 Mar. 2016. <http://www.fordham.edu/halsall/basis/alain-deplanctu.html>.

———. *The Plaint of Nature*. Trans. James J. Sheridan. Toronto: U of Toronto P, 1980. Print.

Albert the Great. *Book of Minerals*. Trans. Dorothy Wyckoff. Oxford: Oxford UP, 1967. Print.

Amodio, Mark C. *Writing the Oral Tradition: Oral Poetics and Literate Culture in Medieval England*. Notre Dame: U of Notre Dame P, 2004. Print.

Anderson, J. J. *Language and Imagination in the Gawain-Poems*. Manchester: Manchester UP, 2005. Print.

Anderson, J. J., and A. C. Cawley, eds. Pearl, Cleanness, Patience *and* Sir Gawain and the Green Knight. 1962. London: Everyman, 1996. Print.

Anderson, Lucy. "The Architecture of Light: Color and Cathedral as Rhetorical Ductus in the Middle English *Pearl*." Diss. New York U, 2009. Print.

Andrew, Malcolm. *The Gawain-Poet: An Annotated Bibliography, 1839–1977*. New York: Garland, 1979. Print.

———. "Theories of Authorship." Brewer and Gibson 23–34.

Andrew, Malcolm, and Ronald Waldron, eds. *The Poems of the* Pearl *Manuscript:* Pearl, Cleanness, Patience, Sir Gawain and the Green Knight. Berkeley: U of California P, 1978. Print.

———, eds. *The Poems of the* Pearl *Manuscript:* Pearl, Cleanness, Patience, Sir Gawain and the Green Knight. 5th ed. Exeter: U of Exeter P, 2007. Print.

———, eds. *The Poems of the* Pearl *Manuscript*: Pearl, Cleanness, Patience, Sir Gawain and the Green Knight. Exeter: U of Exeter P, 2008. Print.

———, trans. *The Poems of the* Pearl *Manuscript in Modern English Prose Translation*. Liverpool: Liverpool UP, 2013.

Aquinas, Thomas. *S. Thomae Aquinatis summa theologiae*. Ed. P. Caramello. 3 vols. 1952. Rome: Marietti, 1956. Print.

Aristotle. *De insomniis et de divinatione per somnum: A new edition of the Greek text with the Latin translations*. Ed. and trans. Hendrik Joan Drossaart Lulofs. Leiden: n.p., 1947. Print.

——. *De somno et vigilia liber, adiectis veteribus translationibus et Theodori Metochitae commentario*. Ed. Hendrik Joan Drossaart Lulofs. Leiden: n.p., 1943. Print.

Armitage, Simon, trans. *The Assembly of Ladies*. Floure and the Leafe, The Assembly of Ladies, The Isle of Ladies. Ed. Derek Pearsall. Kalamazoo: Medieval Inst. Pubs., 1990. TEAMS Middle English Text Series. Web. 7 June 2016. <http://www.lib .rochester.edu/camelot/teams/assemfrm.htm>.

——. *Pearl: A New Translation*. New York: Liveright, 2016. Print.

——, trans. *Sir Gawain and the Green Knight*. New York: Norton, 2007. Print.

Assembly of Ladies. Pearlsall, Floure and the Leafe.

Astell, Ann W. *Political Allegory in Late Medieval England*. Ithaca: Cornell UP, 1999. Print.

——. *The Song of Songs in the Middle Ages*. Ithaca: Cornell UP, 1995. Print.

Auerbach, Erich. "Figura." *Scenes from the Drama of European Literature*. 1959. Trans. Ralph Manheim. Minneapolis: U of Minnesota P, 1984. 11–78. Print.

Augustine of Hippo. *Confessions*. Trans. R. S. Pine-Coffin. New York: Penguin, 1961. Print.

——. *De civitate Dei*. Vol. 1. Trans. George McCracken. Cambridge: Harvard UP, 1957. Print. Loeb Classical Lib.

——. *De doctrina christiana*. Ed. J. Martin. Turnhout: Brepolis, 1962. Corpus Christianorum Series Latina 32.

——. *De genesi ad litteram: The Literal Meaning of Genesis*. Trans. John Hammond Taylor. Vol. 2. New York: Newman, 1982. Print.

——. "Sermon 87." Trans. R. G. MacMullen. *Nicene and Post-Nicene Fathers, First Series*. Vol. 6. Ed. Philip Schaff. Buffalo: Christian Lit. Pub., 1888. Rev. and edited for *New Advent* by Kevin Knight. <http://www.newadvent.org/fathers/1603.htm>.

——. "A Treatise on the Merits and Forgiveness of Sins and on the Baptism of Infants." *St. Augustine: Anti-Pelagian Writings*. 1887. Ed. Philip Schaff. New York: Cosimo, 2007. Print. Vol. 5 of *Nicene and Post-Nicene Fathers, First Series*.

Awntyrs off Arthur. Sir Gawain: Eleven Romances and Tales. Ed. Thomas Hahn. Kalamazoo: Medieval Inst. Pubs., 1995. Print. TEAMS Middle English Texts.

Azéma, Anne. "'Une aventure vous dirai': Performing Medieval Narrative." Vitz, Regalado, and Lawrence 209–22.

Backhouse, Janet. *Medieval Rural Life in the Luttrell Psalter*. Toronto: U of Toronto P, 1989. 47. Print.

Bagby, Benjamin. "*Beowulf*, the Edda, and the Performance of Medieval Epic: Notes from the Workshop of a Reconstructed 'Singer of Tales.'" Vitz, Regalado, and Lawrence 181–93.

Bardavío, José M. "Chaucer: Entorno a cuatro Poemas Mayores." *Estudios de filología inglesa* 3 (1977): 5–17. Print.

Barr, Helen. "*Pearl*: The Jeweller's Tale." *Socioliterary Practice in Late Medieval England*. Oxford: Oxford UP, 2001. 40–62. Print.

Barr, Jessica. *Willing to Know God: Dreamers and Visionaries in the Later Middle Ages*. Columbus: Ohio State UP, 2010. Print.

Barthes, Roland. "The Death of the Author." *Image-Music-Text*. Trans. Stephen Heath. New York: Farrar, 1978. 142–48. Print.

Bauman, Richard. *Verbal Art as Performance*. Long Grove: Waveland, 1977. Print.

Beal, Jane. "The Jerusalem Lamb of *Pearl*." *Glossator* 9 (2015): 264–85. Print.

———, ed. and trans. Pearl: *A Medieval Masterpiece in Middle English and Modern English*. Under review.

———. "The Pearl-Maiden's Two Lovers." *Studies in Philology* 100 (2003): 1–21. Print.

———. *The Signifying Power of* Pearl: *Medieval Literary and Cultural Contexts for the Transformation of Genre*. New York: Routledge, 2017. Routledge Studies in Medieval Literature and Culture.

———. "The Signifying Power of *Pearl*." *Quidditas* 33 (2012): 27–58. Web. 17 Jan. 2014.

———. "Three Approaches to Teaching the Medieval *Pearl*: Introduction to Literature, British Literature I, and the Mythology of J. R. R. Tolkien." *Once and Future Classroom* 12.2 (Spring 2016): n. pag. Web. 8 Sept. 2016. <http://once-and-future-classroom.org>.

Bede. "Bede's Story of *Caedmon*: Text and Facing translation." Ed. Benjamin Slade. Trans. L. C. Jane. 1903. *Beowulf on Steorarune*. N.p., 30 Mar. 2005. Web. 17 Mar. 2016. <http://www.heorot.dk/bede-caedmon.html>.

———. "*Caedmon's Hymn*." *Ecclesiastical History of the English Church and People*. Ed. D. H. Farmer and Ronald E. Latham. Trans. Leo Sherley-Price. 1955. London: Penguin, 1990. Print.

Beidler, Peter G. "Chaucer's *Reeve's Tale*, Boccaccio's *Decameron IX, 6*, and Two 'Soft' German Analogues." *Chaucer Review* 28.3 (1994): 237–51. Print.

Benjamin, Walter. *Illuminations*. Ed. and trans. Hannah Arendt. New York: Harcourt, 1968. Print.

———. "The Task of the Translator." Benjamin, *Illuminations* 69–82.

———. "The Work of Art in the Age of Mechanical Reproduction." Benjamin, *Illuminations* 217–52.

Bennett, Michael J. *Community, Class, and Careerism: Cheshire and Lancashire Society in the Age of* Sir Gawain and the Green Knight. Cambridge: Cambridge UP, 1983. Print.

Benson, Larry D. "The Authorship of 'St. Erkenwald.'" *Journal of English and Germanic Philology* 64.3 (1965): 393–405. Print.

Bestul, Thomas H. *Satire and Allegory in* Wynnere and Wastoure. Lincoln: U of Nebraska P, 1974. Print.

Bishop, Ian. Pearl *in Its Setting: A Critical Study of the Structure and Meaning of the Middle English Poem*. New York: Barnes, 1968. Print.

Blanch, Robert J. "Color Symbolism and Mystical Contemplation in *Pearl*. *Nottingham Medieval Studies* 17 (1973): 58–77. Print.

———, ed. Sir Gawain *and* Pearl: *Critical Essays*. Bloomington: Indiana UP, 1966. Print.

———. "The State of *Pearl* Criticism." *Chaucer Yearbook* 3 (1996): 21–33. Print.

Blanch, Robert J., and Julian N. Wasserman. *From* Pearl *to* Gawain: *Forme to Fynisment*. Gainesville: UP of Florida, 1995. Print.

Blanch, Robert J., Miriam Youngerman Miller, and Julian N. Wasserman, eds. *Text and Matter: New Critical Perspectives of the* Pearl-*Poet*. Troy: Whitston, 1991. Print.

Blenker, Louis. "The Theological Structure of *Pearl*." *Traditio* 24 (1968): 43–75. Print.

Bloom, Harold. *Anxiety of Influence: A Theory of Poetry*. 2nd ed. Oxford: Oxford UP, 1997. Print.

Bloomfield, Josephine. "Aristotelian Luminescence, Thomistic Charity: Vision, Reflection, and Self-Love in *Pearl*." *Studies in Philology* 108 (2011): 165–88. Print.

Bodenham, C. H. L. "The Nature of the Dream in Late Medieval French Literature." *Medium-Aevum* 54 (1985): 74–86. Print.

Boethius. *De consolatione Philosophiae* (*Consolation of Philosophy*). Trans. Victor Watts. Rev. ed. Harmondsworth: Penguin, 2000. Print.

———. *The Consolation of Philosophy*. Trans. W. V. Cooper. 1902. *Electronic Text Center*. Web. 17 Mar. 2016. <http://etext.virginia.edu/etcbin/toccer-new?id=Boe Phil&images=images/modeng&data=/texts/english/modeng/parsed&tag=public &part=1&division=div>.

Boethius of Dacia. *On the Supreme Good, On the Eternity of the World, On Dreams*. Trans. J. F. Wippel. Toronto: Pontifical Inst. of Medieval Studies, 1987. Print.

Boffey, Julia, ed. *Fifteenth-Century Dream Visions: An Anthology*. Oxford: Oxford UP, 2003. Print.

Boffey, Julia, and A. S. G. Edwards. *A New Index of Middle English Verse* [NIMEV]. London: British Lib., 2005. Print.

Bogdanos, Theodore. "*Pearl*: Image of the Ineffable." Diss. U of California, Berkeley, 1975.

———. Pearl: *Image of the Ineffable*. University Park: Pennsylvania State UP, 1983. Print.

Bonaventura. *Doctoris Seraphici S. Bonaventureae S. R. E Episcopi Cardinalis Opera Omnia*. Ed. Fathers of the College of Saint Bonaventure. Florence: Coll. of Saint Bonaventure, 1882–1902. Print; Web. <https://catalog.hathitrust.org/ Record/008603033>.

———. "Vitis mystica sive Tractatus passione Domini." *Opera Omnia* 8: 159–89. Print.

Borgnet, Émile, et al. *B. Alberti Magni ratisbonensis episcopi, ordinis prædicatorum, Opera omnia: Ex editione lugdunensi religiose castigata*. Paris: Ludovicum Vivès, 1898. Print; *Internet Archive*. Web. 4 Nov. 2016. <https://archive.org/details/ balbertimagnira03chgoog>.

Borroff, Marie, trans. *The Gawain Poet: Complete Works*: Sir Gawain and the Green Knight, Patience, Cleanness, Pearl, Saint Erkenwald. New York: Norton, 2011. Print.

———. "Narrative Artistry in *St. Erkenwald* and the *Gawain*-Group: The Case for Common Authorship Reconsidered." *Studies in the Age of Chaucer* 28 (2006): 41–76. Print.

———. trans. Pearl: *A New Verse Translation*. New York: Norton, 1977. Print.

———, trans. *Sir Gawain and the Green Knight*. Ed. Laura L. Howes. New York: Norton, 2010. Print.

———, trans. Sir Gawain and the Green Knight*: A New Verse Translation*. New York: Norton, 1967. Print.

———, trans. Sir Gawain and the Green Knight, Patience, *and* Pearl*: Verse Translations*. New York: Norton, 2001. Print.

———. *Traditions and Renewals: Chaucer, the Gawain-Poet, and Beyond*. New Haven: Yale UP, 2003. Print.

Bowden, Betsy. *Chaucer Aloud: The Varieties of Textual Interpretation*. Philadelphia: U of Pennsylvania P, 1987. Print; CD. *Chaucer Aloud*. Provo: Chaucer Studio, 2012.

Bowers, John M. *An Introduction to the Gawain Poet*. Gainesville: UP of Florida, 2012. Print.

———. "*Pearl* in Its Royal Setting: Ricardian Poetry Revisited." *Studies in the Age of Chaucer* 17 (1995): 111–55. Print.

———. The Politics of *Pearl*: *Court Poetry in the Age of Richard II*. Cambridge: Brewer, 2001. Print.

———. "The Politics of *Pearl*." *Exemplaria* 7.2 (1995): 419–41. Print.

Bradbury, Nancy Mason. *Writing Aloud: Storytelling in Late Medieval England*. Urbana: U of Illinois P, 1998. Print.

Bradley, Henry. "The English *Gawain*-Poet and *The Wars of Alexander*." *Academy* 33 (1888): 27. Print.

Bradley, S. A. J., ed. and trans. "The Dream of the Rood." *Anglo-Saxon Poetry*. London: Dent, 1982. 158–63. Print; Web. <http://faculty.uca.edu/jona/texts/rood.htm>.

Breton, André. "Surrealist Manifesto (1924)." *Manifestos of Surrealism*. Trans. Richard Seaver and Helen R. Lane. Ann Arbor: U of Michigan P, 1969. Print; Web. <http://www.tcf.ua.edu/Classes/Jbutler/T340/SurManifesto/ManifestoOfSurrealism.htm>.

Brewer, Derek, and Jonathan Gibson, eds. *A Companion to the Gawain-Poet*. 1997. Rochester: Boydell, 1999. Print.

Bullón-Fernández, Maria. "'Byyonde the Water': Courtly and Religious Desire in *Pearl*." *Studies in Philology* 91.1 (1994): 35–49. Print.

Buñuel, Luis. *Un Chien andalou*. 1929. Transflux Films, 2004. Videodisc.

Burnley, David, and Alison Wiggins, eds. "St. Patrick's Purgatory." *The Auchinleck Manuscript*. National Lib. of Scotland, 5 July 2003. Web. 15 July 2014. <http://auchinleck.nls.uk/>.

Burrow, J. A. *The Gawain Poet*. Horndon: Northcote, 2001. Print.

———. *Ricardian Poetry: Chaucer, Gower, Langland, and the Gawain Poet*. New Haven: Yale UP, 1971. Print.

———. "'Sir Thopas': An Agony in Three Fits." *Review of English Studies* ns. 22 (1971): 54–58. Print.

———. "Thinking in Poetry: Three Medieval Examples." *The New Compass: A Critical Review* 4 (2004): n. pag. Web. 10 Aug. 2013. <http://people.auc.ca/disanto/dec2004/burrow.html>.

Bynum, Caroline Walker. *Fragmentation and Redemption.* New York: Zone, 1991. Print.

———. *Holy Feast and Holy Fast: The Religious Significance of Food to Medieval Women.* Berkeley: U of California P, 1987. Print.

———. *Jesus as Mother.* Berkeley: U of California P, 1982. Print.

———. *The Resurrection of the Body in Western Christianity, 200–1336.* New York: Columbia UP, 1995. Print.

Capgrave, John. *The Life of Saint Katherine.* Ed. Karen Winstead. 1999. Notre Dame: U of Notre Dame P, 2011. Print.

Carlson, David. "*Pearl*'s Imperfections." *Studia Neophilologica* 63 (1991): 57–67. Print.

Carpenter, Humphrey. *J. R. R. Tolkien: A Biography.* Boston: Houghton, 2000. Print.

———, ed. *The Letters of J. R. R. Tolkien.* Ed. Carpenter and Christopher Tolkien. Boston: Houghton, 2000. Print.

Carroll, Lewis. *Alice's Adventures in Wonderland.* Ed. Donald J. Gay. 2nd ed. New York: Norton, 1992. Print. Norton Critical Editions.

Carruthers, Mary. *The Craft of Thought: Meditation, Rhetoric, and the Making of Images, 400–1200.* Cambridge: Cambridge UP, 1998. Print.

———. "Invention, Mnemonics, and Stylistic Ornamentation in *Psychomachia* and *Pearl.*" *The Endless Knot: Essays on Old and Middle English in Honor of Marie Boroff.* Ed. M. T. Tavormina and R. F. Yeager. Cambridge: Brewer, 1995. 210–13.

Carson, Angela. "Aspects of Elegy in the Middle English *Pearl.*" *Studies in Philology* 62 (1965): 17–27. Print.

Carty, Carolyn M. "The Role of Medieval Dream Images in Authenticating Ecclesiastical Construction." *Zeitschrift für Kunstgeschichte* 62.1 (1999): 45–90. Print.

Cawley, A. C., and J. J. Anderson. Pearl, Cleanness, Patience, Sir Gawain and the Green Knight. 1962. London: Dent; Everyman, 1996. Print.

Chadwick, Whitney. *Women Artists and the Surrealist Movement.* New York: Thames, 1985. Print.

Chaganti, Seeta. *The Medieval Poetics of the Reliquary.* New York: Palgrave, 2008. Print.

Chance, Jane. "Allegory and Structure in *Pearl*: The Four Senses of the *Ars praedicandi* and Fourteenth-Century Homiletic Poetry." Blanch, Miller, and Wasserman 31–59.

Chapman, Coolidge Otis. "Numerical Symbolism in Dante and the *Pearl.*" *Modern Language Notes* 54 (1939): 256–59. Print.

Chase, Stanley P., trans. *The Pearl: The Fourteenth Century English Poem Rendered in Modern Verse.* New York: Oxford UP, 1932. Print.

———, ed. *The* Pearl: *The Text of the Fourteenth Century English Poem.* Ed. Members of the Chaucer Course in Bowdoin College. Boston: Humphries, 1932. Print.

Chaucer, Geoffrey. "The Book of the Duchess." Lynch, *Dream Visions* 3–37.

———. "The Book of the Duchesse." *Poetry Archives*. eMule.com, 1995–2008. Web. 7 June 2016. <http://www.emule.com/poetry/?page=poem&poem=426>.

———. *Chaucer Aloud: The Varieties of Textual Interpretation*. Provo: Chaucer Studio, 2012. CD.

———. "Parliament of Fowls." Lynch, *Dream Visions* 93–116.

———. "Parliament of Fowles." *Poetry Archives*. eMule.com, 1995–2008. Web. 7 June 2016. <http://www.emule.com/poetry/?page=poem&poem=428>.

Chism, Christine. *Alliterative Revivals*. Philadelphia: U of Pennsylvania P, 2002. Print.

Christine de Pizan. *Book of the City of Ladies*. Trans. Rosalind Brown-Grant. Harmondsworth: Penguin, 2000. Print.

———. *Le Livre de l'advision Cristine*. Ed. Christine Reno and Liliane Dulac. Paris: Honoré Champion, 2001.

———. *The Vision of Christine*. Trans. Glenda McLeod and Charity Cannon Willard. Woodbridge: Brewer, 2005. Library of Medieval Women.

Clanchy, M. T. *From Memory to Written Record: England, 1066–1307*. 2nd ed. Oxford: Blackwell, 1993. Print.

Clanvowe, John. "The Cuckoo and the Nightingale." Conlee, *Middle English Debate Poetry* 249–65.

Clark, J. W. "The *Gawain*-Poet and the Substantival Adjective." *Journal of English and Germanic Philology* 49 (1950): 60–66. Print.

———. "Observations on Certain Differences in Vocabulary between *Cleanness* and *Sir Gawain and the Green Knight*." *Philological Quarterly* 28 (1949): 261–73. Print.

———. "On Certain 'Alliterative' and 'Poetic' Words in the Poems Attributed to 'The *Pearl*-Poet'." *Modern Language Quarterly* 12 (1951): 387–98. Print.

———. "Paraphrases for 'God' in the Poems Attributed to 'The *Gawain*-Poet.'" *Modern Language Notes* 75 (1950): 232–36. Print.

Clopper, Lawrence M. "*Pearl* and the Consolation of Scripture." *Viator* 23 (1992): 231–45. Print.

Cohen, Sandy. "The Dynamics and Allegory of Music in the Concatenations of *Pearl*, a Poem in Two Movements." *LQ* 14 (1976): 47–52. Print.

Coleman, Joyce. *Public Reading and the Reading Public in Late Medieval England and France*. 1996. Cambridge: Cambridge UP, 2005. Print.

Coley, David. "*Pearl* and the Narrative of Pestilence." *Studies in the Age of Chaucer* 35 (2013): 209–62. Print.

Condren, Edward I. "Numerical Proportion as Aesthetic Strategy in the *Pearl* Manuscript." *Viator* 30 (1999): 285–305. Print.

———. *The Numerical Universe of the Gawain-Poet: Beyond Phi*. Gainesville: UP of Florida, 2002. Print.

Conlee, John W., ed. *Middle English Debate Poetry: A Critical Anthology*. East Lansing: Colleagues, 1991. Print.

———. "Death and Life." Conlee, *Middle English Debate Poetry* 139–66.

Conley, John, ed. *The Middle English* Pearl: *Critical Essays*. Notre Dame: U of Notre Dame P, 1970. Print.

Cooper, R. A., and D. A. Pearsall. "The *Gawain* Poems: A Statistical Approach to the Question of Common Authorship." *Review of English Studies* ns 39 (1988): 365–85. Print.

Copeland, Rita, and Ineke Sluiter. "Matthew of Vendôme, ars versificatoria, CA. 1175." *Medieval Grammar and Rhetoric: Language Arts and Literary Theory, AD 300–1475*. Oxford Scholarship Online, 2015. Web. 18 Apr. 2016. <http://www.university pressscholarship.com/search?q=Medieval+Grammar+and+Rhetoric&searchBtn =Search&isQuickSearch=true>.

Cotton Nero A.x Project. N.p., 2010. Web. 7 June 2016. <http://gawain-ms.ca/>.

Coulton, George Gordon, trans. Pearl: *A Fourteenth-Century Poem*. London: Nutt, 1906. Print.

Courtney, Charles Russell. "The *Pearl* Poet: An Annotated International Bibliography, 1955–1970." Diss. U of Arizona, 1975. Print.

Cox, Catherine S. "*Pearl*'s 'Precios Pere': Gender, Language, and Difference." *Chaucer Review* 32.4 (1998): 377–90. Print.

Crawford, Donna. "The Architectonics of *Cleanness*." *Studies in Philology* 90 (1993): 29–43. Print.

Crawford, John, and Andrew Hoyem, trans. *The Pearl*. San Francisco: Grabhorn-Hoyem, 1967. Print.

Crawford, Kara. "Linking *Pearl* Together." *Once and Future Classroom* 12.1 (Fall 2015): n. pag. Web. 8 Sept. 2016. <http://once-and-future-classroom.org>.

Daniélou, Jean. *From Shadows to Reality: Studies in the Biblical Typology of the Fathers*. Trans. Wulstan Hibberd. 1960. Raleigh: Ex Fontibus, 2011. Print.

———. *The Origins of Latin Christianity*. Trans. David Smith and John Austen Baker. London: Westminster, 1977. 59–92. Print. Vol. 1 of *A History of Early Christian Doctrine before the Council of βNicaea*.

Dante, Alighieri. *The Divine Comedy I: Inferno*. Trans. and ed. Robin Kirkpatrick. London: Penguin, 2006. Print.

———. *Convivio*. Ed. W. W. Jackson. Oxford: Clarendon, 1909. Print.

Davenport, W. A. *The Art of the Gawain-Poet*. Atlantic Highlands: Athlone, 1978. Print.

———. *Medieval Narrative: An Introduction*. Oxford: Oxford UP, 2004.

"Death and Life." Conlee, *Middle English Debate Poetry* 139–66.

Decker, Otto, trans. "*Die Perle*": *Das Mittelenglische Gedicht. Freier Metrischer Übertragung*. Schwerin: Sengebusch, 1916. Print.

De Ford, Sara, ed. and trans. *The Pearl*. New York: AHM, 1967. Print. Crofts Classics.

De Lubac, Henri. *Medieval Exegesis: The Four Senses of Scripture*. Vol. 1. Trans. Mark Sebanc. Vol. 2. Trans. E. M. Macierowski. 2 vols. Grand Rapids: Eerdmans, 1998–2000. Print.

Dervaux, Isabelle. *Surrealism USA*. New York: Natl. Acad. Museum; Hatje Cantz, 2005. Print.

Diekstra, F. N. M. "Chaucer and the *Romance of the Rose*." *English Studies* 69.1 (1988): 12–26. Print.

Donnelly, C. "Challenging the Conventions of Dream Vision in *The Book of the Duchess*." *Philological Quarterly* 66 (1987): 421–35. Print.

Douay-Rheims Bible Online. N.p., n.d. Web. 10 Aug. 2013.

Douglas, Gavin. *The Palis of Honoure*. Ed. David J. Parkinson. Kalamazoo: Medieval Inst. Pubs., 1992. *TEAMS Middle English Texts*. Web. 7 June 2016. <http://d.lib .rochester.edu/teams/publication/parkinson-douglas-the-palis-of-honoure>.

Draycott, Jane, trans. Pearl: *A Translation*. Manchester: Carcanet, 2011. Print.

Dream of the Rood. S. A. J. Bradley.

Dunbar, William. "The Golden Targe." Dunbar, *William Dunbar* 65.

———. "Thistle and the Rose." Dunbar, *William Dunbar* 30.

———. *William Dunbar: The Complete Works*. Ed. John Conlee. Kalamazoo: Medieval Inst. Pubs., 2004. Print. TEAMS Middle English Texts.

Dunn, Charles W., and Edward T. Byrnes, eds. *Middle English Literature*. Rev. ed. New York: Garland, 1990. Print.

Earl, James. "Saint Margaret and the Pearl Maiden." *Modern Philology* 70.1 (1972): 1–8. Print.

Easting, Robert, ed. *St. Patrick's Purgatory : Two Versions of* Owayne Miles *and the Vision of William Stranton Together with the Long Text of the* Tractus de Purgatorio Sancti Patricii. Oxford: Oxford UP, 1991. Print. EETS os 298.

———. *Visions of the Other World in Middle English*. Cambridge: Brewer, 1997. Print. Vol. 3 of *Annotated Bibliographies of Old and Middle English Literature*.

Edmondson, George. "*Pearl*: The Shadow of the Object, the Shape of the Law." *Studies in the Age of Chaucer* 26 (2004): 29–63. Print.

Edwards, Michael. Rev. of *The Numeric Universe of the Gawain-Pearl Poet*, by Edward I. Condren. *International Journal of the Classical Tradition* 11 (2005): 478–80. Print.

Eldredge, Laurence. "The Imagery of Roundness in William Woodford's *De sacramentis altaris* and Its Possible Relevance to the Middle English *Pearl*." *Notes and Queries* ns 25 (1978): 3–5. Print.

———. "The State of *Pearl* Studies since 1933." *Viator* 6 (1975): 171–94. Print.

Eliot, T. S. "Tradition and the Individual Talent." 1919. *Norton Anthology of Theory and Criticism*. Ed. Vincent B. Leitch. 2nd ed. New York: Norton, 2010. 955–60. Print.

Eller, Vernard. "A Pearl . . . For the Brokenhearted: Translated and with a Commentary by Vernard Eller." Washington: UP of Amer., 1983. Print; Web. <http://www .hccentral.com/eller10/>.

Enders, Jody. "Memory, Allegory, and the Romance of Rhetoric." *Rereading Allegory: Essays in Memory of Daniel Poirion*. Ed. Sarah Amer and Noah D. Guynn. New Haven: Yale UP, 1999. 49–64. Print. Yale French Studies 95.

Erickson, Carolly. *The Medieval Vision: Essays in History and Perception*. New York: Oxford UP, 1976. Print.

Everett, Dorothy. *Essays on Middle English Literature*. Oxford: Oxford UP, 1955. Web. https://archive.org/stream/essaysonmiddleen029939mbp/essaysonmiddleen029939 mbp_djvu.txt.

Fathers of the College of Saint Bonaventure, eds. *Commentaria in quatuor libros sententiarum magistri Petri Lombardi*. Fathers, *Opera Omnia*, vols. 1–4.

———, eds. *Doctoris Seraphici S. Bonaventureae S. R. E. Episcopi Cardinalis*. Fathers *Opera Omnia*.

———, eds. *Opera omnia*. 1882–1902. 10 vols. Florence: College of Saint Bonaventure. Print.

Fein, Susanna Greer. "Of Judges and Jewelers: *Pearl* and the Life of Saint John." *Studies in the Age of Chaucer* 36 (2014): 41–76. Print.

———. "Twelve-Line Stanza Forms in Middle English and the Date of *Pearl*." *Speculum* 72.2 (1997): 367–98. Print.

Field, Rosalind. "The Heavenly Jerusalem in *Pearl*." *Modern Language Review* 81.1 (1986): 7–17. Print.

Finch, Casey, ed. and trans. *The Complete Works of the* Pearl *Poet*. Berkeley: U of California P, 1993. Print.

Finlayson, John. "*Pearl*: Landscape and Vision." *Studies in Philology* 71.3 (1974): 314–43. Print.

———. "The *Roman de la Rose* and Chaucer's Narrators." *Chaucer Review* 24.3 (1990): 187–210. Print.

Fischer, S. R. *The Complete Medieval Dreambook: A Multilingual, Alphabetical Somnia Danielis Collation*. Berne: Lang, 1982. Print.

Fish, Stanley. *Self-Consuming Artifacts: The Experience of Seventeenth-Century Literature*. Berkeley: U of California P, 1972. Print.

———. *Surprised by Sin: The Reader in* Paradise Lost. 2nd ed. Harvard UP, 1998. Print.

Fleming, John V. "The Centuple Structure of the *Pearl*." *The Alliterative Tradition in the Fourteenth Century*. Ed. Bernard S. Levy and Paul E. Szarmach. Kent: Kent State UP, 1981. 81–98. Print.

Fletcher, Alan J. "*Pearl* and the Limits of History." *Studies in Late Medieval and Early Renaissance Texts in Honour of John Scattergood*. Ed. Anne Marie D'Arcy and Alan J. Fletcher. Dublin: Four Courts, 2005. 148–70. Print.

———. *Preaching, Politics and Poetry in Late-Medieval England*. Dublin: Four Courts, 1998. Print.

The Floure and the Leafe. Pearsall, The Floure and the Leafe.

Foley, John Miles. *How to Read an Oral Poem*. Urbana: U of Illinois P, 2002. Print.

Foley, Michael. "The *Gawain*-Poet: An Annotated Bibliography, 1978–85." *Chaucer Review* 23.3 (1989): 250–82. Print.

Foucault, Michel. "What Is an Author?" Trans. and ed. Paul Rabinow. *The Foucault Reader*. New York: Pantheon, 1984. 101–20. Print.

Fredell, Joel. "The *Pearl*-Poet Manuscript in York." *Studies in the Age of Chaucer* 36 (2014): 1–39. Print.

Garbáty, Thomas J. *Medieval English Literature*. Prospect Heights: Waveland, 1984. Print.

Gardner, John, trans. The Alliterative Morte Arthure, *The Owl and the Nightingale, and Five Other Middle English Poems*. Carbondale: Southern Illinois UP, 1971. Print.

———, trans. *The Complete Works of the Gawain-Poet: In a Modern English Version with a Critical Introduction*. 1965. Chicago: U of Chicago P, 1975. Print.

Garrett, Robert Max. *The* Pearl: *An Interpretation*. Seattle: U of Washington P, 1918. Print.

Garrison, Jennifer. "Liturgy and Loss: *Pearl* and the Ritual Reform of the Aristocratic Subject." *Chaucer Review* 44.3 (2010): 294–322. Print.

Gatta, John, Jr. "Transformation Symbolism and the Liturgy of the Mass in *Pearl*." *Modern Philology* 71.3 (1974): 243–56. Print.

Gaylord, Alan T. *Pearl*. Provo: Chaucer Studio, 1997. CD. <http://trove.nla.gov.au/version/8488177>.

Giaccherini, Enrico, trans. *Perla*. 2nd ed. Parma: Luna, 1995. Print. Biblioteca medievale 9.

Gilbert, Jane. "Gender and Sexual Transgression." Brewer and Gibson 53–70.

———. *Living Death in Medieval French and English Literature*. Cambridge: Cambridge UP, 2011. Print.

Gilliver, Peter, Jeremy Marshall, and Edmund Weiner. *The Ring of Words: Tolkien and the Oxford English Dictionary*. Oxford: Oxford UP, 2006. Print.

Ginsberg, Warren, ed. Wynnere and Wastoure *and* The Parliament of Three Ages. Kalamazoo: Medieval Inst. Pubs., 1992. Print. TEAMS: Middle English Texts.

Glare, P. G. W. *Oxford Latin Dictionary*. Oxford: Oxford UP, 1982. Print.

Gollancz, Israel, ed. and trans. Pearl: *An English Poem of the Fourteenth Century; with a Modern Rendering*. 1891. Rev. ed. London, 1897. Print.

———, ed. and trans. Pearl: *An English Poem of the XIVth Century; with a Modern Rendering, Together with Boccaccio's* Olympia. London: Chatto, 1921. Print.

———, ed. St. Erkenwald: *Select Early English Poems*. Vol. 4. London: Oxford UP, 1922. Print.

Gordon, E. V., ed. *Pearl*. New York: Oxford UP, 1953. *Corpus of Middle English Prose and Verse*. Web. 7 June 2016. <http://www.hti.umich.edu/cgi/t/text/text-idx?c=cme;idno=Pearl;rgn=div1;view=text;cc=cme;node=Pearl%3A1>.

Gould, David, trans. *Pearl of Great Price: A Literary Translation of the Middle English* Pearl. Lanham: UP of Amer., 2012. Print.

Gower, John. *Confessio Amantis*. Ed. Russell A. Peck. Vol. 1. Kalamazoo: Medieval Inst. Pubs., 2000. *TEAMS Middle English Texts*. Web. 7 June 2016. <http://d.lib.rochester.edu/teams/publication/peck-confessio-amantis-volume-1>.

Goyne, Jo. "Arthurian Dreams and Medieval Dream Theory." *Medieval Perspectives* 12 (1997): 79–89. Print.

Graves, Pamela. "Social Space in the English Medieval Parish Church." *Economy and Society* 18.3 (1989): 297–322. Print.

Gross, Charlotte. "Courtly Language in *Pearl*." Blanch, Miller, and Wasserman 79–92. Print.

Guidi, Augosto, ed. and trans. "Il meglio di *Pearl*." *AION-SG* 9 (1966): 199–223. Print.

Guillaume de Lorris and Jean de Meun. *The Romance of the Rose*. Trans. Frances Horgan. 1994. Oxford: Oxford UP, 1999. Print.

Hamilton, M. P. "The Meaning of the Middle English *Pearl*." *PMLA* 70.4 (1955): 805–24. Print.

Hanna, Ralph. "Alliterative Poetry." *The Cambridge History of Medieval English Literature*. Ed. David Wallace. Cambridge: Cambridge UP, 1999. 488–512. Print.

———. *Pursuing History: Middle English Manuscripts and Their Texts*. Stanford: Stanford UP, 1996. Print.

Harbus, Antonina. "Dream and Symbol in *The Dream of the Rood*." *Nottingham Medieval Studies* 40 (1996): 1–15. Print.

Harper, Elizabeth. "Gifts and Economic Exchange in Middle English Religious Writing." Diss. U of North Carolina, Chapel Hill, 2009. Print.

———. "*Pearl* in the Context of Fourteenth-Century Gift Economies." *Chaucer Review* 44.4 (2010): 421–39. Print.

Harrington, David V. "Indeterminacy in *Winner and Waster* and *The Parliament of the Three Ages*." *Chaucer Review* 20.3 (1986): 246–57. Print.

Harwood, Britton. "Pearl as Diptych." Blanch, Miller, and Wasserman 61–78. Print.

Haskell, Ann, ed. *A Middle English Anthology*. 1969. Detroit: Wayne State UP, 1985. Print.

Hatt, Cecilia A. *God and the Gawain-Poet: Theology and Genre in* Pearl, Cleanness, Patience *and* Sir Gawain and the Green Knight. Woodbridge: Boydell, 2015. Print.

Hawkins, Peter S., and Anne Howland Schotter. *Ineffability: Naming the Unnamable: from Dante to Beckett*. New York: AMS, 1984. Print.

Herzog, M. B. "*The Book of the Duchess*: The Vision of the Artist as a Young Dreamer." *Chaucer Review* 22.4 (1987–88): 269–81. Print.

Hieatt, A. Kent. "*Sir Gawain*: Pentangle, *Luf-Lace*, Numerical Structure." *Silent Poetry*. Ed. Alastair Fowler. London: Routledge, 1970. 116–40. Print.

Hieatt, Constance B. "*Un Autre Forme*: Guillaume de Machaut and the Dream Vision Form." *Chaucer Review* 14.2 (1979–80): 97–115. Print.

———. *The Realism of Dream-Visions: The Poetic Exploitation of the Dream-Experience in Chaucer and His Contemporaries*. Paris: Mouton, 1967. Print.

Higgs, Elton. "The Progress of the Dreamer in *Pearl*." *Studies in Medieval Culture* 4 (1974): 388–400. Print.

Hillmann, Mary Vincent, ed. and trans. *The* Pearl: *Mediaeval Text with a Literal Translation and Interpretation*. 1961. Rev. ed. Notre Dame: U of Notre Dame P, 1967. Print.

Hilmo, Maidie. *Medieval Images, Icons, and Illustrated Literary English Texts: From the Ruthwell Cross to the Ellesmere Chaucer*. Burlington: Ashgate, 2004. Print.

Irigaray, Luce. *This Sex Which Is Not One*. Trans. Catherine Porter and Carolyn Burke. Ithaca: Cornell UP, 1985. Print.

Jack, Kimberly. "What Is the Pearl-Maiden Wearing, and Why?" *Medieval Clothing and Textiles*. Ed. Robin Netherton and Gale R. Owen-Crocker. Vol. 7. Woodbridge: Boydell, 2011. 65–86. Print.

Jackson, J. A. "The Infinite Desire of *Pearl*." *Levinas and Medieval Literature: The "Difficult Reading" of English and Rabbinic Texts*. Ed. Ann Astell and J. A. Jackson. Pittsburgh: Duquesne UP, 2009. Print.

James I. *Kingis Quair*. Boffey, *Fifteenth-Century Dream Visions* 90–157.

Jauss, Hans Robert. "Theory of Genres and Medieval Literature." *Toward an Aesthetic of Reception*. Trans. Timothy Bahti. Minneapolis: U of Minnesota P, 1982. Print. Theory and Hist. of Lit. Ser. 2.

Jeffrey, David. *A Dictionary of Biblical Tradition in English Literature*. Grand Rapids: Eerdmans, 1992. Print.

Jewett, Sophie, trans. *The Pearl: A Modern Version in the Metre of the Original*. New York: Crowell, 1908. Print; Web. 10 June 2016. <https://LibriVox.org/pearl-by -the-gawain-poet/>. <https://www.youtube.com/watch?v=ZUgHyfEdY-g>. <https://www.youtube.com/watch?v=XYxtX2lYryg>.

John of Salisbury. "Policraticus, Book Six (Selections)." Excerpt from *The Stateman's Book of John of Salisbury*. Trans. John Dickinson. New York: Knopf, 1927. Print; Web. *Internet Modern History Sourcebook*. Ed. Paul Halsall.

———. *The Statesman's Book of John of Salisbury*. Trans. John Dickinson. New York: Knopf, 1927. Print.

Johnson, Lynn Staley (*see also* Lynn Staley). *The Voice of the Gawain-Poet*. Diss. Princeton U, 1974. Madison: U of Wisconsin P, 1984. Print.

Johnston, Andrew James, Ethan Knapp, and Margitta Rouse, eds. *The Art of Vision: Ekphrasis in Medieval Literature and Culture*. Ohio State UP, 2015. Print.

Jones, Michael, ed. *The New Cambridge Medieval History, c. 1300–c. 1415*. Vol. 6. Cambridge: Cambridge UP, 2000. Print.

Jones, Terry, perf. *Pearl*. London: Harper, 1997. Audiocassette.

Julian of Norwich. *Revelations of Divine Love: Short Text and Long Text*. Trans. Elizabeth Spearing. London: Penguin, 1998. Print.

———. *The Shewings of Julian of Norwich*. Ed. Georgia Ronan Crampton. Kalamazoo: Medieval Inst. Pubs., 1994. *TEAMS Medieval English Texts*. Web. <http://www.lib .rochester.edu/camelot/teams/julianfr.htm>.

"Julian of Norwich." New York: Films Media, 2000. DVD. Web. 1 Jan. 1917. <http://www .films.com/ecSearch.aspx?q=Julian+of+Norwich>.

Kalma, Douwe, trans. *De Pearel: in visioen ut it middel-ingelsk oerbrocht yn it nij-frysk*. Dokkum: Kamminga, 1938. Print.

Kean, P. M. "Numerical Composition in *Pearl*." *Notes and Queries* 210 (1965): 49–51. Print.

———. *The Pearl: An Interpretation*. New York: Barnes, 1967. Print.

Keiper, Hugo. "'I Wot Myself Best How Y Stonde': Literary Nominalism, Open Textual Form and the Enfranchisement of Individual Perspective in Chaucer's Dream

Visions." *Literary Nominalism and the Theory of Rereading Late Medieval Texts: A New Research Paradigm.* Ed. Richard J. Utz. Lewiston: Mellen, 1995. 205–34. Print.

Kempe, Margery. *The Book of Margery Kempe.* Ed. Lynn Staley. Kalamazoo: Medieval Inst. Pubs., 1996. *TEAMS Medieval English Texts.* Web. 7 June 2016. <http://d.lib .rochester.edu/teams/publication/staley-the-book-of-margery-kempe>.

———. *The Book of Margery Kempe.* Trans. and ed. Lynn Staley. New York: Norton, 2001. Print.

Kienzle, B. M., ed. *The Sermon.* Turnhout: Brepols, 2000. Print.

"Kind, *Adj. 1.1a, 1.1b, 1.1c,1. 2a,* and *1.3.a.*" *Oxford English Dictionary.* 2nd ed. Oxford: Clarendon, 1989. Print.

Kirtlan, Ernest J. B., trans. Pearl*: A Poem of Consolation, Rendered into Modern English Verse.* London: Kelly, 1918. Print.

Kiser, L. J. "Sleep, Dreams, and Poetry in Chaucer's *Book of the Duchess.*" *Papers on Language and Literature* 19 (1983): 3–12. Print.

Klitgård, Ebbe. "Chaucer as Performer: Narrative Strategies in the Dream Visions." *Revista canaria de estudios ingleses* 47 (2003): 101–13. Print.

Kraman, Cynthia. "Body and Soul: *Pearl* and Apocalyptic Literature." *Time and Eternity: The Medieval Discourse.* Ed. Gerhard Jaritz and Gerson Moreno-Riano. Turnhout: Brepols, 2003. 355–62. Print.

Kreuzer, J. R. "The Dreamer in the *Book of the Duchess.*" *PMLA* 66.4 (1951): 543–47. Print.

Kristeva, Julia. *The Revolution in Poetic Language.* Trans. Margaret Waller. New York: Columbia UP, 1984. Print.

———. *Tales of Love.* Trans. Leon S. Rondiez. New York: Columbia UP, 1987. Print.

Kruger, Steven F. *Dreaming in the Middle Ages.* Cambridge: Cambridge UP, 1992. Print.

———. "Medical and Moral Authority in the Late Medieval Dream." *Reading Dreams: The Interpretation of Dreams from Chaucer to Shakespeare.* Ed. Peter Brown. Oxford: Oxford UP, 1999. 51–83. Print.

———. "Mirrors and the Trajectory of Vision in *Piers Plowman.*" *Speculum* 66.1 (1991): 74–95. Print.

Langland, William. *Piers Plowman.* Ed. Elizabeth Robertson and Stephen Shepherd. Trans. E. Talbot Donaldson. New York: Norton, 2006. Print.

Larkin, David, ed. *Magritte.* New York: Ballantine, 1972. Print.

Latham, R. E., ed. *Revised Medieval Latin Word-List.* London: Oxford UP, 1965. Print.

Lee, Jennifer. "The Illuminating Critic." Diss. State University of New York, Stony Brook, 1977. Print.

———. "The Illuminating Critic: The Illustrator of Cotton Nero A.x." *Studies in Iconography* 3 (1977): 17–46. Print.

L'Engle, Madeleine. *A Wrinkle in Time.* 1962. New York: Farrar, 2007. Print.

Livingstone, Josephine. "The Strange Power of a Medieval Poem about the Death of a Child." *New Yorker* 16 June 2016. Web. 17 June 2016. <http://www.newyorker .com/books/page-turner/the-strange-power-of-a-medieval-poem-about-the-death -of-a-child>.

Lomperis, Linda, and Sarah Stanbury, eds. *Feminist Approaches to the Body in Medieval Literature*. Philadelphia: U of Pennsylvania P, 1993. Print.

Lord, Albert. *The Singer of Tales*. 1960. Cambridge: Harvard UP, 2000. Print.

Lucas, Peter J. "The Pearl-Maiden's Free-Flowing Hair." *English Language Notes* 15 (1977–78): 94–95. Print.

Lydgate, John. *Temple of Glass*. Boffey, *Fifteenth-Century English Dream Visions* 15–89.

Lynch, Kathryn L., ed. *Dream Visions and Other Poems*. New York: Norton, 2006. Print. Norton Critical Eds.

———. *The High Medieval Dream Vision: Poetry, Philosophy, and Literary Form*. Stanford: Stanford UP, 1988. Print.

Macrobius. *Commentary on the Dream of Scipio*. Trans. William Harris Stahl. 1952. New York: Columbia UP, 1990. Print.

Madeleva, Mary. *Pearl: A Study in Spiritual Dryness*. 1925. New York: Phaeton, 1968. Print.

Mann, Jill. "Satisfaction and Payment in Middle English Literature." *Studies in the Age of Chaucer* 5 (1983): 17–48. Print.

"Margery Kempe." Films Media, 2006. Video. *WorldCat*. Web. 6 June 2016. <www .worldcat.org/title/margery-kempe/oclc/707968368>.

Maring, Heather. "Never-the-Less: Gift-Exchange and the Medieval Dream Vision *Pearl*." *Journal of the Midwest Modern Language Association* 38.2 (2005): 1–15. Print.

———. "Oral Tradition, Performance, and Ritual in Two Medieval Dream-Visions: *The Dream of the Rood* and *Pearl*." Diss. U of Missouri, 2005. Print.

Marti, Kevin. *Body, Heart and Text in the Pearl-Poet*. Lewiston: Mellen, 1991. Print.

Masciandaro, Nicola, and Karl Steel, eds. *Pearl: Practice and Theory of Commentary*. Spec. issue of *Glossator* 9 (2015). 1–422. Print; Web. <http://glossator.org/ volumes/>.

Matter, E. Ann. *The Voice of My Beloved: The Song of Songs in Western Medieval Christianity*. Philadelphia: U of Pennsylvania P, 1992. Print.

Matthew of Vendôme. *Ars versificatoria*. Trans. Roger P. Parr. Milwaukee: Marquette UP, 1981. Print. Medieval Philos. Texts in Trans.

McAlindon, T. "Hagiography into Art: A Study of St. Erkenwald." *Studies in Philology* 67.4 (1970): 472–94. Print.

McClung, William Alexander. *The Architecture of Paradise: Survivals of Eden and Jerusalem*. Berkeley: U of California P, 1983. Print.

McColly, William. "Style and Structure in the Middle English Poem *Cleanness*." *Computers and the Humanities* 21.3 (1987): 169–76. Print.

McColly, William, and Dennis Weier. "Literary Attribution and Likelihood-Ratio Tests: The Case of the Middle English *Pearl*-Poems." *Computers and the Humanities* 17 (1983): 65–75. Print.

McGillivray, Murray, ed. "London, British Library MS Cotton Nero A.x. (art.3): A Digital Facsimile." *Cotton Nero A.x. Project*. N.p., 2011. Web. 18 Apr. 2016. <http://content dm.ucalgary.ca/cdm/search/collection/gawain>.

McGinn, Bernard. "The Changing Shape of Late Medieval Mysticism." *Church History* 65.2 (1996): 197–219. Print.

McLaughlin, John Cameron. *A Graphemic-Phonemic Study of a Middle English Manuscript*. Hague: Moulton, 1963. Print.

McNamer, Sarah. "The Literariness of Literature and the History of Emotion." *PMLA* 130.5 (2015): 1433–42. Print.

Mead, Marian, trans. The Pearl: *An English Vision-Poem of the Fourteenth Century Done into Modern Verse*. Portland: Mosher, 1908. Print.

Mearns, Rodney, ed. *The Vision of Tundale: Ed. from B. L. MS Cotton Caligula A II*. Heidelberg: Winter, 1985. Print. Middle English Texts 18.

Medieval Pearl. N.p., n.d. Web. 6 June 2016. <https://medievalpearl.wordpress.com/pearl-poet/>.

Merwin, W. S., trans. *Sir Gawain and the Green Knight*. New York: Knopf, 2002. Print.

Meyer, Ann R. *Medieval Allegory and the Building of the New Jerusalem*. Cambridge: Brewer, 2003. Print.

Middleton, Anne. "The Idea of Public Poetry in the Reign of Richard II." *Speculum* 53.1 (1978): 94–114. Print.

Migne, Jacques-Paul. "Marbodi redonensis epiopi." Ed. Jean-Jacques Bourassé. *Patrologia cursus completus Latina*. Vol. 171. Paris: Garnier, 1854. Cols. 1736–70. Print.

———. "Sancti Brunonis Astensis." Ed. Bruno Bruni. *Patrologia cursus completus Latina*. Vols. 164–65. Paris: Garnier, 1854. Cols. 1736–70. Print.

———. "Walafridi strabi, fuldensis monachii: In evangelium sancti Matthæi." *Patrologia cursus completus Latina*. Vol. 114. Paris: Garnier, 1879. Cols. 863–88. Print.

Mitchell, J. Allan. "The Middle English *Pearl*: Figuring the Unfigurable." *Chaucer Review* 35.1 (2000): 86–111. Print.

Mitchell, S. Weir, trans. Pearl: *Rendered into Modern English Verse*. Portland: Thomas Bird Mosher, 1908. Print.

Miyata, Takeshi, trans. *Shiratama: A Japanese Translation of* Pearl. Kobe: Konan U, Bungakukukai, 1954. Print.

Moorman, Charles. *The Pearl-Poet*. New York: Twayne, 1968. Print.

———, ed. *The Works of the Gawain-Poet*. Jackson: UP of Mississippi, 1977. Print.

Moran, Dennis William. *Style and Theology in the Middle English* Pearl: *Patterns of Change and Reconciliation*. Notre Dame: U of Notre Dame P, 1976. Print.

Morris, Richard, ed. *Early English Alliterative Poems in the West-Midland Dialect of the Fourteenth Century*. 1864. Rev. ed. New York: Oxford UP, 1869. Print. EETS os 1.

Morrison, Geoffrey. "Repetition, Ritual, and Link-Words in *Pearl*: An Expatriate Poetics?" 2013. TS.

Mortimer, Ian. *The Time-Traveler's Guide to Medieval England: A Handbook for Visitors to the Fourteenth Century*. 2008. New York: Touchstone, 2011. Print.

Mossé, Fernand. *A Handbook of Middle English*. Trans. James A. Walker. 1952. Baltimore: John Hopkins UP, 2000. Print.

Mundy, Jennifer. *Surrealism: Desire Unbound*. London: Tate; New York: Metropolitan Museum of Art, 2001. Print.

Murphy, James J. *Rhetoric in the Middle Ages: A History of Rhetorical Theory from St. Augustine to the Renaissance*. Berkeley: U of California P, 1974. Print.

Muscatine, Charles. "Poetry and Crisis in the Age of Chaucer." 1972. *Medieval Literature, Style, and Culture: Essays by Charles Muscatine*. Columbia: U of South Carolina P, 1999. Print.

Naruse, Masaiku, ed. and trans. "A Study of the Middle English *Pearl*: A Text Newly Edited with Japanese Translation." Part I. *Japanese Cultural Studies* 6 (1971): 133–85, 221–88. Print.

Newman, Barbara. "The Artifice of Eternity: Speaking of Heaven in Three Medieval Poems." *Religion and Literature* 37.1 (2005): 1–24. Print.

———. *God and the Goddesses: Vision, Poetry and Belief in the Middle Ages*. Philadelphia: U of Pennsylvania P, 2005. Print.

———. "What Did It Mean to Say 'I Saw'?: The Clash between Theory and Practice in Medieval Visionary Culture." *Speculum* 80.1 (2005): 1–43. Print.

Nicholls, Jonathan. *The Matter of Courtesy: Medieval Courtesy Books and the Gawain-Poet*. Woodbridge: Brewer, 1985. Print.

Nolan, Barbara, and David Farley-Hills. "The Authorship of *Pearl*: Two Notes." *Review of English Studies* ns 22 (1971): 295–302. Print.

O'Donoghue, Bernard. Introduction. *Pearl*. Trans. Jane Draycott. Manchester: Carcanet, 2011. Print.

Olivero, Federico, ed. and trans. *La Perla: Poemetto in "Middle English."* Bologna: Zanichelli, 1936. Print.

Olmert, Michael. "Game-Playing, Moral Purpose, and Structure in *Pearl*." *The Chaucer Review* 21.3 (1987): 383–403. Print.

Olsen, Kenna L., and Murray McGillivray. "Cotton Nero A.x. Project Bibliography, 1994–2008." *Cotton Nero A.x Project*. N.p., 2011. Web. 7 June 2016. <http://people.ucalgary.ca/~scriptor/cotton/CottonNeroBiblio.pdf>.

———. "Cotton Nero A.x. Project Transcription Policy." *Cotton Nero A.x. Project*. N.p., 2011. Web. 20 Apr. 2016. <http://people.ucalgary.ca/~scriptor/cotton/policy.html>.

Olson, Glending. "Making and Poetry in the Age of Chaucer." *Comparative Literature* 31.3 (1979): 272–90. Print.

Ong, Walter. *Orality and Literacy: The Technologizing of the Word*. 1982. London: Routledge, 1991. Print.

Origen. "Origen's Commentary on the Gospel of Matthew." *The Ante-Nicene Fathers*. Trans. John Patrick. Ed. Alexander Roberts et al. New York: Scribner's, 1903. 409–512. Print.

Osgood, Charles G., Jr., trans. *The* Pearl: *An Anonymous English Poem of the Fourteenth Century, Rendered in Prose*. Princeton, 1907. Print.

———, ed. *The* Pearl: *A Middle English Poem*. Boston: Heath, 1906. Print.

Owst, G. R. *Preaching in Medieval England: An Introduction to Sermon Manuscripts of the Period, c. 1350–1450*. Cambridge: Cambridge UP, 1926. Print.

"Paraph, *N. 2*." *Oxford English Dictionary Online*. Oxford UP, 2016. Web. 25 Sept. 2016. <www.oed.com>.

Park, Roswell, IV. "The Authority of the Dream: Geoffrey Chaucer's 'Book of the Duchess,' 'Parliament of Fowls,' and 'House of Fame'." *DAI* 58 (1997): 160A. Print.

Parlement of the Thre Ages. Conlee, *Middle English Debate Poetry* 99–138.

Pearl. Perf. Alan Gaylord. Provo: Chaucer Studio, 1997. CD. <http://trove.nla.gov.au /version/8488177>.

Pearl. *Corpus of Medieval Prose and Verse*. N.p., 2012. Web. <http://name.umdl.umich .edu/Pearl>.

"*Pearl* Free Audiobook." 10 Feb. 2015. *YouTube*. Web. 7 June 2016. <https://www.youtube .com/watch?v=XYxtX2lYryg>.

The Pearl *Manuscript*. Trans. Malcolm Andrew and Ronald Waldron. London: Folio Society, 2016. Print.

Pearsall, Derek. "The Alliterative Revival: Origins and Social Backgrounds." *Middle English Alliterative Poetry and Its Literary Background*. Ed. David Lawton. Cambridge: Brewer, 1982. 34–53. Print.

———, ed. The Floure and the Leafe, The Assembly of Ladies, The Isle of Ladies. Kalamazoo: Medieval Inst. Pubs., 1990. *TEAMS Medieval English Texts Series*. Web. 7 June 2016. <http://www.lib.rochester.edu/camelot/teams/flourfrm.htm>.

———. "The Origins of the Alliterative Revival." *The Alliterative Tradition in the Fourteenth Century*. Ed. Bernard S. Levy and Paul E. Szarmach. Kent: Kent State UP, 1981. 1–24. Print.

Pearsall, Derek, and Elizabeth Salter. *Landscapes and Seasons of the Medieval World*. Toronto: U of Toronto P, 1973. Print.

Peden, A. M. "Macrobius and Mediaeval Dream Literature." *Medium-Aevum* 54 (1985): 59–73. Print.

Peterson, C. J. "*Pearl* and *St. Erkenwald*: Some Evidence for Authorship." *Review of English Studies* ns 25.97 (1974): 49–53. Print.

Petroff, Elizabeth. "Landscape in *Pearl*: The Transformation of Nature." *Chaucer Review* 16.2 (1981): 181–93. Print.

Phillips, Heather. "The Eucharistic Allusions of *Pearl*." *Medieval Studies* 47 (1985): 474–86. Print.

Plotinus. *Enneads*. Ed. and trans. Stephen MacKenna. 1916. New York: Penguin, 1991. Print.

Prior, Sandra Pierson. *The Fayre Formez of the Pearl Poet*. East Lansing: Michigan State UP, 1996. Print.

———. *The Pearl Poet Revisited*. New York: Twayne, 1994. Print.

Pseudo-Dionysius. *The Complete Works*. Trans. Paul Rorem. Mahwah: Paulist, 1987. Print.

Putter, Ad. *An Introduction to the Gawain-Poet*. Harlow: Longman, 1996. Print.

Putter, Ad, and Myra Stokes. "The Linguistic Atlas and the Dialect of the *Gawain* Poems." *Journal of English and Germanic Philology* 106 (2007): 468–91. Print.

———, eds. *The Works of the Gawain-Poet*: Sir Gawain and the Green Knight, Pearl, Cleanness, Patience. London: Penguin, 2014. Print; e-book.

Rankin, Sherri. "'He gef vus to be His homly hyne': Teaching *Pearl* in the Undergraduate Classroom through the Lens of Apostolic Embodiment." *Once and Future Classroom* 12.1 (Fall 2015): n. pag. Web. 8 Sept. 2016. <http://once-and-future -classroom.org/archives/?page_id=815>.

Rastetter, Susan J. "'Bot Mylde as Maydenes Seme at Mas': The Feast of All Saints and *Pearl*." *Bulletin of the John Rylands University Library of Manchester* 74.1 (1992): 141–54. Print.

———. "The Liturgical Background to the Middle English *Pearl*." Diss. U of Manchester, 1989. Print.

Reed, Thomas L. *Middle English Debate Poetry and the Aesthetics of Irresolution*. Columbia: U of Missouri P, 1990. Print.

Reichardt, Paul F. "'Several Illuminations, Coarsely Executed': The Illustrations of the *Pearl* Manuscript." *Studies in Iconography* 18 (1997): 119–42. Print.

Rhodes, Jim. "The Dreamer Redeemed: Exile and the Kingdom in the Middle English *Pearl*." *Studies in the Age of Chaucer* 16 (1994): 119–42. Print.

———. *Poetry Does Theology: Chaucer, Grosseteste, and the Pearl-Poet*. Notre Dame: U of Notre Dame P, 2001. Print.

Riddy, Felicity. "Jewels in *Pearl*." Brewer and Gibson 143–55.

"Right." *Middle English Dictionary*. U of Michigan, 2001. Web. <https://quod.lib.umich .edu/m/med/>.

"Rite." *Middle English Dictionary*. U of Michigan, 2001. Web. <https://quod.lib.umich .edu/m/med/>.

Robertson, D. W., Jr. "The Intellectual, Artistic, and Historical Context." *Approaches to Teaching Chaucer's* Canterbury Tales. Ed. Joseph Gibaldi. New York: MLA, 1980. 129–35. Print.

———. "The Pearl as a Symbol." *Essays in Medieval Culture*. 1950. Princeton: Princeton UP, 1980. 209–14. Print.

Røstvig, Maren-Sofie. "Numerical Composition in *Pearl*: A Theory" *English Studies* 48 (1967): 326–32. Print.

Rolle, Richard. *The Fire of Love*. Trans. Clifton Wolters. London: Penguin, 1972. Print.

Rowland, Beryl. *Blind Beasts*: *Chaucer's Animal World*. Kent: Kent State UP, 1971. Print.

Rumelhart, David E. "Schemata: The Building Blocks of Cognition." *Theoretical Issues in Reading Comprehension*. Ed. Rand J. Spiro, Bertram C. Bruce, and William E. Brewer. Hillsdale: Erlbaum, 1980. 33–58. Print.

Russell, J. Stephen. *English Dream Vision: Anatomy of a Form*. Columbus: Ohio State UP, 1988. Print.

Rust, Martha Dana. *Imaginary Worlds in Medieval Books: Exploring the Manuscript Matrix*. New York: Palgrave, 2007. Print.

Salter, Elizabeth. "The Alliterative Revival I." *Modern Philology* 64.2 (1966): 146–50. Print.

Sanok, Catherine. "The Geography of Genre in the *Physician's Tale* and *Pearl*." *New Medieval Literatures* 5 (2002): 177–201. Print.

Savage, Henry Lyttleton. *The Gawain-Poet: Studies in His Personality and Background*. Chapel Hill: U of North Carolina P, 1956. Print.

———, ed. *St. Erkenwald: A Middle English Poem*. New Haven: Yale UP, 1926. Print.

Schirmer, Elizabeth Kate. "Genre Trouble: Spiritual Reading in the Vernacular and the Literary Project of the Pearl-Poet." Diss. U of California, Berkeley, 2001. Print.

Schmidt, A. V. C. "The Inner Dreams in *Piers Plowman*." *Medium-Aevum* 55 (1986): 24–40. Print.

Schofield, W. H. "Symbolism, Allegory, and Autobiography in the *Pearl*." *PMLA* 24.4 (1909): 585–675. Print.

Schotter, Anne Howland. "Vernacular Style and the Word of God: The Incarnational Art of *Pearl*." *Ineffability: Naming the Unnamable from Dante to Beckett*. Ed. Peter S. Hawkins and Schotter. New York: AMS, 1984. Print.

Scull, Christina, and Wayne G. Hammond. *The J. R. R. Tolkien Companion and Guide*. Vols. 1–2. New York: Harper, 2006. Print.

Sekigawa, Sayko, trans. "*Akoyadama*: A Japanese Translation of *Pearl* (Extracts)." *An Anthology of English Lyrics*. Ed. Konosuke Hinatsu. Tokyo: Kawadeshobo, 1952. 6–12. Print.

Seymour, M. C., ed. *Mandeville's Travels*. Oxford: Clarendon, 1967. Print.

Shippey, Tom. *The Road to Middle-Earth: How J. R. R. Tolkien Created a New Mythology*. Rev. ed. Boston: Houghton, 2003. Print.

Shoaf, R. A. "'Mutatio amoris': 'Penitentia' and the Form of *The Book of the Duchess*." *Genre* 14.2 (1981): 163–89. Print.

Simons, John, ed. *From Medieval to Medievalism*. New York: Palgrave, 1992. Print.

Sisam, Kenneth, ed. *Fourteenth Century Verse and Prose*. Oxford: Clarendon, 1921. Print.

Sisam, Kenneth, and J. R. R. Tolkien. *A Middle English Reader and Vocabulary, 1921–22*. Mineola: Dover, 2005. Print.

Skelton, John. "Bouge of Court." Boffey, *Fifteenth-Century Dream Visions* 232–65.

Spearing, A. C., trans. The Cloud of Unknowing *and Other Works*. London: Penguin, 2001. Print.

———. *The Gawain-Poet: A Critical Study*. New York: Cambridge UP, 1970. Print.

———. *Medieval Dream Poetry*. Cambridge: Cambridge UP, 1976. Print.

———. "Symbolic and Dramatic Development in *Pearl*." *Modern Philology* 60 (1962–63): 1–12. Print.

———. *Textual Subjectivity: The Encoding of Subjectivity in Medieval Narratives and Lyrics*. Oxford: Oxford UP, 2005. Print.

Spyra, Piotr. *The Epistemological Perspective of the Pearl-Poet*. New York: Routledge, 2016. Print.

Stahl, Harvey. "Heaven in View: The Place of the Elect in an Illuminated Book of Hours." *Last Things: Death and the Apocalypse in the Middle Ages*. Ed. Caroline Walker Bynum and Paul Freedman. Philadelphia: U of Pennsylvania P, 2000. 205–32. Print.

Stakel, S. "Structural Convergence of Pilgrimage and Dream-Vision in Christine de Pizan." *Journeys towards God: Pilgrimage and Crusade*. Ed. B. N. Sargent-Baur. Kalamazoo: Western Michigan UP, 1992. Print. Rept. of *Studies in Medieval Culture* 30 (1992): 195–203. Print.

Staley, Lynn (*see also* Lynn Staley Johnson). "*Pearl* and the Contingencies of Love and Piety." *Medieval Literature and Historical Inquiry: Essays in Honor of Derek Pearsall*. Ed. David Aers. Cambridge: Brewer, 2000. 83–114. Print.

Stanbury, Sarah. "The Body and the City in *Pearl*." *Representations* 48 (1994): 30–47. Print.

———. "Feminist Masterplots: The Gaze on the Body of *Pearl*'s Dead Girl." Lomperis and Stanbury 96–115.

———. "Introduction." Stanbury, *Pearl* 1–19.

———, ed. *Pearl*. Kalamazoo: Medieval Inst. Pubs., 2001. *TEAMS Middle English Texts Series*. Web. 7 June 2016. <http://www.lib.rochester.edu/camelot/teams//stanbury.htm>.

———. *Seeing the* Gawain-*Poet: Description and the Act of Perception*. Philadelphia: U of Pennsylvania P, 1991. Print.

Stanton, Bill, trans. *This Being a Translation in Verse of the Middle English Poem* Pearl *by an Unknown Poet*. York: U of York P, 1995. Print; Web. <http://www.billstanton.co.uk/pearl/menu.php>.

Stone, Brian, trans. *Medieval English Verse*. New York: Penguin, 1964. Print.

Taylor, Albert Booth, ed. Floris and Blancheflour: *Edited from the Trentham and Auchinleck Mss*. Oxford: Clarendon, 1927. Print.

Taylor, Karla. "Chaucer and the French Tradition." *Approaches to Teaching Chaucer's* Troilus and Criseyde *and the Shorter Poems*. Ed. Tison Pugh and Angela Jane Weisl. New York: MLA, 2007. 33–37. Print.

Terasawa, Yoshio, trans. "*Shinju*: A Japanese Translation of *Pearl*." *Ancient and Medieval: Anthology of Great Poetry of the World*. Vol. 1. Tokyo: Heibon-sha, 1960. 316–33. Print.

Thompson, N. S. "The Gawain Poet." *British Writers: Supplement VII, Basil Bunting to Sylvia Townsend*. Ed. Jay Parini. New York: Scribner's, 2002. 83–101. Print.

Thundy, Zacharias P. "The Dreame of Chaucer: Boethian Consolation or Political Celebration?" *Carmina Philosophiae* 4 (1995): 91–109. Print.

Tolkien, J. R. R. "*Beowulf*: The Monsters and the Critics." *Proceedings of the British Academy* 22 (1936): 245–95. Print.

———. "Chaucer as a Philologist: *The Reeve's Tale*." *Transactions of the Philological Society* 33.1 (1934): 1–70. Print.

———. *The Fellowship of the Ring*. 1954. Boston: Houghton, 1988. Print.

———. *The History of* The Lord of the Rings. Ed. Christopher Tolkien. Boston: Houghton, 2000. Print. 4 vols.

———. *The Hobbit; or, There and Back Again*. 1937. Boston: Houghton, 1997. Print.

———. "The Nameless Land." *"The Lost Road" and Other Writings: Language and Legend before* The Lord of the Rings. Ed. Christopher Tolkien. New York: Del Rey, 1987. 109–11. Print.

———. *The Return of the King*. 1955. Boston: Houghton, 1988. Print.

———. *The Silmarillion*. Ed. Christopher Tolkien. Boston: Houghton, 2004. Print.

———, trans. Sir Gawain and the Green Knight, Pearl, *and* Sir Orfeo. Ed. Christopher Tolkien. Boston: Houghton; New York: Del Ray, 1975. Print.

———. "Valedictory Address." *"The Monsters and the Critics," and Other Essays*. Ed. Christopher Tolkien. London: Harper, 2006. 224–40. Print.

Tolkien, J. R. R., and E. V. Gordon, eds. *Sir Gawain and the Green Knight*. Oxford: Oxford UP, 1925. Print.

Tomasch, Sylvia. "A *Pearl* Punnology." *Journal of English and Germanic Philology* 88 (1989): 1–20. Print.

"Translate." *Oxford English Dictionary*. Oxford UP, 2010. Print; Web. <www.oed.com/>.

"Translaten." *Middle English Dictionary*. Ann Arbor: U of Michigan P, 2001. Print; Web. <https://quod.lib.umich.edu/m/med/>.

"Translatio, -onis." *Oxford Latin Dictionary*. Oxford: Oxford UP, 2005. Print; Web. <www.oxfordscholarlyeditions.com/page/the-oxford-latin-dictionary>.

Trigg, Stephanie, ed. *Wynnere and Wastoure*. Oxford: Oxford UP, 1990. Print.

Tuchman, Barbara. *A Distant Mirror: The Calamitous Fourteenth Century*. 1978. New York: Ballantine, 1987. Print.

Turnbull, William Barclay, ed. *The Visions of Tundale: Together with Metrical Moralizations and Other Fragments of Early Poetry*. Edinburgh: Thomas G. Stevenson, 1843. Print.

Turville-Petre, Thorlac. *The Alliterative Revival*. Woodbridge: Brewer, 1977. Print.

Utz, Richard J. *Literary Nominalism and the Theory of Rereading Late Medieval Texts: A New Research Paradigm*. Lewiston: Mellen, 1995. 205–34. Print.

Vantuono, William. Pearl: *An Edition with Verse Translation*. Notre Dame: U of Notre Dame P, 1995. Print.

———, trans. Pearl *Poems: An Omnibus Edition*. New York: Garland, 1984. Print. 2 vols.

Vasta, Edward. Introduction. *The Pearl*. Ed. Mary Vincent Hillmann. Notre Dame: U of Notre Dame P, 1961. vii–xiii. Print.

Vitz, Evelyn Birge. "Modalities of Performance: Romance as Recited, Sung and Played; Romance as Read." *Orality and Performance in Early French Romance.* Cambridge: Brewer, 1999. 164–227. Print.

Vitz, Evelyn Birge, and Marilyn Lawrence, dirs. *Performing Medieval Narrative: A Video Showcase.* N.p., 10 June 2014. Web. 10 June 2014. <http://mednar.org>.

Vitz, Evelyn Birge, Nancy Freeman Regalado, and Marilyn Lawrence, eds. *Performing Medieval Narrative.* Cambridge: Brewer, 2005. Print.

Vives, J. L. *Somnium et vigilia in Somnium Scipionis.* Ed. E. V. George. Greenwood: Attic, 1989. Print.

The Vulgate Bible. Ed. Angela M. Kinney. Cambridge: Harvard UP, 2013. Print. Vol. 6 of *The New Testament.*

Vulgate Bible. Vulgate.org. N.p., n.d. Web. 10 Aug. 2013.

Washum, Marley, ed. Pearl*: Bibliography to 1988.* N.p., 2007. Web. 12 Dec. 2016. <http://lightspill.com/schola/nando/pearl_bib.html>.

Wasserman, Julian. "Review of Edward Condren's *The Numerical Universe of the Gawain-Pearl Poet.*" *Arthuriana* 13.2 (2003): 108–10. Print.

Waters, Claire. *Angels and Earthly Creatures: Preaching, Performance, and Gender in the Later Middle Ages.* Philadelphia: U of Pennsylvania P, 2004. Print.

Watkins, John. "'Sengeley in Synglere': *Pearl* and Late Medieval Individualism." *Chaucer Yearbook* 2 (1995): 117–36. Print.

Watson, Giles. Pearl*: A Translation from the Middle English.* Lulu, 2014. Web. 12 Dec. 2016.

Watson, Nicholas. "Desire for the Past." *Studies in the Age of Chaucer* 21 (1999): 59–97. Print.

Watts, Victor, trans. *Pearl.* Ed. David Fuller and Corinne Saunders. London: Enitharmon, 2005. Print.

Watts, William H. "The Medieval Dream Vision as Survey of Medieval Literature." *Studies in Medieval and Renaissance Teaching* 12.2 (2005): 67–94. Print.

Wellek, René. "The *Pearl*: An Interpretation of the Middle English Poem." *Studies in English by Members of the English Seminar of the Charles University.* Vol. 4. Prague: Riváce, 1933. 1–33. Print.

Weston, Jessie L. *From Ritual to Romance.* Cambridge UP, 1920. Print.

———, trans. *Romance, Vision and Satire: English Alliterative Poems of the Fourteenth Century.* New York: Houghton, 1912. Print.

Whatley, Gordon, ed. and trans. *The Saint of London: The Life and Miracles of Saint Erkenwald, Text and Translation.* Binghamton: Center for Medieval and Renaissance Studies, 1989. Print. Medieval and Renaissance Texts and Studies 58.

Whitaker, Muriel. "*Pearl* and Some Illustrated Apocalypse Manuscripts." *Viator* 12 (1981): 183–96. Print.

White, Hugh. "Blood in *Pearl.*" *Review of English Studies* 38.149 (1987): 1–13. Print.

Widdowson, Carolus. *St. Gertrude the Great.* London: Sands and Col., 1913. Print.

Willan, Claude. "*Pearl* and the Flawed Mediation of Grace." *Modern Philology* 112 (2014): 56–75. Print.

William of St. Thierry. *Works*. Trans. Sister Penelope. Vol. 1. Shannon: U of Ireland P, 1971. Print.

Williams, David, ed. and trans. "Pearl." *The Broadview Anthology of British Literature: The Medieval Period*. 3rd ed. *BABL Online* (2015): 1–37. Web. <sites.broadview press.com/bablonline>.

Williams, David H. *Five Wounds of Jesus*. Herefordshire: Gracewing, 2004. Print.

Williams, Margaret, trans. *The Pearl-Poet: His Complete Works*. 1967. New York: Vintage, 1970. Print.

Wilson, Christopher. *The Gothic Cathedral: The Architecture of the Great Church, 1130–1530*. London: Thames, 1990. Print.

Wilson, Edward. *The Gawain-Poet*. Leiden: Brill, 1976. Print.

———. "The 'Gostly Drem' in *Pearl*." *Neuphilologische Mitteilungen* 69 (1968): 90–101. Print.

Wilson, Simon. *Surrealist Painting*. London: Phaidon, 1975. Print.

Windeatt, Barry. *Chaucer's Dream Poetry: Sources and Analogues*. Cambridge: Brewer; Lanham: Rowman, 1982. Print. Chaucer Studies 7 and 8.

Winny, James. *Chaucer's Dream-Poems*. London: Chatto; New York: Barnes, 1973. Print.

Wolff, W. *The Dream-Mirror of Conscience: A History of Dream Interpretation from 2000 B.C. and a New Theory of Dream Synthesis*. 1952. Westport: Greenwood, 1972. Print.

Wood, Chauncey. "Review of Edward Condren's *The Numerical Universe of the Gawain-Pearl Poet*." *Speculum* 80.1 (2005): 208–10. Print.

Wynnere and Wastoure. Conlee, *Middle English Debate Poetry* 63–98.

Young, Frances M. *Biblical Exegesis and the Formation of Christian Culture*. Peabody: Hendrickson, 1997. Print.

Zaerr, Linda Marie. "*The Weddynge of Sir Gawen and Dame Ragnell*: Performance and Intertextuality in Middle English Popular Romance." Vitz, Regalado, and Lawrence 193–208.

Zatta, Jane. "*Pearl*: An Introduction." *The ORB: The Online Reference Book for Medieval Studies*. N.p., 2000. Web. 13 Jan. 2014. <http://www.the-orb.net/textbooks/anthology/middleenganon/zatta.html>.

Zink, Michael. "The Allegorical Poem as Interior Memoir." *Images of Power: Medieval History/Discourse/Literature*. Ed. Kevin Brownlee and Stephen G. Nichols. New Haven, 1986. 100–26. Print. Yale French Studies 70.

Zumthor, Paul. *La poésie et la voix dans la civilisation médiévale*. Paris: PUF, 1984. Print.

INDEX